IN HIS LIVING PRESENCE

3 3 3

Journey Science to Faith

Ramon M. Sanchez, M.D.

Order this book online at www.trafford.com/07-2696
or email orders@trafford.com

Most Trafford titles are also available at major online book retailers.

Note for Librarians: A cataloguing record for this book is available from Library and Archives Canada at www.collectionscanada.ca/amicus/index-e.html

Printed in Victoria, BC, Canada.

ISBN: 978-1-4251-5955-9

We at Trafford believe that it is the responsibility of us all, as both individuals and corporations, to make choices that are environmentally and socially sound. You, in turn, are supporting this responsible conduct each time you purchase a Trafford book, or make use of our publishing services. To find out how you are helping, please visit www.trafford.com/responsiblepublishing.html

Our mission is to efficiently provide the world's finest, most comprehensive book publishing service, enabling every author to experience success. To find out how to publish your book, your way, and have it available worldwide, visit us online at www.trafford.com/10510

www.trafford.com

North America & international
toll-free: 1 888 232 4444 (USA & Canada)
phone: 250 383 6864 ♦ fax: 250 383 6804
email: info@trafford.com

The United Kingdom & Europe
phone: +44 (0)1865 722 113 ♦ local rate: 0845 230 9601
facsimile: +44 (0)1865 722 868 ♦ email: info.uk@trafford.com

10 9 8 7 6 5 4

Dedication and Thanks

I dedicate *this (His) book* and give most loving thanks to my Celestial Mama – *Ave Maria Purisima* - the Blessed Virgin Mary, *Our Loving Mother: "one Mother with many titles" – as Our Lady of Grace - of Mount Carmel – of Charity- of Guadalupe – of Lourdes - of Fatima – of Schoenstatt - of Perpetual Help, Theotokos, the Mystical Rose, The Guardian of Faith, etc. Mother Mary, who prays to bring us - her Son, Jesus - the Living Son of God – the Eternal Word of the Father – the Bread of Life - in His Living Presence.* I also lovingly dedicate *this book* to my dearest wife, whose love and patience is unmatched for putting up with me - during the many years of writing, re-writing and editing *this (His) book.*

I dedicate *this work* and give the most special loving thanks to *God Almighty, Father-Son--Holy Spirit,* Creator of Heaven and earth, for giving us such an amazing *precious gift – the tangible medical and scientific evidence of His Living Presence.* Thank You - *Father God* for allowing it with Your Most Compassionate *Divine Mercy in Your Divine Will.* Thank You - *Jesus* for Your *"sacrifice of praise" and "Precious Blood."* Thank You – *Holy Spirit* for guiding *this work* with Your Anointing *"oil of gladness," "rays of heavenly light"* and *"living waters."*

I give very special thanks to the *three chosen souls: Nancy, the seminarian and Patricia (Pachi)* – for sharing their *heavenly experiences* with us and for all their sacrifices, crosses and prayers. And many thanks to the medical and scientific research team for their work and assistance: Dr. Callahan and Winnie, Dr. Hogben, Dr. Agosto-Maury, Dr. Dalmau, Prof. Castanon, Ph.D., Dr. Velasquez and the radiation team; and to my medical research team. I also give thanks to Dr. Graham.

I give *loving thanks* - to *all my children*; to my dear *earthly* loving mom and dad; and to all my dear family, relatives, teachers, friends and especially Fr. Dan, my spiritual director - for all their love and many, many prayers supporting me through all the years of this - *journey science to faith.* I give thanks to Bridget Hylak with Come Alive Communications, Dr. Petrisko, Fr. Edwin, Fr. Mancini, Fr. Jacque, Archbishop Prata, Archbishop Donoghue, Archbishop Luna, Sr. Dolores, Mother Vicar Sr. Mary Catherine, Mother Angelica / EWTN, TBN, CBN, Beverlee, Beth, Fran, Peter and Marco. Also thank you St. Joseph, St. John, St. Paul, St. Peter, St. Ramon, St. Jerome, St. Anthony, St. Pio, Luisa, St. Faustina, St. Rita, St. Anne, St. Teresa, St. Therese, *St. Michael, St. Rafael* and *St. Gabriel, all holy archangels* and *angels,* my *guardian angel* and my *patron saints,* the *Doctors of the Church,* and *all saints, martyrs* and *holy souls* for their prayers and *heavenly* assistance.

I love you all! --- R.M.S.

TABLE OF CONTENTS

ABOUT THE AUTHOR

Ramon M. Sanchez, M.D., was born in Havana, Cuba. He was educated at Tulane University in New Orleans, Louisiana, and also at the University of Miami, Coral Gables, Florida; receiving in four years both a Bachelor of Arts Degree with honors, *cum laude,* and a Bachelor of Science Degree with honors, *cum laude.* He graduated from the University of Miami - School of Medicine, earning a Degree of Doctor of Medicine. His residency training program consisted of general surgery, neurosurgery and neurology at Jackson Memorial Hospitals/University of Miami School of Medicine and at Thomas Jefferson Medical College in Philadelphia, Pennsylvania. He then studied and completed a two-year fellowship in epilepsy, EEG, neurophysiology, neuropharmacology and sleep disorders at the JMH Jackson Memorial Hospitals/University of Miami School of Medicine/VA Hospitals, Miami, Florida, under the mentorship of Prof. Eugene Ramsay, M.D., Director, International Comprehensive Epilepsy Program.

Dr. Sanchez served our country well in military service as Commander, US Navy, neurology staff physician, clinical instructor and Director of the EEG-Neurodiagnostic Laboratories at the San Diego Naval Hospital, San Diego, California. He was also Director of the Headache and Pain Management Clinic, Director of the Complicated OB/ Neurology Clinic and Director of the Sleep Disorders Clinic at the Naval Hospital, San Diego, California, and assisted in designing a new sleep disorders clinic, sleep disorders laboratory and clinical analysis program. The new sleep disorder program was co-supervised in its initial formation by the Scripp's Clinic/Sleep Disorders Center, La Jolla, California. Cdr. Sanchez received one of the Navy's highest honors in medicine, the Navy Achievement Medal, for his outstanding medical military service and dedication.

Dr. Sanchez is a Diplomate of the American Board of Psychiatry and Neurology and a Diplomate of the American Academy of Pain Management. He is currently in private practice in Atlanta, Georgia. His private practice consists of general neurology, epileptology, headache and pain management, sleep disorders, neurological complications of pregnancy and EEG/neurophysiology diagnostic testing and monitoring. The latter consists of stationary and/or ambulatory intensive audiovisual TV-EEG telemetry, topographic quantitative EEG brain mapping analysis, evoked potential testing, nerve conduction studies/EMG, also ENG, audiometry and polysomnography.

In the 1990's Dr. Sanchez was honored as Chairman of the Professional Advisory Committee for the National Multiple Sclerosis Society, State of Georgia Chapter and was also honored as an *honorary member* of the Board of Trustees for the same Chapter. Currently, he is an active medical staff member at St. Joseph's Hospital of Atlanta and Emory-Johns Creek Hospital, and also an active consultant neurology staff member at the Atlanta Northside Hospital.

At the time of the *testing* for the research in this book Dr. Sanchez's EEG-neurophysiology laboratory had the intensive audiovisual TV EEG telemetry monitoring systems that allowed patients' electrical brain functions to be studied simultaneously along with their behavior using synchronized time-locked TV video monitors. This allowed for moment by moment behaviors to be studied via intensive monitoring audiovisual TV recordings, while at the same time, the electrical brain function are observed, studied and documented via the EEG telemetry monitoring system. This monitoring system is actually a live action EEG tracing hooked up with a live action audiovisual TV monitoring video camera. Thus, the EEG is recorded simultaneously in real time with the same real time - live action filmed of the subject/patient on the video camera. This system allows for continuous and simultaneous real time observations to be conducted in the categories of mental status, psychiatry, neurology, EEG and neurophysiology. The purpose of this intensive type of documentation is to allow for medical and scientific assessments to be made about a given subject/ patient's electrical brain wave function and behavior at any given period of recorded time. The effect is that the TV EEG-telemetry video tracing is reflective of the subject/patient's behavior and mental status at the exact corresponding real time-locked EEG tele-monitoring sequence.

It was for this specialized expertise that Dr. Sanchez was called upon, interestingly, via the *Atlanta Yellow Pages,* to be a part of the international medical and scientific team whose initial purpose was to study the visionary and prophet, Nancy Fowler in Conyers, Georgia, USA. Subsequently, his state-of-the-art EEG-neurophysiology laboratory at St. Joseph's Center for Specialty Medicine became the site of two of the major studies performed on two *chosen souls:* in June 11th, 1993, on Nancy Fowler; and in August 20th, 1993, on Nancy and the young seminarian, who is now an ordained practicing Roman Catholic priest.

Dr. Sanchez is published in medical and scientific newsletters and research publications. His research on the above medical and scientific studies is featured in several chapters of several books, including "*Why Do You Test Me?"* and chapters in *"Documentos para la Ciencia y la Fe (Documents for Science and Faith),"* and chapters in the book, *"La Primavera."* He has made numerous Radio and TV appearances and has been featured in several documentaries. His research has been featured in the FOX Television Network's: *Miracles and Visions: Fact or Fiction?,* which was televised on prime time Fox Network TV. Dr. Sanchez's early research studies were also included in a documentary: *"Why Do You Test Me?"* This video documented the early medical evaluation and scientific testing of the chosen soul, Nancy Fowler.

In the 1990's Dr. Sanchez's medical and scientific studies were also featured on *60 Minutes-* Australian TV, Japanese TV, Spanish News Cable TV/Univision, CNN, and other local Cable News and TV USA Networks. His research was also the subject of interviews for Catholic Radio shows in New Zealand, Australia,

Japan, North America, Canada, Mexico, and South America. In Miami, Florida, Radio Marti - *Cuba Libre,* Free Cuba - Station also broadcasted a two-hour live interview radio show in Spanish with Dr. Sanchez into *Communist* Cuba.

In his *journey of faith,* Dr. Sanchez during infancy was baptized as a Roman Catholic, but left the Catholic Church soon after high-school - looking for God and searching for *the truth.* Some may say *he* was looking for God in all the wrong places. He soon became an agnostic and a hardened skeptic throughout college and early medical school, but found Christianity again and was married in the Presbyterian Church. As a member of the Presbyterian Church he started a family while in medical school with the fruit of two daughters. But sadly, his first young wife found it increasingly difficult to cope and live with all the real life rigors of a resident doctor in training; so, she quickly separated and remarried. Thus, Dr. Sanchez became another casualty of divorce in our modern times during his first years of resident specialty training in general surgery and neurosurgery. Angry with God for being separated from his two beloved baby daughters, he left God again and stopped going to any church. This time he very enthusiastically lived a very secular and worldly bachelor lifestyle throughout most of the early 1980's.

He met his beautiful *Jewish* bride to be during the completion of his neurology residency in Philadelphia. The city where he had re-entered into the Catholic *Christian* faith in the historic St. Joseph's Catholic Church (said to be the oldest Catholic Church in the USA). But soon, like so many young adults today influenced by our modern *"its all about me"* culture of *secular relativism,* he became *a cafeteria Catholic,* picking and choosing what he liked and *looking the other way* for the rest.

While completing his USA military service for our country in the Navy at the San Diego Naval Hospitals, San Diego, California, he was married in a Catholic Church in downtown Atlanta, Georgia, *The Shrine of the Immaculate Conception.* Joyously, Dr. Sanchez now has the wonderful and *good fruit* of four beautiful daughters and two grandchildren. Thanks be to God.

Finally, with abundant prayers from all his family and friends Dr. Sanchez proclaims it was after the hardcore medical and scientific research, especially the meticulous testing and re- testing - of the *chosen souls: Nancy, the seminarian* and *Patricia (Pachi),* that he is now – grounded with a *new* solid *conviction of faith* – a true active, practicing, Bible reading, Holy Spirit filled, sacramental living and Latin Rite - Roman Catholic in his *journey science to faith...and in his journey home.*

~ON THE MATTER OF AN IMPRIMATUR~

HIS HOLINESS, POPE URBAN VIII STATES:

"In cases which concern private revelations, it is better to believe than not believe, for, if you believe, and it is proven true, you will be happy that you have believed, because Our Holy Mother asked it. If you believe, and it should be proven false, you will receive all blessings as if it had been true, because you believed it to be true." (Pope Urban VIII, 1623-44).

OBEDIENCE TO THE CHURCH

According to a decree of the Congregation for the Doctrine of the Faith approved by Pope Paul VI, on October 14, 1966, it is permitted to publish, without an imprimatur, texts relating to new revelations, apparitions, prophecies or miracles. However, in accordance with the regulations of the Second Vatican Council, the publisher states that I do not wish to precede *the judgment of the Church* in this matter, to which I *humbly submit.*

In May 1998 after a private meeting *seeking guidance from the Church,* I was given permission to write *this book (investigating* local *chosen souls,* Nancy Fowler and the seminarian *with heavenly visits)* by the *Archbishop of Atlanta,* Georgia, USA, the Most Rev. Archbishop John Francis Donoghue, D.D.

In November 1994 Patricia Talbot B. and the medical & science research team were *given permission to test* - Pachi, *while receiving the Holy Eucharist* at her home's oratory/prayer room *during a private Holy Communion service* given by a local Catholic priest *after a Roman Catholic Mass, by the Archbishop of Cuenca,* Ecuador, South America, the Most Rev. Archbishop Luis Alberto Luna.

In addition I was given permission to use *the messages of Our Lord and Our Loving Mother* copyrighted by George Collins, which are included in this book.

THE BIBLE SAYS

St. Paul said it best, when speaking about *"the truth"* and *"the church of the living God."* Please read 1Timothy 3:15: *"...the church of the living God, the pillar and ground* (foundation) *of the truth."*

For those of you, who do not need any explanation for reading this book, please skip over the Preface at this time and proceed to the Introduction to the Medical and Scientific Studies.

PREFACE ON THE BIBLICAL LOGIC THAT VALIDATES READING THIS BOOK

I will start with some thoughts and facts in the *Preface on the Biblical logic* available to us that actually clears the way *spiritually* to read *this book* - in anticipation of presenting *new medical and scientific data* recorded in the midst of various *supernatural events* --- ***in the living presence of God*** - with three different *chosen souls: Nancy, the seminarian and Patricia* (prophets/ visionaries/ mystics), who claim to receive *messages from heaven - for us.*

Now, before I go any further into the medical and physical science in *this book* to try to explain our amazing *new data* and findings surrounding our studies of the *supernatural events* involving *three chosen souls,* it is imperative that we use logic and good reasoning skills when approaching the tantalizing subject of possible connections between *the data* I uncovered in *medical science* and *the Bible.* I ask you to please use good *logic,* while we search for *the truth.* Providentially it has come to my attention on several occasions (as I soon sadly learned) while discussing the results of our collective *new medical and scientific data* with family, friends and colleagues, and then relating this *new data* to exciting and intriguing *connections with the Bible* and to a much lesser extent to connections even with the Hebrew Bible codes *(ELS system),* not the *Da Vinci codes (fiction),* that some people will unfortunately reject this *new medical and scientific data,* as well as any premise of *holy connections with the Bible* on purely religious grounds or based on their own individual interpretations. This really puzzled me. So, I researched for clues in the Old and New Testaments that would help me, by simply looking for *verses* that describe being *in His Living Presence.* I hoped to find clues that would somehow help explain the possible rationale for all our amazing *new findings* associated with these *heavenly visitations, visions or apparitions.* Thanks to God, I did find clues, many clues (as you will see) that help identify *God's tapestry of truth.* I also hoped to make the reading of this book more palatable for all who want to *taste and see* the true majesty of God, as *God's harmony of truth and glory* unfolds in our medical and scientific quest for *the truth.* So, please join me in our glorious and *'delicious'* ***journey*** from **science to faith.** Come, *taste* and see.

In a presumed theological basis some Jews, Christians, Mormons, Muslims, Hindu, Buddhists and other religions of the world may never consider the real true ramifications of these *new* medical and scientific findings, let alone allow themselves to even read *this book* because of *fear* of getting some sort *of spiritual contamination* or possibly a misunderstanding or misinterpretation of *the word of God* in the Holy Scriptures as presented here. *What* do I mean? Just look at the ancient Holy Book of Deuteronomy, Chapter 18:9-14. In these verses, God's words given to Moses reveal to us how we should not hearken *(listen to)* soothsayers, diviners, wizards, charmers, fortune tellers, or anyone that: *"consulteth python spirits or seeketh the truth from the dead."* See *why* in verse 12:"For the Lord abhorreth all these things, and for these *abominations* He will destroy them *at thy coming (the coming of the Lord)."* Thus, if you believe in the presumed premise that the *chosen souls* we tested are speaking to *dead spirits,* especially *in lieu* of the above Holy Scriptures, then I can fully understand the concerns and possible trepidation many may have in reading *this book.* So, the next real big question raised by all this is *what* does *the word of God* in Deuteronomy 18:12 really mean by *"consulteth python spirits or seeketh the truth from the dead."* Are the *chosen souls* we tested speaking to *the dead?* Since *the spirits* the chosen souls are speaking to are *alive* and are *living spirits, what* does *dead* really mean in this context?

To help answer these questions, just look at *the word of God* given to Moses as it is written in Deuteronomy 30:15-20: ***"Consider that I have set before thee this day life and good, and on the other hand death and evil:*** That thou mayest *love the Lord thy God, and walk in his ways, and keep his commandments and ceremonies and judgments, and thou mayest live, and he multiply thee, and bless thee...*I call heaven and earth to witness this day, that *I have set before you life and death, blessing and cursing. Choose* therefore *life that both thou and thy seed may live:* And that thou mayest *love the Lord thy God, and obey his voice, and adhere to him* (for *he is thy life* and the length of thy days)*..."* In these passages, it is very clear to me that God wants us to *choose life* and *not death.* In the above verses, God is actually equating *life with good;* and *death (or dead) with evil.* God is, of course, referring to a death of the spirit, not death of the flesh. So, one can extrapolate further from *the word of God* as it is written in Deuteronomy that *"the dead" must mean the evil spirits or evil doers* – man with a spirit prone to do evil. Now the real question is: Did the *chosen souls* we tested speak to *the dead* (evil) or to *living* (good) *spirits? What does God say is a dead spirit vs. a living spirit?* The answer is in Deuteronomy 30:15 and in the following discussions, plus in our meticulous medical and scientific studies. Reading the discussions below will hopefully help answer these questions and make it possible for all who read *this book* to read it without any fear, except for the *holy fear of the Lord thy God,* which in the book of Proverbs 1:7 says - the holy *"fear of the Lord is the beginning of wisdom."* Now, all we need to do is to ask the *Holy Spirit of God* for discernment.

The above passage in Deuteronomy 18:12: *"at thy coming"* or *the coming of the Lord,* is interpreted by most Christian Biblical Scholars and Messianic Jews as *the coming of Messiah. Jesus,* they claim, is *the Anointed One, the Messiah,* in Greek - *the Christos* or *the Christ. "The Christ"* thus *means the Anointed One* or *the Messiah; the Jewish Messiah* as foretold by God in the ancient Holy Scriptures.

"At thy coming" (the first coming of Jesus) many scholars believe is foretold in and associated with all the *(Jewish) Festivals of the Lord in the* **early rains.** Many Christian Bible theologians teach that *through, with and in the mighty name of Jesus, whose name is above all names, all things are possible;* as it is written in Isaiah 45:24*: "For every knee shall be bowed... and every tongue shall swear."* They teach that *in the name of Jesus, the dead* and *evil spirits* are literally cast out, overpowered, and neutralized. Anyone trying to harness truth, power or fortune-telling from *the dead* or *evil spirits* can be delivered or set free from these evil powers *in the name of Jesus.* These evil powers can be cast out and sent to the pit of hell only by the power in *the name that is above all names, Jesus.* One can surmise from this discussion that people, who are *alive but* follow and *do evil,* and thus *choose death over life,* will be considered among *the dead* in the eyes of God. Maybe this is *why,* in the famous Bible story of the *prodigal son,* when the lost *dead* son returns, his long-suffering father becomes joyous and merry and says in Luke 15:24: *"...my son was dead, and is come to life again: was lost, and is now found."*

I believe that *"at thy coming"* (the second coming) is actually and perpetually with us now in *our daily bread from heaven,* the daily *"sacrifice of praise"* (Psalm 49:14, 23) - the *Holy Eucharist (a series of perpetual daily second comings),* through the power of the Holy Spirit *(the Spirit of truth).* This heralds a daily perpetual coming of the Lord in a special way through *the Holy Eucharist* - **until** - as it is written in Rev Chapters 19 and 20: *"The Word of God"* (Rev 19:13) - *Jesus* returns to rule the world with *a rod of iron* (Psalm 2:9; Rev 2:27, 12:5, 19:15) and *Jesus* comes as the *"covenant of peace"/ "the everlasting covenant"* (Ezekiel 37:26) *and* as *"King of kings and the Lord of lords"* (Rev 19:16). He *(Jesus)* is seen in the Bible as riding on a white horse (Rev 19:11), *"with the clouds of heaven"* (Daniel 7:14), and *"the armies that are in heaven followed Him on white horses, clothed in fine linen, white and clean"* (Rev 19:14), as *"heaven opened"* (Rev 19:11). For this reason, I prefer to call this coming - *the final -* ***"at thy coming"*** *(of the Lord),* instead of *the second coming (my preference).* This *final coming (the final Advent)* is associated with the *Festivals of the Lord in the* **late rains,** the heralded *last* and *final coming of the Lord.* Many theologians still prefer to call this *final coming* as *the second coming of the Lord,* and Christian scholars today teach that this *final coming* is *the second coming.* But then how do you explain the daily *sacrifice of praise – the Holy Eucharist?* As you will see, our amazing *new medical and scientific data* actually confirms *the living presence of the Lord in the daily "sacrifice of praise" – the Eucharist.* Thus, the *last* and *final coming* or *the second coming* of the Lord - depending on your personal preference - is akin to the Jewish *Festivals of the Lord* associated with the *late rains,* as it is written in Malachi 4:5: *"the coming of the great and dreadful day of the Lord."* Yes, that *"glorious and terrible day."* I believe it will be a *glorious day,* indeed, *for those who believe in the Anointed One (Jesus)* and a very *terrible day* and *dreadful day for all those who do not believe in and/or reject -*

the One (Jesus) Whom He (Father God) sent.

In Rev: 19 and 20 - it is written that all the evil doers/persons, who continue to do evil and seek truth from *the dead* (evil spirits), will be destroyed and thrown into *hell* for *the first death,* and later thrown into *the lake of fire* forever by God along with all the evil spirits for *the second death.* But *the fortunate,* who follows the Lamb of God *(Jesus),* will be invited *"to the marriage supper of the Lamb,"* and *"blessed are they"* (Rev 19:9). So, of course many Christians and some Jews today joyously welcome the great day *at thy coming,* the *last and final coming (the final Advent)* or the *second coming* of the Lord, again depending on your own preferred interpretation of the Bible. Many are eagerly waiting for this great and glorious day. Our beloved Jewish brothers and sisters today, especially *those who do not believe in Jesus as the Messiah,* believe that *at thy coming* is actually *the first coming* as well as *the final coming,* and the only real true coming of the Lord. Please pray daily (along with me) for the *peace of Israel – Shalom.* Pray for the *"remnant of Israel"*- that *will be saved by the Lord,* see Sophonias 3:5-17: ***"Wherefore expect me, saith the Lord, in the day of my resurrection that is to come...The remnant of Israel...Give praise, O daughter Sion: shout, O Israel...The Lord thy God in the midst of thee is mighty, he will save..."***

After much research, fasting and prayer I have come to believe *"at thy coming"* as portrayed in *the first coming* of the Lord is very well illustrated in Isaiah 45:8: *"Drop down* ***dew,*** ye heavens, from above, and let the clouds ***rain*** *the just (one):* let the earth be opened, and ***bud forth*** *a savior..."* Then *the word of God* proclaims who *the just (one)* and *savior* really is, see Isaiah 45:21-22: *"A just God and a savior, there is none besides me. Be converted to me, and you shall be saved, all ye ends of the earth: for I am God and there is no other."* He is coming to save you and me, Jew and Gentile alike. Can you imagine - ***"A just God and a savior"*** (all rolled up into one), W*ho* ***buds forth from the earth?*** Who could *this person possibly be?* This is a very different portrait of the Lord's coming than what is depicted in Daniel 7:13-14, as seen below that describes what many Bible scholars today believe is *the final coming (the final Advent)* or *second coming of the Lord.* This is clearly *not the prophecy* of the first coming of the Lord. See in the Book of Daniel 7:13-14, as it is written: *"...*One like *the son of man* came *with the clouds of heaven*, and *he* came even to *the Ancient of days*: and they presented *him* before *him.* And *he* gave *him* power, and glory, and *a kingdom:* and all peoples, tribes and tongues *shall serve him: his power is an everlasting power* that shall not be taken away: and *his kingdom that shall not be destroyed."*

As it is written above *"the Ancient of days,"* I believe is *God the Father.* So then, *Who* **is** *"he" ---"one like the son of man came* (coming) *with the clouds of heaven?" He* - that is presented before *"the Ancient of days,"* and was then *given "power, and glory, and a kingdom," "an everlasting power,"* and *given* a *"kingdom that shall not be destroyed?" He* - I believe in these verses **is** *Jesus. The first* *coming* as portrayed in Isaiah 45:8*: "let the earth be opened, and bud forth a* ***savior,"*** shows *a just man* who *buds forth from the earth,* since God created man from *the dust of the earth* (Genesis 2:7). This *savior,* who is further described in Isaiah 45:21 as*: "A just God and savior;"* I believe is *Jesus, the God-man* (Isaiah 9:6). I hope and pray that *understanding the results* of our meticulous medical and scientific studies will soon help you come to the same conclusions as presented in *this book. Jesus* foretold of the *last coming of the Lord* in Matthew 24:30:"And then shall appear *the sign of the Son of man in heaven (the cross)*: and then shall all tribes of the earth mourn: and they shall see *the Son of man* coming *in the clouds of heaven* with much power and majesty."

With testimonies of >500 eyewitness accounts (1 Corinthians 15:6) of His resurrection, one of my favorite testimonies as it is written in the New Testament, that portrays exactly *who Jesus is* and relates to me as a physician, is in John 3:13-21. Recall as physicians, we have a *medical insignia* in our profession and *healing ministry that* is actually portrayed within *the beginning* of these verses. *Jesus* speaks to a ruler of the Jews, a man of the Pharisees named Nicodemus, saying in John 3:13-21:*"And no man hath ascended into heaven, but he that descended from heaven, the Son of man who is in heaven. And as Moses lifted up the serpent in the desert, so must the Son of man be lifted up: That whosoever believeth in him, may not perish; but may have life everlasting. For God so loved the world, as to give his only begotten Son; that whosoever believeth in him may not perish, but may have life everlasting. For God sent not his Son into the world to judge the world, but that the world may be saved by him. He that believeth in him is not judged. But he that doth not believe is already judged: because he believeth not in the name of the only begotten Son of God* (see Psalm 2:7). *And this is the judgment: because* ***the light*** *is come into the world and men loved darkness rather than the light: for their works were evil. For every one that doth evil hateth the light, and cometh not to the light, that his works may not be reproved. But he that doth truth, cometh to the light, that his works may be made manifest, because they are done in God."* These verses are indeed very, very important, so please read them again slowly. The words in parenthesis, I added for clarity only.

Now I know *"at thy coming"* was and still is so very, very important to us all. This fact may help explain why *Jesus* made sure there were at least three eyewitnesses of the heavenly kingdom of God - even *before* his crucifixion, death, and 3 days later, his glorious resurrection. So, w*hy three witnesses?* See Deuteronomy 19:15: "One witness shall not rise up against any man, whatsoever the sin or wickedness be: but *in the mouth of two or three witnesses every word shall stand." Remember the empty tomb!* The empty tomb had many, many eyewitnesses - including the powerful Roman guards. Now, go read about the *transfiguration of Jesus* as witnessed by Peter, James and John on Mt. Tabor *(three eyewitnesses)* and as it is written in the New Testament. Just as *Father God* *foretold* future events before they happened, *Jesus also foretold* many future events before they happened. One example is seen in Luke 9:27 when *Jesus* said to his apostles: *"...*There are some *(of you)* standing here that shall not taste death, till they see the kingdom of God.*"* Then fulfilling His own prophecy, Jesus took three of his disciples up to Mt. Tabor and there moments later - *Jesus was transfigured* before them, *showing* them *His divinity.* See Luke 9:30-31: "And behold two men were talking to him *(Jesus).* And they were Moses and Elijah; appearing in majesty. And they spoke of his decease that he should accomplish in Jerusalem.*"* And Peter, James and John fell into a ***deep sleep.*** Later in this book, we will explore the genesis of *deep sleep* while *in His living presence (the True Peace of God).* Recall that the above three chosen apostles *did see the kingdom of God,* see Luke 9:32-35: *"*...they saw *his glory,* and the two men that stood with him *(Jesus).* And it came to pass, that as they were departing from him, Peter saith to Jesus: Master, it is good for us to be here; and let us make three tabernacles, one for thee, one for Moses, and one for Elijah; not knowing what he said. And as he spoke these things, there came a cloud, and overshadowed them; and they were afraid, when they entered into the cloud. And *a voice* came out of the cloud, saying: ***This is my beloved Son; hear him."***

So, in Luke 9:27: *"some standing here,"* three privileged apostles did see *the kingdom of God before tasting death,* just as *Jesus foretold.* They also saw *two living, not dead* men: *Moses and Elijah* standing with Jesus. These two men were obviously *living, not dead.* Moses and Elijah are *the first coming - prophets* or the first two *(true) prophetic witnesses of Jesus* associated with the *early rains,* as it is written and foretold by God through Moses in the Book of Genesis Chapter 15:17. These *two great living lights* are seen as the *"smoking furnace"* by Moses (Exodus 19:18) and the *"lamp of fire"* by Elijah (3 Kings 18:38). Interestingly, in Matthew 17:1-8, we read a slightly different account of the *transfiguration of Jesus: "*...He *(Jesus)* was transfigured before them *(Peter, James and John).* And His face *(the face of Jesus) did shine as* **the sun;** and *His garments became white as snow.* And behold there *appeared, Moses and Elijah* to them talking with him (just like in Nancy's *apparitions of Jesus* with other saints) ... And...behold a bright cloud overshadowed them. And lo, a voice out of the cloud, saying: ***This is my beloved Son, in whom I am well pleased: hear ye him."***

All the New Testament Gospels plus the Acts of the Apostles give testimony to the *Risen Jesus,* as well as over 500 (1 Corinthians 15:3-8) *eyewitness accounts* of seeing *Jesus appear* - as *the Risen Lord* - after His *resurrection* and before His glorious *ascension into heaven, as witnessed by the apostles* (Luke24:51). *Remember the empty tomb of Jesus!* Please *do not believe* in the silly old *lie* that *the body of Jesus was stolen.* Recall, the devout Jew and *doubting* apostle, Thomas placed his fingers into the flesh wounds of Jesus days *after His resurrection,* then declared, *"My Lord and my God."* Traditions of the Church, as well as Holy Scriptures say *Jesus appeared* many times *as the Risen Christ to His apostles, disciples and many of the new Jewish and Gentile converts. Jesus* even appeared to one of the most famous of the Jewish zealots, Saul of Tarsus. Initially, Saul did not understand *the truth* about *Jesus.* In his zeal for the Jewish faith with the uttermost hatred and disgust of any Jew who dared to follow Jesus, he almost single-handedly destroyed *the good news,* the gospel, and *"the Way"* movement (Acts: 24:14; St. Augustine: Sermons 51-60, No.4) of *Jesus* before it even had a chance to prosper. But if *"the way"* is really part of God's plan, *who* can stop it? Can *anyone* stop God's plan? (Acts 5:38-39) In the Bible, Saul was miraculously converted to *the truth* soon after *Jesus appeared to him on the way to Damascus.* Yes, the same Saul who had just been given the authority and permission by the Jewish chief priests to retrieve, persecute, put in prison and even help sentence to death Jews following Jesus. Then, *Saul* with the grace of the *Risen Jesus* became *Paul,* the most famous *apostle of Jesus to the Gentiles.* Later acting as a Roman citizen, Paul deliberated in his own legal defense after being placed in prison by the same Jewish chief priests. In the official legal hearings in Jerusalem Paul told King Agrippa how *Jesus appeared to him* (much like Nancy's apparitions). See Acts 26:13-18: "At midday, O king, *I saw in the way a light from Heaven above the brightness of* **the sun** *(a light brighter than the sun), shining round about me,* and them that were in company with me. And *when we were all fallen down on the ground,* I heard a voice speaking to me in the Hebrew tongue: Saul, Saul, why persecutest thou me? It is hard for thee to kick against the goad. And I *(Saul)* said: Who art thou *Lord?* And *the Lord answered:* ***I am Jesus*** whom thou persecutest. But rise up, and stand upon thy feet: ***for this end have I appeared to thee, that I may make thee a minister*** *(to the Jews and Gentiles),* ***and a witness of those things which thou has seen, and of those things wherein I will appear to thee,*** *delivering thee from the people, and from the nations,* unto which **now I send thee: to open their eyes,** ***that they may be converted from darkness to light, and from the power of Satan to God, that they may receive forgiveness of sins, and a lot among the saints, by the faith that is in me (Jesus).***"

Now you are probably starting to wonder: *"What* is the point of all this dialogue*?"* It was unbeknownst by me at the beginning of these medical and scientific studies, how crystal clear history repeats itself, especially in God's masterful handiwork of the human experience. *Our three chosen souls: Nancy Fowler, the seminarian and Patricia Talbot;* as well as many other *chosen souls,* saints and martyrs throughout history, especially during the last 2,000 years, I now believe have been *commissioned* after exercising their own free will, *like Paul,* to be *a witness* and *a minister of God's kingdom* - among us and within us - on this planet earth. And just like *Jesus* appeared to *Saul* saying, *"I will appear to thee"* and later *did appear* to *Paul* many times, to help open the eyes of all the people, so *"they may be converted from darkness to the light, and from the power of Satan to God"*

(Acts 26:16), there are *new* apostles like *Nancy and the two other chosen souls* we tested, who are *new witnesses and ministers of God's kingdom* and receive lots of help from *Jesus* and the *Holy Spirit of God* (Joel 2:28-30; Isaiah 44:3) to accomplish *the holy works* of God the Father. As you will see, *Jesus appeared* to the *three chosen souls* we tested in different ways. Now according to our *new data*, we, the medical and scientific research team along with Nancy, the seminarian and Patricia are true legitimate eye-witnesses to the most amazing *tangible evidence of God - in His Living Presence* --- through medical and scientific testing.

I can only imagine, that if *Jesus* said He *will appear* to Saul/Paul for *God's Divine Will,* plan and purposes, and indeed did so repeatedly over 2,000 years ago (right after His resurrection), then I ask and ponder *why not now?* Recall, *God is the same yesterday, today and tomorrow. Jesus* gave very special instructions to all of His apostles during *His ascension into heaven.* See, as it is written, in Matthew 28:18-20: "All power is given to me in heaven and in earth. Going therefore, teach ye all nations; *baptizing* them *in the name of the Father, and of the Son, and of the Holy Spirit* (see - *the Holy Trinity* of God). Teaching them (all nations) to observe all things whatsoever I have commanded you: and behold I am with you all days, even to the consummation of the world *(the end of time)."*

Are the witnesses and ministries of *Nancy and the two chosen souls* we tested really and truly part of God's *Divine Will,* plan and purpose just like Saul's/Paul's witness and ministry? If so, it now makes perfect and logical sense to me that *Jesus* would also want to assist and *appear* to Nancy and/or any other *chosen souls as God wills,* in order to accomplish God's Almighty *Divine Will,* purpose and plan for all of us in this world. Yes, in this world we all live in, that unfortunately is so full of *His* very sinful, rebellious, ungrateful and yet beloved adopted children.

Despite the information on the Biblical logic just presented - to read this book, certain Jews, Christians, Mormons, Muslims, Hindu, Buddhists and other religions and religious faithful may still *not want to read this book,* if they still think they will somehow be *contaminated* or they think that *Nancy and the two other chosen souls* are somehow listening to, consulting or seeking truth from *"the dead."* Amazingly, our medical and scientific studies will show you that *Jesus is* indeed *not dead,* but ***alive.*** The studies will also show you that *His heavenly court is not dead,* but ***alive.*** Based on our medical and scientific research and *new data* to be presented in this book, it is correct to say that *Jesus, the Holy Trinity* and Almighty God's awesome heavenly court: His Blessed Mother Mary, *Our Loving Mother,* St. Joseph, all saints, martyrs, archangels and a myriad of countless multitudes of holy angels are indeed *not dead, but* ***alive.*** *Jesus appears* in a *bright glory cloud of light* or in a *white luminous vapor* to *Nancy Fowler and to the seminarian and Patricia Talbot, the* two other *chosen souls.* The heavenly visits, visions and apparitions of Nancy and the two other chosen souls are interestingly very much like the heavenly visitations, visions or apparitions as it is written and recorded in Sacred Scriptures. Likewise concerning the *transfiguration of Jesus,* an obviously *living* Moses and Elijah *appear* on Mt. Tabor *to three eye-witnesses:* the apostles Peter, James and John. Now, the *living* Mother of Jesus, the Blessed Virgin Mary*, Our Loving Mother,* the *living* holy saints - just like Moses and Elijah - and the *living* holy angels *appear* to these new *three eye-witnesses* and *chosen souls.* Can you imagine we had the great privilege to test and test, and to test again, these *3 chosen souls (three eye-witnesses)* during their *supernatural experiences* with *heavenly* **living** *souls?*

As you will soon hopefully see in *this book,* we now have evidence that demands a verdict. Our medical and scientific studies completed clearly demonstrate *hardcore proof and confirmation* that *the living presence of God (alive not dead)* truly changes us, and changes our surrounding atmosphere/external environment. *In the living presence of God* in all His glory, the physiology and neurophysiology of a person really *changes.* This was indeed recorded in Nancy and the two chosen souls to limits and ranges never thought physiologically possible, until now. *We actually have proof that God's true living presence really changes us within, and also really changes our surrounding atmosphere (our external environment).* In fact, *the living presence of Jesus* alone or along with His Mother or *living* heavenly court caused such astronomical changes in *the light* energy, especially *the sun* light and the *lightning*-light as recorded and documented, that all of us were astonished and confused about what all this *new data* really means, especially me. As you will also see, *the living presence* of *Jesus alone or with His living Mother Mary* produces and evokes *physiological changes* in the *chosen souls* we tested that were previously thought to be *impossible.* We also demonstrated *in His Living Presence* an alarming and obvious *oxymoron* or *contradiction* to otherwise known medical science.

Now, to make matters really interesting, while I was reviewing our collective medical and scientific research data repeatedly over the past decade, I slowly discovered, admittedly only by *the graces of the Holy Spirit of God,* that all of our *new data* has Biblical significance! So read on, *be not afraid* and *fear not* to read this *(His)* book, because according to our medical and scientific studies *(give praise, glory and thanks to the Lord, our God), Jesus, His Mother Mary, His heavenly court of holy angels and saints are all* indeed *not dead, but* ***alive!*** Therefore, I now strongly believe, Nancy and the other *chosen souls* we tested do not seek truth from *the dead,* but seek *the truth* from *the living Son of God – Christ Jesus,* and His *living* holy messengers - *His Holy Mother Mary, holy angels and saints.* Even Moses writes about *the Lord with saints* in Deuteronomy 33:2: *"...he (God) hath appeared from mount Pharan, and* ***with him (God) thousands of saints.*** *In his right hand a fiery law."*

In Deuteronomy **33:3**: *"He (God) hath loved the people,* ***all the saints are in his (God's) hand:*** *and* ***they that approach to his feet, shall receive of his doctrine (the Word of Father God /Jesus).****"*

See in the verses above how *the Lord God appears with thousands of (living) saints*, just like in many of Nancy's apparitions.

I give thanks to my son-in-law who graduated with a Masters Degree from Oral Roberts University, Tulsa, Oklahoma and is now just completing missionary work with a non-denominational Christian ministry in Berlin, Germany, for inspiring me to write this longwinded, but necessary – PREFACE ON THE BIBLICAL LOGIC - that actually clears the way *via the word of God* for reading of this book. This Preface is indeed especially suited for and directed towards sincere God-fearing souls in search of *the truth,* who may have *a learned and educated slant towards an anti-Catholic bias* in their knowledge and understanding of the Holy Scriptures.

I believe the material in this *(His)* book with *the truth* discovered in our medical and scientific studies of *His Living Presence* **in** - *His Living Word, His Living Light, His Living Touch* and *His Living Bread* has the real potential of having a *unifying effect* on *the Church* universally - once this *new data* and its amazing solid connections with the ancient Holy Scriptures is understood - for whatever *God Wills* for us to understand. I believe God wants us *to live in His Divine Will* always and to *let His Divine Will reign* in our souls, in our hearts, in our minds and in all our strength. Just look around and see all the trouble our *human will* has managed to get us into, from the time of Adam and Eve to the present. So, please pray for God's *Divine Will* to be our every thought, word, act, work and prayer.

Do you think it was *God's Will* for us to have so many different *churches?* Just look at what *Jesus* said in Matthew 16:15-19: *"Jesus saith to them* (His apostles)*: But whom do you say that I am? Simon Peter answered and said: Thou art Christ, the Son of the Living God. And Jesus answering, said to him: Blessed art thou, Simon Bar-Jona: because flesh and blood hath not revealed it to thee, but my Father who is in heaven. And* ***I say to thee****: That thou art* **Peter***; and upon this* **rock** *I will build* **my church,** *and the gates of hell shall not prevail against it. And* ***I will give to thee the keys*** *of the kingdom* **of heaven.** *And whatsoever thou shalt bind upon earth, it shall be bound also in heaven: and whatsoever thou shalt loose on earth, it shall be loosed also in heaven."* Notice how *Jesus* says, *"upon this rock I will build my church." Jesus - did not say – my churches.* Also, notice how in Matthew 16:19 *Jesus gives His authority to His Church.* Additionally, please read 1Timothy 3:15: *"...the church of the living God, the pillar and ground* (foundation) *of the truth."* Notice how St. Paul says, *"the church..."* and **not** *the Bible.* I hope this information helps you (and me) better understand *the truth* about *His church.*

Finally, I believe there is a hidden message in the ancient Holy Scripture verse of Deuteronomy 8:3: *"...Not in bread alone doth man live, but in every word that proceedeth from the mouth of God."* This verse strongly connects with how the *early Christians* acted out their *faith in Christ "in one accord."* Read The Acts 2:46. This topic on the *"bread" / "word of God"* will be further expanded in my next book.

Thanks be to God! The journey science to faith now begins....

INTRODUCTION TO THE MEDICAL AND SCIENTIFIC STUDIES

Unbelievable...unbelievable...unbelievable... This is undoubtedly one of the most exuberant and emotion filled phrases I repeatedly heard expressed when pondering the extraordinary events recorded *in His Living Presence* and associated with the *heavenly visits* or *apparitions* claimed by prophet Nancy Fowler and similar *supernatural events* associated with two other *chosen souls,* a seminarian *(now a Roman Catholic priest)* and a young Ecuadorian, Patricia Talbot Borrero. Also **unbelievable...** is a personal statement I continue to make even today, while reviewing the astonishing *new data* and results of a series of meticulous medical evaluations and scientific studies that were conducted on Nancy and the two other *chosen souls.*

Even more unbelievable is God's awesome love and mercy in clearly showing faithless skeptics like me (a super *doubting Thomas* to the max), the true medical and scientific evidence of being *in His Living Presence.* Also quite amazing are God's unfathomable boundless blessings and graces in showing us *His Living Presence* in our medical and scientific *hardcore* data. As you will see, our *new data* can convincingly demonstrate to most hardened skeptics (like me) the most incredible *tangible evidence* of His Living Presence in *His living words,* His Living Presence *in His living light,* His Living Presence in *His living touch,* and most radically important and revolutionary *good news* for this new millennium - His Living Presence in *His living bread: "I am the living bread which came down from heaven"* (John 6:41) - the consecrated *Holy Eucharist.* With this *new data* we can also see *His Living Presence* in and with His Mother Mary, *Our Loving Mother, "Hail, full of grace"* (Luke 1:28) bringing her baby Jesus to us.

The *new data* was obtained through the extensive medical and scientific testing of the above *three chosen souls,* and the study of Nancy Fowler's external environment or atmosphere during the *heavenly visits, visions* and *apparitions* in Conyers, Georgia, USA. The atmosphere was studied according to our experiment design method of testing - *before, during and after the apparitions* - for the following scientific goals:

1) To measure the surrounding atmospheric radiation energy fields.

2) To study the atmosphere to skin boundary radiation energy fields of the *chosen soul.*

3) To study the atmosphere to wall boundary of the apparition rooms' radiation energy fields associated with the *supernatural events.*

4) To study the paramagnetic energy of the *holy sites* or *holy grounds (clay, rock and soil)* and perform a comparative analysis with some Church-approved and some yet unapproved but pilgrim-recognized *holy sites* around the world.

The members of our international medical and scientific team included atheists, agnostics, Jews, and Christians (skeptical like me of *apparitions* in general). In search of *the truth* all of us were in one accord. For her part, Nancy Fowler, R. N., a registered nurse and mother of two adopted boys has claimed and still claims to receive *private messages from heaven* since the early 1980's until the time of this writing (1995-2007). The other two *chosen souls* involved in our studies also claimed experiences of heavenly visits somewhat similar to Nancy's, though distinctly different and unique, as you will see. The questions that were raised by the international medical and scientific team, I was privileged to be part of, was basic and direct: Were these *mystical, supernatural events* and *heavenly visits* or *apparitions* claimed by these visionaries *true or false?* Is it *fact or fiction?* Could their *experiences* be scientifically explained away, or was there something deeper and potentially more meaningful at their core?

To answer these questions, an international group of independent medical doctors and scientists gathered. Among them were: Professor Philip S. Callahan, Ph.D., entomologist, biophysicist and inventor, University of Florida, USA (now retired). He is a renowned international authority on *low* and *extremely low frequency ionization radiation energy* fields and *paramagnetic studies* of historical, sacred, holy sites/holy grounds *(clay, rock, soil).* Professor Ricardo Castanon-Gomez, Ph.D. is a self-proclaimed atheist for over twenty-five years and is Director of the Neuropsychology Department at the State University of La Paz, Bolivia. Radiation specialist Humberto Velasquez, M.Sc., University of Miami, Florida, is a Ph.D. candidate at Florida International University and is a doctoral physics researcher and expert in high frequency *gamma* radiation energy fields from the University of Antioquia, Colombia South America. He has the title of doctor of physics in Colombia and out of respect I will refer to him in this book as Dr. Velasquez. During the studies he was working with the State Department of Radiation in South Florida, USA. Also included in our team was George Hogben, M.D., a New York psychiatrist *(Board Certified),* with expertise in the role of prayer and Catholic sacramental practices in mental illness and health. Adjunct Professor of Neurology Norma Agosto-Maury, M.D., neurology and electroencephalography *(Board Certified),* Department of Neurology/EEG-Neurophysiology at the University of Puerto Rico, School of Medicine; and Adjunct Professor of Clinical Neuropsychology and Neurophysiology Teresa Dalmau, Ph.D., who also teaches at the same medical school, were both welcomed to the team. Completing the team was Ramon M. Sanchez, M.D., Diplomate of the American Board of Psychiatry and Neurology *(Board Certified),* with a two year certified fellowship training in epilepsy, EEG/intensive audiovisual TV EEG telemetry, topographic quantitative EEG brain mapping analysis, neurophysiology, sleep disorders, sleep analysis and neuropharmacology at the University of Miami, School of Medicine, Miami, Florida, USA. Dr. Sanchez is also a Diplomate of the American Academy of Pain Management and is currently in private practice in Atlanta, GA USA. Our research began with the full intent of revealing and possibly exposing the mystery of these s*upernatural events,* which has so profoundly affected and continue to affect the lives multitudes, and even today continue to magnetize and mobilize huge congregations of faithless, skeptical, nonreligious, hopelessly lost and searching souls (like me) towards the path of faith. Our results, as will be shown, shocked even the most ardent atheist and hardened skeptics (like me) on our medical and scientific team of experts. **Our (my) journey in search of the truth** took us (me) on the most unbelievable, yet glorious ride of our lives, one which continues even today and I predict will continue forever, as the very results we (I) sought have led us (me) far, far beyond the realm of what science could explain. I looked and searched hard and deep in science and in the realm of medicine and found no satisfactory answers to my many questions raised by our unprecedented *new data.* Then, my hunger and thirst for *the truth* and quest for the real true meaning of our astonishing results became very personal. Does God really exist? Is God *alive* today? Does God really speak to us through the new *prophets* or *chosen souls?* Now, I wanted to know. But incredibly, and much to my surprise, in my many years of research the only recourse in finding true logical answers to my many questions was to seek and search in the spiritual realm of faith and religion. Wow!

Very unexpectedly, it was while researching the ancient Holy Bible, the sacred Holy Scriptures plus recent theology books concerning the ELS Hebrew Bible codes, that I soon discovered, quite amazingly, medical and scientific *holy biblical connections.* And this, many years later after all the studies were completed. Our provocative findings slowly, painstakingly, and then finally so very convincingly, led me to some illuminating conclusions and interpretations of all our unprecedented and astonishing *new data* associated with and *in His Living Presence.* These later discoveries were the real and fundamental basis for the writing of this *(His)* book, **In His Living Presence – 333** Journey Science to Faith. Can you imagine, discovering and documenting a specific mathematical and numerical pattern in the brain that occurs *only in His Living Presence?* Then many years later, finding this same identical mathematical and numerical pattern associated *only in His Living Presence* in the Bible and in the ELS - Hebrew Bible codes - encoded in *the Torah,* as researched and written by different brilliant Biblical Hebrew scholars. Can you imagine also discovering and documenting another different and specific mathematical and numerical pattern in the brain that occurs only when the Blessed Virgin Mary brings us Jesus (the baby cradled in her loving arms) - *in His Living Presence* or *His living words in His light.* And then many years later, finding a distinctly different and specific mathematical and numerical pattern seen in the Bible to be associated with specific symbolic foreshadows of *the ark of the new covenant* and *the virgin birth of Jesus, the Holy Incarnation,* seen respectively through the two *first coming* prophetic witnesses of Jesus as mentioned earlier, Moses and the prophet Elijah (John 1:45). So now, the Blessed Virgin Mary speaks to Nancy *(the prophet)* in Conyers, Georgia, USA, and *Our Loving Mother, a holy* *messenger* sent from heaven, *brings Jesus to us all* and *speaks or echoes the living words of Jesus.* Unbelievably, I found a distinctly *new and* different EEG pattern *only associated with* specific symbolic numbers and *Biblical foreshadows of things to come* that specifically and *prophetically depicts the new Eve* or *"woman"* of Gen 3:15, Jeremiah 31:22, and Revelation 12:1.

Every Friday evening as rehearsed by all traditional Jews around the world, and at the beginning of each Sabbath day celebration, the *new Eve* or *"woman"* of Genesis 3:15, Jeremiah 31:22 and Revelation 12:1 *prophetically brings* back *the light, the fire of God* that was lost originally in paradise by *the first Eve.* Recall, Eve ate the *forbidden fruit* from *the tree of life* in the Garden of Eden, after the *old serpent* tricked Eve and Adam into eating it. So, who is the *new Eve* or *"woman"* that brings back *"the light," "the word of God," "justice and peace"* and *"the life"* and *fire of God?* Incredibly and much to my surprise, our medical and scientific studies will show you that the same specific EEG pattern of numbers found during the testing specifically and symbolically identifies the prophesized *"woman"* and *new Eve* numerically by *the gold of the ark of the covenant of Moses* and by *the "Fill four buckets with water"* times *three of Elijah* - to be *the Blessed Virgin Mary.* Studying the *feast of the Sabbath,* you will see that during each Sabbath celebration, it is the *woman* of the house (symbolically *the new Eve)* who brings back *the light* of paradise *(lost by Eve)* to our dark world by *lighting the two candles* on the Sabbath table representing the *two great lights - God's law and word - a revelation to the Jews.* In Genesis 15:17: the *"burning furnace"* and the *"lamp of fire"* represent the *two great lights* (the two lighted Sabbath candles) as *the first two great witnesses of God.* The first candle to be lighted by the *woman* of the house is placed on the right side of the table and represents *"Moses our teacher," the teacher of the law of God.* The second candle to be lighted by the *woman* of the house is placed on the left side of the Sabbath banquet table which represents Elijah and the prophets given *the word of God.* Thus, *"woman" (the Virgin Mary), the new Eve* brings *the light* of paradise, *"...the true light, which enlighteneth every man that cometh into this world"* (John 1:9) back to us.

So, the *"woman"* of the house brings back to us *"the light"* of God in three steps:

1) Through *"the light"* given to Moses our teacher of *"the law",* the *"Torah"* or the *Holy Bible.*

2) Through *"the light"* in *the word of God* given to Elijah and the prophets of God; and finally in the culmination and combining together of the *two great lights.*

3) Through *the woman's seed, her Son* (Genesis 3:15; Isaiah 7:14; and Jeremiah 31:22), *Emmanuel, Jesus,* Who is *"the law" of God* and *"the word of God" made flesh* (John 1:14), *"the light"* (John 8:12) and the living *"fire of God"* (Isaiah 10:17), *"justice and peace"* (Psalm 84:11) and *"the living bread"* (John 6:41) *of God, which comes down from heaven* (John 6:33) for us. I ask you, *are you hungry and* *thirsty for God?* If you are, then please read on because your *journey science to faith* has just started with a pure explosion, an atomic and cosmic blast into an *uncharted harmony of truth* in the *holy fields of God - in His Living Presence.* So, hold on tightly to your seats.

The above mathematical and numerical pattern that I discovered in the medical and scientific testing, *when Mary brings Jesus to us,* is depicted as follows:

1) The *Ark of the New Covenant* brings us *His Living Presence in* ***light*** and both ***the word of God*** *in* **the light** *and in* (manna) ***"the bread of God,*** *is that which cometh down from heaven, and giveth life to the world" (John 6:33).* Both *the life giving words* and *the life giving bread* are *given to us by God - in, with and through the Blessed Womb of Mary, the (living) Ark of the New Covenant* (Rev 12:1). See the 4 golden wings of the two cherubims and 4 golden rings and the 4 golden bars or golden posts (exactly 4- 4- 4 pieces of gold), and even *the height* of a *golden crown round about the holy of holies was 4 inches or 4 finger breadths high,* where *the testimony of God - the word of God* was placed and later through tradition *a jar with a gomer of manna - the bread of God* was also placed *inside the ark,* as it is written in Exodus, Chapters 25 and 37.

2) The holy Singular Vessel of Honor, *God's bucket* filled with water *(the Holy Spirit -"living waters")* as it is written in 3 Kings18:34-39, which actually shows a numerical sequence in a series of exactly 4- 4- 4. *"Fill four buckets with water*" three times *"and pour it upon the burnt offering, and upon the wood" as prepared by Elijah. "Then the fire of the Lord fell" – "the lamp of fire"* (Genesis 15:17), yes, ***fire*** literally *fell from heaven* and *"consumed the holocaust, and the wood, and the stones and the dust...," which* I believe is *Jesus, the cross, the church and us.*

What was in the *water* that is so very special to God? In the Book of Numbers 24:7: *"Water shall flow out of his (God's) bucket, and his seed (the seed of God) shall be in many waters."* The first part of this verse foreshadows the *Incarnation,* but the last part of this verse is made possible only through the passion, crucifixion, death, resurrection, and ascension of Jesus and Pentacost. Recall John 7:38: *"...out of his belly shall flow rivers of living waters."* The *"many waters"* and the *"living waters"* above describe *the living Holy Spirit of God.* See Genesis 1:2: *"...the spirit of God spread over the waters,"* and in Ezekiel 36:25-27, *the word of God* to Ezekiel foretells of the water God will use to cleanse His people and says, *"I will put a new spirit within you,"* here describe the *baptismal living waters.* In the *living water is God's* seed *(the Son of God)* and *"water shall flow out of his bucket" - God's bucket* (Numbers 24:7; 3 Kings18:34) or *God's Singular Vessel of Honor,* which **is** *the Blessed Virgin Mary.* Recall *the seed of the woman (the Son of man)* in Genesis 3:15 & Jeremiah 31:22. And all this finally points to a special *divine offspring* (Ecclesiasticus 39:17), *"the Son of God" and "the Son of man,"* (Psalm 2:7; Isaiah 7:14; 9:6-8). Thus, the imagery presented in the Old Testament foreshadows *the virgin birth of the only begotten Son of God, the God-man* and the *Holy Incarnation* *of both the living word of God and the living bread of God* - all in Mary's *blessed womb!* In history both *the ark of the covenant* of Moses and later *the 4 buckets of water x 3* of Elijah - with their fervent prayers called down and brought forth *the holy living presence of God,* the *Shekinah, the glory cloud* or *the living fire, "the lamp of fire,"* as revealed in the ancient Old Testament -*Torah* and the Book of Kings, respectively.

As a medical doctor and scientist, can you imagine my incredible surprise when I discovered these astonishing *Bible holy connections,* while reviewing the *new data?* And then realizing that this *new medical and scientific data* actually *connects with ancient Holy Scripture writings* that describe being *in His (God's) Living Presence.*

God really has a good sense of humor. I had never personally or seriously read the Bible until after my 40th birthday, approximately one to two years after these amazing studies were completed. As I began searching for answers to my very personal questions, *the Holy Spirit of God,* I believe, prompted me a self-proclaimed *poor* writer to write this book (privately I call it *"His"* Book). I now know that my *only hope* for this book's true success is that *God really loves to exalt the poor* (even a poor writer like me) and *with God's awesome love and mercy - nothing is impossible.*

It is the prime purpose of this *(His)* book to reveal the astonishing medical and scientific tests results *in His Living Presence.* And later to show you the Biblical holy connections *the Holy Spirit has guided me to discover.* Hopefully to increase whatever *faith* we have or do not yet have. While the original impetus, which guided our medical and scientific team's very skeptical scientifically-trained minds was initially to search for *the truth* concerning the claims of *heavenly visits* and *messages from heaven* to *prophet* Nancy Fowler. This search soon led to more research and testing which we did not originally anticipate. Now the search for *the truth* has wholeheartedly unified the collective medical and scientific endeavors of our entire research team.

The hallmark of validating medical and scientific studies is its *reproducibility.* This refers to the ability to reproduce identical results under the same testing parameters in order to ensure the validity of the scientific methods and findings. As our initial results were so astounding and totally unprecedented, we were led to study Nancy many times over and over again repeatedly. Plus, later we were also led to study two other *chosen souls* and other historical *sacred holy sites* further. Indeed, as scientists we were professionally charged with the duty of documenting the reproducibility of our medical and scientific data. However, the logic of the scientific method guided us to study the two other *visionaries* in this book in order to confirm and validate our unprecedented and amazing *new data.*

So, in addition to Nancy, as noted above, we had the pleasure of studying two other *chosen souls;* a young seminarian (now a Roman Catholic priest), whom we will refer to as *the seminarian* in order to maintain the anonymity he and his religious order have requested; and Patricia Talbot B., a young and beautiful former model, nicknamed *Pachi,* from Cuenca, Ecuador, South America. The astonishing results obtained from these two other *chosen souls* solidly furthered the cause of validating the claims of Nancy and much, much more. To our surprise, we discovered a repetitive, identical and specific brain wave pattern that until now was considered *physiologically impossible* in all three visionaries --- occurring *only* during uniquely different experiences or *heavenly visitations of Jesus - in His Living Presence,* in *the light,* in *His living words,* in *His living touch,* and in *His living bread.* Interestingly, I repeatedly recorded and documented an EEG pattern of *deep sleep,* while also simultaneously recording another EEG pattern superimposed of an *awake and alert state with focused attention.* This is a spectacular, unprecedented *oxymoron* and a pure *contradiction* of physiological terms and principles as we know it. This perplexing mixed new EEG pattern was considered until now to be physiologically impossible. Additionally, as was proclaimed by our *three chosen souls,* all of these heavenly visitations or apparitions of *Jesus - in His Living Presence* was always associated with a deep genuine feeling of profound interior *peace, love and joy.*

So, what does *deep sleep - in His Living Presence* and *peace* have in common? Hopefully, this question will be answered both medically and scientifically by the end of Chapter 8 of this book. However, if you are still not satisfied with the answers given there, then please read the last chapter, Chapter 9.

Astonishingly as noted above, I also discovered a totally different and uniquely repetitive specific brain wave pattern that has a different mathematical and numerical sequence from the scientifically documented *visitations of Jesus.* I recorded this uniquely different EEG pattern only during the *heavenly visits of the Blessed Virgin Mary bringing baby Jesus or speaking (echoing) His living words* in His light to all of us. It is now clearly revealed in our medical and scientific studies that the heavenly visitations of *Mary bringing baby Jesus (to us),* as well as, the uniquely different types of heavenly visitations of Jesus (bringing God to us) evoke a very special, definite and specific, yet different unprecedented physiological brain wave responses. I repeatedly documented stimulus specific evoked brain wave responses that have never before ever been recorded, and until now was thought to be *physiologically impossible.* Also much to my surprise, I even twice recorded an *encounter or attack* on Nancy *from the enemy,* yes - *the serpent* – Satan, during one of the final medical and scientific tests performed on Nancy and the seminarian, see Chapter 7 for more details. Can you imagine my great surprise as to *what number* I discovered? A very specific and different EEG mathematical and numerical pattern was recorded and documented *only* during these two eerie attacks on Nancy by Satan. **Hint:** a very specific mathematical and numerical pattern found in the Book of Revelation, concerning the number of the name of the

Anti-Christ (*the anti-*Messiah) or *the number of the beast.* This is still really and truly un-be-liev-a-ble!

Furthermore, our scientific investigations unquestionably documented the actual presence of statistically significant increases in low ionization radiation energy fields (light energy) from the *visible light* radiation energy fields range down to the extremely low ionization radiation energy fields range. Which basically means we measured astronomical increases in *photons* (light particles) released from the orbits of atoms in the atmosphere of the testing sites and/or measured astronomical increases in *the light* present in the testing sites *during the apparitions.* Can you imagine how exciting it was and still is to repeatedly observe and measure scientifically these tremendous increases in *the light* energy (in the range of visible and invisible light, especially the low and extremely low ionization radiation energy fields) *only during the heavenly visitations* or *apparitions?* So, what does *the light* and *Jesus – in His Living Presence* have in common?

We also documented and then measured using advanced computerized digital photo-spectroscopy analysis an even more astronomical 30-90% of statistically significant increases in *sun light* radiation energy fields discovered only *in His Living Presence.* Just *how* is it possible that we were able to measure 90% *more sun light,* when in fact there is only *one sun?* Or is there another *sun* or *Son* that actually appeared? And exactly what does *sun light* and *Jesus - in His Living Presence* have in common?

Can you imagine, we actually documented *flashes or bolts or darts of lightning* light radiation energy fields that incredibly occur only and always *during the heavenly visitations of Jesus - in His Living Presence.* The *flashes or bolts or darts of lightning* light radiation energy fields were also repeatedly documented when the Blessed Virgin Mary, *Our Loving Mother,* appears bringing baby Jesus to us, as well. So, what does *flashes or bolts or darts of lightning* and *Jesus - in His Living Presence* have in common? And what does *flashes of lightning* have in common with *the Blessed Virgin Mary bringing baby Jesus?* Please see Revelation 11:19 and 12:1-5.

Our astonishing medical and scientific *new data* with some surprises and the unprecedented *specific mathematical and numerical brain wave patterns* we recorded and documented quite amazingly, somehow *appear to have deep biblical significance.* It is this *last statement* that I hope will capture your attention (as it surely did mine) in my **journey science to faith.** After completing our studies and realizing that *medicine and science* alone could not fully explain all the *phenomenon of heavenly visits or apparitions*, nor fully explain all of our *new medical and scientific findings,* we were compelled to ponder **another kind of power**, another *power source of energy* to help explain and answer our very real yet inexplicable *new data.* If this *power source* is really and truly *- the Almighty God,* then to *the Bible* we must go, since it is here in *the Bible* where scholars, theologians and believers say we can find *wisdom, truth* and *His living words* and *find God.* So, what does *the Bible* say about *God's living presence?* And is this the same *living presence* we recorded?

As a medical doctor and scientist, I pondered these questions: *What* really did happen to all the *chosen souls* portrayed in the Bible *in God's living presence*? Is it similar to our experience? How does *the Bible* describe the external, visible and many different *manifestations of God? What* does *the Bible* say about *"a certain pure emanation of the glory of the Almighty God" (Wisdom 7:25)?* Can you imagine what will actually happen to you, me or anyone *in God's living presence - in His Living Presence? What* happens to our external environment *(our atmosphere)* in God's living presence - *in His Living Presence?* Will it be similar to what happens in *the Bible?* Just *what* is this awesome *power source of energy?* Can we measure it? Is this great *power source of energy* just a mere glimpse of the real true *presence of God?* Does God really exist? Is God alive? ***Is Jesus God?*** The answers directly and indirectly to all these universal and yet very personal questions are all in this *(His)* book.

After many (~10) years of trying to grasp the full impact of our new medical and scientific data and findings, and finally reaching my 49th birthday, I am often led to ponder the message foretold by Jesus to Nancy long before our medical and scientific team arrived and indeed, before this research was even a thought in my mind. In a message documented in Nancy's diary on April 29th, 1993, *Jesus* said, *"Scientists are coming. You (Nancy) will outwit all of them, because I will do this. Watch what I will do. The results of the scientific team will be astonishing."*

I now truly believe what was foretold to the prophet Nancy above on April 29th, 1993 was most definitely and unquestionably fulfilled. The results of our *new medical and scientific data* continue to amaze both our research team and our colleagues alike, and seem to cry out for an explanation beyond them, an explanation which, after many years of searching, seems only available in the realm of *faith and religion.* But each person will decide for himself or herself, which is as it should be and is apparently as *the Lord wills. The truth* need not be defended, promoted nor advertised; its purity and clarity in itself sways and persuades, defends and convinces.

I feel so unworthy in even attempting to write a book of this magnitude and scope; that gives genuine true facts and heavenly guidance to all mankind concerning the medical and scientific evidence we recorded *in His Living Presence.* His Living Presence: in His living words, in His living light, in His living touch, in His living bread, and also in and with His Loving Mother, *Our Loving Mother.* Only by the graces and mercy of God have we uncovered the astonishing *new medical and scientific data,* during the extraordinary series of *supernatural events* that occurred in places around the world, and during our medical and scientific testing, and in particular those events that took place in Conyers, in Atlanta (my lab), in Puerto

Rico and Ecuador from 1988 to the present.

If these events had not so impacted my entire being, I know I would never have had the courage to write this *(His)* book. Again I give Him all the credit, honor and glory. But as my own life has been so dramatically and permanently changed, along with the lives of those around me—my family, friends, and those whom God has placed in my path, (in Spanish*: "quen Dios a puesto en mi camino")*—I draw strength from *the call of truth.* Now I cannot turn away, nor back; forward is my only option, and my prayer is that this very truth which science herself delivered to my lap may be as clear to you as it soon became to me. Despite my incredible, initial and hardened skepticism towards these visionaries and apparitions in general, I found myself humbled by the realization of **WHO** is really and truly in control of all medicine, science and faith, physics, mathematics and all of the cosmos.

My little prayer for all who read this *(His)* Book:

May the *God of Abraham, Isaac and Jacob; Jesus* - the *Holy Word of God* and *Wisdom Incarnate;* and the *Holy Spirit* show us **the truth** that will give us **the light** to see clearly what God's *Divine Will* is for each soul on this planet we call earth, the *blue planet.* [Interestingly, *blue* is Mary's color]. May the Lord God, *"the Lord is One,"* always guide our Holy Living Church and help us to see *Mary,* the most Blessed Virgin, according to *His Divine Will* and through *His eyes* - to see *the woman,* the living **blue-**print for the Church, who brings us back *the light* and *peace of paradise* lost by Eve. I cry out to You Lord and shout: *Praise Elohim! Praise You, Lord God!* So please, *Holy Spirit,* anoint us with *the fire of God* to enlighten our minds. Please, *Jesus,* let *Your Precious Blood* wash away all of our sins and *save us.* Please, *Father God, remove the veil* from the eyes of **all** your children. Open all our senses to know You better - our eyes, ears, minds, hearts, hands and even our mouths - to see, hear, know and understand, feel and taste *His tangible Living Presence - the way, the truth, and the life.* And *Behold, the Lamb of God! Behold Him, Who takes away the sins of the world; the true light and peace of the world! Holy Spirit of God* anoint us with *Your "oil of gladness."* Lead us. Teach us - *to live always in God's Divine Will, truth* and *wisdom* -- as we read this *(His)* book. **Amen.**

This prayer to let *the Holy Spirit of God* lead was already expressed in one of the very first messages given to Nancy on August 26th, 1990. Nancy asked *Jesus, "What* do you ask of me? I am troubled that people want me to be silent.*" Jesus* replied, *"Don't be. I do not want you to be completely silent. I want you to bear witness that I am the Living Son of God. How can you be silent and bear witness? You are not to be a silent witness, but a public witness. Look in the Bible and find out what the word witness means. A witness does not go before the Holy Spirit of God. Therefore, Nancy, allow the Holy Spirit to direct you. Let the Holy Spirit lead."*

So, may *the Holy Spirit of God* lead you to ***the truth*** *about His Living Presence:* **1)** His Living Presence in His living words; **2)** His Living Presence in His living light; **3)** His Living Presence in His living bread; and **4)** His Living Presence in His living touch and finally **5)** His Living Presence in and with the Blessed Virgin Mary, *Our Loving Mother, as she brings her baby Jesus to us and to all nations...*

...as we **journey science to faith...**

Now before you start traveling on this very difficult and bumpy *road of science to* reach a treasured, profitable and joyous *faith* - let me first give you some words of inspiration from *the word of God,* as it is written in Zachariah 2:10-13: *"Sing praise, and rejoice, O daughter Sion: for* ***behold I come,*** *and* ***I will dwell in the midst of thee: saith the Lord.*** *And many nations shall be joined to the Lord in that day, and they shall be my people, and* ***I will dwell in the midst of thee:*** *and* ***thou shalt know that the Lord of hosts hath sent me to thee.*** *And the Lord shall possess Juda his portion in the sanctified land: and he shall yet choose Jerusalem.* ***Let all flesh be silent at the presence of the Lord: for he is risen up out of his holy habitation."*** *God* is getting ready to come to you. Are *you* ready for *Him?*

As for me, my personal journey from *science to faith* has led me to feel *on fire for God,* with a *fire* that cannot be quenched. This *fire* inside me drives me onwards and upwards with an incredible and tremendous *zeal.* Yearning, thirsty and panting to always learn more about God's *Way, His Living Presence* and *Divine Will.* I now not only have *faith,* but I have a *real conviction of - the truth, God's truth.* I also have the deepest profound love for God with *a daily, genuine hunger and thirst for the living presence of God and living in His Divine Will.* So, my daily prayer with the utmost fervor is indeed best expressed by one of David's famous Psalms 41:2-3: ***"As the hart panteth after the fountains of water; so my soul panteth after thee, O God. My soul hath thirsted after the strong living God;*** *when shall I come and appear before the face of God?"*

Now ask yourself this very important question:

Are you hungry and thirsty for God?

Let us now --- Come taste and see the goodness of the Lord...

Come journey science to faith...

CHAPTER I

THE CALL

PREVIEW TO THE BASELINE STUDIES

It was early May 1993. I received a long distance telephone call from Bolivia, South America, in the middle of the afternoon, during my busiest and most hectic hours of the day in the clinic. The call was from Prof. Ricardo Castanon, Ph. D., who introduced himself as Director of the Neuropsychology Department at the State University of La Paz, Bolivia. He was soliciting my participation in a medical and scientific study of the supernatural events and mystical phenomena occurring in a local horse town in the U.S. named Conyers, Georgia, USA, which was the actual *equestrian riding site* of the 1996 Atlanta Summer Olympics. The professor asked me directly whether I would be willing to participate in the research and study of these phenomena.

Catching me by surprise, I remember quickly responding, asking him, *"What phenomena* in Conyers, Georgia*?"*

The professor answered, "To study Nancy Fowler, a middle-aged woman who has been having *visions, apparitions* and *receiving messages* from *Jesus* and *the Blessed Virgin Mary."*

I have to admit that, at the very moment I heard this statement, I started laughing to myself and immediately thought this was a crank call. I have a very dear friend from Colombia, a neuro-ophthalmologist in the U.S. Navy, whose wife is from Bolivia. For a time I suspected that it was he who was calling me with this crank call. So playing along with the joke, I said to the professor that I would be very interested; but that I needed him to send me a formal letter of invitation and then I would get back in touch with him. With that, our conversation ended and I certainly didn't expect the joke to go any further. I had been to the Conyers apparition site once before to meet my parents who had come as pilgrims on a bus tour from Miami, Florida, on July 13^{th,} 1992. I recall my true hardened skepticism. I was even worried about my parent's involvement with the *apparitions.* However, I do fondly remember bringing my daughters during their preteen age years to a horse-back riding camp at Conyers (Camp Hope) during the summer vacations in the early 1990's. So, I was at least somewhat familiar with the area.

Much to my surprise, within a few days of this curious telephone call, I received a formal letter of invitation from the State University of La Paz, Bolivia, from the Director of the Neuropsychology Department, the very same professor person who had phoned me. I instantly realized that this was indeed a real bona fide invitation to be part of an international medical and scientific team to study and investigate these *heavenly visits,* as well as, to test the authenticity of Nancy's experiences in

Conyers, Georgia, USA.

At that time I did not realize it, but *my journey* had already begun...

Soon after receiving the letter, I received another telephone call from the professor. Wasting no time, we soon began discussing the logistics of the testing to be done and the types of investigations. During a lengthy and thoroughly technical exchange, I elaborated upon the various conditions and stipulations I would require in order to take part in such a project. I also discussed the $ costs involved in my fees. First and foremost, I wanted to be sure that baseline studies could be done in a sterile laboratory environment so that we would have an opportunity to study the subject's mental status, cognitive behavior and electrical brain function simultaneously. Such meticulous *baseline* studies were primary to a careful following of the scientific method. I was insistent that they needed to be done, and done properly.

These baseline studies could then be compared with others performed elsewhere— for example, at the subject's home, or at the place of her public visionary experiences and so on. Nancy's mental status and electrical brain activity could then be analyzed before, during and after her heavenly visits or experiences, and then comparisons could be made with the baseline studies. The professor wholeheartedly agreed with this established scientific approach. He was very excited that my medical team had the technology available to study the subject, Nancy, not only in the laboratory, but also in the field, as we had at our disposal intensive ambulatory audiovisual TV-EEG telemetry monitoring systems with real time-locked synchronized TV monitors and event markers.

The benefits of this state-of-the-art equipment were many. This ambulatory audiovisual TV-EEG telemetry monitoring system equipment provides the technology to study the mental status, cognitive behavior and electrical brain wave data of any subject simultaneously. Thus, recording audio-visually on a time-locked TV-monitor, which was simultaneously linked to a time-locked EEG telemetry system monitor at the same time, a subject can be clinically observed audio-visually as recorded on a TV screen to study the mental status and cognitive behavior, while the electrical brain wave activity (EEG telemetry) can also be observed and studied on a screen simultaneously.

During any given sequence of time, then, both the subject's cognitive behavior, mental status, as well as the topographic electrical brain function could be recorded, studied and reviewed simultaneously. Thus, the precise moment-by-moment real time cognitive clinical behavior, the psychiatric and neurological mental status examinations via clinical observations, along with the EEG (a topographic electrical neurophysiology study of the brain which is a timed-sequence electrical behavior of the brain and brain wave activity), allows us to record and thoroughly study the subject's psychiatric and cognitive behavior and EEG simultaneously. This gives us an excellent opportunity for a thorough clinical neurological mental status evaluation and a topographic electrical brain wave activity picture or an electroencephalographic evaluation (EEG) to be made simultaneously for comparisons and ultimately for diagnoses and treatment, if needed.

This technology was, and continues to be, very important. Over the past few decades, in fact, a multitude of scientific textbooks and journals dedicated to studying this process have been published. In the 1990's, with the advanced sophistication of computers, vital and important scientific equipment evolved to both qualify and quantify the electrical brain wave activity function of any human being from pre-maturity to old age, for the purposes of studying normal versus abnormal electrical brain wave activity and brain function. We already know that, as our brain matures throughout life, certain known EEG patterns are recognized at certain pivotal approximate dates of maturation with great predictability.

For example, normal EEG patterns change during different levels of wakefulness and during different stages of sleep. These EEG changes also vary in accordance with the age of any given subject. With the advent of computerized topographic and quantitative EEG brain mapping analysis, the medical world has recently become privy to an immense and reliable data bank of statistics reflective of the various normal and abnormal EEG patterns. Many different and specific brain wave activity patterns have been identified which are associated with neurological and psychiatric disorders and all of the normal states of human brain function in both the awake and sleep stages.

The professor was elated by the welcome news that my medical team and I had agreed to participate in this international medical and scientific team endeavor, and especially since we had such sophisticated hi-tech, accessible and reliable equipment to contribute to the effort. I related to him that our EEGs and neurodiagnostic equipment in the laboratory was shielded with a state-of-the-art *platinum mesh,* produced locally by well respected Georgia Tech University in Atlanta, Georgia. Platinum mesh is superior to the conventional lead shielding used in most laboratories around the world. It will allow us to study Nancy in a true, sterile scientific laboratory environment without any chance of data contamination by artificially-produced artifacts (*artifact:* meaning electrical activity recorded not produced by true electrical brain wave activity) which are sometimes frequently seen in field studies.

The date for the *baseline studies* was set for June 11th, 1993. The tests would be performed at the Peachtree Neurology Associates - EEG/neurodiagnostic laboratory at St. Joseph's Hospital Center for Specialty Medicine in Atlanta, Georgia. We agreed to start in the early afternoon hours. The professor informed me that he would be performing neuropsychophysiological tests on Nancy using the

EMG of La Fayette technology, and that Dr. George Hogben, a brilliant psychiatrist from New York with expertise in the psychiatry of mystical experiences etc., would also be present. I then learned that the entire sequence of baseline studies and the subsequent field studies on the appointed day of June 13th, 1993 was to take place at a site known as *the farm*, would be filmed and documented by an Australian film crew headed by Ron Tesoriero with the assistance of a former Australian ABC television documentary producer, Bill Stellar. This Aussie film crew produced several television documentaries on apparitions of the Blessed Virgin Mary in various places around the world, and the question they sought to answer in this documentary was: *"Does the Virgin Mary appear to Nancy Fowler at Conyers, Georgia, USA?"*

I remember the Australian film crew was quite uncomfortable with the way the media at large was handling the whole issue of *apparitions,* particularly those relating to Nancy Fowler. They felt that no journalist, especially in Atlanta, thought it was worthwhile to truly investigate and evaluate Nancy's claims and that no serious journalist would even report on the subject, but only a courageous few.

However, one serious journalist, Lee Green of Atlanta TV channel 46, did air for three separate nights, a one-half-hour documentary on Nancy and the very special Conyers events. Green produced a very fair and objective presentation, showing little doubt from his interviews with me, the other doctors and scientists that Nancy was basically a normal person having very gifted, blessed and special extraordinary experiences.

In the Australian Ron Tesoriero's documentary entitled *Mother of Great Love, Mother of Great Sorrow*, recorded during the May 13th, 1992 apparition of the Blessed Virgin Mary in Conyers, it was reported that earlier in the day Nancy had received a message conveyed to her from *Our Loving Mother,* promising *a sign* would be given *during the apparitions.* In the documentary, they filmed people obviously witnessing and reacting to the inexplicable phenomenon of *the sun spinning and emitting different rainbow colors,* as well as, to an awesome *cloud formation* which actually *formed the silhouette of the Blessed Virgin Mary in the sky during the apparitions.* They felt this was obviously *the sign* that was promised earlier that day. Each of these events was most extraordinary. Photographs that were taken by many pilgrims clearly show *the image of the Blessed Virgin Mary* formed out of white clouds in the blue sky. This *sign of Mary* impressed and increased the Aussie film crew's desire to further investigate Nancy's claims.

I finally had the opportunity to meet the professor in person and the entire Australian film crew when they arrived at my medical office at St. Joseph's Hospital Atlanta for the *baseline studies* on June 11th, 1993. At that time, I also had the opportunity to meet George Collins (Nancy's friend and transcriber of the heavenly messages) and the subject in question, Nancy, *the prophet* and *visionary* in Conyers, Georgia, USA.

After all the formal introductions, we led Nancy back into the EEG/neurodiagnostic laboratory suite in order to set up all the electrical and audiovisual equipment required for the medical and scientific testing. While my EEG technicians, an agnostic and an atheist respectively (at that time), were preparing Nancy for the *baseline studies*, the Australian film crew shared with me a conversation they had in Australia with a well respected neurologist there, Dr. John Graham, in October of 1992. Apparently, Dr. Graham had been given one of the 1992 videotapes of Nancy filmed during the apparitions. Basically, he said that if someone claims that he or she is seeing and speaking to the Blessed Virgin Mary, while others do not see the Virgin Mary, then that person must have a brain problem or abnormality that causes them to *hallucinate.* He also added that this person may even be psychotic, living in a world of their own, where things seem very real to that person only.

In an attempt to convince Dr. Graham of the apparent genuineness of Nancy's claim, the Aussie film crew showed the doctor another videotape of Nancy during the October 13th, 1992 apparitions. This footage impressively attested to the fact that Nancy was undergoing some sort of unique and valid experience. However, upon seeing these tapes, Dr. Graham's response was basically that she (Nancy) did look as if she were really talking and interacting with something. Her actions were indicative of that something being very real to her. But, if she were indeed having a *psychotic hallucination,* this is just the way Dr. Graham would expect her to act (becoming part of a *crazy cycle*). Dr. Graham informed the Aussie film crew that this psychotic behavior may have been triggered in Nancy's case by her going into a prayer state. I was told by the Aussie film crew that Dr. Graham had speculated that by using repetitious prayer (like the Rosary) Nancy could activate a process of *self-hypnosis.* But after reflecting on the videotape, Dr. Graham discussed with the crew that if he had to identify Nancy's medical condition, it probably is *the face of a flagrant psychotic talking to a hallucination.* Thus, he said that *if we were to subject Nancy to a psychiatric examination and an EEG test, we then should be able to determine* what *her problem* is.

Dr. Graham was apparently totally unwilling to concede to the Aussie film crew that there could be any possibility of a *supernatural explanation* for these occurrences. This information turned out to be very insightful for our investigation, as Dr. John Graham, a skeptic of apparitions in general *(like me)* with professional medical and scientific expertise, clearly pinpointed and confirmed *(to me)* the basic approach that our medical research team and I had already planned to undertake.

The tests we proposed to conduct—namely an EEG *(electrical brain wave activity function study)* and a psychiatric examination, plus a clinical neuropsychological battery, neuropsychophysiological testing and neurological examinations were all studies to be done - *before, during, and after the apparitions*—should be more than sufficient to yield the answers to our many numerous, yet intrinsically related questions: Was Nancy (and the other *chosen souls* studied) *crazy?* Were they all flagrant *psychotics?* Were these visionaries *lying, malingering,* or *telling people stories for secondary gain?* Were they having *visual hallucinations* on the basis of *focal seizure activity* over the visual related cortex of the brain? Were their *apparitions* in essence just a *trance state* produced by *self-hypnosis* or *self-induced hypnosis* by *repetitive prayer?* Were they hallucinating from some *organic* or *mental disorder?* Were the *heavenly visits, apparitions or visions* a product of *mass hysteria* or *mass suggestion?* In short, were these experiences *true* or *false?* Is it *fact* or *fiction?* We wanted to know. I *(personally)* wanted to know.

We also wanted to thoroughly examine the external environment *before, during, and after the heavenly visits or apparitions* to see if, indeed, any changes can be detected during these *visits* that will help explain the extraordinary *supernatural events* reported by countless pilgrims in Conyers on the 13th of each month in the early 1990's. Especially with the numerous assortment of reported phenomena like smelling a *scent of roses,* silver medals or rosaries *turning a golden color,* many pilgrims seeing *flashes, bolts or darts of light,* seeing the *sun spin with different colors, or feeling a profound peace* and much, much more. What are these *phenomena?* As a medical scientist, *I ask:* if heaven truly visits Nancy, *what* do or should we look for, and *what* will we find?

Each of these questions, and the answers they eventually reaped, was significant, as our quest was to find out the **truth** in this entire matter— *the whole truth and nothing but the truth, so help me God.* And the Lord God surely did help, as you will see! I felt these questions could be answered with a systematic approach by studying Nancy's cognitive behavior and mental status state using psychiatric, neuropsychophysiological and neurological examinations; plus by studying the EEG/electrical brain wave function using the state-of-the-art intensive audiovisual TV-EEG telemetry monitoring systems previously described. Some of the questions would be answered *in the field,* especially those pertaining to *mass hysteria* or *mass suggestion,* while other questions would be answered *in the laboratory setting.* Also intriguing to ponder is what type of energy we will find in the surrounding atmosphere and external environment *during the heavenly visits and* as we will discover --- *in His Living Presence?*

During the setup of the *baseline studies* in our neurodiagnostic laboratory at St. Joseph's Hospital, Center for Specialty Medicine, I was informed that for the upcoming testing *in the field* at the farm house scheduled two days later on June 13th,, 1993, a crowd of pilgrims in excess of eighty thousand was predicted. I was initially shocked at the prospect of such a large number, but then it was explained to me that such crowds were not unusual at the monthly apparitions of the Blessed Virgin Mary to Nancy, which occurred on the 13th of every month. We were then informed that a group of independent international scientists would also be present to monitor the different radiation energy fields - before, during and after the apparitions - in order to find out whether any external environmental stimuli or energy changes in the atmosphere of the room could be measured, qualified and quantified.

I also soon learned that our medical team's New York psychiatrist, Dr. George Hogben, would not be attending the baseline studies scheduled because of a prior engagement. But, that he would be performing his own baseline studies and psychiatric mental status examinations - before, during, and after the apparitions - on the appointed June 13th, 1993. This series of tests would indeed be satisfactory to complete all the requirements for his psychiatric clinical observations and evaluations of Nancy - before, during and after the apparitions. As will soon be demonstrated, Dr. Hogben's brilliant in-depth insights, professional opinions and impressions regarding his professional medical and clinical psychiatric observations and also his very thorough clinical psychiatric evaluations were indeed most critical for our overall *data* recorded and documented.

With most of the details now out of the way, Nancy plus the medical and scientific team prepared for the upcoming tests, we were ready to begin.

Now the *journey science to faith* begins...

CHAPTER II

"NOTHING IS IMPOSSIBLE"

BASELINE STUDIES OF JUNE 11th, 1993

We were just about ready to commence our testing of the June 11th, 1993 baseline studies, when George Collins approached me. Mr. Collins describes himself as Nancy's good friend who volunteers literally most of his time to help with the original mission requested by *Jesus and Our Loving Mother.*

A single man who leads a prayerful life, as well as a graduate and instructor of the well-respected Mississippi State University Engineering School, it is George's responsibility to record all of the messages Nancy claims to receive from heaven. As quickly as Nancy receives messages from heaven and verbalizes them, George writes the words onto paper. According to many priests and other eyewitnesses, George has been given a special gift from heaven in being able to record every word so precisely. Often Nancy speaks so softly that without a micro-phone, it is all but impossible at times for others (like me) to hear her well. Charged with his mission, George has become proficient in this important craft. *Jesus* has requested through Nancy that George categorize all the messages and teachings from heaven. He has now spent well over a decade dedicated to compiling these heavenly messages with *the living words of God.*

George once remarked that, as an engineer and a very logical thinker, he ***needed signs*** in order to believe that these messages were really coming from Jesus and the Blessed Virgin Mary. Eventually, George received *the signs* he asked for, and in fact these *signs* were so convincing, that he now devotes most of his life to propagating *the messages.* George is an eye witness to these *supernatural events* and gives his testimony concerning what he believes is the truth about the apparitions in Conyers. George has witnessed, in amazement, the fulfillment of many prophecies foretold by *Jesus and Our Loving Mother* through Nancy. George said, *"Jesus reads my heart and mind and answers my many questions through Nancy before I even verbalize them."* George has now come to know and believe these messages are truly of *divine origin.*

Now approaching me with obvious purpose, George indicated that Nancy had some concerns to discuss. I entered the EEG/neurodiagnostic laboratory, while Nancy was seated and the EEG technicians were attaching the EEG scalp electrodes to her head. Looking at me with concern, Nancy asked, *"Do you have a blessed crucifix in this office?"* I became very perplexed, and said with some regret, *"No."* Nancy then asked, *"Can you please get a blessed crucifix for these tests, so that I can focus on Jesus and pray during the testing?"*

I remember becoming a bit frustrated, and thinking to myself, *"Great...* here we are on a Friday afternoon... and where in the world am I going to get a *blessed crucifix*... at this time?" I must admit I became a little upset at not being informed of this particular and peculiar request and obvious requirement prior to setting up for the *baseline studies.*

Since our professional medical office is attached to the St. Joseph's Hospital of Atlanta, I immediately called *pastoral care services* and spoke with one of the *Sisters of Mercy* answering the phone. I asked if she knew where I could buy or borrow a *blessed crucifix* right now for the purposes of the *baseline studies.* The kind Sr. Mary Sue said, *"It is just not possible to obtain a blessed crucifix on such short notice."* As she was saying these words, she suddenly remarked, *"Oh,* wait a minute... there is a beautiful crucifix in the gift shop...but is *not blessed."* And before I even had the chance to react with any further frustration, she quickly added, *"Oh wait ...Father* Cummings is walking through the door *right now."*

In less than five minutes, the kind sister delivered a *blessed crucifix* from the gift shop *to my office!* I was indeed delighted on the one hand, but was simultaneously perplexed and intrigued on the other hand at the prospect of this very unlikely accomplishment that had just occurred. Imagine, first locating a *crucifix* and then finding a *priest to bless* the crucifix in a very busy Hospital Medical Center on a Friday afternoon within five minutes of asking for it. Though I may not have recognized it at the time, it was indeed a small lesson and foreshadow of what I would soon later learn so powerfully via the awesome results of our tests, *that* ***nothing is impossible with God!*** I thanked the tall, gentle and smiling sister for bringing the *blessed crucifix,* and I quickly placed it on the wall in the intensive monitoring audiovisual TV-EEG telemetry room. Then, I diligently proceeded with the medical history and neurological examinations.

MEDICAL HISTORY

HISTORY OF PRESENT ILLNESS: Nancy Fowler was a forty-five years old right-handed (at the time of our initial studies) very pleasant overweight Caucasian female. She was shy, humble and prayerful, and spoke softly with a slight Boston accent. Boston was the place of her birth. The history of present illness was significant only for problems concerned with weight gain; otherwise, she had been in good health.

PAST MEDICAL HISTORY: Significant for an acute Guillain-Barre syndrome, which is an acute post viral inflammatory demyelinating polyradiculoneuropathy affecting predominantly the myelin in the peripheral motor roots of the spinal cord. This malady causes severe motor weakness and loss of deep tendon reflexes. Fortunately, Nancy experienced a 100 % recovery which was evident in her normal neurological examinations.

PAST TRAUMA HISTORY: She was involved a motor vehicle accident wherein the car spun, but she endured no closed head trauma or loss of consciousness.

She denied having any history of post-traumatic brain syndrome symptoms or any neurological deficits, and has no history of any psychiatric disorders or disturbances.

PAST PSYCH HISTORY: Nancy claimed starting *to see mystically,* when she was a young girl; but it later intensified, while she was working as a registered nurse in the CCU Cardiac Care Unit of a local Hospital in Boston, Mass. It was during that time that she began to have many unexplained mystical experiences. She recounted, *"I thought* I was going crazy." So, Nancy took herself to see a psychiatrist, who, after a complete psychiatric evaluation, told Nancy that she was perfectly *normal.* But soon after this evaluation, as a result of some ongoing marital problems, Nancy claimed to feel knocked down. So, she sought another evaluation from a different psychiatrist in a local Hospital in Boston where she was still working as a registered nurse. This other psychiatrist told Nancy that she did not meet any of the criteria for clinical depression. No psychiatric prescription or psychotherapy was ordered. No mental illness was found.

ALLERGIES: None known.

MEDICATIONS: Currently Nancy is on no medications, but does take over the counter vitamins.

SOCIAL HISTORY: Married with children, two adopted boys, at the time of the testing. She is now divorced and has been granted an annulment from the Roman Catholic Church. No history of tobacco, drug or alcohol abuse.

FAMILY HISTORY: History of heart disease on the paternal side and diabetes in two siblings. No seizures, neurological or psychiatric disorders.

REVIEW OF SYSTEMS: Non-contributory.

NEUROLOGICAL EXAMINATION

HEAD: Normal with no deformities.

NECK: Supple with normal range of motion.

No evidence of meningeal irritation with a negative Kerning's sign and a negative Brudzinski's sign, negative Forbes-Norris sign, negative L'hermitte's sign, and negative Spurling's sign. Normal auscultation was noted of both carotid arteries with no bruits.

SPINE: Normal with no deformities and normal range of motion in the trunk and lower back.

MENTAL STATUS: Awake, alert, oriented to name, place and time. Higher cortical function was highly intact with normal fluent speech with a slight Bostonian accent. No anomia, aphasia or apraxia was noted. Her attention span, immediate memory, short-term memory and long term memory was normal. She is highly intelligent and articulate with a normal full and supple affect and animation. Nancy graduated *summa cum laude,* the highest honors at the University of Maryland. She demonstrated is no evidence of any psychiatric disturbance, mood disorder, thought disorder, affective disorder or personality disorder. No evidence of any delusions, paranoia, hallucinations or delirium was identified. Thus, no evidence of psychoses was identified. No evidence of hysteria or evidence of malingering was identified. And there was no evidence of any epileptic behavior or seizure activity clinically observed or recorded.

CRANIAL NERVES I-XII: Grossly normal with bilateral pupils that were equally round and reactive to light and accommodation. Normal corneal reflexes were noted bilaterally. Visual fields were full to confrontation and to double simultaneous stimulation. Fundi were normal with no evidence of papilledema and with normal venous pulsations noted bilaterally. EOM's were normal with no nystagmus. The Facial smile was symmetrical with normal sensations. Uvula, palate and tongue were all midline with normal gag reflex, and normal bilateral shoulder shrugs.

MOTOR: No drift or fixation, and normal 5/5 motor strength and tone were noted throughout all muscle groups tested with no tremors, tics, twitching or myoclonus noted. No other adventitious movements were identified. No cramps or spasms were noted. No myotonia, myokymia or dystonia was noted. No atrophy or fasciculations were identified. And there was no evidence of any spasticity or cogwheel-rigidity or any extra-pyramidal signs identified.

POSTURE, STANCE AND GAIT: Normal.

COORDINATION: No ataxia or dysmetria was noted. Normal rapid alternating movements were noted bilaterally and normal checking was noted in all extremities.

DEEP TENDON REFLEXES: Normal 2+ and symmetrical throughout with no pathological spread of reflexes. No cross adduction was noted. No clonus was elicited, sustained or un-sustained type.

ABDOMINAL REFLEXES: Normal in all four abdominal quadrants.

CORTICAL REFLEXES: No grasp reflex/palmomental reflexes identified.

TOES: Negative Babinski's sign with toes that were downward pointing bilaterally. There were no pathological reflexes recorded.

SENSORY: Normal in both primary and secondary sensory modalities throughout and bilaterally.

ROMBERG SIGN: Negative and normal.

WARTENBERG SIGN: Negative and normal.

SCHWARTZMAN SIGN: Normal.

In short, Nancy's complete cognitive/mental status and neurological examinations and general physical exam (not shown) other than her obesity was **normal** for her stated age of 45 years. A complete clinical neuropsychological examination and psychiatric evaluations will be conducted by Prof. Castanon, Ph.D. and George Hogben, M.D., respectively. Additional neuropsychophysiological studies will also be performed by the professor during the upcoming studies using the EMG system of La Fayette.

Just after having finished with Nancy's neurological examinations, which was as stated entirely normal, I was struck by my initial impressions of her overall demeanor—a normal, pleasant, loving, shy and humble person, with an almost childlike honesty in her remarks. As producer Bill Stellar began to film Nancy while she was still being hooked up by my two EEG technicians, he unintentionally, though providentially, recorded this conversation between Nancy and the professor (Prof.).

Nancy*: "Our Lord told me* a few days ago*, 'you will be a busy one this weekend and there will be many tests done.* ***Watch, what I will do.***' So, I know that something will show from these *tests."*

Prof.*: "But He* (referring to *Jesus*) agrees that we can do these *tests?"*

Nancy*: "I* guess so, because *Jesus* did say, '*Watch, what I will do.'"*

Shortly afterward, the entire Australian film crew and I were observing my medical team and registered EEG technicians as they meticulously continued placing the EEG scalp electrodes on Nancy. Later during a spare minute, they related the details of a very pleasant exchange they had had with Nancy on the way to our office. The Aussie film crew asked her*, "Nancy,* do you know *why* you have been *chosen?"*

Nancy hesitated slightly and then replied*, "Jesus* once said to me*, 'if I wanted to show the world my love and mercy, I would choose a person who is in most need of it. Nancy, you are that person.'"* Consequently, Nancy indicated that *the grace* she receives is a *pure gift from God*, and not something that she has earned or even merits.

After all the EEG scalp electrodes were placed along with ECG (electrocardiography), EMG (electromyography) and EOG (electro-oculography), Nancy was taken to the intensive monitoring audiovisual TV-EEG telemetry laboratory suite where several cameras were ready to record her and document the entire event. Our cameras time-locked to the EEG equipment were carefully stationed to focus on Nancy. At the foot of the bed another stationary camera was placed by the Aussie film crew, plus a hand held mobile camera that was ready to film any of the reactions, actions and comments of the doctors and EEG technicians, and also film the electrical activity of Nancy's brain waves on the electroencephalographic paper as needed. Once Nancy was inside the audiovisual TV-EEG telemetry room, she was perfectly visible via the large double glass two-way mirror which allowed for easy viewing from the audiovisual TV-EEG telemetry monitoring station. The room provided a very quiet and relaxing setting for Nancy. George Collins then asked my permission to stay in the audiovisual TV-EEG telemetry laboratory suite during the testing for purposes of recording any visions or messages Nancy might possibly receive during the medical and scientific baseline study and testing. I quickly showed him different areas where he could comfortably stand or sit and be still able to see and hear the entire baseline study testing event. George complied with no complaints.

Once inside the audiovisual TV-EEG telemetry laboratory suite, Nancy was asked to lie down on the EEG bed for the baseline study testing to begin. By way of explanation, an EEG or electroencephalogram is a graphic visible record of amplified electrical cerebral activity generated by the millions of nerve cells in the brain. Thus, by placing electrodes on the scalp and then amplifying the electrical activity, we can record a timed electrical brain wave picture on a graph paper, so that from one moment to the next we can see the rising and falling of electrical brain cell potentials called *brain waves* in different head regions or topography of the brain. During approximately the first two hours of the intensive monitoring audiovisual TV-EEG telemetry testing, Nancy's electrical brain wave activity picture was completely normal in states of awake and alertness and also in states of drowsiness and in all stages of sleep. A series of activation tests were performed, designed to bring out various EEG responses and reactions to known stimuli. These provocative EEG tests include the prolonged photic stimulation using different color filters and prolonged hyperventilation studies. The activation studies on this day of testing demonstrated absolutely no abnormal paroxysmal discharges and produced no abnormal brain wave activity. The activation tests did not precipitate any ictal or interictal epileptic discharges. The EEG tests also did not activate any epileptic potential activity nor produce any electrographic seizure activity or seizure behavior. Thus, these prolonged activation studies importantly did not activate or stimulate or produce any visual hallucinations or any visions or apparitions in the subject, Nancy.

After the prolonged EEG activation procedures were completed, I entered the audiovisual TV-EEG telemetry laboratory suite and stood next to Nancy at the foot of the bed. She remained lying on the EEG telemetry bed. Then the professor entered the room while opening his legal size notebook pad to a series of prewritten questions, and began to speak to Nancy in a very controlled, monotone and deep voice, which had a hypnotic tone type quality. His deliberate purpose was *to test* whether hypnotic suggestions could somehow precipitate Nancy's *visions or heavenly visits or apparitions.* I remember the professor saying to Nancy, who had her eyes closed.

Prof.: *"Open* your eyes and try to see something. Anything you want, anything you can.*"*

Nancy replied, "I don't see anything.*"*

Prof.: "Try to see something.*"*

Nancy replied, "I don't see anything.*"*

Then the professor moved to another position inside the room and said:

Prof.: "If I move over here in front of you, do you see anything *(mystically)?"*

Nancy paused and softly replied, *"No."*

Then, the professor said in a deep monotone voice:

Prof.: *"Nancy,* have a vision... *"* Nancy shook her head as if to say she was not seeing anything. And then the professor said:

Prof.*: "Nancy,* see something*... " - a long pause-..."Nancy,* see something*..." – pause--*

This type of questioning was repeated several times and produced absolutely no changes. Neither in Nancy's behavior nor in the electrical brain wave activity picture as seen on the audiovisual TV-EEG telemetry display monitors did we see any changes.

Then, the professor moved back closer to the right side of Nancy and said:

Prof.: *"Begin* to pray*."*

The professor then asked Nancy to close her eyes and then open them. And he asked the same sequence of commands again a few seconds later. Then, the professor again tried to use hypnotic type suggestions to induce Nancy to have a *vision.*

Nancy (paused again) said*, "*Boy, one thing is for sure, it is a pure gift from God, and He *(God)* is in total control... because I can't make it happen*..."*

Prof.: *"Even* if you pray*?"*

Nancy could now be seen closing her eyes and praying intensely and reverently for a while, at this time. Then after a pause of about ten seconds, Nancy became very excited and happy. Her facial expression actually lit up with a radiant glow of joy and ecstasy. Nancy then said*, "*A light just flashed*."*

A few seconds later with a joyful, radiantly beaming face, loud voice full of excitement,

Nancy proclaimed*, "Now* I have a vision. I just saw *the Risen Christ. He* was faint. I saw *His* head and shoulders and light just burst onto you, doctor (she was referring to me, Dr. Sanchez, as I stood at the foot of the EEG telemetry bed), on the right side of your face*."*

As Nancy said those words, Bill Stellar with the hand-held mobile camera rolling quickly moved to where the EEG technicians had written on the EEG record, *Christ.* The time 14:21:00 was written on the EEG tracing. At the precise moment when the word *Christ* was written on the EEG epoch (a timed sequence section of EEG graph paper)—during Nancy's vision of *Jesus*—there was an immediate, drastic and definite change in the electrical brain wave activity that was recorded and documented.

Nancy said*, "Jesus* has just appeared again*."* Nancy pointed just behind me, slightly off to my right. She was obviously very joyous, happy and ecstatic that *Jesus* was present. Nancy then said in a very soft and gentle voice*, "I see* a small rim of light, on your right shoulder, doctor (referring again to me, Dr. Sanchez) and a beam of light *(like a flash or dart or bolt of lightning)* just went through your chest*..."*

Nancy said*, "*Thank you*, Jesus."* Then looking at me (Dr. Sanchez) intently she said, *"You* need to pray more*."* Immediately after saying these words, she blushed with childlike embarrassment and quickly tried taking back her words.

Nancy said, *"Oops* (looking very embarrassed), I shouldn't have said that."

The medical and scientific testing with the intensive EEG monitoring continued. Then moments after the first apparition of Jesus, Nancy once again became visibly excited. Nancy in a louder voice said, *"Jesus* has just appeared again." Nancy also said a very bright light appeared on my right shoulder again, that was two to three inches high in brightness. Then, she saw another larger beam of light flash through my chest (like lightning). Nancy became very excited. She looked over to the professor, who was standing adjacent to her near the TV-EEG telemetry bed.

Nancy quickly said to him, "It is happening again, it's happening again, it's happening to this doctor (again referring to me) just like it happened to you professor, in Bolivia."

Then *looking at me* (Dr. Sanchez) with a smile softly said, *"You* have a good heart."

I do remember this moment very well. Unable to relinquish my very hardened skeptical and scientific mindset, I was thinking to myself, *"Jesus...* if you are really here... behind me... I am sorry for not kneeling... but I just do not believe this. Lord, please help me understand all of this." I remember that, despite my hardened skepticism, I slowly turned my head gently to the right just slightly for a quick peek behind me. I did not see *Jesus,* so initially I was feeling somewhat relieved. Then, I felt a tremendous and virtually indescribable calm and profound peace all around me. This *peace* was indeed profound.

As time passed and more of the audiovisual TV-EEG telemetry testing continued, Nancy now for yet a third time became visibly excited once more. And beaming with joy and *ecstasy* she shouted out, *"Jesus* just appeared again."

Prof.: *"How* do you see Him *(Jesus)?"*

Nancy: *"In the spirit form...* in a *glorified state."*

Prof.: *"Big?* Small?"

Nancy retorted, *"Life-size,* and then...*the light* just flashed on you again (addressing *me,* Dr. Sanchez). *This message is* intended *for you* (Dr. Sanchez). *Praise you, Jesus. It's now gone..."*

Nancy later explained, *"When the Risen Christ appeared, He* was *life-size* and then *light flashed onto you, doctor* and you had an *aura of light* about five or six inches coming from *all around you. Jesus* gave me *visions* again and *now it's gone. Thank you, Jesus!" (**Note:*** Nancy sees *visions of light,* so when she says *"now It's gone,"* she is actually referring to *the visions of light* - that are *now... gone.)*

In trying to really understand what had just happened, I nervously asked Nancy to explain further. Nancy said that she later saw a much more intense and brilliant beam of light *like a bolt or dart or flash of lightning* literally *flash* or *dart* through my chest, while a larger and brighter *aura of light* about five to six inches was seen over my entire head, shoulders and torso area and round about me. It was at this point that she looked straight at me.

Nancy said, *"Doctor* (referring to *me*), *Jesus* has a *message* for you. I will tell you in private, when we finish with *the testing."*

I now have to admit that I initially felt a little scared and nervous about this particular news. While my hardened skeptical, scientific mind wondered, *"Wait* a minute *who* is being tested here, *Nancy* or *me?"* I did not know *what* all this meant, but I was eager to find out. I especially wondered *what* kind of EEG brain wave activity would be recorded *during the three separate appearances of Jesus (in His Living Presence).* The intensive monitoring audiovisual TV-EEG telemetry studies continued for at least another thirty minutes. During this time we attempted to reproduce all the known physiological and electrical artifacts for comparison with the EEG data we had acquired *during the three separate apparitions of Jesus* (i.e., eye blinking, eye movements, head movements, muscle, swallowing, chewing, startle, glosso-kinetic artifacts, ECG, sweating, etc.). After exhausting all our options and curiosities, the nearly four hours of intensive baseline studies ended.

While we were discussing the just-completed studies in the audiovisual TV-EEG telemetry laboratory suite, none of the doctors, medical EEG technicians, the professor or the Aussie film crew present---no one said they saw *the visions of light* or *apparitions* claimed by Nancy. Only Nancy claims to have witnessed seeing *the light,* flashing lights, a beam of light *(like lightning),* auras of light and *Jesus* - life size in a *glorified state - in light (in His Living Presence)* and *Jesus* **after** *His* 3rd appearance *with His light still present, heard Jesus speaking - His living words.*

To explain further Nancy said, "All of *God's words* give *life* to the soul." Then while discussing this same topic many years later, she asked me to read John 1:1-14. In these verses *Jesus* **is** the true *personification of living word of God made flesh.* John 1:4: *"In Him* was *life,* and *the life* was *the light of men."* So if this is *true,* all of *His words* (the word of God/see *Jesus* in Rev19:13) are indeed *life giving* and true *living words. The word of God* thus, gives us *the light* that shows us *"the way, the truth and the life,"* and *the life* **is** *eternal life.*

I then dispatched my EEG technicians to start removing the EEG scalp electrodes from Nancy's head. And after they completed disconnecting the audiovisual TV-EEG telemetry monitoring systems, Nancy asked where we might go in private, to give me this private *message* from *Jesus?* I took Nancy into one of my neurology clinic examination rooms and closed the door. As I sat down and observed Nancy, I could see clearly that she was visibly shy and looking embarrassingly sort of uncomfortable with the *message* she was about to give me.

Nancy said, *"Dr. Sanchez,* I say this... only out of obedience to *Jesus...*

...Jesus said, "Ramon (Dr. Sanchez) *if you want to get closer to me* (Jesus)... *stop worrying about money."*

[**Note:** Nancy says that *Jesus* calls everyone by their *first name.*]

As I heard these words, I became aghast, open-mouthed and stunned frozen for a few moments. I asked myself, *"How* could Nancy know this about me*?"* This message *Jesus* had for me (Dr. Sanchez) was so deeply personal that I must admit that even despite my severe hardened skepticism over the entire issue concerning visions and apparitions in general; it was at this point in time that I began to really contemplate with wonder, "Are these *heavenly visits, visions* or *apparitions* to Nancy for real*?* How could Nancy have known this very deep and personal part of my current private life without ever meeting me before? And without knowing my thoughts, how could she have known, since this issue (of money) was not even on my mind the day of the testing*?"* I simply could not come up with any good logical explanations or answers to my queries. I began to question, perhaps for the first time in my life: Was there a *power* beyond our understanding that was aware of all our thoughts and our deepest, darkest secrets? Or was this just a mere *coincidence?* As a young professional at that particular time in my life and career, I must confess, I had just become increasingly obsessed with the idea of making lots of money. Having just met her, how could Nancy possibly know this fact?

I was reminded of a conversation with George Collins concerning his personal conversion, particularly regarding his comment that he needed signs to help him, which he eventually received. Nancy would tell George things that Jesus or the Blessed Virgin Mary would say to Nancy about him that no one could possibly know. And George speaking about them said*, "*They were right.*"* At times, George said, he would just be thinking about something, and then Jesus or the Blessed Virgin Mary, through Nancy, would address those things that he had just been thinking about. George once said to a group of pilgrims*, "*I have been around Nancy long enough to know how she talks, what she will say or not say. I definitely know that *the messages* that she tells me to write down are not coming from her*, no way.* No way could she write such profound and deep life changing words, only God can say those words. Nancy's apparitions are real. I was converted by these *signs* and by *His living words."* Now I could not help but wonder if these *signs* George Collins was speaking of *had just occurred* ***to me***...

With the *baseline studies* now ended, I was left literally amazed, confused, and even a bit flattered (Oh, how vain!) after having just received *a private message from Jesus,* despite its content and *personal wake up call* ***for me.*** Then, Nancy and the entire group left my office and headed back to Conyers. I was so anxious to review the audiovisual TV-EEG telemetry monitoring systems data just completed that day.

Little did I know that the amazement and *confusion* I felt was not even the tip of the iceberg...?

The journey science to faith is now just starting to rev up...

RESULTS OF BASELINE STUDIES

Armed with the assurance that our thorough neuropsychological cognitive testing and mental status examinations showed Nancy to be absolutely **normal**, we proceeded wholeheartedly with the EEG testing.

Our combined clinical observations during the EEG testing were astounding:

-Subject Nancy Fowler was awake, alert and oriented with clear logical thinking; normal fluent speech with normal prosody and a Boston accent; and no anomia, aphasia, or apraxia; normal content of thought and speech; no evidence of a thought or mood or affective or personality disorders. No hysteria or malingering. Normal immediate, short-term and long-term memory:

-Nancy's train of thinking was completely clear and logical. She was able to describe what she was seeing in vivid detail during the three apparitions or visitations of *Jesus (in His Living Presence).* She demonstrated no loss of reality contact with herself or with the people around her—in itself this is very good evidence that there was no psychotic disturbance of any kind. Moreover, we saw no clinical evidence of a hypnotic trance despite the repeated attempts by the professor to produce or induce this response from Nancy through a trial of numerous hypnotic suggestions given.

-Nancy's affect was indeed normal, full and supple with no evidence of hysteria or depression or anxiety or any mood disorders. With her steady affect, she reacted appropriately to the thoughts that she was expressing as well as to the visions she saw, as seen in the audiovisual TV-EEG telemetry system in the laboratory suite during the *three separate visits of Jesus.* These *heavenly visits of Jesus (in His Living Presence)* also *included* in the 3rd visitation as *Jesus* speaks to Nancy - *His Living Words.* Recall, *Jesus* gave Nancy a private message to give to me. During the moment *Jesus* was *speaking,* (Nancy *did not see Him,* but *did see the light)* the same stimulus specific evoked EEG pattern 333 was also identified.

-Nancy's mood was at all times appropriate for what she was expressing to be seeing. Indeed, during the moments that Jesus appeared, Nancy's mood was very lovingly joyful, excited, yet profoundly calm and peaceful. According to the professor, there was no evidence of a personality disorder, no affective disorder and no malingering (or lying) found in the extensive testing.

-It was obvious during the review of the intensive monitoring audiovisual TV-EEG telemetry system testing, that during the three separate *heavenly visits of Jesus,* Nancy was indeed, awake, alert with very focused attention while concentrating on the heavenly visits of Jesus and retained the ability to intelligently relate what she was *seeing* and *hearing* to us, the medical doctors and the research medical team around her throughout the study.

-There was absolutely no evidence of any epileptic seizure activity or epileptic behavior: before, during or after the three separate visits of *Jesus.* This was eye witnessed and testified by all the members of my medical research team present for the baseline studies this day. And this was also personally reaffirmed by me, a USA Board Certified neurologist plus completion of two year fellowship training program in epilepsy / EEG / neurophysiology / sleep disorders / neuropharmacology. Even more significantly, there was absolutely no seizure activity seen electrographically on the audiovisual TV-EEG telemetry system during the three separate *visits of Jesus.* Also, no seizures were recorded electrographically on EEG during any of the prolonged *baseline studies* just completed. Thus, there was absolutely no evidence of any pathology in any of the EEG activity recorded: before, during, or after Nancy's *visits of Jesus* that can potentially produce audiovisual hallucinations or possibly explain the experiences Nancy claims.

-A complete and thorough neurological, neuropsychological, cognitive-mental status examinations and a prolonged EEG battery conducted for the baseline studies was entirely ***normal*** *for her stated age of 45 years.*

-The prolonged EEG testing, which lasted over three and one-half hours and included prolonged activation studies using different color filters, was also entirely *normal (for subject's stated age).* The background activity was normal displaying posterior symmetrically rhythmic alpha 9-10 Hz with eyes closed. Normal beta activity was seen in the anterior head regions with eyes closed and in all channels with eyes open. A ***normal variant*** was seen *rarely* and *only in the drowsy state - a psychomotor variant* ranging 5 to 6 Hz (avg. 5.5 Hz) observed over the bi-temporal head regions. Normal sleep stages I and II were recorded with no activation of any seizure activity, thus no ictal or interictal epileptic discharges were noted. No paroxysmal or epileptic seizure activity or epileptic behavior was identified. Basically, no pathological EEG activity was recorded, and no evidence of a sleep disturbance was found.

Only during the three separate *heavenly visits of Jesus - in His Living Presence (Jesus in light - Nancy's words)* or *when Jesus speaks His Living Words* in *the light* - did we record dramatic and unprecedented changes in the EEG tracing - producing the 333 pattern. These amazing changes began *only* with the immediate or sudden *appearances of Jesus* to Nancy and abated immediately and *only* when Nancy said that *Jesus* was no longer present, seen or heard (audibly or interiorly). It is extremely important to emphasize that these clear-cut electrographic (EEG) changes that occurred *only* during the three separate EEG epochs (periods of time) when *Jesus appears* or *speaks* to Nancy were clearly astonishing and ***unprecedented*** in even in today's current medical, scientific and neurophysiology literature. Specifically the changes were:

1) The sudden appearance of higher amplitude, medium to high range voltage, rhythmic 3 Hz delta rhythms, ranging from 2.5 to 3.5 Hz, but with a clear average and preponderance of 3 Hz delta activity was recorded. The rhythmic 3 Hz delta rhythms was best seen over the frontal, temporal and central regions, bilaterally, and at times spread to the parietal occipital regions, bilaterally, and had the same characteristic brain wave topography EEG pattern and distribution that is typically *only* seen in *deep sleep stages* in *normal* subjects.

2) There was no lateral focal slow activity recorded.

3) No sharp transients, no sharp waves, no spikes, no poly-spikes and wave discharges, no paroxysmal activity, no epileptic discharges and no seizure activity was recorded. Also no epileptic behavior was identified.

4) Typical beta activity seen and recorded with her eyes open as observed throughout the baseline studies only abruptly changed during each of the three separate EEG epochs (periods of time) when the Nancy claimed *Jesus is here.* The beta activity with eyes open became accentuated with slightly higher amplitude (voltage) in all the brain wave EEG channels only during the three separate EEG epochs recorded of the heavenly visits of Jesus *(in His Living Presence).* The accentuation of the beta rhythms recorded in all brain wave EEG channels verifies Nancy's recorded behavior of being *in a wakeful state, alert with focused attention and eyes wide open with dramatically reduced blinking whenever she claimed to see Jesus.* Nancy on the first two occasions saw *Jesus* without receiving any messages. On the third *heavenly visit* during the *baseline studies,* after initially claiming *to see Jesus*, Nancy started *to hear Jesus speaking* to her *audibly then interiorly, while still seeing the light, but did not see Jesus.* During these 3 very special EEG epochs, Nancy appeared excitedly joyful and was in *ecstasy,* and yet *very calm* as she later claimed *a feeling of profound peace, love, and joy.* This was clearly documented on the audiovisual TV-EEG telemetry display monitors.

5) The prominent 3 Hz delta rhythms were recorded only during the three separate EEG epochs in which *Jesus* was visually present as reported by Nancy and on the third visit - *Jesus* spoke to Nancy and *gave a message* to her. Somehow this EEG epoch also produced the same EEG pattern of three 3Hz delta brain waves in succession, jointly forming a recurring mathematical and numerical pattern of **333** – which is 3 cycles in 1 second. This EEG pattern was associated with no sharp waves, no spikes or poly-spike wave discharges and no pathology was seen interspersed with these 3 Hz EEG patterns recorded. There was no epileptic behavior. And no petit mal seizures were documented.

6) There was no evidence of artifacts such as eye movements, eye blinking, or glosso-kinetic artifacts; and no head movements, muscle, sweating, swallowing, or jaw movement artifacts; and no other physiological or any electrical artifacts to possibly explain the appearance and disappearance of the 3 Hz delta rhythms, deep sleep pattern, which repeatedly appeared along with the overriding slightly accentuated beta activity *(with eyes open),* an awake state, alert with focused attention pattern superimposed, as was seen in all the brain wave EEG channels-- *only in the living presence of Jesus* and *during the time when Jesus speaks to*

Nancy. This is unbelievably amazing, astonishing and unprecedented, as it undoubtedly proves that what I really recorded was truly a *contradiction* of true cerebral (electrical) brain wave activity patterns that is brain-produced and was not produced by any artifact.

7) The brain wave topography distribution of the 3 Hz *delta rhythms* recorded is typically seen in normal adult subjects only during the stages of *deep sleep.* But how is this possible, since Nancy was obviously *awake, alert with focused attention,* as confirmed by the audiovisual TV-EEG telemetry system video display monitors and also confirmed by the diffuse accentuated beta rhythms recorded superimposed on the EEG? This EEG recording on this day of testing is indeed astonishing, amazing and unprecedented and a true *oxymoron* and *a contradiction* of basic pure physiological principles. **Note:** It's just like taking the most extreme opposites and placing them together simultaneously; it is like *"the first and the last, the beginning and the end, the Alpha and the Omega"* all at once, simultaneously. Sound familiar? Now here is some EEG technical information for those who want to know. It is important to note that **delta** activity is the s*lowest brain wave activity range*. In Greek it is the sign of the *triangle* or *one form with three sides*. Most of the available scientific literature refers to *delta activity* as being *in the range of 0.5 to 3.5 Hz,* while other sources indicate that it *may go as high as 4 Hz.* However, the majority of all the neurophysiology literature resources available today would concur with a delta frequency range of 0 to 3.5 Hz. See Neidermeyer and Lopes de Silva, 3rd edition. The range of **theta** activity, on the other hand, begins at 4 Hz and may go as high as 7.5 Hz. The average theta frequency range generally agreed upon in most of the international neurophysiology literature is 4 to 7.5 Hz. There are still other brain wave activity frequency ranges which should be explained **alpha** activity, which ranges from 8 Hz to about 13.5 Hz, is logically followed by **beta** activity, which ranges from 13.5 Hz upwards. As the beta range is so broad, newer literature made public in the 1980's and 90's described slow beta and fast beta activity, in order to differentiate the 13.5 to 25 Hz range versus the 25 to 40 Hz range. Also *the alert with focused attention beta activity frequency range* is in the 20 to 40 Hz range. Furthermore, very familiar to all experts in this field is the old 60 Hz *electrical artifact,* which is nowadays usually filtered out by the majority of most sophisticated EEG machines *(like ours)* available in today's EEG market.

Now with a basic explanation of brain wave activity frequency ranges under our belts, it is important to understand that particular and specifically different brain wave activity patterns occur with different ages of subjects. Different EEG patterns are also seen in the different stages of sleep. Neurophysiologists (like me) also study as part of our neurophysiology training in EEGs, the location or topography of these EEG patterns or where on the brain are these normal EEG patterns typically found. And we study different levels or stages of awake and alert consciousness and stages of sleep as typically seen in the normal range. Much of the normal brain wave activity frequencies we study are also determined by the maturity of the brain; hence, when recording and analyzing our *new data,* we must always take into account the subject's age in deciding if the observed EEG pattern or frequency range is normal for the particular stated age of the subject. Thus, in any discussion of EEG results, the clinical conclusion of normal vs. abnormal should always be followed by a qualifier, for the stated age of the subject or patient, as has been repeatedly done in our analysis of all our raw data. Current medical and scientific literature holds that the brain matures according to the following information:

Delta brain wave activity is first observed starting in premature infant brains. Soon delta activity begins to diminish in quantity and continues this rapidly decrease in the first few years of life. By the pre-teen and teenage years, the only remnant of delta activity rarely seen is the normal variant, posterior slow waves of youth, seen in the posterior Head regions in the awake to drowsy states. By adulthood over the age of twenty-one years, no delta activity should be seen in normal subjects, especially while in the awake and alert state, unless the subject is in the stages of *deep sleep.*

Alpha brain wave activity in normal adults is seen typically (in an awake state) in the posterior head regions with *eyes closed.* However, alpha brain wave activity seen with *eyes open* typically represents a *reflective* or *contemplative state* and/or a relaxed brain wave active state.

Beta brain wave activity in normal adults is typically seen (in the awake state) in the anterior head regions with eyes closed. However, with eyes open beta brain wave activity is seen in the anterior and posterior head regions, and when alert with focused attention is seen basically all the brain wave EEG channels, as was repeatedly seen on Nancy *only* during the three recorded EEG epochs of *Jesus - in His Living Presence* along with the *deep sleep* patterns recorded.

Theta brain wave activity is seen normally in the drowsy sleep stage I, as well as in various variants of normal. Sleep stages are represented by EEG brain wave patterns which are truly unique from the brain waves observed during wakefulness. Thus, it is just as important to carefully observe the awake, alert with focused attention states of our subjects when making any conclusions on the raw data EEG obtained. Such observations are recorded in *this book* and presented without fail for anyone who wants to decipher our data and should be taken into account by the layman or expert interested in really understanding the significance of the amazing results I incredibly obtained in the *baseline studies.* Sleep stages progress from stage I to IV, with stages III-IV representing the *deep sleep* stages, and then REM (rapid eye movement) sleep. In adults no delta activity is seen in drowsiness stage I of sleep, only theta activity with some mixed alpha activity in lower amplitudes. In stage II of sleep, however, we do begin to observe some delta activity, which is typically intermixed with sleep spindles and vertex sharp waves forming the typical K-complexes [this EEG data has clinical significance to experts in EEG, neurology, neurosurgery, psychiatry, neuropsychology, neurophysiology, sleep disorders as well as EEG and sleep disorder technicians]. While progressing to the *deep sleep* stages III and IV, however, a tremendous increase of delta activity is seen. Stage III typically involves > 50% delta activity, while stage IV involves >75% delta activity. In REM sleep, the rapid eye movements can actually be clinically observed along with total relaxation of the EMG (electromyography) and *low voltage diffuse beta activity* heralding the dreaming stage. No delta activity is seen in REM sleep.

Again **Delta** brain wave activity quantity as measured in %'s increases in accordance with the deepness of a subject's stages of *deep sleep*. In simple terms, delta activity has, or should have, nothing to do with the brain of an adult, awake, alert with focused attention and conscious subject. More specifically, in adults >21 years of age, ***no delta brain wave activity is seen in the awake state*** unless there is some pathology or artifact or the subject/patient is in normal stages of *deep sleep*. What we recorded then is an obvious *contradiction,* since Nancy during these EEG epochs of the testing is fully awake and normal. This very real and unprecedented *newly discovered data* was precisely my problem in deciphering *what* I recorded, during Nancy's three separate *heavenly visits* or *apparitions of Jesus in light* (Nancy's words) or *when Jesus speaks in the light,* in which I documented a recurring **3 *Hz delta rhythm - deep sleep - topography*--- 333 *EEG pattern.*** Then, how can I also explain that Nancy was in a state of mental alertness, fully awake with focused attention and fully conscious with eyes open, and in total touch with reality? Yet, we recorded the onslaught of the medium to high amplitude rhythmic 3 Hz delta rhythms ranging from 2.5 to 3.5 Hz frequency, but predominantly 3 Hz *delta rhythms* typically *only* seen *in the* ***normal deep sleep stages III-IV,*** forming the stimulus specific evoked EEG *brain wave* pattern of **333.**

The overriding accentuated *beta activity* recorded *(ridding) on top of the rhythmic 3 Hz delta rhythms* is the most plausible answer to this question, since normally beta activity represents an *awake, alert, focused attention* type of brain wave pattern. But how could anyone be awake, alert with focused attention and also be in the deep stages of sleep simultaneously? This is definitely an *oxymoron* and a *contradiction of neurophysiology terms* and *principles* as we know them. Also, this was *once believed,* until now, *to be a physiological impossibility.*

As noted above, there was no evidence of any seizures, ictal or interictal EEG activity recorded. Nancy exhibited normal speech, thought, content and train of thought processes throughout the testing even when *Jesus appears.* Nancy was visibly excited, loving and joyful, and yet very calm and peaceful during the three occasions in which *Jesus appears and speaks.* Her excitedly joyful, alert with focused attention status can be easily supported by the accentuation of beta rhythms seen with higher voltages in all the brain wave channels during the three EEG epochs that *Jesus appears.* Now for the 1st time in medical history, rhythmic delta brain wave activity with an average range of 3 Hz is recorded with the same brain wave topography seen in the *normal deep sleep stages* III-IV of adult brains, while the adult brain is fully alert, awake with focused attention. This unprecedented EEG pattern is repeatedly recorded with no associated sharp transients, sharp waves, or spikes; no spike wave complexes, poly-spike wave complexes, or spike slow wave complexes; no paroxysmal activity, epileptic potentials, or epileptic discharges; and no seizure activity, epileptic behavior or artifacts.

This new 3 Hz EEG pattern of *deep sleep* is now somehow simultaneously recorded with a slightly accentuated beta activity overriding on all the EEG brain wave channels with eyes open. The type of *beta activity* recorded actually documents a *normal awake, alert and fully conscious with focused attention* subject or patient. This is just like the clinical observations we recorded of Nancy earlier. Thus, as never previously seen nor documented before --- *a normal adult EEG* ***deep sleep*** *recording* was repeatedly documented *only* during the *heavenly visits of Jesus - in His Living Presence* and when *Jesus speaks His living words in the light, while simultaneously* the same adult subject Nancy was *fully awake, alert and fully conscious with focused attention* as recorded *with the overriding beta brain wave activity.* What an *oxymoron* and a *contradiction* of known *physiological principles.* As medical scientists and hardened skeptics *(like me)* interested in *"the truth"* and the real true facts, I suddenly realized we had a lot of explaining to do...

REFLECTIONS ON THE JUNE 11th, 1993, BASELINE STUDIES

My *new data* had, without a doubt, unveiled an *oxymoron in pure physiological terms.* Simply put, I had uncovered (discovered) something *previously thought impossible.* This was exciting and yet somehow frightening. *What* does all this *new data* mean? In most complex terms, I had recorded brain wave activity associated with deep sleep states in an awake individual while simultaneously also recording the most alert with focused attention brain wave state possible—and these unprecedented, mixed extreme opposite ends of the spectra and *contradicted* EEG patterns occurred **only** during the three separate EEG epochs when Nancy proclaimed *Jesus - in His Living Presence or when Jesus speaks in the light.* It became very apparent to me that the very specific stimulus of *Jesus - in His Living Presence* somehow evokes a stimulus specific *brain wave EEG response pattern of 333,* as I had recorded *only* during the three separate EEG epochs. This stimulus specific evoked EEG pattern was seen within milliseconds of Nancy *seeing Jesus.*

A number of wondrous reports surfaced surrounding Nancy, the miraculous healings and occurrences in Conyers on the 13th of every month - since Oct 13th, 1990. But as is the case with most apostles and true prophets of God - as seen in many historical accounts of the ancient *Holy Bible* - Nancy has been painfully tested, used, abused, persecuted, criticized, and falsely accused by many including some of her own family members and friends. These random, unfounded rumors, some of which claim Nancy is mentally ill, lying, malingering, or simply making up stories for her own secondary gain, have caused her great grief, personal sadness and painful interior suffering. Certain individuals have even aggressively attacked Nancy's character, credibility and integrity, as well as the validity of the all apparitions themselves. The following *new medical and scientific data* actually squashes to smithereens all the negative false accusations and publicity against Nancy. A passage in the New Testament by *Jesus* in Luke 4:24: *"Amen* I say to you, that *no prophet is accepted in his (her) own country...,"* might help us have a clearer understanding of *what* has occurred to Nancy.

Nancy has been and is still being persecuted so viciously for the sake *of Jesus.* But with these same persecutions, Nancy should *"Rejoice and be glad ..."* as it is written in the *New Testament - Beatitudes.* Now concerning Nancy's true character, credibility and validity of her *heavenly visits,* I do believe that our medical and scientific data will confirm and reveal *the truth* in these matters and prove that the amazing *new data* is contrary to the vicious rumors and bogus attacks directed against Nancy for writing and speaking *the truth.* First, in order to dispel any possibility that Nancy may be lying, consider the mechanics of a *lie detector machine.* Indeed, a careful examination of such an apparatus reveals that there is *absolutely no EEG equipment attached;* this is due to *the fact that* ***brain waves do not change when someone is lying. Nancy's*** *brain waves,* however, ***did change!*** The EEG *did change* so significantly whenever Nancy said, *"Jesus is here."* On the three separate occasions when Nancy indicated *Jesus is present,* as seen above, the dramatic and inexplicable EEG variances were recorded. By EEG definition and criteria: *Brain waves do not change during the moment someone is telling a lie* or *even conjuring up a lie.* Thus, *Nancy was not lying* or *malingering* (as supported by our new data) *during the three separate heavenly visits or apparitions of Jesus - in His Living Presence and* later *when - His living words were spoken in the light* and we were very fortunate again to record the same amazing EEG variances. Recall that during the *baseline studies,* no epileptic behavior or seizure activity was recorded electrographically (EEG), which included the three EEG epochs when Nancy claimed - *Jesus is here.* Once again, our medical science leads us to the following conclusions: Nancy's *heavenly visions and apparitions* were not a product of any focal parietal-occipital seizures potentially inducing visual hallucinations. Thus, Nancy was not hallucinating on the basis of any abnormal repetitive electrical excitation of brain neurons or seizures; in simplest terms, she was not seeing and not hallucinating or imagining things on the basis of seizure activity.

No hypnosis was induced in Nancy by the professor during his repeated trials of hypnosis with hypnotic suggestions. There was no evidence of any presumed self-hypnosis induced by *repetitive prayer* as recorded. We know this, since there was no production of the a*lpha-theta rhythms typical for a hypnotic trance.* Thus, no *hypnotic trance state* was identified *clinically. No hypnotic trance was recorded by*

EEG at any time during the *baseline studies. No hypnotic trance was recorded during the three visits of Jesus. And no hypnotic trance was recorded when Jesus speaks to Nancy.*

Note: The *alpha-theta rhythms* evident in *hypnotic trance states* are very different from the *beta-delta 3Hz rhythms* recorded with the specific EEG pattern 333 during the three epochs (time periods of EEG) when *Nancy sees Jesus in light - in His Living Presence* or *when Nancy hears Jesus speak audibly and/or interiorly - His living words in - the light/His Light.*

Thus, the medical and scientific evidence uncovered suggests that *His Living Presence and His living words* are *one.* Jesus is One and the same source of energy, since the same new EEG data was and is produced when *Jesus appears* and/or when *Jesus speaks* to Nancy.

Yes, both *seeing Jesus - in His Living Presence* and *hearing Jesus speaking - His living words in the light* gave us *the same new data,* the astonishing 333 EEG pattern. So, *what* is the significance of this mathematical and numerical 333 EEG pattern? This 333 EEG pattern in EEG terms is actually 3 cycles in one second of time or rather simply put: *"Three in One." What* does *Jesus - in His Living Presence* or *Jesus speaking in the light - His voice and His living words* have in common with *333 (three in one)? What* does *Jesus in light; His voice* and *His living words in the light - have in common?* Recall Genesis 1:3: *"And God said: Be light made. And light was made."* You can make a case for the following Biblical fact: *God's voice and living words,* brought forth together at the same time *in the beginning of time* **is *the light (flames)!*** In Exodus 20:18:*"all the people saw the voices and the flames;"* this is the same source: *the voices/the flames/the fire/the light - that* wrote on the tablets of stone. Thus, *the sound and the light* do go together – from *the beginning.*

EEG brain waves of subjects with psychosis-induced hallucinations or with mental illness diseases like schizophrenia do not change during the psychotic audiovisual hallucinations. In fact, the EEG *remains unchanged* throughout the psychosis, as well as before, during and after any audiovisual hallucinations. Likewise, in organic brain disorders with abnormal EEG's, which include episodes of delirium and hallucinations, the EEG does not change before, during or after any hallucinations or during periods of delirium. The unchanging abnormal brain waves *remain abnormal,* throughout the disorder or disease or delirium state - before, during and after any periods of hallucinations. Many different organic diseases like cancer, leukemia, lymphoma, different types of CNS infections, meningitis, encephalitis, trauma, hypoxia, vascular diseases, stroke, multiple sclerosis, dementia, degenerative brain diseases, toxic-metabolic derangements, systemic organ failure, sleep disorders, nutritional deficiencies, medication effects, chemotherapy/radiation effects which may occur *(just to name a few)* - can give rise to numerous CNS electrolyte or hormonal imbalances/derangements that can cause hallucinations. Other conditions such as drug-induced toxicity/adverse effects or alcohol/drug withdrawal can also potentially cause different states of delirium with active hallucinations. In all these different clinical settings, the abnormal EEGs do not change during the active hallucinations caused by all these different organic brain disorders. The brain waves *remain abnormal* throughout the altered mental status state, and absolutely no changes in the abnormal EEG patterns are observed before, during or after any active hallucinations in these clinical settings.

Finally, based on the results of our *baseline studies* and just given the above information to try to explain the *apparitions* or *heavenly visits of Jesus* or *seeing Jesus in light* (Nancy's words) as claimed by Nancy, our research team-- who were eye-witnesses to these *supernatural events* during the testing that took place in the state-of-the-art neurodiagnostic laboratory suite on June 11th, 1993 -- we can now both medically and scientifically *exclude* as possible explanations the following: malingering, lying, epileptic behavior, epileptic seizures, hypnotic trances, hysteria, psychotic disturbances or psychotic reactions both from mental and/or organic diseases, also all forms of delirium, and obviously all possible drug-induced hallucinatory phenomena since no drugs were administered and Nancy was on no current medications and no over-the-counter remedies except for a daily multi-vitamin. This solid and objective clinical, medical and scientific conclusion is significant, as all the above conditions are known to potentially produce or be associated with visual and audiovisual hallucinations clinically.

How then, can we explain Nancy's *experiences?* How can we explain the *new data?* How can we explain the *new phenomenon* of a mixed beta-delta activity -- diffuse overriding beta rhythms on top of the 3 Hz delta rhythms in a *deep sleep* topographic pattern forming the very specific 333 pattern? Recall, this was recorded on EEG electrographically *only* during the three EEG epochs that Nancy was clinically *awake and alert with focused attention and* somehow *simultaneously,* as recorded on EEG also, *in a deep sleep state.* This *new* unprecedented EEG pattern was recorded ***only*** when Nancy claims *to see Jesus in light* or then *hears audibly the sound of His voice* or *hears interiorly* ***His living words in - the light*** *= while still seeing and/or feeling/receiving* **His light.** Indeed, to be *awake, alert with focused attention and* at the same time be *in a deep sleep state* **is** *a contradiction!* So, *what* does - *a sign of contradiction* and *Jesus - have in common?* We found ourselves at a medical and scientific impasse. Recording the data was one thing; explaining it was yet another. The astonishing findings were indeed *unprecedented* and to our knowledge had never been seen before in any medical or scientific neurophysiology adult or pediatric literature. In an attempt to reach some conclusions, I posed the following questions: *What* did all the scientists actually record? *What* is the true significance of this recorded phenomenon? Could these results be reproduced with other EEGs or even with EEG computerized testing? Can this *new data* be ever reproduced in any other subjects exposed to similar heavenly experiences?

Because my incredible hardened skepticism persisted despite the above *new data* and even after studying all the raw *data* at hand, I felt uncomfortable making any conclusions until further medical and scientific testing could be performed to see if this *new data* could be reproduced and validated. In planning the medical and scientific testing for the June 13th apparition, I decided to change equipment and use my intensive monitoring ambulatory audiovisual TV-EEG telemetry and computerized digital Oxford II equipment, and also to combine two separate eight-channel recorders together to increase the EEG channels for a total of sixteen channel EEG recordings and cover more of the brain's topography for the appointed testing date of June 13th, 1993. I also contacted the Nihon-Kohden EEG representative and requested that he please come as soon as possible to evaluate our EEG equipment. I wanted to be absolutely sure that our EEG equipment had been functioning properly during the entire *baseline studies* of June 11th, 1993. I also wanted to be sure *(as a true skeptic)* that no electrical artifacts could have possibly produced what we were interpreting to be of real true cerebral brain activity, a step I needed to take, since our *new data* and findings recorded were so incredibly unprecedented.

I had been extremely careful to perform these studies in my state-of-the-art EEG/ neurodiagnostic laboratory that was entirely shielded with a new platinum mesh produced by Georgia Tech University, in order to give us the highest degree of artifact free purity possible for collecting EEG and neurophysiology data. As we had already excluded all possible physiological artifacts, we now needed to scientifically rule out all possible electrical artifacts as well as all other types of artifacts that could have somehow produced this astonishing data.

After sharing the significance of the initial data with the Aussie film crew, they immediately wanted to speak with the Australian neurologist, Dr. Graham, and present him with my *new data*. Recall, Dr. Graham had the opportunity to review a videotape of Nancy during a May 1992 apparitions without the advantage of having an EEG test or a psychiatric evaluation to review. So, Dr. Graham surmised that Nancy's experiences were *not authentic.* Now based on my *new data,* the Aussie crew was hopeful Dr. Graham might reconsider re-evaluating his opinion expressed so enthusiastically in their May 1992 video documentary. Our medical team was beside itself with all the potential ramifications of the *new data.*

Had I discovered a new variant of a normal EEG pattern or rather a new stimulus specific evoked brain wave response pattern in a subject - to the specific stimulus of Jesus - in His Living Presence and/or to His voice and living words in His light? I say *living* because *Jesus* **is** *alive* according to Nancy.

Thus, if Nancy was **not** crazy, **not** a flagrant psychotic, **not** in a hypnotic trance, **not** having epileptic seizures or epileptic behavior and **not** lying or malingering or hysterical, and not taking any medications; then what other possible explanations were available? A thorough survey of the situation revealed that one more option remained: Could these *experiences* be explained by *mass hysteria?* This question would soon be re-addressed again in *the testing* scheduled for the appointed date of June 13th, 1993, as the media had already predicted over eighty thousand pilgrims to converge on the small town of Conyers for the apparition that day. Obviously with that many people predicted to be present, the question of whether *mass hysteria* could explain some of the reported phenomena associated with the heavenly visits or apparitions will be re-addressed.

However, the above baseline studies just completed definitely demonstrated no possible *mass hysteria* induction, since there was no *mass of people* present in my laboratory suite to generate the type of stimulus required to warrant the label of *mass hysteria.* Recall, we were in a very private EEG-neurodiagnostic laboratory suite surrounded by very hardened skeptic scientists (like me), except for only one person (the scribe) George Collins. Although George is considered a gentle *God-fearing* big man, he is definitely not a *mass of people.* Thus, I was facing a rapidly shrinking lack of concrete, non-supernatural, scientific viable options to explain or that can possibly ever explain the astonishing and unprecedented *new medical and scientific data.* What does *Jesus in His Living Presence in light* and *Jesus speaking the sound of His voice (audibly or interiorly) - His living words in the light have in common?* The answer for now on the surface appears to be in the words *living, light and the new* amazing *EEG 333 brain wave pattern* recorded that I discovered during the *baseline studies* testing. So, *what* does *the light* and *the sound of His (living) voice* and *His (living) words* have *in common* with *His Living Presence?*

Now please ponder Genesis 1:3. Interestingly, scientists have discovered that all light travels in electro-magnetic wavelengths of which *we only see 3%.* This means *we do not see 97% of the light around us.* Also more recently scientists have discovered that *all sound travels in the same electro-magnetic wavelengths.* Thus, all *light* waves and all *sound* waves *travel* in space and in the atmosphere on earth *in the same electro-magnetic wavelengths.* In other words, *light and sound (the voices* of the word of God/*the light)* spoken *travel together.* Recall, Nancy saw *Jesus in light* as we recorded the 3 Hz delta rhythms forming the 333 pattern three separate times. On the 3rd visit, initially ***while still seeing the light/His light*** *Nancy started to receive a message.* Nancy first heard *Jesus - the sound of His voice speaking His words (His living words) audibly and then later interiorly* as well, *but did not see Jesus-only His light.* Above I said *living* because *Jesus is alive speaking His words to Nancy,* as we once again recorded 3 Hz *delta rhythms* forming the 333 pattern. Thus, seeing *Jesus in light* or separately *hearing the sound of His voice audibly or interiorly in the light (without seeing Jesus) – as Jesus speaks His living words* ***in - the light/His light*** incredibly *evoked the same brain wave responses on EEG* with the 3 Hz delta rhythms forming the astonishing 333 brain wave pattern.

Since scientifically we now know that *light and sound* energy travels in the same electro-magnetic wavelengths, and as above *the light of Jesus* or the sound of *the voice(s) - with the living words of Jesus in the light* all generated the same EEG brain wave responses; then, it is logical (to me) and also makes perfect sense that the specific source of energy that produced or evoked this amazing *new unprecedented* and very specific *EEG 333 pattern* - must certainly be *one and the same source of energy, Jesus - in His Living Presence.* Now re-read and ponder Genesis 1:3*: "And God said: Be light made. And light was made."* So, again as *science* has just recently discovered that *light and sound* travel in the same *electromagnetic wavelengths,* we can now see the incredible depth and true meaning of this famous verse of Holy Scriptures in the Book of Genesis: *the sound of God's voice speaking the living word* of the living God was *light (the fire of God).* Thus, in simple terms, *light and sound* really do *travel in the same electromagnetic wavelengths* and have done so from ***the beginning.*** See in Exodus 20:18: "And *all the people (the children of Israel) saw the voices (of God)* and *the flames,* and *the sound of the trumpet,* and the mount smoking*...*" This great historical and monumental event occurred, while *God was actually speaking and* simultaneously *writing the Ten Commandments* as it was *given to Moses* and *all the people (the children of Israel).* Recall, the *Ten Commandments (the fiery law)* were *written by the finger of God.* Is it possible for you or me or anyone *to see the voices of God? How* did *"all the people"- the children of Israel -* ***see the voices*** *of God?*

As it is written in Exodus 20:18, I now believe that *the voices of God* were *the flames, the living fire of God and the living flames* - that the *children of Israel* saw write the *Ten Commandments on the two stone tablets.* And since *science* has now shown us that all *light and sound travel in the same electromagnetic wavelengths,* then it is logical to deduce that once again *science has proven the Bible to be absolutely correct and truthful.* What do I mean? Just look at Genesis 1:3*: "And God said: Be light made. And light was made."* So, now pay close attention: *the sound of the voices of the living God* - speaking *the first living words* of God, **--- "*light.*"**

Questions: "Be *light* made," ***of what? And... "Be light made" by what?***

I believe this *light* was *made of* and *made by* the created *living flames of God,* since in those days ***light*** *came mostly from* **the sun** *(Rev 22:16: "the bright and morning star")* or *the reflections of the sun on the moon and stars* at night or from a *fire* or *flames.* And *the sounds of the voices of the living God* and *the light* or *fire* or *flames* were all actually traveling in the same electromagnetic wavelengths together from *the* very *beginning* of time on earth, according to Genesis 1:3. Thus, *the sound* (heard audibly or interiorly) *of God's voices, the light* or *the living flames* or *fire of God, and the living word of God all travel together in the same electromagnetic wavelengths* as clearly portrayed in Exodus 20:18. Recall, that in Holy Scriptures it is written that *God* was actually simultaneously speaking and writing on the stone tablets with *"the finger of God,"* now please read Deuteronomy 9:10; and then see how *God gave Moses* and *all the people: His living words, the living words of God, the law, the ten commandments of love* as it is written in *the Torah,* the Bible. In Exodus 33:2: *"in His right hand a fiery law."* See Deuteronomy 4:24: *"Because the Lord thy God is a consuming fire, a jealous God."* Interestingly, science has now shown that - *the light, the sound and the voice* - are each *individually* made up of three parts. Thus, *the three* together form a pattern of 3 -3 -3.

See in Isaiah 10:17: "And *the light of Israel* shall be as a *fire* and *the Holy One* thereof as a *flame."* So, what is *God* trying to tell *us?* In Zachariah 2:1-5, the prophet beholds *a man with a measuring line* (in Hebrew this means *circumference)* to measure Jerusalem: "And *I will be to it, saith the Lord, a wall of fire round about:* and *I will be in glory, in the midst thereof."* In Psalm 96:2-6: *"...justice and judgment* are the establishment of *his throne.* A *fire* shall go before him, and shall burn his enemies *round about. His lightnings have shone forth to the world:* the earth saw and trembled. The mountains melted like wax, *at the presence of the Lord: at the presence of the Lord* of all the earth. *The heavens declared his justice:* and *all people saw his glory."* Recall *a bush not burnt/in flame of fire/spoke,* Exodus 3:1-14.

Hopefully, later in Chapter 9 of this book, I will humbly attempt and try to show you through our astonishing and unprecedented *new medical and scientific data* the incredible importance of these last three verses given above; as they relate to the awe and wonder of God's glorious mystery of *the living Son of God, Jesus, the Anointed One of God, the Jewish Messiah* and *the Christ,* the second person of *the Holy Trinity of God* & *God's signature: 333!* This material is *deep* and a truly profound *revelation --- in science and faith.*

Questions arise relating the above Holy Scriptures to Nancy's *heavenly visits:* Is *Jesus in light* or **the light** *Nancy sees, while Jesus speaks* - ***the word of God*** somehow related to *the voices* and *the flames* or *a fire* or even *a flame* - as it is written in Holy Scriptures? Do these *verses* vividly portray being *in His Living Presence?*

A hint to help answer these questions is connecting these *three verses* in Holy Scriptures:

(1) "And God said: Be ***light*** made,*"* Genesis 1:3;

(2) "And *all the people (the children of Israel) saw* ***the voices and the flames"*** (*flames* actually wrote *the law* - the *Ten Commandments* of love), Exodus 20:18;

(3) "And ***the light of Israel*** shall be as ***a fire*** and ***the Holy One*** thereof as ***a flame,"*** Isaiah 10:17. Maybe this is *why* on October 7th, 1998, the Blessed Virgin Mary, *Our Loving Mother,* gave Nancy this short, yet very profound unpublished message: *"Please keep the living flames of love alive in your hearts, dear children. The living flame of love is the living word of God."* The Blessed Virgin Mary was obviously speaking about her dearly beloved Son, *Jesus, the living word of God* and *the Holy One of Israel* - as ***"a flame," a living flame of love.***

Pondering the scientific reality or facts that we only see 3% of all *light* makes me wonder and ask this question: Is God somehow or in someway allowing certain *chosen souls (like Nancy)* to actually see some of the other 97% of *light* around us in the atmosphere on earth and in space that we cannot see? To answer this question scientifically, on the *appointed field study* at Conyers, Ga., June 13th, 1993, we decided to measure and to study the external environment in various ways:

1) To measure the low and extremely low ionizing atmospheric radiation light energy fields in both the visible range (the 3% we see) and the invisible range (the 97% we do not see) that surround the *mystical supernatural events.*

2) To measure the atmospheric-skin boundary radiation energy fields.

3) To measure the atmospheric-wall boundary radiation energy fields in the rooms were the heavenly visits or apparitions usually take place *(especially near - the cross/the crucifix on the wall).*

4) To measure the general atmosphere radiation energy fields within the rooms of the apparition sites.

5) To measure the high ionizing *gamma* radiation energy fields surrounding the apparition sites, and record and document any *visible light* energy range changes that can be seen with our naked eyes or be recorded possibly on video or photographs.

Hopefully, all these measurements of the external environment and of the atmosphere's *light* radiation energy fields will shed some light on the *next series* of medical and scientific studies scheduled for June 13th, 1993:

1) Recently retired from the University of Florida, Professor and Dr. Philip Callahan, an expert and world authority on low and extremely low ionizing radiation energy fields, and an expert in many other areas as you will see later in this book, will measure the external environments of Nancy before, during and after the *heavenly visits,* as outlined in 1, 2, 3, and 4, above.

2) Dr. Humberto Velasquez and his radiation team from south Florida will measure, as outlined above 5, the high ionizing gamma radiation energy fields in the external environment of Nancy before, during and after the heavenly visits, and will have professional photographs taken of the exterior façade and surface of the farm house chimney: *before, during and after the apparitions* for advanced digital computerized photo-spectral analysis of the three separate series of professional photographs recorded in the field to measure *the sun light* energy reflection.

3) In another area of great interest of study is *the mental status* state of Nancy *before, during and after the apparitions.* Though the brilliant New York psychiatrist Dr. George Hogben had initial scheduling problems which prevented him from attending the June 11th, 1993 baseline studies, he planned to arrive on June 12th, 1993, to begin his clinical psychiatric observations and follow the established experiment design's protocol for the medical and scientific testing of Nancy.

Dr. Hogben planned to perform his clinical psychiatric observations and mental status examinations before, during, and after the apparitions on the appointed day of June 13th, 1993. See Chapter 3 for a full and comprehensive report of Nancy's complete *psychiatric evaluations.*

Now before we go any further, please ponder again the above *new data* that is generated *in His Living Presence - the living presence of Jesus in light* (just how Nancy usually sees Jesus). Also ponder *His Living Presence* in the sound of *His voice* and/or *in His living words* (as *Jesus speaks to Nancy - in the light*). Can you imagine the unprecedented *new data* I just recorded was generated by both types of *heavenly experiences?* Both forms of stimuli produced the same new unprecedented 3 Hz EEG *delta rhythms* forming the pattern 333. Given this *new data,* we can now speculate that *His Living Presence (in light) and His living* words *(Jesus speaks - in the light)* are *one;* since, *one and the same* 333 EEG pattern was produced by the same specific stimuli of being *in His Living Presence.* So, it is no surprise that in the *messages* given to Nancy, *Jesus* said, *"My living presence and my living words are one."* Now this *new medical and scientific data* is *beginning* to make more sense to me after reading Jeremiah 23:9: *"My heart is broken within me, all my bones tremble:* ***I am become as a drunken man, and as a man full of wine, at the presence of the Lord, and at the presence of his holy words."***

As we move on to the next phase of study, we will hopefully see if the rigors of medical and scientific research can truly *shed some light* on this mystery of *heavenly visits, visions and apparitions* and on *His signature – 333.* So, the journey *science to faith* continues... But wait, one more point needs to be mentioned before we go on.

Namely, Nancy's very own words and description of her *heavenly experiences* is solicited. So, after asking Nancy on numerous interviews: *What* do you (Nancy) *see or hear or feel* during these *mystical experiences?* Nancy gave me *a very special insight into the mystery of God,* saying: *"When* I experience *the Almighty God* - He is so awesome and great and loving that it is difficult to articulate... *God* is so much more... So much more... I can not do justice in trying to describe *Him (God)...*any of the words that I think about to describe *Him* though grand are still very inadequate in describing *His Holiness... His Glory and Awesome Majesty...* You see *God...***is**...truly much, *much more than this."*

Below, Nancy describes *3 dimensions* as to what she *sees, hears* and *feels:*

1a) A *vision of light* is usually seen suspended in the air, as in the *atmosphere.* It is seen *over* people or *coming from within* people. It is seen over objects like holy images, medals, pictures, sacred art or statues etc. It is seen simultaneously, suspended over and coming from within, people or objects. Sometimes, she sees the *visions of light* like a 3-dimensional, *bright cloud of light* superimposed on people, objects, nature, but especially over *the holy words of God* in the Bible! It is seen especially over priests during their reading of the *Gospel.* She sees *visions of light* like *beams, flashes, bolts or darts of lightning,* and also sees *light, visions or apparitions* in the sky.

1b) *God* at times makes the *visions of light appear life-like and animated.* For example: the *visions of light will appear to have real life-like animated movements,* like the moving of lips or turning of the head. Sometimes, in the animated life-like *visions of light, Jesus* can be seen *looking upward* and *praying to Who* Nancy understands to be *God the Father.* Sometimes, *Jesus* appears to be *suffering for us* while *praying.* Sometimes, *Jesus* shows His *sense of humor* and has a *warm smile.* It is truly remarkable how *human Jesus* actually appears, which *makes Him* very, very *approachable.* This is probably *why He visited* His people as a newborn baby in *Bethlehem (the city of David,* also called *the city of Bread*) in a *manger wrapped in swaddling clothes* - that special *holy night on Christmas Eve.*

Recall, *His* ***star*** had *risen out of Jacob over Bethlehem,* just as prophesized in the Book of Numbers 24:17 and was sought out by the three wise men (kings) from the East. *What a God we serve!* What an approachable and awesome God. The *Jewish Messiah* from the *house of David* came down from heaven as an infant boy *child* born in poverty, but *God the Father* provided *Him* with more than enough provisions *(Isaiah 9:6: "For a child is born to us, and a son is given to us...").* Recall, the three kings came from Arabia, Tharsis and Saba bearing truly *prophetic gifts* for the *King of Kings and Lord of Lords (Rev 19:16).* The *gold* was given for *His anointed kingship* of heaven and earth; the *myrrh* was given for the *anointed prophet,* who would *speak the bitter truth* to all peoples as it is written in the Bible; and finally, the *frankincense* was given for *the anointed high priest in the order of Melchisedech (Psalm 109 (110):4).*

2) The *audible* sound of *His voice* or the more frequent *inaudible* sound of *His voice (heard interiorly) in the light,* that is somehow *heard* very distinctly, clearly and more often even louder than audible. Nancy says, *"His voice* resounds deep in my heart, *burning* like ***a fire*** *from within. The voice* I hear and understand *interiorly* is clearly that of *my Lord and my Savior, Jesus, the Living Flame of Love... Whose love surpasses all - human love."*

3) Nancy *feels the tangible Holy Living Presence of God* in many ways. She feels a deeply *profound interior peace, an unconditional love and joy* and an *unfathomable Divine Mercy* that surpasses all our grandest possible imagination. Nancy feels that *His* tender and awesome *love* is greater than the greatest father, brother, husband or best friend could ever give; all rolled up into one, but yet, still so *"much, much more than this."*

The following excerpts are taken from various *messages Jesus gave to Nancy* that indeed sheds *light* on Nancy's mission*:*

"You are not a false prophet. You are My prophet."/ "You are called to bear witness that I Am the Living Son of God."/ "You are called to bear witness to My Living Presence and to show the world my love and mercy through the cross."/ "Bring My Living Presence to My children. Bring My Living Presence to My children."/ "The world needs to know about My Living Presence. The time is now."/ "Nancy has been given the rarest of gifts."/ "Nancy has direct communication with Me."/ "I choose to show the world My love and mercy through a weak, simple, sinful soul"/ "Even though you are disobedient at times, even though you lack many virtues, through you I will show the world My love and mercy."/ "My dearest Nancy, you are My wayward daughter and through your faults and failures I am teaching the world."/ "I liken you to Moses. He talked to God and you talk to Me."

Finally, a prophetic message *Jesus* gave to Nancy concerning *the second coming* or *the last coming of the Lord* that connects as a revelation, a part of Nancy's true mission, with that of another chosen *Servant of God, Luisa Piccarreta* from Corato, Italy*: The Little Daughter of the Divine Will.* Luisa's cause for beautification/sainthood is currently under investigation by *the Vatican,* Rome, Italy.

In August 27, 1994, while Nancy was praying the *Lord's Prayer* with a priest, a friend and George*, Jesus* interrupted them and said*, "Too fast. Go back."* And the friend stopped and repeated, ***"Thy Kingdom come, Thy Will be done..."****Jesus* said*, "Stop there." As they were saying, "on earth as it is in heaven." Jesus* continued to say, *"The Spirit of God, My Holy Spirit, is* **the gift** *that I have given to mankind to live in My Will. The more you desire My Will, the more I desire to have you in Me...This is the highest truth for all My created Kingdom...Mankind is being given a special grace to have this 'truth of all truths' revealed. It offends Me when this prayer* (the Lord's Prayer) *I have given to My children is pronounced from the lips. When the Will is merged, the heart is merged. All become one in perfect union with Me, every action, every thought, every word. Divine Will for My created Kingdom will be restored after purifications have been completed. The highest happiness is living in My Will."* Then Nancy asked *Jesus, "How* am I connected to all this, since I am *to bear witness to the Living Son of God*?" Jesus replied*,*

"My Living Presence and living in My Divine Will merge in perfect union."

Thanks to Sr. Gabrielle and my friend, Robert, for recently introducing me and encouraging me to read *Luisa's writings* (1898-1938) *from Jesus, as He teaches us how to live in the Divine Will of God.* To my surprise *some of her writings* incredibly connect with our *new medical and scientific data of His Living Presence* and point to our future hopeful fulfillment - as pointed out above by *Jesus* in the *Lord's Prayer.*

Journey science to faith now gets a big, big *burst of light...*

CHAPTER III

VISIONS OF "THE LIGHT"

APPOINTED APPARITION DAY - JUNE 13th, 1993

I received a phone call from George Collins very early on the morning of June 13th, 1993. George called to inform our medical team that we needed to head out to the farm house, much earlier than we had originally planned due to the unusually large crowds. While an estimated eighty thousand pilgrims had been predicted for that day, George indicated that the latest counts were now well over one hundred thousand pilgrims expected. The monthly apparition of the Blessed Virgin Mary bringing us baby Jesus, *Our Loving Mother*, was always a special event in the horse town of Conyers. Somehow this particularly special and appointed *apparition day* of June 13th *(613)* was selected by *providence* for our medical and scientific testing out of the lab and in the field seemed unusually popular.

Can you fathom one obvious reason *why* this date was so popular? *Faith was being put to the test by science.* Can you imagine the intrigue, the wonder, the excitement this testing day generated? So, I now hurried our medical team toward Conyers...

The legacy of Conyers was impressive. According to Nancy, every 13th of the month since October 13th, 1990, the Blessed Virgin Mary bringing baby Jesus to us had appeared to give *heavenly messages (echoing the living words of God)* to the United States of America and to the world. Asking to be invoked by the title of *Our Loving Mother* given to her by God, the Blessed Virgin Mary would often identify herself before she began speaking to Nancy in order to help Nancy verify the authenticity of the *visions, heavenly visits and apparitions* by saying, *"I am the Blessed Virgin Mary, the Holy Mother of God and your Loving Mother. I bow down to God the Father. I adore, I worship, I love Him with my whole heart, mind and soul and all my strength. Jesus is the Son of God and I serve Him."*

Much had been written about the monthly apparitions and our impending scientific studies before the appointed June 13th, 1993 apparition date. It was difficult to know exactly what influence these publications may have had on the number of people who came, but judging by the excitement of the crowd, one could conclude that many of those present were convinced about the authenticity of Nancy's claims and the *divine origin of the messages* given to Nancy.

Wondering how so many people had been drawn to these apparitions, I as usual wanted an explanation. I was told that some people believed in this because of the supernatural phenomena seen in the sky, such as *the sun spinning, pulsating and changing colors or clouds forming the silhouette of the Virgin Mary,* which was actually photographed and filmed during the apparitions of May 13th, 1992.

Others were influenced by reports of *rosaries or other religious medals turning a golden color.* Still others reported an inexplicable, *gold-like dust sprinkling from the sky over the pilgrims.* During the March 13th, 1992 apparitions, close to forty thousand pilgrims even witnessed *miraculous rose petals* raining down and falling from the clear blue sky in large numbers. This was actually videotaped and included in a recent Fox TV broadcast documentary: *Miracles and Visions: Fact or Fiction?* Many people also experienced the phenomena of *smelling* a perfume-like *scent of roses,* and hearing *birds chirping just before Mary appears to Nancy.* Still others claim taking very unusual photographs in which they can see different *lights or light rays* or *bright beams of light* not apparently seen by the naked eye of the photographers while taking the pictures. Other *miraculous photographs* show the *silhouettes of angels* or the *silhouette of Jesus* or the *silhouette of the Blessed Virgin Mary* or the recently sainted *Padre Pio* by Pope John Paul II – the *silhouette of St. Pio* seen in the sky clouds. There was even one faint photograph of apparently *the spirit of Moses holding the Ten Commandments on Holy Hill,* and numerous *door to heaven* photographs taken by many pilgrims. One very unusual photograph actually shows a *shadow cast in the form of the number 7 behind the statue of Our Loving Mother.* The *Blessed Virgin Mary* in this statue *is* caressing and *bringing her baby Jesus to us.* Later in this Book, you will see the significance of the *number 3* and the *number 4* which does add up to the *number 7.* In Hebrew *7* is *the perfect number* (representing *the perfect plan for salvation,* see Gen 3:15). But as expected, I believe many pilgrims came merely out of curiosity.

And yet, there were still others—perhaps the most noteworthy of all—who saw no unusual signs or wonders, but instead experienced a *profound interior peace, a peace* that they said they had never before known. Despite the overwhelming proof of unusual phenomena, most of the people present, it seemed, were genuinely convinced of the *divine origin of the messages* given to Nancy, **not** because of the *supernatural phenomena and signs witnessed* by others, but because they found the *heavenly messages* to be Biblically sound and theologically correct and profoundly inspiring. Many, many countless pilgrims, too many to count, reported a profoundly deep *life changing* inner healings of their spiritual lives, *a renewed faith* and *a return to the Church* and to the Holy Sacraments. But most important, they had *a new zeal* and *an inner thirst and hunger for the true living presence of God.* Despite the excellent crowd control procedures implemented by the Sheriff's Office of Rockdale County, the Fire Rescue Department officers, state troopers and numerous volunteers, our travel to the farm house was indeed slow. As we crawled into the already-packed town of Conyers well ahead of our scheduled arrival time, I had to place a big sign on the front of my car indicating that we were part of the medical and scientific team, so that the Rockdale county sheriff officers would allow us to move ahead. It was imperative that we set up our testing equipment on time for the preliminary testing *before the apparitions.*

The day was brimming with excitement. An impressive mass of humanity, excellent for the *mass hysteria* question and thousands of pilgrims could be seen in all directions. And much to my surprise they were not pushing, shoving or yelling. On the contrary, the crowd was unusually peaceful, with many people holding rosary beads and religious objects or taking pictures of the sun and sky. Most were praying, singing religious songs or simply quietly waiting. As we made our way into the farm house, I saw many colorful religious, priests and nuns present from different countries. I even met an invited Archbishop from Rome, Italy, to be an eye witness to the testing *(for the Church)* and witness the *heavenly visits or apparitions* of that day.

It was a wonderful and hot day with a deep blue sky and no clouds, full of hope, intrigue and still a lot of hardened skepticism on my part and in the minds of most of my colleagues. Numerous questions occupied us, which would hopefully be answered during the course of this testing day. What would we find? What would we record? Would we encounter the same EEG patterns in Nancy's brain, electrographically *(on EEG),* that we recorded *during the living presence of Jesus?* Or would there possibly be a different brain wave pattern when the Blessed Virgin Mary appears bringing us baby *Jesus (in His Living Presence)* or a different pattern when Mary speaks *echoing* the words of *Jesus (His living words)* to Nancy? These and many more questions kept each of us individually absorbed and deeply curious.

We all certainly wanted accurate answers to our questions. So in order to avoid the possibility of any *contamination* by my baseline studies EEG Nihon-Kohden equipment, for this appointed *(out of the lab) field study* day of June 13th, 1993, I decided to use distinctly different equipment. *(See above)* My digital computerized Oxford-II ambulatory intensive monitoring audiovisual TV-EEG telemetry system equipment was then selected as best for the job.

Just to satisfy my curiosity, I had the EEG equipment used for the *baseline studies* technically checked for any flaws, by the makers of the EEG equipment, the Nihon-Kohden Co. A conclusive report from the technical support representatives of this company found absolutely no flaws in the EEG equipment that could possibly help explain the dramatic new unprecedented EEG pattern changes recorded on Nancy's brain during the baseline studies conducted just two days ago. So, I made the decision to use my other equipment - the digital computerized ambulatory audiovisual TV-EEG telemetry monitoring systems that is preferred for *out of the lab* or *out in the field* use.

Many other questions also hounded our scientific minds: *What* was the significance of the *beta-delta 3 Hz rhythms* and especially the specific EEG *333 pattern?* Were these brain wave changes true cerebral brain wave activity or false? False or non-cerebral brain wave activity is typically called *an artifact.* An artifact is not produced by the brain's own electrical output of living brain cells. If *Jesus* does appear to Nancy during this appointed apparition day, would we ever again record the astonishing EEG pattern documented during the baseline studies? And if so, *what* is the significance of the amazing *new data* and unprecedented findings?

It was just after 10:00 o'clock in the morning when we finally made our way into the farm house. My medical team and two EEG technicians started setting up the necessary equipment in the apparition room, and also in the room adjacent to the apparition room for the *before the apparitions,* testing. I then had the pleasure of meeting the rest of the medical and scientific team. Present for this remarkable round of studies were George Hogben, M.D., a brilliant psychiatrist from New York. Prof. R. Castanon-Gomez, Ph.D., of Clinical Neuropsychology from the State University of La Paz, Bolivia, a very prolific author of many published *(over 300)* scientific papers in neuropsychological and psychology scientific journals in Europe and South America and has written several books, the professor is also a researcher for the European Institute of Neuroscience.

Dr. Philip Callahan, *(now retired)* University of Florida Professor of Entomology, a Biophysics world expert who is also a prolific author of many published *(over 150)* papers in scientific journals, has several scientific patents for new inventions and has published over 14 books in North America; Dr. Callahan's wife, Winnie, who assisted with the recordings and documentation of his different experiments. Colombian Dr. Humberto Velasquez, a radiation specialist with the Florida State Department of Health *(at the time of this testing),* and present for the testing is his radiation team and a professional photographer. And on this appointed day, my medical team was also present: the certified EEG technicians; my wife, who assisted with the medical photography plus the organization and time synchronization of our medical and scientific teams working together with my EEG technicians; and she also assisted in the coordination of the ambulatory EEGs with the audiovisual TV display monitoring systems and all recording equipment; an expert technical video assistant was in charge of all backup medical audiovisual video monitoring for background documentation of all the testing done on this day; and finally *(me),* Ramon M. Sanchez, M.D., a physician in Atlanta with expertise in general neurology, epileptology, EEG/neurophysiology/sleep disorders, neuropharmacology, headache/pain management and other areas of interest.

In our spare time before the testing began, we had the opportunity to thoroughly discuss ***the experiment design*** and ***focus for the testing,*** which included:

1) To study the concentrations of low and extremely low radiation energy fields in the atmosphere, all the radiation *light* energy fields from the *visible light* range to the *invisible light* range in the *extremely low* energy fields; to measure and study the general atmosphere radiation energy fields at different locations around the apparition site; and to measure the skin-atmospheric radiation boundaries of Nancy *before, during, and after the apparitions.* All this will be orchestrated by Dr. Philip

Callahan and Winnie, his wife and assistant. Dr. Callahan also planned to measure and to study the *paramagnetic energy* in the soil/clay/rocks at various *apparition sites* like in Nancy's home*, the Holy Hill,* and the farm house in Conyers, Ga., USA, for scientific comparisons with internationally recognized *holy sites or sacred grounds* around the world. Dr. Callahan studied *holy sites* of both approved and some yet to be approved *sites* by the Church, as well as some other *famous sites* where *Jesus actually walked and taught - the good news.*

2) To study and measure the *invisible light* energy presence of high ionizing *gamma* radiation *before, during and after the apparitions.* This study will be performed by Dr. Humberto Velasquez and the radiation team. His other experiment was to professionally photograph the external environment outside of the *apparition site before, during, and after the apparitions.* Then to perform *advanced digital computerized photo-spectral analysis* on these three series of photographs to *quantify statistically the relative amount (in %'s) of the sun light energy's total reflective light intensity actually present on the external (outside) facade and surface of the farm house's chimney.* Recall that inside the apparition room's fireplace wall is hanging a very special Ecuadorian *crucifix of Jesus. Jesus is said to appear on this cross* to Nancy on the 13th of each month *during the heavenly visits or apparitions* of the Blessed Virgin Mary and *pilgrims report seeing* an *increase in the brightness of the sun light reflections - during the heavenly visits.*

3) To study and register the cutaneous bioelectrical discharges from muscle fibers emanating from Nancy's head and body, at Nancy's pre-frontal head region and the distal 2nd and 3rd fingers of her right hand, using the EMG system from La Fayette for measurements *before, during and after the apparitions.* This will be under the direction of Prof. R. Castanon-Gomez, Ph. D. The professor will also perform a battery of clinical neuropsychological and neuropsychophysiological tests *before, during, and after the apparitions* along with his clinical observations.

4) To study and evaluate with very thorough psychiatric clinical observations and mental status examinations *before, during, and after the apparitions.* This will be under the direction of George Hogben, M.D., a Board Certified psychiatrist practicing in New York.

5) To study Nancy's neurological examinations and the intensive ambulatory audiovisual TV-EEG telemetry monitoring systems, allowing us to intensively study Nancy's neurological mental status and neuro-cognitive behavior, while simultaneously studying the EEG Electrical brain wave activity picture along with the other neurological and physiological parameters via the continuous EEG, ECG, EOG, EMG intensive monitoring before, during and after the apparitions. This portion of the experiment design was under my direction, Ramon M. Sanchez, M.D. along with my medical team.

It was difficult to explain, but there was already a slight *tangible sense of peace and love* in the room with a relaxing calm and tranquility in the air and surrounding atmosphere with lots of people praying. At the same time there was a very palpable *joyous excitement* and anxious anticipation of what was to happen. This *tangible feeling* and oxymoron of a deep interior peace and love and yet joyful exciting energy reminded me briefly of *what* Nancy had experienced in my medical office's laboratory during *the baseline studies*, when we were able to record two extreme opposite frequencies of slow rhythmic *3 Hz delta* rhythms (*deep sleep* pattern) and the faster overriding *beta rhythms* (*awake and alert with focused attention* pattern) of slightly higher amplitude recorded and documented during the three separate EEG epochs when *Jesus appears to Nancy or speaks*—while her eyes were wide open and Nancy was indeed awake, alert and fully conscious.

Once *the experiment design* was made clear to the entire medical team and scientists present, each of us individually began setting up our own specialized equipment in the *apparition room.* This room was a large, rectangular area with oversized windows and a beautiful stone fireplace. Over the mantle, a white board with a beautiful crucifix from Ecuador hung on the wall. Off to the right, front corner of the farm house room was a three-tiered, triangular, wooden shelf. On the top shelf sat a statue of *Our Loving Mother*, the Blessed Virgin Mary caressing baby Jesus in her arms, surrounded by statues of angels praying. The second shelf held a very large portrait of the image of *Jesus, Divine Mercy*. Note: The original image of *Jesus* as *Divine Mercy* was given to a Polish nun *(now St. Faustina)* in a vision that depicts the *Risen Glorified Lord Jesus* in a white robe with *rays of blood and water* emanating from *His heart.* Near the bottom of the portrait of *Divine Mercy* it says*: "Jesus, I trust in you."* This *Divine Mercy* picture was flanked by a statue of *Jesus* praying at Gethsemane, and another statue of *Jesus all bloody* holding and carrying *the cross* on the road to Calvary in Jerusalem, Israel. On the third tier of the shelf was a statue of the *Infant of Prague (the Infant Jesus)* adorned with a crown, statues of angels and other religious statues. I later learned that this three-tiered, triangular, wooden shelf was actually *a replica of the original apparition site in Nancy's home*. Nancy first started *seeing* and *receiving messages* from Jesus and the Blessed Virgin Mary at this site in her home.

I was later informed that at the beginning of the public *apparitions* due to the very large crowds which had made a habit of gathering at Nancy's home on the 13th of each month, the Rockdale County Sheriff's Department had issued citations to put a stop to the gatherings for various reasons: zoning laws, safety issues, crowd control and complaints from surrounding neighbors, etc. Thus, the monthly pilgrimage to the 13th of the month apparitions of *Our Loving Mother with Jesus* after *receiving permission* was then later moved to a local farm house. I also met a skeleton group of *volunteer pilgrims* who totally believe in the authenticity of Nancy's claims. These pilgrims are convinced that *the messages* given to Nancy are of *divine origin.* These groups of volunteers were completely dedicated to *the perpetual adoration of Jesus in the Most Holy Blessed Sacrament* and *to increasing the honor and respect for the Blessed Virgin Mary.* Their loyalty and their devotion appeared noticeably reverent and profound.

Both Jesus and the Blessed Virgin Mary had asked that the *messages given to Nancy* be printed and distributed *for the United States and for the world* to read. In a message to Nancy from *Our Loving Mother* dated August 20th, 1992, the Blessed Virgin Mary said, *"Please spread my messages. Help others to hear them. I am only a messenger sent from heaven to echo my Son's words. I ask each of you to be a messenger for me... for my Son."* Heeding what they considered to be heaven's request, the volunteer pilgrims' mission involved the printing, publishing and distribution of all of Nancy's *visions, heavenly visits and experiences,* and *messages* not only from *the Blessed Virgin Mary* but also from *Jesus* directly *(the living Son of God).* They pointed out that in one of the messages *Jesus* Himself had said, *"My Mother's words and My words are one,"* which echoed another message given to Nancy on September 13th, 1992, when *Jesus* told her, *"Fear not, little one, speaking my Mother's words. Know that she speaks mine. Sometimes I speak to you, sometimes my Mother does. We are one. Come, little children, and be one with me and then you will speak my words too."* Without a doubt the entire group of pilgrim volunteers had their work cut out for them.

Many of the pilgrims present and thousands just like them believe that both *Jesus* and *Our Loving Mother* are using Nancy as an instrument to convey *God's words* with *messages to America and the whole world.* This was and is significant *(they feel)* as ***the messages contain a constant and urgent invitation from Jesus and His Loving Mother, Our Loving Mother, to our erring world to repent, amend our lives and come back to God,*** such as in the message of April 13th, 1991, in which the Blessed Virgin Mary, *Our Loving Mother* had said, *"Dear children of America, as your Loving Mother, I am calling you. Take my hand and walk with me on a path to my Son. Children of America, take my hand... Many of you are walking on a path away from my Son and you are in danger of losing your life with God forever. Repent and turn back to God. Children, please come. With tears I am pleading with you. I bless you." Our Loving Mother* was *crying* while she was pleading with us her children to *come back to God.*

As I walked around the *apparition room* to supervise the continuing setup of my equipment, it was impressive to see the large number of religious present from all over the world—in different colored robes, different religious orders of both priests and nuns, speaking many different languages. The priests and nuns were allowed to make private pilgrimages to Conyers, but were not permitted by the Catholic Church *(at the time of the testing) to lead* any pilgrimages to the *apparition site* since it was yet unapproved by the Church.

Immediately outside the *apparition room,* a very impressive yet peaceful mass of humanity, thousands of pilgrims and the media, were intently focused on the apparition room. Just beyond the front porch of the farm house were numerous journalists and television camera crews from local and international news media stations ready to film and record the events of the *appointed day.* It never occurred to me how important that appointed day was until I first set foot into the *apparition room* and felt the odd yet exciting combination: a profound sense of peace and love and yet a joyous anticipation on the part of all the devout and religious present, in stark contrast to the hardened *skeptical minds (like me)* and intrigue on the part of the media and unbelievers.

My EEG technicians were quickly at work finishing the setup of all the equipment in the apparition room and making sure the intensive audiovisual TV-EEG telemetry monitoring systems were all in working order. The actual arrangement of the apparition room, where Nancy prays and receives messages from the Blessed Virgin Mary and Jesus, had to be altered slightly so that our cameras and other audiovisual recording equipment could be placed in front of the kneeling pews in order to allow for a full frontal view of Nancy's face. This was done much to Nancy's initial objection. But, when she was asked to put this to prayer, we were told she had just received a *message from heaven* telling Nancy to *"submit to all tests."* Cameras were placed in front and back and on both sides, so that Nancy could be monitored and filmed from all four angles.

An additional hand-held camera would be used by one of our audiovisual monitoring technical staff. He would film Nancy from behind, primarily to document the actual testing itself and get the reactions of the pilgrims and religious in the apparition room. While I continued to supervise the ambulatory audiovisual TV-EEG telemetry monitoring systems setup in the room, I could see the other scientists also busy at work setting up their own specialized equipment and display monitors. The research teams would now be ready to test, record and document the energy changes *before, during, and after the apparitions.* Dr. Velasquez was placing magnetic strips geometrically on the floor of the apparition room and around the farm house in order to test and later compare radiation changes at the different sites.

At this point, I was asked to go back into the room next to the apparition room (which we referred to as *the adjacent room*) to meet Nancy, who had just arrived to pray before the *noontime apparitions.* I quickly reintroduced myself and then instructed my medical team and EEG technicians to start placing the EEG scalp electrodes on Nancy's head and to start the set up the ambulatory EEG Oxford II audiovisual TV-EEG telemetry monitoring system for the testing scheduled on this appointed day. We had decided to use two separate eight-channel EEG recorders in order to have the luxury of monitoring additional brain waves and topographic surface head regions for a more complete *electrical brain picture analysis.* While the EEG technicians were busy at work placing the EEG scalp electrodes, I initiated my second series of neurological examinations of Nancy; and this was filmed by the Australian film crew for their documentary.

Nancy's second neurological examinations were once again **normal**. Her mental status examination was normal and demonstrated that Nancy is a very shy, humble, honest person with a childlike quality as she spoke with a slight Boston accent of the heavenly visits and messages she had received the night before and during our initial *baseline studies* testing. My medical clinical observations of Nancy were that Nancy appeared sincere, genuine, trustworthy and sane. I detected no form of hysteria, psychosis, affective or personality disorder, and no mood disorder, thought disorder or malingering.

After I completed my neurological examinations and clinical observations, Dr. George Hogben, the renowned psychiatrist from New York, came into the room and began to perform his psychiatric mental status examinations on Nancy while my medical team's EEG technicians continued the placement of EEG scalp electrodes on Nancy's head. Dr. George Hogben recorded detailed observations of Nancy: *before, during and after the apparitions,* that are fully disclosed in the results section of this chapter. His in-depth view of Nancy's make-up from his professional perspective is very insightful.

After our medical and scientific testing, I spoke with Dr. George Hogben whose professional impressions were documented and summarized, and said, "I had been asked to give a testimony as to whether Nancy showed any psychiatric disturbance especially: *before, during, and after her visions* and I can say unequivocally, no. There is no evidence of any psychiatric disturbance at all." After Dr. George Hogben completed his *before the apparition psychiatric evaluation,* Prof. Castanon went quickly to work setting up his own instruments. He began applying the EMG of La Fayette by placing the recording electrodes on Nancy's pre-frontal region which the professor claims enables the identification of electrical discharges that are continuously being emitted from the muscle fibers, as long as the subject/patient is *alive* and *zero discharges only* when the subject/patient is *dead.* Modern technology with supersensitive electrical instruments has now made it possible to measure very weak electrical currents, which change in response to stimuli resulting from emotional excitation, known as *cutaneous resistance.* Scientifically, the responses to stimuli from emotional excitation have been measured to increase under conditions of *stress / anxiety* and decrease under conditions of *rest / relaxation.*

In these studies the professor used surface electrodes, which enable the measurements of bioelectrical potentials in concomitance with certain conditions such as stress and tension or with stimuli of a different nature such as light, sound, etc. These surface electrodes conform to an interphase between the biological tissue and that of the electrical apparatus. The data thus collected is measured by their direct visual, auditory and sensory expressions as a result of the use of electrical amplifiers that register the intensity of the electrical discharges on a visual display screen and the amplitudes of the electrical discharges are recorded in micro-volts. Amplifiers attached register the sound or the auditory activity of the electrical discharges that are emanating continuously from the muscle fibers - as long as the subject is *alive.* Thus, the supersensitive EMG system from La Fayette actually enables the identification and measurements of these very weak electrical discharges from muscle fibers, quantifying the contraction as well as the relaxation of muscle fibers. These instruments were designed to help demonstrate and document varying levels of intensity concerning different emotional states such as stress, tension, anxiety, etc. Prof. Castanon, Ph. D., is a clinical neuropsychologist and neuropsychophysiologist, who has taught at different Universities in Italy, Germany and Bolivia, South America. He has published over 300 scientific papers and authored numerous books on the topics of the brain, the nervous system and stress. The professor has advanced the understanding of stress in regard's to bio-feedback stress management techniques by utilizing the EMG system of La Fayette which can identify weak cutaneous bioelectrical discharges emanating from muscle fibers during contraction and relaxation from a subject's body. His work has shown that patients who are in an absolutely *relaxed state* will typically demonstrate on the EMG system's display screen an amplitude range electrical discharge of 0.2 to 0.5 micro-volts, while those patients in a state of *stress, tension or anxiety* will register a reading of greater than 1.2 micro-volts (1.3 to 2.0µV or greater). Thus, *readings >1.2 micro-volts usually suggest a person is undergoing tension or anxiety.*

The professor's preliminary tests on Nancy recorded *tension levels* of 1.5 -1.7 micro-volts just *before the apparition,* which logically corresponded to the increased high tension or anxiety that this study (before a very large crowd) may have caused Nancy; however, as soon as Nancy began to pray and *the heavenly visits, visions and apparitions* began, then the readings ***instantly*** and ***dramatically dropped*** *from 1.5-1.7 micro-volts down* ***to 0.2 micro-volts!***

After his preliminary studies on Nancy before June 13th, 1993, the professor claimed that in over 25 years experience in this field he has never witnessed anyone ever *relax so abruptly like Nancy* with such lightning speed. He has studied relaxation and biofeedback techniques for stress, tension and anxiety management using the EMG system of La Fayette for many years and has never witnessed or seen any subject/patient relax that quickly. Nancy dropped from a high tension/anxiety level to a profound and completely relaxed level within a millisecond of time. Not only was the dramatic drop in high tension and anxiety itself very significant, but the actual blazing *speed (within milliseconds)* with which Nancy's amplified muscle fiber bioelectrical discharges shifted down so rapidly, that this event according to the professor was truly unprecedented, and until now was previously considered *biologically and physiologically impossible.*

The professor privately told me that in his neuropsychology clinic in Bolivia, he teaches patients *to relax* using various biofeedback techniques and hypnosis; simultaneously, he uses the EMG of La Fayette system display monitors for objective documentation of the patient's success in reaching varying levels of relaxation and whenever possible to reach a completely relaxed, stress-free state. The professor said that even the most highly-trained subjects with expertise in *biofeedback* and *hypnosis* that he has worked with are not able to ever reach such a deeply profound and *completely relaxed state* as was attained by Nancy in this study. Moreover, the incredible lightning speed *(within milliseconds)* with which Nancy's body and physiology accomplished this feat was indeed absolutely mind-boggling. He stated that with over 25 years experience in this specialized scientific field he has never encountered such dramatic and unprecedented *new data.* The professor's clinical observations and documented scientific evaluations of Nancy during these studies were also truly astounding.

The professor proceeded to perform the neuropsychophysiology tests and clinical observations, while my medical team and EEG technicians completed the intensive ambulatory TV-EEG telemetry monitoring systems *hookup.* It was at this point that Dr. Philip Callahan and his wife, Winnie, entered the room, greeted Nancy and set up their specialized equipment. They handed Nancy one of the *probes of the photonic ionic cord amplifier*—a device that Dr. Callahan has patented to scientifically measure the atmospheric *extremely low and low* ionizing radiation *invisible* light energy in the form of Schumann waves, target waves, Soliton waves, radio waves, infrared maser-like waves and visual coherent bursts of laser-light. The other such probe was going to be held literally in the air or the atmosphere of the apparition room by Dr. Callahan.

Dr. Callahan *(now retired)* was recently a consultant with the Bio-Information Institute, and was formerly a Professor of Entomology and Biophysics who taught at the University of Florida in Gainesville. Dr. Callahan has now authored over 14 books and well over 150 scientific papers in the fields of zoology, entomology, insect biophysics, antennae of insects, paramagnetism, lasers, insights into treating the AIDS virus as antennae, electromagnetic communication of insects, radiation environment, and low energy electromagnetic radiation amplification. His credentials also included studies on the photonic ionic radio amplifier, infrared low ionization radiation studies on the *Tilma of Our Lady of Guadalupe* in Guadalupe, Mexico, and studies on the authenticity of the miraculous shroud in Liverpool, England, under the invitation of St. Joseph's Hospice Association.

Dr. Callahan has led a very colorful and diverse life. He pioneered studies on the importance and uses of paramagnetic soil, which led to an invitation by members of the Shinto religion for him to deliver a speech to the Prince and Princess of Japan regarding the utilization of paramagnetic forces to save the sacred groves of Japan. He has completed three scientific expeditions sponsored by the Bio-Information Institute to visit the Achuara Headhunters in the Amazon Jungle, in order to study the paramagnetic forces in the soil and to study the region's atmospheric low and extremely low radiation energy fields of activity. Dr. Callahan has also participated in expeditions to Ireland to study the ancient stone structures and other places.

But Dr. Callahan's impressive qualifications do not end there. With four U.S. patents to his credit, he has also done consulting work with Temple University Medical School and the Center for Study of Human Functioning in Wichita Falls, Kansas, and has traveled the world over visiting holy religious sites, in order to study the *paramagnetic energy* in the soil and surrounding rock. In addition to his consulting work, Dr. Callahan has been spending his retirement by conducting continued research in the use of nonlinear far infrared radiation by biological systems. His studies have demonstrated that trees and people always amplify radiation when waves pass through them, similar to the way that the reception of a radio or television signal typically improves when an antenna is used. This radiation measured in Schumann waves ranges from 1 Hz to 40 Hz, and in most areas of the world the atmospheric range is indeed from 2 Hz to 40 Hz.

During his extensive research of the effects of radiation on humans, Dr. Callahan recorded that when subjects touches the photonic ionic cord amplifier probe instrument, such as the one he intended to use that day on Nancy, he was able to measure *Schumann waves* in a frequency from 14 to 20 Hz. In his many years of research,

Dr. Callahan had never seen the *extremely low* ionizing radiation energy fields measured at the skin-atmospheric boundary change to frequencies lower than 14 Hz, unless the subject had undergone many hours of training using electronic biofeedback or meditative techniques. Likewise, Dr. Callahan has never recorded *Soliton waves* with an amplitude intensity of more than 25 mV anywhere around the world. The significance of these last statements would later come to light with full impact as you will hopefully see as you read *this book,* though none of the members of our medical and scientific team could have predicted it at the time of the testing.

Dr. Callahan took readings in the adjacent room and in the apparition room before the apparitions took place. Schumann waves of 14 Hz frequency with 1 mV intensity were recorded; this was considered to be in *normal range*. With all the doctors, scientists, and medical team busy at work making last minute preparations *before the apparitions,* and the time continuing to tick away toward the 12:00 noon hour, I could definitely feel the excitement and wondrous anticipation as to what would possibly occur. I began to ponder the statement Nancy made during the *baseline studies*, when she quoted *Jesus* as *saying, "**Watch what I will do**."* These words definitely heightened my interest and intrigue, despite my very hardened skeptical mindset.

In the adjacent room Dr. Callahan placed *the probe* in Nancy's hand to get baseline recordings before the apparitions. After Dr. Callahan and the professor finished their own preliminary recordings, Nancy said she was ready. We all walked into the apparition room in the farm house and everybody took their places. Nancy, with George Collins and the Spanish translator-Juan Ruiz to her left, all knelt down and started to pray. It was at this point that an announcement was made over the loudspeaker to the waiting crowds that the *Rosary prayers* were to begin.

At this point members of our medical and scientific team made one last check of the cameras and made sure that everything was working. We wanted to be certain that Nancy could be seen on the audiovisual TV-EEG telemetry monitoring screen, which was time-locked in synchrony with the event marker. The event marker itself was pressed by me several times to make sure it was operational. Each time the event marker was pressed, an *asterisk* would appear on the TV screen, recording that precise moment in time.

As mentioned, Nancy had been given different scientific probes and devices to hold in her hands during the testing. And with all the religious items and rosary in her hands, it was clear that someone would have to push the event marker for her during the testing. So, I willingly volunteered. I knelt immediately adjacent to Nancy, on the right and still slightly behind her, so that I could be in a position to hear everything she was saying. I would then press the event marker each time it was necessary to highlight and study Nancy's electrical brain wave picture and behavior during different specific EEG epochs (short periods of EEG recorded time) of special interest for comparative analysis.

Once my medical team and certified EEG technicians confirmed that all the equipment was in order and operational, I gave my nod for clearance to *start the testing.* The professor checked his instruments and Dr. Callahan, who was assisting in this *new data* collection, started recording with his equipment and sat on the edge of the fireplace just to my right. In that position, he was close enough to monitor *the atmospheric radiation changes within one foot of the actual apparition site,* the place where the Blessed Virgin Mary brings baby Jesus appears to Nancy. Behind me and to my left was Dr. George Hogben, who was to make his clinical psychiatric observations and evaluations of Nancy during the apparitions. Adjacent to Dr. Hogben was the radiation team and scientific crew who had come with Dr. Humberto Velasquez. This group had their Geiger counters in place to measure the high ionizing *gamma* radiation energy field changes in the room and in predetermined locations along strategically-placed, magnetic strips on the floor of the room for all the recordings during the apparitions.

Everything was finally ready. Nancy started to pray, beginning with the first of the fifteen mysteries of the rosary. I knelt along with Nancy with the rest of the medical and scientific team. Surrounding us were cameras inside the apparition room and media cameras outside the apparition room, as literally thousands of people began to pray even more intensely. Over the loudspeaker I heard the crowd begin to sing the famous *Fatima song chorus: Ave, Ave, Ave, Maria...* Moments after the singing and prayers began, Nancy joined in with the singing and then paused and said, *"Oh,* I see beautiful angels. There are one, two, three, four, five angels. Oh! They are beautiful." Shortly after I learned from our medical team that my wife had taken a picture with a Polaroid camera the moment Nancy said there were *"one, two angels"* present. Surprisingly, on this photograph *"two oval-shaped, golden, transparent lights" are visible,* in the same corner that Nancy said she was seeing *"one, two... angels".* The photographer, my wife, did not know how to explain these two images of the *"oval shaped golden lights" photographed,* since these *two golden lights* were not visible to her or our eyes, and none of the stationary lights present in the room could possibly have produced such an artifact. Recall, our medical and scientific team had total control of all the lighting fixtures in the apparition room, and we definitely have no explanation for this unusual documented phenomenon.

Another source of excitement was soon evident in the *chirping sounds of birds,* followed by the *clicking sounds of the Geiger counter monitors* under the direction of radiation specialist Dr. Humberto Velasquez. I looked around to see where the Geiger counter monitor had been placed, and I could see the radiation team busy at work recording the appointed event. My level of curiosity drastically increased at this point. Alerted by Nancy's words, *"Oh, I see beautiful angels,"* we all moved closer to Nancy in order to listen and observe her more intently. The soundtracks from our audiovisual TV-EEG telemetry monitoring system recorded Nancy saying, "A light just appeared on the statue of *Our Lady*... I can hear her. I can hear her call my name. She is here. Please, *in the name of Jesus* I ask you to identify yourself... pause... If anything here is not of God, let it be gone in *the holy name of Jesus...* pause... Oh! A beautiful crown appeared above her head! Oh! I love you so very much Blessed Mother." *Our Loving Mother* then said, *"Please tell the children that I am here."* Nancy then gently described how beautiful and awesome the Blessed Virgin Mary was while holding her baby *Jesus* with such tender love and offers her Son, *Jesus - in His Living Presence* to us.

As noted above immediately after the first pause, Nancy explained the Blessed Mother said, ***"I am the Blessed Virgin Mary. I am the Mother of God and your Loving Mother. I come in the name of my Son Jesus. Thank you, children, for joining us in prayer. Thank you for your prayers and sacrifices."***

At this point the professor leaned over Nancy's shoulder and placed an instrument on her right wrist and took some readings. It appeared that this particular action somehow interrupted Nancy because she then went on to say, "Can you please repeat that again, Blessed Mother?" On the audiovisual TV-EEG telemetry monitoring system one can actually see Nancy asking the Blessed Virgin Mary for *the message* to be repeated, and then she nodded saying, "Yes, Blessed Mother..." If this was acting, then Nancy should be considered for an Academy Award (an Oscar) or a Golden Globe Award.

Nancy then reported that the Blessed Virgin Mary said, ***"I will give the message for the United States at the end of the sorrowful mysteries. I will***

depart at that time, yet I will remain with you."

Nancy then exclaimed, *"Behold* the Mother of God in her radiant beauty...Behold her ...pause... pause... Behold her baby, Jesus... Behold Him...pause...Glory to the Lamb...Glory to the Lamb of God, Who takes away the sins of the world...*Glory!"* Nancy at first said she saw the Blessed Virgin Mary appear alone briefly and then saw *baby Jesus in great burst of light appear in all His Glory on her loving arms.* The Blessed Virgin Mary then said, *"Please tell my children."*

At that point, Nancy turned to George Collins and said, *"She* wants us to continue to pray*."* The information that *"the Blessed Virgin Mary is here"* was then relayed over the loudspeaker by the Spanish translator Juan Rivas to all the pilgrims present outside the farm house. It was fascinating to hear the entire massive crowd become immediately silent. As they continued *the rosary,* their prayers seemed increasingly more serious and more reverent. Nancy continued to experience *visions* during the recitation of the fifteen decades of the rosary. Nancy said she saw the radiant *Blessed Virgin Mary* lovingly holding her *baby Jesus,* preceded by an *army of holy angels* and an *array of saints.* Nancy said, "The *Blessed Virgin Mary* has appeared with the *heavenly court."* During the early part of the *sorrowful mysteries,* St. Padre Pio appeared to Nancy on her left side, almost in front of his own photograph that was hanging on the wall on that side of the apparition room. St. Padre Pio died in 1968 and is a renowned Catholic Italian Capuchin monk of the Franciscan Order. He is one of the most famous and amazing mystic of our times. Historically, he is a known true *miracle worker,* who suffered the intense agony of the *stigmata "the five wounds of Jesus" for more than 50 years,* as documented by the Roman Catholic Church. A famous confessor during World War II, St. Padre Pio was reported to possess all the marvelous gifts and chrisoms of the *Holy Spirit.* One of his gifts was the *ability to read souls - to see* deeply into the human spirit *with eyes of God,* which made him an incredible, amazing and highly-sought out confessor. According to Nancy, St. Padre Pio visits her in many of the apparitions.

Of interest, numerous pilgrims have also reported seeing St. Padre Pio in Conyers. Some pilgrims have even taken photographs at the Conyers apparition sites wherein an image of St. Pio is seen in the silluotte of the clouds. Nancy continued to speak privately with the Blessed Virgin Mary throughout the recitation of *the rosary.* It was a real treat to hear the rosary prayers, i.e., the Our Father prayer *(The Lord's Prayer)* and *the Hail Mary prayer* being recited in many different languages and tongues, by people from all over the world. Part of *what the Blessed Virgin Mary said to Nancy* privately was recorded by our equipment as follows:

"I will return next month. You can record those words. I am preparing you (Nancy) for a time when you will no longer give a message for the United States, by my silent visits during the month. My children (referring to all God's children all over

the world) are fighting with each other, because they have walked away from God. ...So many of my children are not allowing me to help them. Please, pray for our children who are suffering in Yugoslavia, Africa, Cuba, India, and Ireland. My children, we are suffering for each child that has pushed God away. My children are suffering everywhere. There is hatred in the hearts of men. There should be love in the hearts of men. Please, children, it is time to wake up. Turn your lives around and come to my living Son. Implant His words deep within you. Know we are with you always. I am patiently enduring these tests. My children have too little faith. It makes me very sad. He died for you, dear children. He died for you. He lives and you do not know Him. Man is always testing God."

When the Blessed Virgin Mary says, *"He died for you,"* she means *her Son Jesus (the living Son of God)* died for you. When she says, *"He lives and you do not know Him,"* as foretold in the Bible, she means *her Son Jesus* who resurrected 3 days after His death lives on to this day and forever more. *Remember the empty tomb in Jerusalem!* Yearly, the *resurrection of Jesus* is celebrated on *Easter Sunday.* At that point, the increase in background noise of the Geiger counter radiation detector's clicking, *"click, click, click,"* was obvious. The readings caused some excitement among the onlookers present, as well as the scientific team, for they signified the potential detection of energy changes and the presence of increased high ionizing radiation in the apparition room that was possibly not present before Nancy's announcement that the Blessed Virgin Mary was present.

For their part, Dr. Callahan and his wife, Winnie, were both very excited about their own readings registering from the photonic ionic cord amplifier *probe* placed in Nancy's hands. While this probe had been measuring *14-20 Hz Schumann waves* with *the amplitude intensity (mV) 1mV Soliton waves* just *before the Blessed Virgin Mary appeared. As soon as Nancy* said that she *could hear then see the Blessed Virgin Mary, the Schumann waves dropped to 8 Hz.* And when the *baby Jesus* appeared in the loving arms of the Blessed Virgin Mary, she said, *"Please tell my children that I am here,"* during this exact time period the signal frequency in *Schumann waves dropped instantly to 4 Hz!* And the *Soliton wave's amplitude jumped up to >25 mV with an average 40 mV!* Interestingly, the *4 Hz Schumann waves* were recorded *only* when *the Blessed Virgin Mary was bringing her baby Jesus to us* or when *the Blessed Virgin Mary was echoing His (Jesus) words.*

I then heard Dr. Callahan saying, "The drop to 4 Hz when the Blessed Virgin Mary appeared holding baby Jesus and began *speaking* to Nancy was also puzzling for another reason, because between 4 and 8 Hz that person should be *asleep*; yet Nancy, as we all saw, was wide awake and communicating what she was *experiencing* at the moment to the transcriber George Collins next to her." Not only did the frequency drop to 4 Hz while the Blessed Virgin Mary was holding and caressing and bringing her baby Jesus to us, but also when she began *speaking His words* to Nancy, at the same time, *the amplitude intensity (mV) in Soliton waves increased from 1 mV to >25mV with an average of 40 mV!* Then, Dr. Callahan shouted out, ***"I have never recorded Soliton waves with amplitudes of more than 25 mV anywhere else in the world!"***

Dr. Callahan claims that if you were actually standing on top of an active volcano and simultaneously you were also closely nearby an electrical *(lightning)* thunder storm while still holding the probe in your hands, only in that type of setting has he recorded Soliton waves that come near or even close to approaching 25 mV. But, Dr. Callahan has never recorded Soliton waves above 25 mV, unless *flashes or bolts or darts of lightning* actually struck very close to and near to the actual recording probe. I then raised this question: Had real *flashes or bolts or darts of lightning* just entered into the *apparition room?"* Recall, it was a hot and very dry June 13th summer day with *a clear blue sky* and definitely no rain clouds around. How can we possibly explain *flashes or bolts or darts of lightning* energy being recorded and documented inside the apparition room at the exact and precise moments in time Nancy says the Blessed Virgin Mary appears *bringing her baby Jesus to us and/or echoes His living words?*

In 1989 Dr. Callahan wrote an article on the maser-like nonlinear scatter from *human breath,* which is a unique enhanced surface for the infrared scatter effect. Prior to this in 1978, he also wrote a paper on nonlinear radiation and life, namely *the human breath,* as a low intensity gas-dynamic laser. Armed with this type of very highly specialized and unique expertise in the relationship between the human breath and special minute extremely low forms of ionizing radiation energy detectable in the human breath and in the human voice, Dr. Callahan used his patented picram oscilloscope to record the maser-like non-linear (coherent) scatter of extremely low ionizing radiation energy atmospheric field waves, which were created from the emission of Nancy's *voice and breath* as she spoke to the Blessed Virgin Mary. Thus, the data registered *Nancy's specific human voice and human breath pattern* at the precise moments Nancy spoke. This pattern was very specific for Nancy's voice and breath which according to Dr. Callahan had clearly demonstrated the *normal range* of spikes typically seen *for a human voice* and/or *human breath patterns.*

All of us in the room witnessed with intensely curious anticipation *what* was being recorded. I watched Dr. Callahan become quite excited as he began to observe *a new specific* and *very different human voice pattern* on the display monitor. This distinctly different voice pattern was *associated with a normal range of larger amplitude* spikes as seen, recorded and documented on his picram oscilloscope display monitor. This *new data* was recorded *only* while Nancy was *listening to* and *receiving private messages from the Blessed Virgin Mary, Our Loving Mother.*

All the people in the apparition room including Nancy were very still and reverently *silent,* yet Dr. Callahan still noted the *new distinctly different changes in the pattern and amplitude* of the spikes registering on his display monitor. He clearly demonstrated a distinctly different but normal typical human voice and human breath pattern registering on his display instruments that was *clearly not Nancy,* which Dr. Callahan so excitedly pointed out to me and to the entire medical and scientific team. I was an eye-witness to seeing these distinctly different and slightly larger spikes registering on Dr. Callahan's picram oscilloscope display monitor, which scientifically corresponded to a distinctly different and normal human voice and human breath pattern of another person speaking other than Nancy. According to Nancy the Blessed Virgin Mary, *Our Loving Mother* was the *only one* ***speaking*** *to her (Nancy)* at that precise moment in time. And there was total *silence* in the apparition room. Obviously, the only clue or indication that anyone was actually speaking at those precise moments of total silence, besides Dr. Callahan documenting a human voice and human breath pattern of a distinctly different person on his patented picram oscilloscope, was Nancy's claims that the Blessed Virgin Mary was *giving her a message* - at those precise moments of time. *Wow!* Was the Blessed Virgin Mary's *voice* really detected?

Later in many private conversations with me, Dr. Callahan said he could *only speculate* that his findings were indeed the human voice or human breath pattern of the Blessed Virgin Mary. He added that, to be absolutely sure, he would need a photo-acoustic antenna, which was not available for these tests, to more accurately document these human voice and human breath patterns (see Dr. Callahan's work on *dolphin ears* in the book titled *Exploring the Spectrum*). Nonetheless, it was amazing to me to actually see (and to personally eye-witness) these distinctly different larger spikes registering on Dr. Callahan's patented picram oscilloscope display monitor which occurred during the precise moments in time that the *Blessed Virgin Mary was giving Nancy a message from Jesus.* Thus, the above recorded *new data* actually documented the real presence of a distinctly different ***human voice pattern*** and ***human breath pattern*** of another person (not Nancy) really speaking. Can you imagine? ***The Blessed Virgin Mary is speaking to Nancy while the rest of us in the apparition room heard complete and total silence. Repeatedly, whenever (and while) Our Loving Mother is speaking to Nancy, Dr. Callahan's equipment scientifically detected, registered and actually documented another human voice pattern (not Nancy's voice pattern), while the rest of us in the room were hearing - complete and total silence.***

As the fifteen decades of the rosary continued at a very slow and reverent pace, I remember for the first time beginning to feel quite moved and touched by the entire experience, seeing all those thousands of pilgrims praying and sensing a very sweet peaceful calm. While I was actually feeling interiorly this profound peace, love and joy, I soon started to feel externally, uncomfortably warm and hot. It was a very hot and dry day with almost no breeze. The only ventilation inside the apparition room was a small fan that appeared to be malfunctioning, and it was certainly not efficient enough to adequately cool down the large number of people (mostly priests and nuns from all over the world) crowded in the rather small apparition room. As sweat rolled off my brow, I began to feel intense pain and discomfort in my knees from the prolonged kneeling that was seemingly required in respect of the *heavenly visits.*

For almost one hour and forty-five minutes, the recitation of the fifteen-decades of the rosary continued. I became increasingly fidgety due to my painful knees, so I tried to adjust my lower body to find a more comfortable position. This was most embarrassing. I couldn't seem to control my fidgeting. Shifting my weight from side to side, my knees started burning with pain. Several times I started to feel my legs go numb. I observed this was in stark contrast to Nancy, who was in a loving, joyful, calm, peaceful state of *ecstasy* with absolutely no signs of discomfort during the entire recitation of the rosary.

Throughout Nancy's encounter with the Blessed Virgin Mary, Nancy's voice with a slight Bostonian accent was soft and gentle with an almost childlike-quality. She was very reverent and humble in her demeanor and expressions, as she spoke with *Our Loving Mother.* It reminded me of what we expect to see when a little girl is speaking tenderly with her loving mother and asking for advice and consolation, while also demonstrating and showing great respect and love. I continued to marvel at how long Nancy actually could kneel for such a prolonged period of time without ever flinching even once or showing any discomfort whatsoever. My Cuban-American machismo tendencies were now beginning to come to life and soon started to take charge. I now wanted more than ever to endure any pain whatever-the-cost, simply because Nancy was able to kneel without a flinch or even a trace of any pain whatsoever. Now see my typical *Cuban* bravado!

As the pain in my knees fired up a few notches and persisted, I continued to shift my body weight from knee to knee to try to get more comfortable. At times I experienced severe spikes of pain in my knees, reoccurring at increasing intervals, to a point where it was now really beginning to distract my attention away from what I was supposed to be doing. So I said no, no to my increasing desire to sit. But, the pain in my knees became so excruciating that I finally sat down, much to my chagrin and my *macho whatever,* for moments of delightful relief. Embarrassed, I remained sitting immediately behind Nancy, until the numbness in my knees dissipated. Quickly recognizing the work at hand, again I grudgingly got back on my knees and looked at Nancy's face. She had such a peaceful and radiant glow. I witnessed then in Nancy a tremendous *joy and ecstasy* that was so transparent. I immediately sensed that Nancy indeed has a very genuine and deep love for Jesus and the Blessed Virgin Mary, *Our Loving Mother.* It was as if the energy source of Nancy's *heavenly visits or apparitions* was somehow reflecting or shining from her face. During the visions, I also noted that Nancy was able to stare, rarely blinking, as if she were transfixed by the heavenly visits or apparitions and not wanting to lose not even a millisecond of the *majestic vision.* Just by looking at Nancy's face made me somehow feel an immense sense of ***peace.*** I soon found myself *joining in the rosary prayers* along with the pilgrims *for the first time.* Then somehow *miraculously, I felt no more pain in my knees.* This was unbelievable! Recall, I am a very well trained medical doctor and neurologist. How could this happen? *I felt no more pain in my knees... only* moments after *I started to pray the rosary prayers. What in the world - does this mean?*

Jesus appeared once during the sorrowful mysteries and a second time during the glorious mysteries. Jesus appeared full size and as an adult according to Nancy. *Jesus* gave Nancy a private message during His second appearance. After the sorrowful mysteries were completed, the Blessed Virgin Mary gave the monthly message of June 13th, 1993 to the United States and the world. There was silence before the Blessed Virgin Mary delivered *the words of her Son, Jesus.* Nancy privately said the Blessed Virgin Mary comes as a *loving mother* and as a *heavenly messenger to echo the words of her Son, Jesus.* I remember looking around and seeing so many religious. Some were literally in tears, crying while others looking like little children anticipating a loving word from their *heavenly Mother.* I looked outside the window and I could see thousands of devout God fearing pilgrims surrounding the farm house accompanied by all the local TV-networks, cable-TV and foreign TV-Networks camera crews, and many local and foreign journalists with their cameras rolling, anticipating any of the many purported *heavenly signs.*

I looked forward and observed Nancy nod her head, and at that point in time *the Blessed Virgin Mary* began to give her message *(a message from her Son, Jesus)* to the United States and the world. Nancy repeated it word for word:

"My dear little children, do you understand the times in which you are living? Do you see any signs? Do you hear the voice of my Son in your hearts? Do you know Him? Please children it is time to wake up. Turn your lives around and come to my living Son. Implant His word deep within you. Know that we are with you always. Children please know He is the living bread come down from heaven. Eat **(of His body)** ***and drink*** **(of His blood),** ***then you will have His life within you. Please listen; please do not deny my Son any longer. I love you, dear little ones, and I bless you. As you make the sign of the cross, I will bless you and I will depart, yet, I will remain with you. I will now bless everything you have brought with you."***

Note: It is a *Catholic* and traditionally *universal Christian* dogma that teaches and proclaims that *the Most Holy Eucharist* is the *"sacrifice of praise."* This *holy "sacrifice of praise" is perpetual,* ongoing and *offered daily in the worship to God and to God alone.* This *daily offering to Father God at Holy Mass* is more than just *the new covenant memorial service.* The *"bread and wine" offered daily to Father God,* after the *holy consecration* is offered by a Catholic priest in the true authoritative succession, *the Church* still teaches, **is** now the true *Precious Body, Blood, Soul and Divinity of Jesus Christ; the real true presence of the unblemished Lamb of God, Who takes away the sins of the World;* the *only begotten Living Son of God, the Second Person of the Most Holy Trinity; One God in the Mystery of All Mysteries.* In John 6:51-52 *Jesus says: "I am the living bread which came down from heaven. If any man eat of this bread, he shall live for ever..." Jesus, the true manna,* feeds and fills the hungry soul with *His* ***life giving*** *bread* (see John 6:54). Jesus *gives* us *His flesh* as true *food (meat)* and *His blood* as true *drink* for all souls as *"the blood of the grape," the Precious Blood,* to *inebriate the weary, thirsty soul.*

As the heavenly message was being delivered to Nancy, Dr. Callahan who was immediately to my right again showed me the larger now more familiar spikes which were registering on his picram oscilloscope. He once again demonstrated to me that another human voice or human breath pattern was being generated, that was different from Nancy's breath pattern. I recall there was absolute and complete silence at the precise moments when *no one was speaking* according to Nancy *except for the Blessed Virgin Mary,* who was giving the monthly 13th day of the month *messages.* The moment Nancy begins to give us *the message* of the Blessed Virgin Mary, the typical normal human voice and human breath spike pattern specific for Nancy's voice pattern was once again recorded.

Dr. Callahan was smiling at the exciting prospects of all the amazing results. He later said in private to me that his wife, Winnie had witnessed, at the precise moment Nancy proclaimed *the messages* were now being spoken, a *myriad of lights* emanating or coming from the same corner where *the Blessed Virgin Mary* was supposed to be present according to Nancy. Though Winnie had been sitting right next to me, I did not personally see or witness *the light or lights* that she (Winnie) was privileged to see; however, later I was informed that other people inside the apparition room, namely, several priests, nuns and religious, as well as a visiting Archbishop from Rome, also reported seeing some of these same *myriad of lights. What* does this all mean? Why some were people privileged or blessed to see *the light* while others *(like me)* were not? Or *does faith suffice?*

Moreover, some pilgrims outside the farm house also claimed to witnesses what they referred to as *a light show.* These lights intensified greatly the moment *the Blessed Virgin Mary,* according to Nancy, said she was departing. Nancy went on to describe *the Blessed Virgin Mary* as *ascending through the roof,* at which point the crowds outside literally and noticeably went wild with excitement. With the cameras rolling, many pilgrims excitedly reported seeing *the Blessed Virgin Mary* on the rooftop of the farm house, while others adamantly claimed to have seen a *myriad of lights;* some saw *the light or lights* and others even saw *the silhouettes of angels on top of the roof.* A very large number of people also reported *smelling a sweet* ***scent of roses*** that pervaded the entire apparition room and the surrounding farm house area at that precise moment in time. Still other pilgrims reported that ***the sun*** *had immediately begun to spin* and *radiate different colors like an array of rainbows,* as if ***the sun was dancing*** with celestial and cosmic joy.

Throughout this exciting period of time in which so many pilgrims, skeptics and religious alike reported *a myriad of mystical* and *optical phenomena,* the Geiger counter monitor was intermittently clicking away with its *"click, click, click..."* The brisk scientifically unanticipated *clicking* seemed to reach a faster frequency when Nancy said the Blessed Virgin Mary was departing, and according to many pilgrims at this point in time *the light show* dramatically intensified.

All of a sudden, the readings on all of our equipment, detectors and monitors immediately returned to near baseline values with a silence noted from the Geiger counters' decreased clicking without an apparent cause, except for Nancy's claim that the *heavenly visits* (*Our Loving Mother brings baby Jesus and the heavenly court*) had just departed. The near baseline normal range readings similar to *before the apparitions* were once again recorded across all the display board monitors, now *after the apparitions.* The readings from the picram oscilloscope had ranged from 25 mV up to 40 mV during the time *the Blessed Virgin Mary bringing baby Jesus was present* and increased to well above **40 mV,** while *Our Loving Mother* was departing with *the heavenly court.* After the *heavenly visitors* departed the mV Soliton wave readings returned quickly to the previous baseline readings of 1 mV.

Dr. Callahan, who had never recorded Soliton waves with amplitudes of more than 25 mV anywhere else in the world, was now equally impressed by the stunning and unprecedented changes in the voltage intensity recorded. Dr. Callahan said, "It was as if *flashes ...or bolts... or darts of lightning* had just *entered the room." What* does this *new data* of energy voltage mV change signify? *What* did we actually record? Dr. Callahan says this astronomical increase in the voltage energy just recorded in *the apparition room* is similar to recording *real live flashes or bolts or darts of lightning energy.* So, *what* does *flashes or bolts or darts of lightning* have *in common* with *the Blessed Virgin Mary bringing baby Jesus to us?*

Unbeknownst to me earlier in the *appointed day,* Dr. Velasquez had sent a professional photographer from his radiation team to take pictures of the chimney and the outside façade of the farm house *before, during, and after the apparitions.* An analysis of the above series of photographs was performed using the new and highly sophisticated *advanced computerized digital photo-spectroscopy analysis* equipment (similar to the equipment utilized on satellites for weather detection analysis used by NASA). Much to our surprise the photographic analysis of the farm house chimney and outside facade demonstrated astronomical and statistically significant increases in quantified low ionizing radiation energy fields in the form of reflected *sun light energy.* A much simpler analysis of the 3 series of photographs could be conducted by anyone—that is, a *simple visual glance* clearly reveals an obvious higher intensity of *sun light energy* being reflected on the chimney photographs at the precise moments of time the *apparitions of Jesus – in His Living Presence* and *the Blessed Virgin Mary bringing baby Jesus to us* - were occurring.

Dr. Velasquez scientifically recorded *30-90% more sun light* reflected off the outside chimney façade *during the apparitions* as *compared to before or after* the heavenly visits or apparitions. So *what* is the real significance of the photographic analysis just completed? According to Dr. Velasquez, he unequivocally recorded and documented an unprecedented and astronomical *(statistically significant)* increases in the presence of reflected *sun light energy* on the chimney and outside façade of the farm house as *measured only during the apparitions.* The tremendous quantified increases in the *sun light* energy were *not present before or after the apparitions, but **only** during the apparitions.*

These scientific tests helped to validate the claims of many thousands of pilgrims, devout believers and many of the religious outside the apparition room, who excitedly reported ***seeing bright, very bright light outside***. Plenty of comments were heard by my staff that *the sun* was somehow really *extra bright during the apparitions.* So, *what* does it mean for *the sun* to be *extra bright* only *during the heavenly visits?*

While the fifteen decades of the rosary was being prayed *Jesus appeared twice* to Nancy as the *Risen Lord.* The first time *Jesus* appeared was during the sorrowful mysteries, but without giving any message. The second time *Jesus* appeared was during the 3rd glorious mysteries in the 3rd decade of the rosary prayer, *"the coming of the Holy Spirit at Pentecost"* when *Jesus in light* did speak to Nancy. *Jesus* said He was going to give the medical and scientific team *a private message* after the *Blessed Virgin Mary* had completed her monthly message for the USA *(echoing His living words).* So after witnessing the fact that *Jesus appeared on two occasions during the testing,* I became even more excited over the prospect of possibly detecting the same dramatic EEG changes that I had just recorded on the June 11th, 1993 *baseline studies.* I pondered the sobering fact that a tremendous surge in *the light* energy quantified scientifically in very significant amounts by the scientists could now also be *visibly seen* on the series of photographs taken professionally by one of Dr. Velasquez's radiation team researchers.

I pondered these questions: Are *the visions of light* that Nancy sees similar to *the light* that many people report seeing, especially at the end of the apparitions especially when the *Blessed Virgin Mary is departing (ascending back to heaven)?* Is *the light* mentioned here *the same light* referred to many times over in the Old Testament by Moses, David, Isaiah and all the prophets? Is this *the same light* quoted in the famous New Testament verse as it is written in John 8:12? Where *Jesus* says: *"I am the light of the world: he that followeth me, walketh not in darkness, but shall have the light of life."*

See *Reflections on the Light* later in this chapter. Is *the light* that *Jesus* Himself refers to (above) *the same light* when He said to Nancy, *"I am the light,"* on September 1st, 1989, and *"I am the true light and source of all light,"* on January 19th, 1995? If this is so, then our medical and scientific findings can be and should be interpreted for their clear Biblical significance. Wow!

I told my medical staff and EEG technicians that I could not wait to see our EEG telemetry findings of that appointed day of testing. We had used an Oxford II digital computerized system, and obtaining the results for analysis proceeded according to the following process: the EEG, which had been recorded on magnetic tape, would be downloaded to a computer tower, the Oxford II system, which could then generate a printout of the entire testing on EEG paper for analysis and study. I wondered if the same 3 Hz delta rhythms 333 pattern would be found *during the two times Jesus appeared* to Nancy during this testing. Would Nancy's brain wave activity be similar as when *the Blessed Virgin Mary bringing baby Jesus to us appears?*

Despite my eager and curious anticipation of what we would possibly find, I strongly felt that more testing was definitely needed. Nancy indicated that *Jesus had promised to give a message to the medical and scientific team,* so we started to set up our equipment in the room adjacent to the apparition room, in accordance with all *the experiment design* directives. At this point Prof. Castanon approached me. He was bewildered yet elated about his findings. He could not understand *what* had happened? The professor explained that during the tests he had actually observed *Nancy's EMG of La Fayette measurements* to have *registered* a reading on the display screen of ***0 micro-Volts!*** He also heard absolutely no auditory sounds coming from the EMG amplifiers as recorded and documented by his EMG of La Fayette bio-feedback monitoring system. The professor claims this heralded an astonishing and unprecedented *new level of relaxation never seen before in modern science,* since basically *nil or no neurobioelectrical emissions* were recorded emanating from Nancy's body, specifically *no cutaneous/skin resistance and no neurobioelectrical discharges* were recorded emanating from Nancy's pre-frontal region and distal *2nd/3rd* fingers right hand muscle fibers. The professor could not explain *why* the EMG system from La Fayette *did not emit any electrical signals during the heavenly visits or apparitions of Jesus* or *when the Blessed Virgin Mary brings her baby Jesus to us and/or echoes the words of her Son, Jesus.* He checked and re-checked the EMG system and found it working in perfect order. He commented that recording this type of *data* was virtually *impossible for any living human being to ever attain.* Such a reading was *only consistent with a non-living* or ***dead*** *subject/patient.* He was exceedingly perplexed by the ramifications of this *new data.* Thus, *only during the heavenly visits or apparitions of His Living Presence* did we scientifically record and *document Nancy as "dead,"* according to the EMG system from La Fayette. But obviously, Nancy was *alive.* So, *how* can we explain this? How can anyone explain this new extraordinary phenomenon? Can *you* explain being - at the same time - a*live and dead, or "as dead?"*

Recall that during the preliminary *baseline studies*, the professor was likewise amazed that when Nancy would begin to pray, her cutaneous/skin resistance and neurobioelectrical discharges from the pre-frontal region muscle fibers and the right hand distal *2nd/3rd* fingers muscle fibers *instantly dropped from a level of 1.5 to 1.7 micro-Volts (interpreted as a measure of high tension and anxiety)* ***down to 0.2 micro-Volts.*** He repeatedly indicated that a 0.2 micro-Volts level represented the *most complete state of relaxation ever.* In over 25 years of neuropsychophysiology research and study, the professor had never known anyone to achieve such a complete and total state of relaxation with such an abrupt and blazing speed. Especially coming down from such a *level* or *state of high tension and anxiety to a level of profound relaxation,* as was so vividly recorded and documented in Nancy.

Now adding to the amazement and intrigue was the fact that on several occasions as noted above during the testing, while Nancy was receiving messages from *the Blessed Virgin Mary (echoing the words of Jesus)* as well as *when Jesus appears in His Living Presence, the cutaneous/skin resistance* and *neurobioelectrical discharges emanating from muscle fibers in Nancy's body* ***measured 0 micro-Volts!*** The professor said when *a person is* literally medically and scientifically *dead - is the only time a level of 0 micro-Volts is reached.* Nancy at the time of *the testing* was *alive;* and after the writing and editing of *this book,* Nancy is today still very much *alive.* Needless to say, the professor had absolutely no explanations for the *new data.* All his instruments were checked and again rechecked. His device was found to be working in perfect order throughout the entire testing. Now just imagine - Nancy is *alive,* awake, alert with focused attention and fully conscious, *but with the measurements of 0 micro-Volts on the EMG of La Fayette* - Nancy is *dead.* So, since we see *Nancy* **is** *alive* and *yet* on the EMG readings recorded *she is dead, then* ***Nancy*** **is** ***"as dead" in His Living Presence.*** These measurements of *0 micro-Volts* occurred *only* with the *apparitions of Jesus in His Living Presence* or *with baby Jesus in the arms of the Blessed Virgin Mary.* Wow! Now *what* does all this *new data* really mean to us?

In pondering the many new amazing results just obtained, we anxiously braced ourselves for the promised additional *message from Jesus for the doctors and scientists present* on this appointed June 13th, day for the testing of Nancy. We then quickly started to get ready to receive this *private message from Jesus* in the room adjacent to the apparition room, so hold on to your seats.

RESULTS OF THE JUNE 13th, 1993 APPARITION ROOM TESTING

The following were the results of the appointed June 13th, 1993 apparition room testing, according to the different scientists and medical team members. **The following *new data testing results* are provided according to each medical team member and scientist as per the experiment design directives:**

A) Professor (retired) Philip Callahan, Ph. D.

On June 13th, 1993, Dr. Callahan found that Nancy's atmospheric-skin boundary radiation energy field readings, measured by his patented photonic ionic cord amplifier monitoring system yielded *Schumann waves* of 14 Hz frequency with *Soliton waves* of 1 mV intensity. These readings were definitely in the *normal range.* These same measurements were recorded both in the adjacent room and in the apparition room prior to the onset of any claims of celestial phenomena *(i.e., light, angels, saints, Jesus and the Blessed Virgin Mary appearing).* As soon as Nancy said that *the Blessed Virgin Mary* had arrived in the apparition room, her atmospheric-skin boundary radiation energy field readings dropped to 8 Hz. When *the Blessed Virgin Mary* is seen caressing baby Jesus and *brings baby Jesus to us* or *speaks (echoing the words of Jesus)* to Nancy, the frequency readings dropped to 4 Hz. While the Schumann waves frequencies dropped to 4 Hz activity, the amplitude intensity of the Soliton waves increased to 25-40 mV range. At the height of the readings, when the *Blessed Virgin Mary speaks (His living words) to Nancy,* Dr. Callahan's equipment measured 4 Hz in Schumann waves with an average amplitude intensity of 40 mV in Soliton waves. Thus, the surface area of Nancy's atmospheric-skin boundary radiation light energy fields was dramatically and astronomically increased.

This was truly a *heavenly light show invisible to our eyes, but visible to Nancy and to Dr. Callahan's scientific equipment.* He said that the Schumann waves measured, when the Blessed Virgin Mary appears to Nancy, carried on top of them *piggyback-style special waves* called *Soliton waves* of varying amplitude intensity. Later, Dr. Callahan claimed these Soliton waves appeared in groups to form what are known as *target waves.* Recall, Dr. Callahan claims he has never recorded Soliton waves with amplitudes of more than 25 mV anywhere else in the world. So, the amplitude of Soliton waves increasing beyond 25 mV to 40 mV when the *Blessed Virgin Mary appears bringing baby Jesus* or *speaks (His living words)* to Nancy was indeed scientifically mind-boggling and never seen before. This *new data* result is important to keep in mind, because *during the testing before the crucifix* – with the documented *pulsating (living) light* - in the adjacent room (see Chapter IV), the *Soliton waves* recorded demonstrated unprecedented increases in the amplitude intensity to an amazing high reading of 80-90 mV!

On the picram oscilloscope, Dr. Callahan recorded wave forms created from the emission of Nancy's voice and breath that was in the *range of normal spikes for the human voice and breath patterns.* An interesting and very remarkable *new finding,* however, occurred when Nancy claimed that the Blessed Virgin Mary was speaking to her. During this time of complete and total silence, for us in the room, Nancy was seen *looking up* reverently, nodding her head at times, while she was *receiving messages* from the Blessed Virgin Mary *(echoing the words of Jesus).* As Nancy was observed to be listening and then receiving the *messages from heaven,*

I (and the rest of the research team) heard *only total silence* in both the apparition room and outside of the farm house. During these moments of *total silence,* surprisingly much larger spikes were now being recorded on the picram oscilloscope. Dr. Callahan said *the larger spikes* he detected can *only* be produced by *a voice or breath from a human person,* who was *really speaking at that precise moment in time.* While mere observation of Nancy would indicate the opposite, since we heard only *total silence.* This *new finding* was repeated several times during the testing, but *only when* Nancy was *receiving a message from the Blessed Virgin Mary.* All the medical team members and scientists, including *me,* were eye-witnesses to this astonishing *new data.* We all saw the *new readings* on the picram oscilloscope display monitor *documenting* that we had recorded *another human voice* or *human breath speaking* at that precise time. However, at those same precious moments of time when Nancy said she was receiving *heavenly messages* from *Our Loving Mother* – we witnessed *only* periods of *total silence.*

Dr. Callahan reported it is a pure speculation that *the Blessed Virgin Mary's voice and breath pattern was recorded,* as represented by the different pattern of *larger spikes* detected. Since, Dr. Callahan is relying solely on whom *Nancy claims is speaking to her* at that precise moment in time. However, this different pattern recorded with the *larger spikes* does indeed confirm that a *real true human voice* or *human breath* was recorded, *during the precise moments of total silence.* This different *new pattern of spikes* documented was definitely *not Nancy's voice and breath pattern.* Dr. Callahan said that if a *photon-acoustic antenna* had been used like in his *studies on dolphin ears,* we may have been able to better confirm this unique supposition. Unfortunately, this equipment was not available for today's tests. But still this *new data* is quiet tantalizing, when viewed with our other data.

So, in retrospect and after very careful review of the *new data,* the majority of the medical and scientific team members now believe that in all probability *the human voice* and *human breath pattern* detected was indeed that of the *(invisible to us, but not to Nancy) heavenly visitor, the Blessed Virgin Mary.* We can say this *only* because of all the other astonishing surrounding *new evidence* and *data* collected, as you will see, that collectively shows and clearly points to *the truth* concerning the claims of *heavenly appearances* of the *Blessed Virgin Mary bringing* her baby *Jesus* to us and *speaking* or *echoing the words of Jesus* to us - *His Living Presence in His living words.* Furthermore, Dr. Callahan's *new findings* also scientifically proved there was a statistically significant increase in the *presence of* ***the light*** *energy* in the room only *during the heavenly visits* or *apparitions;* thus, verifying the astronomical increases in *the light* energy radiation fields recorded *only - in His Living Presence* with or without *His heavenly court. His court* includes all of the *(living) heavenly visitors* appearing *with Jesus.* See Reflections. This *new data* reminds me of the events surrounding the *transfiguration of Jesus,* as it is written in Matthew 17:1-7 and Luke 9:27-35, already mentioned in the Introduction.

Another new result which further added to our scientific intrigue was the fact that whenever the Blessed Virgin Mary brings baby Jesus to us and/or speaks (echoes His living words) to Nancy at those precise moments Dr. Callahan repeatedly detected a tremendous surge in *the light* radiation energy fields in the atmosphere of the apparition room. Scientifically *the light* energy detected, whenever the *Blessed Virgin Mary brings* baby *Jesus* or speaks *(echoes) His living words* to us, was indeed astronomical.

As Dr. Callahan repeatedly demonstrated Nancy's atmospheric-skin boundary radiation energy fields to be 4 Hz Schumann waves, he also recorded the incredible increases from 1 mV to 40 mV amplitude intensity - Soliton waves, thus increasing the surface area of light intensity at the atmospheric-skin boundary. *This powerful surge of energy* 25-40 mV mostly averaging 40 mV as recorded, Dr. Callahan said, **is** very similar *to the surge of energy - produced by flashes or bolts or* ***darts of lightning*** *light energy.* I also remind you that the *flashes of lightning* light energy fields were recorded *inside the apparition room* during a long drought season on a very hot, dry and clear-blue sky day, when the *Blessed Virgin Mary appears* to Nancy *bringing* baby *Jesus* (to us).

Using another scientific probe, Dr. Callahan recorded yet another specific range of atmospheric energy in the apparition room that is typically seen in the North American Aviation Radio Band Spectrum. Within a 2,000 - 4,000+ Hz range, an average of 3,000 - 4,000 Hz was recorded during most the *heavenly visits* or *apparitions.* This range of low radiation light energy fields is interestingly called the *electrical anesthesia* region. In the 1800's this energy was used by Dentists with a very low voltage *to relax* and help *anesthetize* people. Dr. Callahan said this low radiation *radio light* energy range should be called *electrical-magnetic-anesthesia* region. Thus, this *radio light energy* he recorded *in His Living Presence* actually helps generate a soothing, peaceful, tranquil, calming and very relaxing atmosphere: *a true, peaceful light energy.*

As you will later see in Dr. Sanchez's section of the medical and scientific testing data, Nancy's brain wave activity at these precise moments in time, whenever the Blessed Virgin Mary brings Jesus to us, amazingly measured 4 Hz theta rhythms with a *specific pattern of 444!* Thus, just looking at all the above *new data* the number four (4) for some reason appears to be significant. Interestingly, in all our recorded and documented *new medical and scientific data, the number 4* is somehow always associated with the *Blessed Virgin Mary bringing* her baby *Jesus - His Living Presence and/or His living words* to us. The same inexplicable *new data* seen above was repeatedly recorded and documented by many different types of medical and scientific equipment (just to be sure the *new data* was valid). All the various equipments utilized at different times and locations during our meticulous medical and scientific investigations of the *heavenly visits* recorded the same data.

Dr. Callahan also performed another series of scientific studies that compare the paramagnetic properties of the *holy sites* or holy grounds at the heavenly visits or apparition sites in Conyers, Georgia, USA, to other famous holy sites around the world. Dr. Callahan documented the measurements of approved as well as some popular but still unapproved sites by the Catholic Church. See **Table 1** page 97 for a fascinating outline of Dr. Callahan's *comparative study of holy sites* or holy grounds from many different locations throughout the world, that are still being visited yearly by literally thousands of pilgrims. His comparative study consisted of measuring and recording the paramagnetic properties of the -clay, soil, and rocks- on and also surrounding the holy sites. He studied many different *holy sites* throughout the world of historical significance. He even studied *the holy sites where Jesus walked,* taught and preached the good news to the Jews and to all the people around the Sea of Galilee 2,000 years ago in Israel. Dr. Callahan wanted to compare all of these known *holy sites* with the measurements and recordings he had repeatedly documented over a span of eight years in the 1990's at the apparition sites in Conyers, Ga., USA.

Dr. Callahan's interest in paramagnetic fields and properties first began with one of his best known international scientific studies, which was accomplished in 1979 with Prof. Jody Smith. Both of them (professors of science) collaborated on an infrared study of the sacred image of *the Virgin of Guadalupe* that was published (see *The Tilma under Infrared Radiation*, Cara, 1980). After completing this work, Dr. Callahan remembers picking up a piece of *(paramagnetic)* basalt rock from Tepeyac Hill, Mexico, where the apparition of the Virgin of Guadalupe had occurred on December 12^{th,} 1513. When he returned home to Gainsville, Florida, USA, Dr. Callahan noticed that a small chip of the Tepeyac Hill rock was strongly attracted to a magnet. At that time he believed that *apparition sites* had a magnetic force inherent in them, since when he traveled to Lourdes, France and Kerrytown, Ireland, in particular, he felt in his own body a subtle difference in the surrounding atmosphere. This then lead him to the physics handbook table of paramagnetic properties of all the elements.

A simple definition of paramagnetism is the ability of a substance like rock, clay or soil, to take in (absorb) and transmit magnetism. In short a paramagnetic rock for example, is not magnetic, that is, it does not store a fixed amount of magnetism, but when placed in a magnetic field it absorbs the cosmic magnetic energy and transmits it to the environment. Thus, it is like the *antennae* of your cellular phone. It receives the alternating magnetic energy and retains it for nature's use. Then like the cellular phone antennae, it takes this alternating voice current and transmits it to someone's ear. But in the case of a paramagnetic rock, it takes in the magnetic field of the earth and cosmos and then if there are any plants in the area (as Dr. Callahan discovered) transmits this paramagnetic energy to plants for more excellent root growth. Reviewing this new discovery Dr. Callahan now believes that plants grown in highly paramagnetic soil, clay or rocky areas require no fertilizer, and no weed killers or insecticides. He has actually done numerous experiments to prove his claims. He now proclaims that plants grown in highly paramagnetic areas are so healthy that they tract neither disease nor even insects (see Acres USA, August 1996). Just think what this new information can do to deter world hunger.

Paramagnetism is measured by CGS, which means centimeters per gram per second, or how far will one gram of rock travel towards a magnet in one second (distance x weight x time). CGS is then the measurement of the force (needed). The force needed to move one gram of rock towards a magnet in one second. The higher the number of CGS measurement, then translates into the greater the force needed and available.

Dr. Callahan's studies show that any number above 500 CGS is considered good. A poor number of CGS is < 200, a *normal number is 200-500 CGS,* and an *excellent number is >1000 CGS* (any soil with a >1000 CGS value is excellent for farming).

He has traveled all over the world to visit many *holy sites,* shrines and places where *apparitions of the Blessed Virgin Mary* were said to have occurred, and he also visited *the places where Jesus was said to have walked* on this earth over 2,000 years ago. Interestingly, all these historical spots where the *Blessed Virgin Mary* has appeared, as well as where *Jesus* mostly walked, taught and preached the *good news* to the people located along the shores and rim bowl of rock around the Sea of Galilee, Israel, were indeed all very highly paramagnetic. This means that, either the rock, clay or soil analyzed has a measurement well above 500 CGS. In none of the *Marian apparition holy sites* Dr. Callahan tested was the soil, clay or rock measuring any less than 500 CGS, except at Conyers the farm (USA) in August of 1999 when it measured only 280 CGS (low normal CGS measurements), when for the years 1992-1998 the measurements there were excellent.

After Dr. Callahan's miraculous cure of a 5.5 cm lung mass, documented on CT chest (appearing like a large cancer mass), totally disappeared while on Conyers Holy Hill in 1998 (with no chemotherapy, no radiation therapy, no surgery, no antiviral or antibiotics, no steroids and no medical treatments), he and his wife Winnie came back to Conyers Holy Hill on their 50th wedding anniversary in August 1999 *to give thanks to Jesus* and *Our Loving Mother* for his amazing healing and miraculous cure. During their week long visit in Conyers, Dr. Callahan out of curiosity and on his own initiative re-measured the paramagnetic energy of the clay on Conyers Holy Hill and of the rock and soil at the farm with his special equipment. He found that the farm's CGS measurements had substantially dropped from the consistently high paramagnetic energy 1480-1490 CGS with an average of ~1486 CGS, that Dr. Callahan had recorded yearly from 1992-1998 at the farm, to a low normal paramagnetic energy measurement of 280 CGS. It is very interesting and indeed intriguing that the values of CGS force of energy measured on Conyers Holy

Hill had remained essentially the same from 1992 through August 1999. *Why?* These high values remained in the same range and original amazingly high CGS force of energy 2,000-3,700 CGS on Conyers Holy Hill, in contrast to the big drop of CGS values recorded at this same time in 1999 on the farm. Ponder this. Only the *soil at the top of the mountain* immediately *over The Grotto in Lourdes, France,* and the *soil on the bowl rim of rock along the shores of the Sea of Galilee,* where *Jesus* spent 3+ years of *His* ministry teaching *the way, the truth and the life* of love, did Dr. Callahan measure the same astoundingly high paramagnetic energy of 2,000-3,700 CGS as he had recorded on Conyers Holy Hill (USA).

Incredibly, these same high paramagnetic energy CGS values were repeatedly recorded and documented yearly from 1992-1999 on Conyers Holy Hill. But though the high paramagnetic energy CGS values remained in this high range for his August 1999 analysis of the Conyers Holy Hill clay; interestingly, and for some reason the formerly high CGS values (~1486 CGS recorded from 1992-1998) had dropped significantly at the farm in Conyers, when measured by Dr. Callahan in August 1999. *Why* then, I ask, was there such a dramatic drop and change in the paramagnetic energy, as measured in CGS values at the farm in Conyers, from the high paramagnetic energy measured yearly from 1992-1998 to the low normal soil and rock CGS values as recorded in August 1999? The CGS values actually dropped from an excellent high average of 1486 CGS to a low normal (approaching a poor CGS value) 280 CGS in August 1999.

When the farm organization managing Nancy's *original mission* decided to go in a new direction in early 1999 --- without Nancy's approval, she publicly separated from them. See the Catholic newspaper *The Georgia Bulletin* March 11th, 1999. Is it possible that, what *Our Loving Mother* foretold in a message to Nancy in the early 1990's, has come true? In one of her messages of the 1990's to Nancy, *Our Loving Mother* foretold specific information about *"graces and signs."* By March 11th, 1999, Nancy was no longer associated with the organization at the farm, which originally had promoted and had helped spread the messages Nancy had received from *Jesus* and *Our Loving Mother* for America and the world. After this date, Nancy was publicly separated from the not-for-profit corporation, which, from the early years of her ministry, had operated the *apparition site*, owned the farm and all the land properties and resources. This was the organization that originally promoted the *heavenly messages* given to Nancy. Therefore, I ask again*, why* did the consistently excellent high paramagnetic energy CGS values, recorded yearly from 1992-1998, drop so dramatically to levels of low normal (approaching poor) CGS values --- at the farm --- as recorded in August 1999*?*

Historically, Nancy had received her early *heavenly visits* inside her former home, located on the same property where the Conyers *Holy Hill* site is located. As of 2007 Nancy still lives in Conyers, but in a different home. Nancy's *original apparition room,* located inside of Nancy's former home, and the C*onyers Holy Hill* property (in Nancy's former backyard) is owned by loving family supportive of Nancy. Nancy is currently trying to keep her *original ministry and mission from Jesus* alive. And no, ----- Nancy is *not* living in Florida --- as rumored after the October 13th, 1998 apparitions and *final messages given* in Conyers from *Our Lord and Our Loving Mother* for the USA and the world.

So, I ask again, *why* did the CGS measurements at the farm land drop so precipitously from the excellent high paramagnetic energy recorded yearly and repeatedly from the rock underneath the farm *while Nancy was still associated with the organization at the farm* from 1992 through 1998 --- to the low normal (approaching poor) CGS values recorded *when Nancy was no longer associated with the organization operating the farm* later in August 1999? The answer to this question has many curious and intriguing implications. So, were the *"graces and signs"* on the farm land by 1999 --- somehow *being changed?* If *yes why?*

From 1992-1999 the rock and clay being analyzed on the *Conyers Holy Hill* was literally taken from Nancy's backyard, while she still lived there. The other measurements (see below Table 1) were taken from the farm. The farm is a real estate property located, geologically speaking, on a white granite dome of rock in Conyers. Have we by *co-incidence* scientifically measured the *"graces* and *signs"* somehow from the Almighty God upon a land mass like the Conyers Holy Hill and the farm? Or is this another *God-incidence? Why* did the CGS values drop so dramatically at the farm and yet remain so high on Conyers Holy Hill in Nancy's own backyard *after Nancy dissociated from the farm's organization* in 1999? And now that Nancy is *no longer associated* with the farm organization, I must ask, as a scientist, *why* did *the science* of the farm's property of rock and top soil *change so drastically --- after Nancy's dissociation?* So, do *"graces and signs"* really *follow Nancy?* The answer to this question is probably in the following *short message* the *Blessed Virgin Mary gave to Nancy* on May 13th,, 1994. At the end of 31/2 years of monthly 13th day scheduled *apparitions from heaven, Our Loving Mother* said, *"Wherever you go, my Son will bestow on you* ***graces and signs*** *about you."* Ponder this 44th message. Look below at the amazing scientific *new data* collected over the years by Dr. Callahan. Dr. Callahan has completed other agricultural studies showing that a farm with soil above 500 CGS can basically grow a healthy disease-free crop with no chemical fertilizers needed; interestingly, like what is currently seen in the farm lands of Israel. But, since most of the *chemically treated soil* around the world measures less than 100 CGS, of interest, Dr. Callahan says this type soil with *"poison farming"* can unfortunately lead to starvation.

Note: In the following **Table 1**, Dr. Callahan presents --- a series of *"holy apparition sites"* --- matched with their corresponding CGS values and substance measured and listed for comparisons.

TABLE 1

PLACE	CGS VALUES	SUBSTANCE	DATE
Lourdes (France)	3700	Soil	1992
La Salette (France)	850	Rock	1988
Guadalupe(Mexico)	1800	Rock	1992
Knock (Ireland)	Unknown	Church Wall	1983
Kerrytown (Ireland)	1443	Rock	1984
Fatima (Portugal)	1340	Clay	1989
Conyers farm (USA)	1486	Rock	1992-98
Conyers farm (USA)	280	Rock	1999
Medjugorje (Yugoslavia)	700	Soil	1988
Betania (Venezuela)	550	Soil	1989
House of Loreto (Italy)	800	Rock	1997
Shore-Sea of Galilee	>2,000-3,700	Rock & Soil	1997
*Conyers Holy Hill (USA)	>2,000-3,700	Rock & Clay	1992-98
*Conyers Holy Hill (USA)	>2,000-3,700	Rock & Clay	1999

*(Holy Hill is on a private property in Conyers)

Unlike other historical *"holy apparition sites"* Conyers is unique in that it has a rocky terrain, but with a thin top soil. The top soil at Conyers is really poor measuring only 60-70 CGS, presumably because of many years of poor farming practices in that area, according to Dr. Callahan. However, this top soil is in reality only a thin layer covering a huge white granite dome. The edge of the dome of granite can be seen in the woods just south of the farm house cross. In the years 1992-1998 this Conyers white granite dome of rock measured an average of 1486 CGS (See Table I), which is very close in CGS value to the measurements found in Fatima (Portugal), Kerrytown (Ireland), and Guadalupe (Mexico). Interestingly, one of the messages *Our Loving Mother* gave Nancy in Conyers in the early 1990's said, *"I want the world to know that my appearances here (in Conyers) are linked directly to Fatima. No other appearances are you linked more strongly with than Fatima. The world would come to know in time."* During the years when the *Blessed Virgin Mary* was still giving messages from her Son *Jesus* to the USA and the world through Nancy, the actual CGS energy measured on the farm property from 1992-1998 was indeed very close to the CGS values Dr. Callahan recorded in Fatima, Portugal. Of interest, these *similar findings associated with Fatima existed only while Nancy was still associated* with the farm organization, *but not after Nancy severed all connections and her association* with the farm organization.

Even more interesting, amazing and astonishing are the measurements of the rock and clay on *Conyers Holy Hill.* Remember, Nancy's former home in Conyers (USA) is the original site of the *heavenly visits* or *apparitions.* In Nancy's former backyard sits the *Conyers Holy Hill* (USA). Interestingly, this blessed *Holy Hill* has the same identical CGS values as the measurements of the rocky bowl rim of land and soil *along the shores around the Sea of Galilee, where Jesus walked 2,000 yrs ago!* In the New Testament Holy Scriptures they refer to *Jesus* as *the Galilean,* though *born in Bethlehem,* because *He* spent so much time there preaching the *good news* to the people, first to the Jews and then later to the Gentiles.

Dr. Callahan when summarizing his data stated that Lourdes was very difficult to measure. The limestone grotto has a CGS of only 20 or less. But at places on top of the mountain immediately over the grotto, the CGS values range from a level of 200 CGS closer to the limestone to a very high 3,700 CGS on the top soil directly above the grotto. Thus, the mountain top soil just above the grotto in Lourdes (France) is just as highly paramagnetic as the Conyers Holy Hill (USA) CGS measurements recorded from 1992-1999 (while Nancy lived in her former home), and as the bowl rim of rock and soil along the shores of the Sea of Galilee in Israel where *Jesus* lived and walked. Wow!

It is now clear to me after reviewing the above data just presented, that the *fingerprint of energy* (as Dr. Callahan likes to call it) measured in *Conyers Holy Hill* (USA), more than matches the best CGS values of all the measured and documented paramagnetic energy of the other famous and internationally known *holy sites,* and most of the Church approved apparition sites around the world that Dr. Callahan has tested. Also *Conyers Holy Hill* matches the very high CGS values of the paramagnetic energy in the rock and soil from the bowl rim of land and shores along the Sea of Galilee where *Jesus* walked and taught the *good news,* healed the sick, opened the eyes of the blind and the ears of the deaf, cleansed the lepers, healed the withered, lame and paralyzed, cast out demons, walked on water, calmed the storms and performed many more astonishing miracles like *raising the dead,* including *Himself* - in Jerusalem in *the resurrection* (Isaiah 33:10). Remember the empty tomb! Recall the 500 eye-witnesses (1Cor 15:6), who also saw the *Risen Jesus* after His passion, crucifixion and death. In fact in the New Testament, all of nature obeyed *Jesus.* Recall, the *multiplication of bread and fish* for literally thousands of people to eat, the incredible *catch of fish, the calming of storms* and *walking on water* witnessed by Peter and His apostles. And through it all, *Jesus* lived as a just, sinless man, *the expectation of nations* (Genesis 49:10) over 2,000 years ago. Dr. Callahan wrote to me saying, *"I would have a difficult time with the overused word coincidence, if it were used here to try to describe the marvelous magnetic antennae properties of all the Marian apparition sites I studied all around the world, especially at Conyers Holy Hill (USA)."*

B) Dr. Humberto Velasquez

Reference graphs which show the geometric placement of magnetic strips in the apparition room, round about the *apparition site,* and surrounding the farm house with the tabulated measurements of *gamma* radiation energy fields are available for review for those who are interested. Dr. Velasquez's recordings of *gamma* radiation energy fields were taken *before, during and after the apparitions* on June 13th, 1993. *Gamma* radiation energy fields were detected in all of the three time periods mentioned above, as per *the experiment design* directives and documented on the Geiger counter display monitors. This meticulous comparative statistical analysis of *gamma* radiation energy fields identified in the apparition room, as well as around the farm house, is displayed as tabulated data available for review. It clearly shows *no statistically significant changes in gamma radiation energy fields - before, during and after the heavenly visits, visions or apparitions.* Dr. Velasquez and the radiation team demonstrated that *before, during and after the apparitions,* the changes in *gamma* radiation energy fields detected were indeed definitely **not** mathematically or statistically significant.

In my many private conversations with Dr. Velasquez, he reiterated that the *new data* and findings were very significant, because *gamma radiation* energy fields are potentially very harmful. Intuitively Dr. Velasquez had found it difficult to believe that any real true authentic *(God sent)* heavenly visits or apparitions would co-exist with any significant increases in *gamma radiation* energy fields, since *gamma* or high ionizing radiation energy fields could potentially harm the *chosen souls* or *visionaries* as well as all the pilgrims present. Apparently, erroneous rumors concerning the *radiation studies* done by scientist Dr. Lipinski in Medjugori, Yugoslavia, had already surfaced suggesting the very possibility of a potentially harmful toxic exposure *during the apparitions* (as per Dr. Velasquez).

Thus, Dr. Velasquez's *new data* and findings demonstrated (once and for all) that no harmful *gamma* or high ionizing radiation energy fields were associated with the *heavenly visits* or *apparitions,* we tested. Dr. Velasquez really feels this *new data* was and is a definite vote in favor of the genuine and heavenly nature of these *supernatural events.* Any other result would have been questionable or open to suspicion. He said, *"Can* you imagine *God appearing* to His children and lovingly exposing them to harmful radiation*?" God forbid.*

All those present in the apparition room (like me) could hear the increases in the Geiger counters display monitors activity at various times *during the apparitions.* The clicking sounds did appear to us (to me) at times to increase in intensity during the times when Nancy claimed Holy Angels, St. Michael the Archangel, the Blessed Virgin Mary, Holy Saints, Padre Pio (now St. Pio) or *Jesus -in His Living Presence* appeared. But, Dr. Velasquez clearly demonstrated that the Geiger counter clicking sounds *did not change* during these precise moments of time in a mathematical and statistically significant manner. Initially like many others in the apparition room, we

(I) *assumed incorrectly* that the increasing clicking activity of the Geiger counter monitors had recorded an apparent increasing level of *gamma* radiation energy fields in the room. But, after a very careful review and statistical mathematical analysis, the scientific *new data* was proof enough to clearly showcase that no harmful radiation energy fields were ever recorded or documented (in our testing) to increase in a statistically significant manner during the *heavenly visits* or *apparitions.* These studies clearly show that no statistically significant changes were detected in the apparition room or round about the apparition site and farm house; and the *normal range of gamma radiation* energy fields already present in our natural and normal atmosphere is indeed what was only measured: before, during and after the apparitions.

Dr. Velasquez claimed that the equipment used for the appointed testing of June 13th1993 was modeled after the studies done by a radiation scientist, Dr. Lipinski. Dr. Velasquez's instruments were not calibrated to record changes in the ranges of low or extremely low ionizing radiation energy fields, but only calibrated and able to detect and quantify levels of *gamma* or high range ionizing radiation energy fields. Dr. Velasquez had just recorded and documented for us *new scientific data* that *gamma* or high ionizing radiation energy fields *did not change - during the heavenly visits* or *apparitions.* So, I asked him, *"What* does the astronomical and statistically significant increases recorded and documented by Dr. Callahan in the ranges of low and extremely low ionizing radiation energy fields mean to you as a radiation scientist?" Dr. Velasquez answered, "It means Dr. Callahan measured *the essence of light* or rather as it can be simply explained... Dr. Callahan recorded astronomical and *increasing surges of photons being released into the atmosphere* – thus, *giving light* in the rooms being tested *only during the heavenly visits* or *apparitions."* He actually documented the *pure essence of the light energy* present in the apparition rooms tested. And especially with all the amazing increases and surges of *the light* energy measured Dr. Velasquez then added, *"You* see... when electrons from atoms are driven out of their orbit - leaving a low energy ion - they emit *photons of light.* Thus, when this occurs in high concentrations of atoms, Dr. Callahan can record these increases of low and extremely low energy ions, which emit *photons of light energy,* with his newly patented and sophisticated equipment." His device is calibrated to detect the levels of low and extremely low ionizing radiation energy fields of *the light* energy (invisible light) present in the atmosphere of the rooms. Therefore, the astronomical increases in photons being emitted were actually equal to the astronomical increases of low energy ions being detected and *the light* energy measured.

Scientifically, we can now say that the *heavenly visits* or *apparitions* recorded and documented in our studies were most definitely associated with truly unprecedented and statistically significant increases in the *pure essence of light. The light* energy recorded in the surrounding atmosphere while *in His Living*

Presence was detected to increase amazingly to new unprecedented heights both inside and outside the apparition room. Recall, Dr. Velasquez's equipment was calibrated only to register and measure high ionizing radiation energy fields (e.g., *gamma* radiation), which comes from the splitting of the nucleus of an atom, as his original intent was to verify or discount the rumors that harmful *gamma radiation* energy increases in association with the *heavenly visits* or *apparitions.* Though Dr. Velasquez detected the presence of *gamma* radiation already present in the atmosphere of both the inside and the outside of the apparition room tested, the high *gamma radiation* energy *did not* statistically significantly increase *before, during and after the heavenly visitations* or *apparitions.*

Now reviewing the other studies conducted by Dr. Velasquez, it was obvious he was very excited about the series of professional photographs taken of the chimney outside façade of the farm house *before, during and after the apparitions.* These photographs clearly demonstrated statistically significant and mathematically quantified astronomical *increases* in ***the sun** light* (visible light) *energy* measured, which occurred *only during the heavenly visits* or *apparitions.* An advanced computerized digital photo-spectroscopy analysis was conducted on the series of photographs. Moreover, a graphic statistical analysis of the *new data* using the above advanced computerized digital photo-spectroscopy clearly shows that **statistically significant changes were documented when the astronomical increases of 30-90% more *sun light* energy was recorded on the outside façade of the farm house chimney. These unprecedented, mind-boggling and powerful *sun light* energy increases were *only* detected *during the heavenly visitations* or *apparitions of Jesus* and the *Blessed Virgin Mary bringing* baby *Jesus - in His Living Presence* or *echoing the words of Jesus - His living words to us.* These astonishing increases in *the sun light* energy were never detected *before* or *after the heavenly visits* or *apparitions,* but *only during.***

REFLECTIONS ON THE EQUIPMENT ANDTHE CULTURE OF DEATH

This highly sophisticated analysis equipment, employed in our studies above to obtain these very precise results, is actually the same device utilized by weather satellites for NASA; and is also used by the Mexican born scientist and computer expert, Dr. Jose Tonsmann, in studying *the eyes of the Blessed Virgin Mary* on the famous *Tilma* from Guadalupe, Mexico. Guadalupe is a famous internationally renowned Mexican pilgrimage *"holy site."* It is the oldest *approved holy site of the apparitions of the Blessed Virgin Mary bringing baby Jesus in her blessed womb* to the Americas. Historically, it is claimed that the Blessed Virgin Mary *appeared* to the humble and devoted Mexican Indian *campesino, Juan Diego.* St. Juan Diego is the first indigent American Indian canonized by Pope John Paul II in 2003. He was unique in his day for his conversion and zealous devotion to the Catholic faith

(*Catholic* which means *universal Christian*) amidst a thriving community of *Aztec pagans, who offered human sacrifices.* Many of whom were *mostly young babies offered to the pagan gods.* This sounds so familiar. Isn't this just like the numerous *abortions* that are occurring here in our current day and age amidst a thriving community of citizens in the USA and around the world. Now, in our *culture of death,* are we not just like the Aztec pagans *offering human sacrifices* of many young *unborn babies, the unborn embryos and fetuses to the pagan gods* of Pro-choice and offering them up to the *abortion* l*egalized murder clinics* of the unborn? Millions are legally murdered yearly. Over 50 million *abortions* have been performed in the USA alone since *Roe* vs. *Wade* and still counting. This is so bloody outrageous! Maybe this is the reason *why Jesus* and *the Blessed Virgin Mary* have been so frequently seen by many *chosen souls* around the world to be very sad and literally *crying tears of blood,* because of all the horrible, diabolical and grotesque sins - *man's human will* is repeatedly committing indeed with government approval and with laws that actually protect the *legalized murder of the unborn* by *choice of the mother* called *abortion.* With all of today's advanced medical science, pure and simple and without any doubt, we now know **abortion is murder (legal murder).**

The word of God in Jeremiah 1:5 said it best*:* "Before I formed thee...I knew thee: and before thou camest forth out of the womb*..."* In Isaiah 44:2:"Thus saith the Lord that made and formed thee, thy helper from the womb*..."* and in Genesis 1:26: *"Let us make man to our image and likeness..."* Thus, if God formed us and knew us even before we came out of the womb (Psalm 138(139):13-17), and we are made in the image and likeness of God (and God is forever Sacred and Holy), just by using pure logic ---*we are sacred and holy! Life is* indeed *sacred!* Medical and scientific evidence today clearly demonstrates that ***life*** *begins at the very beginning of conception,* which by the way, is what the Church still teaches and has always taught *(thank God).* But, our current rapidly growing and liberal *culture of death* mentality in America proudly boasts, protects and promotes this insidious rampant *legalized murder of the unborn,* and even defends it with all its very might, heart and soul. No one should have a *legalized choice* to kill.

Now ask yourself, are we really any different from the horrible blood-thirsty murdering Aztec pagans? What or where are the *human rights* of our unborn children? ACLU who are you really fighting for? You hypocrites! Why are you not protecting the *human civil rights* of the largest silent majority in America today *the unborn?* Apparently, it seems *the majority* in our righteous democracy is either asleep in deep somber or in a stupor and coma or maybe they just don't really care? So, sound the alarm: All *embryos, fetuses* and *the unborn, the true silent majority in America* unite, band together, pray and write to your Congressmen. Let us all get together and march to Washington, D.C. to protest these real gruesome acts of violence. Demand a stop to all forms of *legalized murders.* Let us all ***say yes to life*** and *stop all abortions* in this land. Now let all the *embryos, fetuses* and *the unborn* shout out in one accord: *"Stop killing us! Stop selling our body parts (embryonic stem cells),* we are *alive* you know. This is *America - land of the free.* We have rights too! You can use *adult stem cells* and *umbilical cord stem cells.* Abortionists stop crippling our nation of *good* American stock. *Stop our genocide!"*

Obviously, *the unborn* in reality have *no voice* here. So, now while literally millions of human beings are silently slaughtered yearly in the wombs of America, I ask where are the tears and the cry of outrage and lamentations from our modern day society. The blood of millions of aborted and murdered babies is *on all of us* who do not speak up and especially on all those *politicians* who call themselves *Christian* and still fight for the *death culture* or the *Pro-Choice* movement. Also know - the blood of all the murdered unborn babies - is on all of us, who vote for those *Pro-Choice politicians.* So, be careful *who you vote for.* Sadly, this deeply sour and bitter commentary on our current modern day society may just be one of the main reasons *why* the Blessed Virgin Mary is again appearing in the Americas after almost 500 years later *crying* and pleading with all of us in America and around the world to stop the brutal killings and murders of our unborn children. *So repent, turn back to God and **stop all abortions!*** Thousands of *wombs in America* and all over the civilized world have sadly become *the silent* legalized butchering *concentrations camps* of our present day human history. What a bloody dreadful holocaust? The *apparitions of Guadalupe* occurred in the year 1531, and *Our Lady of Guadalupe* is recognized by the title *Patroness of the Unborn* due to the infanticide and injustice wreaked upon the *innocent children* by the *Aztec pagans* at that time of history. Are we any different today? Unfortunately, *history has a habit of repeating itself.* And apparently in today's thriving *culture of death* that is quickly spreading in America and all over the world, we are again in desperate need of the *Blessed Virgin Mary* to once again *bring the light* - her baby *Jesus* back to us again, again and again, just to remind us all of *the most precious gift* we have – ***life!*** Father Emmanuel Charles McCarthy, on a EWTN documentary covering the life of little Audrey Santos – an adult patient in a chronic neurovegetative state since the age of 5yrs old, said*: "*Either all life is sacred or all life is meaningless, either we are all made in the image and likeness of God or we are not.*"*

Recall, in Deuteronomy 30:15, 19: "Consider that I have set before thee this day *life and good* and on the other hand, *death and evil...* I call heaven and earth to witness this day, that I have set before you life and death, blessing and cursing. Choose therefore life that both thou and thy seed may live.*"* So, *choose life!* Do not be fooled any longer by the phrase Pro-Choice. In God's own words given to Moses ~ 3,300 years ago as it is written above, it is indeed very clear and please make no excuses: Pro-Choice = Pro-Legal Murder = Pro-Evil = Pro-Death! Who says women have less rights, then men in this country? The women in the USA, indeed have more rights then men; they have the *legal right* ***to choose*** *to kill, murder, and abort* God's awesome *gift of life.* What a crying shame. Please, wake up America...wake up world...and wake up all churches and civilized societies to *the truth* about these heinous acts of terror. As a token final gift and proof of Mary's real presence bringing *the unborn baby Jesus in her blessed womb* to all of us skeptics, *Our Lady of Guadalupe* secretly left a miraculous, full-color image of herself on the inside of Juan Diego's coat, known as a *Tilma*, which today is still admired and revered. Inside the *Tilma,* there is an image of the Blessed Virgin Mary wearing a very traditional *Indian maternity dress.* So, just like in Rev 12:1 *"a woman clothed in the sun,"* the woman *(Mary)* is carrying an unborn man child in her blessed womb Who was to *"rule all nations with an iron rod"* (Rev 12:5 and Psalm 2:9).

Interestingly, Dr. Tonsmann, previously a professor at Cornell University and a specialist in computers who works for IBM in Mexico City, found the imprints of thirteen different people in each of the Virgin's eyes in the *Tilma.* Seven of them, located in the pupil, comprise an entire family unit—specifically, an Indian family unit with a father, mother, two toddlers, an infant, and what appears to be two older looking grandparents. The six other people were scientifically identified anatomically correct in the reflection from the cornea of Mary's eyes on the *Tilma* and were thought to represent the *visionary* Mexican Indian Juan Diego *(now St. Juan Diego),* the Bishop, the Indian-Spanish interpreter, two other tribal Indians and the Bishop's house servant. All the true and historical accounts surrounding the meeting of Juan Diego with the Bishop has been studied in great detail by the Church and the *apparitions* were later approved as authentic.

In short, Dr. Tonsmann's state-of-the-art advanced computerized digital photo-spectroscopy analysis of the *Tilma* was indeed the same equipment utilized by Dr. Velasquez that scientifically detected and analyzed the actual presence of statistically significant increases in *the sun light* energy on the outside façade of the farm house chimney in Conyers, *during* the appointed *heavenly visitations* or *apparitions* of June 13th,, 1993.

The N*ew Data* and Results of Dr. Velasquez's testing were remarkable for three separate findings:

1) The Geiger counter equipment used for this experiment design detected the presence of *gamma* radiation energy fields at normal levels *before, during and after the apparitions. During the apparitions* there were *no statistically significant changes in the gamma radiation detected.* Thus, *no harmful radiation* energy occurred in conjunction with the presence of the *heavenly visits* or *apparitions.*

2) The medical and scientific research team, as well as all those present in the apparition room, clearly heard the clicking sounds emanating from the Geiger counters. Although these sounds audibly seemed to increase in intensity while Nancy's *apparitions* were occurring, there were absolutely no statistical significant increases in the readings recorded (see above). However, the video cameras filming the Geiger counter display monitors by accident or *coincidence (or God-*

incidence) captured and demonstrated coherent bursts of laser white light (with a silver hue) on the back wall of the apparition room during Nancy's *visions of light,* which many pilgrims in the room also reported they were seeing! So, Dr. Velasquez logically speculated that he detected on video some of the increases in low ionizing radiation energy fields that somehow literally spilled over into the 3% visible light spectrum, as was already confirmed by Dr. Callahan's amazing *new findings and data.* Dr. Velasquez believes this surge in low ionizing radiation energy recorded by Dr. Callahan is in fact the essence of *the light* energy surge that was detected in the rooms tested and that was documented *only in the living presence of Jesus (in His Living Presence)* or during the presence of the *Blessed Virgin Mary bringing* baby *Jesus* to us and/or *speaking (echoing) the words of Jesus* to us, which is actually *His living words.*

3) Dr. Velasquez's second experiment with the series of photographs using advanced digital computerized photo-spectroscopy analysis was also statistically significant. The measurements and comparative analysis of the quantum of light energy detected in the photographs during the *heavenly visits* or *apparitions,* when compared to before or after the apparitions, clearly demonstrated the astronomically significant increases in *the sun light* energy. Therefore, the third and most significant of the *new findings* were the documentations and demonstrations of *statistically significant increases of* ***30-90% more sun light*** *energy being detected only during the heavenly visits of baby Jesus with His Mother Mary* and *His heavenly court* or *the apparitions of Jesus - in His Living Presence.*

C) Professor R. Castanon, Ph.D., Clinical Neuropsychophysiology

The neuropsychophysiology studies began by placing the EMG system from La Fayette on the prefrontal regions of Nancy's head and on the distal right 2nd and 3rd fingers of her right hand to measure different levels or states of relaxation, tension or anxiety. This test was conducted first in the room adjacent to the apparition room. This is where the hookup of the ambulatory audiovisual TV-EEG telemetry monitoring system was completed. Then, the test was done in the apparition rooms during the apparitions. The studies measuring Nancy's cutaneous/skin resistance and neurobioelectrical discharges from the pre-frontal region and distal fingers of the right hand muscle fibers demonstrated a *tension* level of 1.7 micro-Volts *before the apparitions* started. According to the professor this level corresponded to a person with *high tension* or *anxiety,* such as Nancy might logically have been experiencing just before the apparition especially on that particular day with the onslaught of reporters, medical doctors, scientists, religious, etc. and over 80,000 pilgrims gathered for the celebrated apparitions. Instantly upon Nancy praying and then saying, "The Blessed Virgin Mary is here," the registered measurements dropped to a level of **0.2 micro-Volts!**

The professor reiterated that he has never seen nor ever eye-witnessed such an immediate, instantaneous drop from a level of *high tension and anxiety* to a level of extreme calm, peace and such *total relaxation.* The professor was very surprised and baffled by this finding, especially knowing that Nancy has never received biofeedback training, nor was she experienced in self-hypnosis techniques. He explained that even the most skilled subjects with years of training in both biofeedback and self-hypnosis are ***unable*** to instantaneously drop from a level of high tension and anxiety to a level of extreme peace and complete relaxation with the amazing speed as was witnessed in Nancy.

Much to the professor's surprise, at precisely 12:25:04 as noted on our ambulatory audiovisual TV-EEG telemetry system, his instrument registered no auditory signals on his amplifiers and no electrical signals on the display screen. He recorded and documented a reading of 0 micro-Volts! At first he thought his instrument was broken, but after 40 seconds of a 0 micro-Volts reading, a registered reading of 0.2 micro-Volts reappeared. This new, surprising and yet very baffling finding was repeated several times during the recitation of the fifteen decades of the rosary, and this phenomena occurred only during the moments when the Blessed Virgin Mary was lovingly caressing and bringing her baby Jesus to us and/or echoing the words of *Jesus (His living words)* to Nancy. As already noted the professor's equipment was functioning perfectly (as it was checked many times over by the self-proclaimed atheist). He had had an opportunity to test it and re-test it, to make sure it was completely operational. Despite this, these *new findings* were a definite scientific curiosity and yet revealed a profound *contradiction,* since Nancy was obviously awake and alive, as documented by our equipment and seen with his and our own eyes.

He later explained that a 0 micro-Volts level of measurement is only seen in patients with basically no neurobioelectrical emissions flowing forth from their bodies—in other words *in patients, who are dead.* It was as if Nancy's entire body ceased to emit neurobioelectrical energy. This finding was in stark contrast to what we visually were eye-witnessing in the apparition room as well as what we filmed and documented by our ambulatory audiovisual TV-EEG telemetry intensive monitoring systems. The professor again had no possible scientific explanation for these *new* findings. He said these findings were *physiologically impossible.* The professor also conducted a battery of neuropsychology tests and made clinical neuropsychological observations *before, during and after the apparitions.* All the tests performed were completely *normal* for a person of Nancy's stated age and level of education. He found Nancy to be truthful with no malingering, no evidence of hysteria or mania or depression or psychosis. He found no personality disorder and no mood or thought disorder. Thus, no clinical neuropsychological disturbance was identified during any of the examinations *before, during and after the apparitions.*

D) George Hogben, M.D., Psychiatry

Dr. George Hogben is a brilliant New York Board Certified Psychiatrist who is a Catholic Christian and at the time of this writing, practices in the state of New York, USA. He is well-known in the psychiatric literature. He has lectured extensively on the role of prayer and Catholic sacramental practices in mental illnesses and health. Dr. Hogben believes that he attended Nancy's apparition experience of June 13th, 1993 with a very open and non-prejudicial mind. He did stipulate, however, that he wanted to do this work voluntarily, and received no monetary compensation for his work.

Likewise, Dr. Callahan, Dr. Velasquez and I (Dr. Sanchez and my entire medical team) also dropped our fees for this extraordinary research to $0.00.

I have been given permission by Dr. Hogben to reprint all his clinical psychiatric observations and examinations of the subject Nancy Fowler *during the visionary experience* as well as during the private meetings before and after the apparitions of June 13th, 1993; and Dr. Hogben also gave me permission to reprint all his psychiatric impressions and other the reported commentaries and remarks he made shortly after the testing was completed. His clinical observations and commentaries are as follows:

PRIVATE MEETINGS BEFORE AND AFTER OBSERVATIONS
By DR. GEORGE HOGBEN

Mrs. Fowler is a warm, friendly woman who related in a very open, humble manner. She maintained steady eye contact. She had an excellent sense of humor even when she described people who act maliciously toward her. She was most serious when she described her experiences of Jesus and Mary and discussed their meaning. These experiences are quite obviously the central focus of her life and she treated them with reverence and humility.

Mrs. Fowler was completely in touch with all her feelings. Her affect was full and supple, well modulated and fully integrated with her thoughts, facial and bodily experiences. She was basically a peaceful, joyful woman, but also readily experienced the sorrow and emotional urgency of the apocalyptic messages she is receiving. She was able to exhibit anger with forcefulness and control.

Mrs. Fowler's thought processes were goal directed. Her sentence structure was intact and quite complex. She showed no looseness in her association or tangentiality. There was no evidence of autistic thinking, delusions, or hallucinations. Mrs. Fowler was completely oriented. Her memory was excellent. She seemed to be well above average in intelligence.

VISIONARY EXPERIENCE OBSERVATIONS
By DR. GEORGE HOGBEN

Mrs. Fowler received her visual and auditory experiences of Jesus and Mary in a large room. She knelt in one corner of the room and described the visions as being on the wall in front and slightly above her. There was a group of thirty or so priests and religious observing her. She was also observed by a team of Neurologists and Neuropsychologists, so she was wired to various EEG and Neuropsychophysiological recording apparatus. The visions lasted approximately one hour and thirty-five to forty minutes and occurred while the group and large crowd outside prayed aloud the joyful and sorrowful mysteries of the holy Rosary.

During the visionary experience, Mrs. Fowler's attention was riveted on what she was seeing and hearing. However, she was able to describe in complete detail the visual and auditory material to a man kneeling next to her who transcribed her words onto paper (reference to George Collins).

Mrs. Fowler's running commentary exhibited vivid detail about the experience of Jesus and Mary to her, with precise quotes of what she was being told. There was no break in her linguistic stream, except, when the scene or verbal content was changing. There was no evidence of loosening of associations or tangentiality.

Mrs. Fowler's affect remained full and well-modulated throughout the experience. There was absolutely no evidence of labile or inappropriate affect. Mrs. Fowler remained peaceful throughout this session, but became quite sad at several moments. She was reverential throughout.

***Psychiatric Impression**: Mrs. Fowler's behavior during the visionary session demonstrated extremely mature, healthy, and complex cognitive abilities. Mrs. Fowler became completely immersed in the visionary experience. Her whole attention was involved in what she heard and saw. Her affect modulated with the visionary material and her mood was congruent with her witness.*

Mrs. Fowler was able to maintain ego objectivity and observational skills, and to describe the experience in vivid detail with elaborate quotations of the verbal messages. Maintaining observing ego in the face of the type of experience she was having is an extraordinary ability which Mrs. Fowler performed effortlessly.

This data shows that Mrs. Fowler maintained ego control, throughout the visionary experience, indicating that the experience was not the result of any mental or emotional disturbance or disorder. In essence, there was absolutely no evidence that psychosis, hysteria, dissociation or any psychiatric disturbance formed Mrs. Fowler's visual and auditory experience of Jesus and Mary.

Mrs. Fowler's personality was quite definitely intact. She was a strong woman, who was serious and humble about what is happening to her. Yet, she was able to maintain an excellent sense of humor about her life. Her affect was appropriate and well-modulated and her feelings and emotions exhibited full healthy range. She had excellent insight into herself.

These observations indicate that Mrs. Fowler's visionary experiences occur to a woman who is healthy and mature. While I am not a theologian and cannot judge the supernatural origin of her experiences of Jesus and Mary, my observations indicate that this must be taken seriously and not simply be passed off as the aberrant products of an unbalanced person.

Speaking from my own personal convictions, gained from talking with and witnessing Mrs. Fowler, I believe that her experiences of Jesus and Mary are from the Lord and our Blessed Mother. Many of the things that Mrs. Fowler described to me, about the role of the supernatural in our daily lives, confirmed my own impressions gained from thirty years of professional experience with mental illness and healing. I do not think that Mrs. Fowler could have gained the insights and knowledge she has otherwise, unless she had lengthy, clinical experiences with mental illness and witnessed many people growing in the Lord.

When journalists and the Australian film crew asked again what he thought of Nancy Fowler (as above, Dr. George Hogben gave me the privilege and permission to print this material as well) Dr. Hogben answered: "I had many impressions of her. But I would like to discuss it from a psychiatric point of view first because that is my training. I had been asked to give a testimony as to whether she *(Nancy)* showed any disturbance–whether her behavior during the visions showed any evidence of psychiatric disturbance, and I can say *unequivocally no, there is no evidence of any psychiatric disturbance at all."*

Dr. Hogben continued, *"Nancy's* thinking was absolutely clear. She described what she saw in very good and vivid detail. There was no evidence of any thinking disorder, any confusion, any loss of contact with myself, or with the people around her. We call this *ego reality* or *ego control,* and she maintained that throughout the entire time, and her train of thinking was completely clear and logical. As far as her affect was concerned, her affect showed no evidence of hysteria or depression. Her affect is what we call full and supple. Her affect was neither too high nor too low. Neither excessive, or down in the dumps, and it did not show any evidence of ups and downs, rapid ups and downs. It was this normal, steady affect which reacted appropriately to the thoughts that she was expressing and the visions that she saw, and her mood was joyful and peaceful except when she was describing visual elements that were sad, and then she became appropriately sad, but not overwhelmingly so."

"There was no evidence of a mood disorder, or depression, or manic depression and no evidence of a personality disorder or hysterical personality. *A psychotic person would get lost in the visions and would not be able to maintain a distance from it and be able to describe it in a clear, concise and vivid way, as Nancy did. So that was a very positive sign that there was no evidence of psychotic disturbance. I also saw no evidence of a hypnotic trance at all. When she was in the vision, she was concentrating on the visions, but she did have the ability to relate to the outside as she would talk to the transcriber* (reference to George Collins). *She would keep her contact with the vision but talk to the transcriber at the same time and give details both of what she was seeing and what she was hearing..."*

In summary then, as recommended by Australian neurologist Dr. John Graham, Nancy was subjected to a psychiatric examination and an EEG test in order to determine *"what her problem was."* The thorough meticulous psychiatric examination yielded a *normal result before, during, and after the apparitions of Jesus and the Blessed Virgin Mary.* The amazing unprecedented results of the EEG tests obtained by my medical team and myself will be reviewed in the next section. However, the results did not show Nancy to have a problem, but rather a very, very special *gift (from God).*

E) Ramon M. Sanchez, M.D., Neurology/Epileptology/Neurophysiology

Before the visionary experience, a neurological exam was conducted in the adjacent room while the ambulatory audiovisual TV-EEG telemetry monitoring system was being hooked up. This examination was entirely normal for the forty-five year-old subject in question, Nancy. And her mental status examination included in this evaluation was *normal.* Once the visionary experience began, our medical team's clinical neurological observations were all reviewed to be *normal.* The subject was awake, alert and oriented, with normal speech, without anomia, aphasia, or apraxia. Her mood and affect were all normal and appropriate for the different elements of her visionary experience. Because of my unique position in the apparition room throughout the entire visionary experience, allowing me an excellent view of her facial expressions and overall bodily movements, I was able to closely observe Nancy. Recall, that I was immediately adjacent to her right side at a slight angle so that I could press the event marker for the ambulatory audiovisual TV-EEG telemetry system. Nancy's physical movements were symmetrical and expressive. Her facial movements were also symmetrical, with appropriate tone and strength and with movements of normal coordination. I was amazed at the prolonged period of time that she was able to kneel, without exhibiting any discomfort, pain or anguish from her arthritis-stricken knees. Even though I could not see what Nancy was seeing, it was obvious by her expressions and the movements of her eyes that she was indeed undergoing a very real auditory and visual experience. These visions were very real to Nancy and interactive. I say *interactive*, because Nancy was interacting and conversing with the *visions or heavenly visits or apparitions* and was receiving messages. Nancy's interaction with the visions appeared very candid and real. Nancy conversed in a very intelligent, clear manner. She exhibited no psychotic behavior and maintained good reality contact with herself and those around her in the room. Her thought processes were normal with no evidence of delusions or paranoia. I thought to myself that if we were somehow to conclude that these events were not authentic, Nancy should indeed and most certainly receive an *Academy Award* or a *Golden Globe Award* for her acting performance. During the visions, Nancy's voice and expressions did change, becoming very humble, reverent with a refreshing honest childlike quality. At times it appeared as if this 45 year-old woman was instantly transformed into a meek and gentle little girl speaking with her loving mother. It reminded me of those Hallmark moments of loving endearment. Like so many scenes Hallmark has crafted over the years, of a joyful child gazing into the eyes of the affectionate and doting parent. Another surprising observation worthy of record was Nancy's markedly *decreased eye-blinking* noted *throughout the visions.* It almost appeared as if Nancy didn't want to blink, for fear that she might lose an instant of the glorious beatific vision or that blinking would somehow deter the visual communication. Both of her eyes remained wide open with dramatically decreased blinking. And the expression on her face exhibited a radiant glow with the most incredible love, joy and peace I have ever witnessed. Indeed, Nancy appeared to glow and radiate the profound love and affection she was feeling. When the vision was completed, her expression became somewhat sad but appropriately so, like the child who must say good-bye to a loving mother.

My clinical neurological observations of Nancy during her visions demonstrated that she was indeed in a state of *ecstasy,* while somehow retaining the ability to interact with those around her in a limited but normal and intelligent manner. *During the visionary experience,* Nancy had a *normal* neurological examination. She exhibited all the manifestations of a visionary in *ecstasy,* while remaining still awake, alert, oriented, and in touch with reality, with normal speech, speech content, train of thought, and normal affect and mood. No anomia, aphasia or apraxia was noted. She likewise exhibited no evidence of delusions, psychosis, paranoia or epileptic behavior. Thus, no psychiatric disturbances were found. The interpretation of the ambulatory audiovisual TV-EEG telemetry monitoring systems analysis yielded *new findings* that were quite remarkable and indeed astonishing—in fact the *new medical and scientific data* is unprecedented in the history of adult neurophysiology.

In summary, Nancy's complete neurological examination was *normal* for her stated age of 45 years. Nancy's electrical brain wave activity (EEG) baseline studies were also *normal* for her stated age, and Nancy's EEG brain wave activity *before and after the apparitions* was indeed identical to the results seen during our baseline studies and all of the medical and scientific data were **normal.**

Before I describe the unprecedented and remarkable EEG results documented *during the apparitions,* I would like to repeat the message Jesus gave to Nancy just a few days before the testing. Jesus said, *"You will be a busy one this weekend, and there will be many tests done. Watch what I will do."* These last few words, *"Watch what I will do,"* resounded in my thoughts as I began to analyze Nancy's EEG electrical brain wave picture recorded *during the heavenly visits* or *apparitions* of that appointed day.

In the early 1990's most ambulatory EEG systems contained only eight channels. As I wanted to cover more brain surface area *(topography)* for the investigations, so we devised a system which involved hooking up two ambulatory EEG systems together to form a sixteen-channel ambulatory audiovisual TV-EEG telemetry monitoring system. All this brain wave electrical data would be recorded on a digital collecting system, brought back to my laboratory and then downloaded into our Oxford II Tower - computer and digital scanner which would then print out this digital information to hard copy for analysis and interpretation. The first time this information was downloaded to the Oxford II Tower, extraordinary results were obtained which contained evidence of an *electronic artifact.* ***Artifact meaning electrical activity not produced by the brain,*** occurring during the times that the Blessed Virgin Mary was apparently speaking *(echoing the words of Jesus)* to Nancy.

The first printout of this electronic artifact started at 12:25:05, but just milliseconds before the professor's EMG system from La Fayette recorded a total of *0 micro-Volts* emanating from Nancy's body at 12:25:04. This first, unusual, EEG *artifact* was recorded for approximately 40 seconds, which coincided with the *0 micro-Volts* emission of bioelectrical discharge signal reading and lasted 40 seconds as well. I must say that this unusual brain wave activity was so bizarre in appearance that it had to be *artifact* and I questioned whether any human brain could ever produce this activity.

The highly unusual electrical behavior and activity made me feel certain and more comfortable that it was some form of *electrical artifact,* and *not produced by Nancy's brain waves.* During these epochs of *electronic artifact,* Nancy as recorded and witnessed by all present showed no evidence of epileptic behavior. Nancy instead displayed a uniquely shy, humble, reverent adult with innocent childlike qualities, and with an obvious love and honest reverence for the Blessed Virgin Mary while speaking or *echoing the (living) words of her Son, Jesus* at those precise moments.

In addressing the problem of the *electronic artifact,* we initially considered that it might be related to a computer scanning malfunction. We contacted the manufacturer of the equipment so that they would come to analyze it and make sure it was running satisfactorily. A letter from the Consumer Service Product Support Group of Oxford Instruments, Medical Systems Division, after their complete evaluation is summarized here: "After a diagnostic check of the internal hard drive was performed, no computer viruses were found nor any corrupted data files. A surface analysis was also performed with no problems reported. The technician proceeded to test the functionality of the replay and system software by playing a tape, storing a fragment and replaying from the hard drive. All signals displayed were clean and artifact free. The technician then performed some preventative maintenance on the system, pulling and receding all of the electronic circuit boards in the tower which is commonly done to alleviate any possibility of contact problems, present or future. The technician again tested the functionality of the replay, once re-assembled he reported no problems.*"*

In reference to the actual *electronic artifact* printout sent by our office on June 16th, 1993 to the Consumer Service Product Support Group, they claimed that they had never seen this type of signal, but that it appeared to be an *electronic artifact.* They were unable to duplicate this printout from the hard drive, and reported that this type of *electronic artifact* was not present on the tape itself. The final conclusion from the Oxford II Instruments Medical Systems Division that our system was free of defects and was working perfectly to all of their specifications, made me all the more suspicious that we were dealing with a real artifact, and not actual brain wave activity. With equipment malfunction ruled out, we also considered the possibility that since we were combining two different digital magnetic tapes of analysis onto one hard copy EEG paper, that maybe the digital tapes were recorded *out of sync* with each other, millisecond to millisecond, during the scanning. This would certainly have produced a *liaising--electronic artifact.* For this reason we then printed out each digital tape alone, then again two more times. Then we reprinted them together again this time making sure that every millisecond of tape was in sync from one tape to the other. Confirming our suspicions, this bizarre *electronic artifact* **was now absent and not seen** on the three separate printouts or when reprinted together again. We therefore concluded that **the first printout demonstrating bizarre brain wave activity was purely an *electronic artifact* produced by human error** in playing the two tapes simultaneously *out of sync.* The first printout most likely caused a *liaising--electronic artifact.* **Thus, Nancy's brain waves did not produce this *electronic artifact,* but rather human error did.**

We shared this information with other university neurophysiologists who were also very well-trained with many years of experience using the same type of ambulatory EEG systems. When we informed them of our *electronic artifact* and the fact that we were downloading two digital magnetic tapes, taken from two different ambulatory EEG recorders, they also confirmed our conclusions of a *liaising--electronic artifact.* All who have reviewed our data agreed that the bizarre electrical activity captured with the first printout was an *electronic artifact,* and that it was not Nancy's true brain wave activity that produced this bizarre electronic artifact activity on the first EEG initially printed. Such were the results of the first instance the *Blessed Virgin Mary was speaking or echoing the living words of Jesus* while appearing to Nancy on that June 13th, 1993 appointed day. Indeed, *the data* was correct but the *liaising electronic artifact* just described was *due to human error.* Significantly, we found no such human error occurred on the second, third and fourth printouts and all of the later printouts were identical to each other. Thus, this verified our conclusions that the bizarre EEG epochs were indeed just *human error.*

Now, I can finally say it is the professional opinion of our medical and scientific research team that the following three printouts were accurate and free from any *liaising--electronic artifacts,* and contain a true electrical picture of Nancy's real brain wave activity. On these three separate printouts, starting at 12:25:05, Nancy's brain wave EEG pattern registered an astonishing and unprecedented *4 Hz rhythmic theta rhythms only during the times Nancy claims to be receiving a message from the Blessed Virgin Mary (speaking the words of Jesus - His living words);* recall that the Blessed Virgin Mary has repeatedly told Nancy, that she *(Mary) is only a messenger sent from heaven to echo the words of her Son.* Thus, the *Blessed Virgin Mary speaks or echoes the (life giving) words of her Son, Jesus.*

Moreover, it was extraordinarily interesting to see how Nancy's brain wave activity dramatically decreased in frequency from an alpha-beta activity in the posterior head regions to 4 Hz theta rhythms in the frontal head regions as soon as the Blessed Virgin Mary appeared lovingly holding and caressing her baby *Jesus.* The 4 Hz rhythms were recorded whenever *the Blessed Virgin Mary was bringing her baby Jesus to us or when Nancy claimed the Blessed Virgin Mary was not holding her baby Jesus but was speaking or echoing the words of her Son, Jesus (His living words).* While *Mary was bringing Jesus or speaking the words of Jesus (His living words) the fast beta activity in the alert with focused attention range was seen overriding the frontal 4 Hz rhythms in the anterior head regions.* And when Mary appeared to Nancy alone not with baby Jesus and Mary was speaking her (own) words, a predominant rhythmic 8-8.5 Hz *alpha brain wave activity* was recorded *with eyes open* in the occipital, parietal and posterior temporal head regions bilaterally with occasional 9 Hz activity recorded as well. The recorded rhythmic 8-9 Hz *alpha brain wave activity with eyes open* is an alpha brain wave activity called *the reflective* or *relaxed state.* Of interest the 8 Hz alpha rhythms recorded on EEG simultaneously coincided with Dr. Callahan's 8 Hz Schumann waves recorded on Nancy's atmospheric-skin radiation boundary energy fields.

Thus, at the instant the Blessed Virgin Mary began to speak or echo the words of her Son Jesus, Nancy's brain wave activity simultaneously demonstrated rhythmic 4 Hz rhythms. This also simultaneously coincided exactly with Dr. Callahan's picram oscilloscope data of recording a *different voice pattern* with slightly larger spike signals that clearly represented *a different and real human voice or human breath pattern.* As mentioned, Dr. Callahan's photonic ionic cord amplifier probe recorded at the atmospheric-skin boundary energy fields in *Schumann waves.* These are atmospheric measurements of *extremely low ionization radiation energy fields.* The *Schumann wave's frequency dropped immediately from 14 Hz to 8 Hz when the Blessed Virgin Mary first appeared* and then *quickly dropped to 4 Hz when* Nancy indicated that *the Blessed Virgin Mary, Our Loving Mother, was now appearing - bringing her baby Jesus to us and then began to speak or echo the words of her Son, Jesus (His living words).*

Dr. Callahan's readings of *unusual* atmospheric-skin boundary radiation energy fields at 4 Hz Schumann waves coincided with Nancy's 4 Hz theta rhythms I recorded on EEG. This occurred despite the fact that both types of equipment were measuring something totally different. So, at the precise moments Nancy indicated that *the Blessed Mother was speaking or echoing the words of her Son, Jesus – 4Hz theta rhythms were recorded on EEG.* Frequently, the 4 Hz theta rhythms formed *a pattern of three 4 Hz waves in sequence 444!* This occurred *only during the apparitions* just mentioned. So, when *the Blessed Virgin Mary was bringing her baby Jesus to us* or *echoing the words of Jesus (His living words) to us the EEG pattern 444 was recorded.* This sequence of 444 can now be considered a type of stimulus specific evoked EEG brain wave pattern. Meanwhile, the predominant *4 Hz brain wave activity* was seen over the frontal head regions including the anterior temporal, central areas and at times less frequently the *4 Hz theta rhythms* spread over the posterior temporal, parietal and rare occipital head regions, but with lower amplitude. *Beta activity in the alert with focused attention range* was seen mainly overriding the anterior head regions, but also throughout all channels with eyes open. Beta activity could be seen *riding on top* of the predominant rhythmic *4 Hz theta rhythms.* During the two times that Jesus appeared, once briefly - and the second time - giving Nancy a message for the medical and scientific team, the medium to high amplitude rhythmic 3 Hz *delta rhythms,* recorded during the *baseline studies* of June 11^{th,} 1993, were again recorded. During the second visit of *Jesus* to Nancy, *3 Hz delta rhythms were recorded,* and seen predominantly over the frontal, temporal and central regions bilaterally. Occasionally, low amplitude *3 Hz delta rhythms* spread over the parietal and posterior temporal regions but rarely over the occipital regions, bilaterally. No spike wave discharges, sharp waves, or epileptic discharges were seen. No electrographic seizures were recorded during the entire apparitions. No ictal or interictal brain activity was recorded before, during or after the apparitions, on the audiovisual TV-EEG telemetry monitoring systems and in person, no epileptic behavior and no psychotic behavior was ever noted.

Nancy's expressions with a radiant glow could be seen to reflect a deep *love, joy and a* profound *peace.* During these times the beta activity seemed to slightly increase in amplitude especially over the anterior head regions. Beta activity was seen riding on top of the 3 Hz delta rhythms *only* on the two occasions *when Jesus appeared - in His Living Presence. Beta activity* was seen *riding on top of the 4 Hz theta rhythms only* during the times *when the Blessed Virgin Mary appeared bringing her baby Jesus to us or was echoing the words of her Son, Jesus (His living words).* During the two times that Jesus appeared, 3 Hz delta waves were frequently seen in succession of three times, *forming a distinct EEG pattern of 333.* This is similar to the amazing EEG pattern I recorded in the *baseline studies* of June 11^{th,} 1993, during the three EEG epochs of *Jesus.* It was uncanny for the scientifically trained members of our team to see the 3 Hz delta rhythms, while Nancy was still very much awake, alert with focused attention, and with normal speech, and normal content of speech without anomia, aphasias, and apraxia. Also, there was no evidence of any loss of time or memory, and there was no evidence of a cognitive brain dysfunction. As explained above, the *3 Hz delta rhythms* are *only seen in normal adults - during deep sleep stages III-IV.* And riding on top of the *3 Hz delta rhythms* - I clearly saw a slight accentuation of the beta activity, while her eyes were open. This is a normal response. Whenever there is an increased level of alertness with focused attention recorded (imagine when seeing *Jesus*), it is indeed typical for the subject to experience an increased level of cognitive brain activity function. No sharp waves, spike wave discharges or epileptic activities were seen. And there was no evidence of any epileptic seizures recorded - causing the amazing EEG brain wave changes.

There was no evidence of a hypnotic trance recorded since *no alpha-theta trance state* pattern was seen or documented. The beta-delta 3 Hz rhythms pattern I recorded was only documented during the *heavenly visits or apparitions of Jesus - in His Living Presence* while Nancy's eyes were open. This EEG pattern has never been described before in *normal* awake, alert and fully conscious subjects and has been thought to be *physiologically impossible* until now. I have no current medical explanation for the amazing and astonishing test results. However, from a clinical neurophysiology observation, I could honestly say that no one would have ever predicted these EEG brain wave patterns especially after studying the ambulatory audiovisual TV-EEG telemetry monitoring system recordings of Nancy during the apparitions. Nancy's demeanor with a peaceful radiant glow in fact did change in regard to the way she addressed *Jesus* and *the Blessed Virgin Mary.* Nancy became very reverent, shy and humble with innocent childlike qualities and with *a holy fear of God,* which was at times quite striking. Anyone who was present during the apparitions of the Blessed Virgin Mary and was close enough in proximity to Nancy *(like me)* could actually hear the tone in her voice change from that of an adult parent to a very soft spoken tender loving adult daughter with an endearing honest child-like quality and slight Bostonian accent. Comparing Nancy's appearance and demeanor with many other documented mystics and visionaries in states of *ecstasy,* Nancy seemed to be obviously sharing and enjoying the same type of experience or *supernatural event.* Nancy also succeeded in peacefully radiating and reflecting the *love, joy and peace* to others in the room, as Nancy was seeing *Jesus* and *the Blessed Virgin Mary* and the *heavenly court,* it seemed logical to conclude that at the very least, Nancy was indeed in *ecstasy,* if only in the layman's sense.

Two articles concerning the topic of *Pleasure Rhythms* or *Hedonic-Theta Rhythms* by Dr. Maulsby appeared in the clinical neurophysiology literature, Journals of Clinical Neurophysiology in 1971. Therein, Dr. Maulsby wrote a case report of a nine month-old girl being kissed by her mother while simultaneously being monitored on EEG equipment. During this experience Dr. Maulsby reported that rhythmic 4 Hz theta rhythms were recorded. Two other scientists, Drs. Kuglar and Laub, also conducted a 1971 study in which the EEG's of small children from six months to six years of age were monitored while the children were watching a toy/puppet show. During the times of particularly great enjoyment while watching the show, the children demonstrated rhythmic *4 Hz theta rhythms.* Drs. Kuglar and Laub concluded that in the pediatric population, 4 Hz rhythmic theta brain waves can be interpreted as an *expression of extreme pleasure.* These scientists also noted that the so-called ***pleasure theta rhythms had never been recorded in the adult population, but only in children.*** One might speculate that this can be attributed to the fact that children's emotions are arguably the purest and most sincere of all humankind. Children's minds are generally free from the clutter, cynicism and general hang-ups we adults seem to engender. The above information compared to and analyzed in conjunction with the results obtained from medical and scientific studies on Nancy is fascinating. These findings are indeed quite remarkable especially because of the previously-mentioned childlike quality Nancy exhibits when she speaks to the *Blessed Virgin Mary* or to *Jesus.* One might arguably conclude that the *ecstasy* experience itself must be one of supreme pleasure which thus allows Nancy (and other visionaries, as we shall see) to manifest these 4 Hz theta rhythms during her *ecstasy experience.*

Though the above-mentioned instances of *4 Hz theta rhythms (pleasure rhythms)* recorded among the pediatric population do exist, a careful search of the literature for any documented or published data on delta rhythms seen in awake and normal adults yielded absolutely no published sources. In fact there were no published reports describing or even mentioning delta rhythms (or more specifically the 3 Hz delta rhythms I had recorded) in association with normal adult subjects on no medications who were awake, alert with focused attention and a normal higher cortical and cognitive functioning. According to all the known and recorded precedent to date, the rhythmic 3 Hz delta rhythms I repeatedly recorded in the *living presence of Jesus* was and is only supposed to be seen in normal adult subjects during *normal deep sleep stages.* We may now conclude that the EEG *3 Hz delta rhythms* (I recorded) only formed this EEG pattern of 333 during the *heavenly visits or apparitions of Jesus - in His Living Presence.* This is definitely a *new EEG brain wave pattern* that is not only unprecedented but also astonishing for all its implications. This EEG brain wave pattern of 333 was indeed puzzling. *What* does it mean? Remember, delta brain wave activity is only seen in normal subjects in *deep sleep* stages. On the audiovisual TV-EEG telemetry monitoring system display screen Nancy was obviously **awake**, so *how* could we explain this *3 Hz delta rhythm pattern?* Did this new EEG pattern represent an even more profound *peace* and supreme *pleasure rhythm in His Living Presence?* Or were the

3 Hz delta rhythms describing some yet unknown deeply profound *peace* and/or a spiritual state of *ecstasy*, now with new neurophysiological parameters that have never been published to date in any of the adult clinical EEG and neurophysiology international literature? So, does the *3 Hz delta rhythm* represent another form of *ecstasy* or a *more profound interior peace and pleasurable state of ecstasy?* Many of these new concepts themselves needed explanation as the term *ecstasy* itself, I soon discovered, has different meanings in different circles.

The validity of any scientific study rests in its *reproducibility.* Thus, we now have five documented apparitions of *Jesus (in His Living Presence);* in which each recorded EEG epoch clearly **reproduced** the same amazing and unprecedented *3 Hz delta rhythms.* As a neurologist and *not* a numerologist, I could not help but notice the repeated frequency patterns of *4 Hz slow theta rhythms* seen only in the presence of *the Blessed Virgin Mary bringing baby Jesus to us, or speaking the words of Jesus (echoing His living words).* And the repeated frequency EEG patterns of 3 Hz seen only *in the living presence of Jesus. Why?* These astonishing and **unprecedented** EEG patterns were indeed identical during the second, third and fourth printouts of the ambulatory audiovisual TV-EEG telemetry monitoring system, digital magnetic tapes, and predictably reproduced the same EEG patterns as were noted above. As discussed, the *4 Hz slow theta rhythms* recorded only in the presence of the Blessed Virgin Mary bringing her baby Jesus to us or speaking the words of her Son, Jesus formed a definite EEG pattern of 444. This is unprecedented, since 4 Hz theta *Pleasure Rhythms* have never been described in the adult population. One can only speculate that I inadvertently measured a supreme form of EEG *hedonic/pleasure rhythms* that were previously only seen in the pediatric population, but are now seen and recorded in an adult in our testing. Recall, Nancy (and later you shall see *other visionaries* or *chosen souls* with similar findings) was in a *state of ecstasy* with the typical peaceful radiant glow when these results were recorded and documented.

Consider the imagery and symbolism of Dr. Maulsby's 1971 case report, in which a baby girl of nine months develops the *4 Hz theta pleasure rhythms* just as she is kissed by her mother. Nancy claims to believe and fully acknowledges that the Blessed Virgin Mary is her heavenly mother. While Nancy is *seeing and receiving messages* from her *heavenly loving mother*, she reacts with a radiant glow and tender childlike quality that visually overflows with a sense or feeling of pleasure received as only a loving daughter can evoke or muster. This tender love giving pleasure to Nancy was easily recognized and observed during the ambulatory audiovisual TV-EEG telemetry recordings. This *new data* beautifully correlates Nancy's experiences with Dr. Maulsby's case report. It is as if Nancy were being kissed by her *heavenly loving mother* while with a pure child-like quality Nancy lovingly receives supreme contentment, pleasure and a very large dose of tangible motherly love that somehow scientifically evokes or produces the

4 Hz theta brain wave pleasure rhythms in Nancy (an adult). ***Until now these pleasure/hedonic theta rhythms were seen and recorded only in infants and very young children.***

In conclusion: Nancy was found to be normal before, during and after the apparitions, as per our repeated numerous and meticulous neurological examinations, and clinical observations. The *EEG brain wave activity recorded was also* ***normal*** for Nancy's stated age of 45 years. Thus, *the astonishing new results of 4 Hz theta rhythms seen only during the heavenly visits of the Blessed Virgin Mary bringing her baby Jesus to us and/or echoing the words of Jesus (His living words) to us;* and the *3 Hz delta rhythms seen only during the heavenly visits of Jesus (in His Living Presence),* can now be acknowledged as being *truly unprecedented* by all the currently known medical, scientific and EEG criteria. This *new data could never have been predicted nor even concocted, based on all the currently available medical and scientific research to date.* Wow! Just as exciting as our *new findings* of extraordinary EEG brain wave patterns, were the test results of measurable changes in *the light energy* found by the other scientists. Due to the astonishing nature of these new findings, and their potential impact on the scientific community, a series of scientific conferences on all the results obtained by our scientific research team have been presented. Can you imagine actually *confirming* to the world *the truth* about Who Father God, His only begotten Son and the Holy Spirit really **is**? I say **is**, because God **is** truly One. The *Holy of Holies* **is** *One substance undivided: 3 in 1 and One in Three.* Just like *David's Star* --- with the *delta triangle pointing upwards,* that a local rabbi said *represents God.* The rabbi also said the *delta triangle pointing downwards (God's reflection) represents us (mankind)* - God's creation: *"let us make man in our image and in our likeness"* (Gen.1:26). So, with our generation's tremendous *faith in science,* just imagine the potential *eternal life-saving* blessings harnessed by finally being able *to confirm* ***the truth*** *of what we believe in* via our faith, *which is a pure gift from God --- through science, with science and in science. God's gift of* ***the truth*** is given to us via *the word of God,* as it is written in the *Holy Bible* and taught by *traditions* and *the Church.* But, is it really science that confirms *the truth?* Or rather God (Elohim) the Master Scientist, Creator of *"heaven and earth"* (Gen 1:1) Who *"through Him, with Him and in Him" and His Church* confirms *the truth?* Through this scientific journey, many (including me) have been graciously given God's loving *gift of faith.*

Although there are no current medical or scientific explanations for these *new test results,* I now believe these unprecedented yet measurable EEG brain wave rhythms might express a true state of the most profound interior *peace* and *pleasure (love and joy)* ever recorded and documented, but yet, only *in His Living Presence, the living presence of Jesus,* as claimed by Nancy. One can now speculate that these EEG unprecedented brain wave patterns must represent new EEG patterns that can be seen only in normal adult subjects during different states of spiritual *ecstasy* and with a specific heavenly stimulus. The word *ecstasy* with our *new medical and scientific data* can now be loosely used to describe an intensely supreme form of peace, love, and joy and a deeply profound and interior *pleasurable state.* As emphasized, EEG delta rhythms are seen in adults normally only in the *deep sleep* stages. As such *deep sleep* no doubt represents one's most peaceful, calm and relaxed brain wave state. Therefore, Nancy's repeated claims and testimonies of feeling a deeply profound *peace, love and joy* while experiencing *visions, heavenly visits or apparitions of Jesus and the Blessed Virgin Mary, Our Loving Mother* was more than just hearsay, more than just her words or opinion. This ***profound interior peace was actually measurable by EEG.*** For many years after the medical and scientific testing was completed, I deliberated as to the meaning of these different specific mathematical and numerical frequencies of EEG brain wave patterns, since the numbers associated with the frequencies recorded were uniquely different and stimulus specific for the experiences of the Blessed Virgin Mary bringing her baby Jesus and/or speaking *(echoing)* His living words to us and for all the *heavenly visits or apparitions of Jesus.*

I am not a ***numerologist*** *nor a* ***theologian,*** but in the following section, I will cite certain religious Biblical sources and holy scriptural texts ***as a physician journeying science to faith and as a medical scientist who discovered with much frustration that most of our new data and results left me and our entire medical and scientific research team baffled, confused and indeed very astonished.*** We had no medical or scientific explanations for the *new data* we obtained. It took a courageous leap of faith, and humility, to recognize that these *new results* did have significance in ***science*** *and* ***faith (and even religion).*** The two *did not contradict, but rather* almost for the first time actually *complement one another.* Indeed, our collective *new data* seemed clearly pointed in the direction of this merger. Never in my wildest dreams would I have thought that our *new medical and scientific results* would squarely lead us or me (for that matter) to a greater faith and truth about God and religions for their clearest, and indeed, their most basic interpretation.

Unfortunately, such a conclusion is considered mostly *unacceptable* to most of our medical and scientific circles today. Sadly enough, such *new data* may be even considered *politically incorrect;* as it seems with most of the current trends in both our local and international *secular news media* of the world today will likely try to portray it. As it will be clearly shown and this is *in black and white* hardcore-science to the max, the mathematical and numerical EEG brain wave patterns we observed, recorded and documented are significant. These *new EEG patterns* are indeed significant particularly when this *new data* is considered in conjunction with various sources of the ancient Holy Scriptures, the Holy Bible, different scholarly theological and religious literature, and also including the now famous and renowned Hebrew ELS Bible codes, that was discovered by a Jewish rabbi and recently rediscovered by many Biblical Hebrew *(Jewish and Christian)* scholars.

The *journey science to faith* continues...

REFLECTIONS ON NUMBERS

Years after the testing, I was still searching for the significance of the EEG *patterns of numbers* which our testing had yielded. I was shown a book written by an Italian priest, Father Stephano Gobi, entitled *The Marian Movement of Priests.* This intriguing volume of messages contains a number of apocalyptic type messages received by Fr. Gobi from *Jesus and the Blessed Virgin Mary.* Much to my surprise *message number 407* entitled *The Number of the Beast,* talks specifically about *the number 333,* and also *the number 666.* In this message the former *number 333 is equated with the Holy Trinity of God,* while the latter *number 666 is equated with the beast (the old serpent, Satan).* This squarely confirmed in a way I never imagined my *new data* in association with Nancy's claims regarding all her *visions, heavenly visits or apparitions* recorded thus far and would later record.

See Chapter 7 in this book for more information concerning the *new medical and scientific data* associated with the latter and most unwelcome visitor. I also recently learned of two Biblical Hebrew Scholars whose research pointed squarely to the significance of *the number 333.* Both Grant R. Jeffrey and Yacov Rambsel separately found ***three hundred thirty-three (333) prophetic phrases* that say - *Jesus, the Messiah* - en*coded via the ELS Bible Codes in the five Books of Moses,*** known as ***the Torah,*** *the Bible* or *the Law.* Thus, as per these two Biblical experts a total of *333 prophetic phrases* were found *encoded in the Jewish Hebrew Torah* that *proclaims - Jesus as the true Jewish Messiah.* Wow! Somehow little by little, *the new unprecedented EEG pattern - 333,* I had discovered and observed on all our EEGs - *in His Living Presence* - seemed less and less mysterious.

Soon after, I spotted a *message* given by *Jesus* to Nancy on August 26th, 1990. In this message, *Jesus* asked Nancy, *"What is the greatest life in you? Eternal life... It is the life of the soul."* George (Collins) then asked, *"Please...* explain more about *eternal life."*

Jesus said through Nancy, *"I am the way, the truth and the life. That is eternal life. I am the author of life. The way, the truth and the life add up to eternal life. Look at each one individually. Walk in my way. That is life. Live my words. That is life. Take my body and blood. That is life. In my words find everything–truth, way, wisdom; find love, find me. Walk my way. You will find truth. You will find life. You will find love. You will find wisdom.* ***I am taking you in a circle. You can start at any point and come to eternal life. Remember the number 3.*** **It is the Holy Trinity. *I am the way, the truth, and the life."*** *Now* just *look at the forehead of Jesus on the Shroud of Turin* and *see the number "3" written in His Precious Blood.*

In discussing this *topic of numbers* with many religious and Biblical scholars, I further discovered that *the number three (3)* also had great significance in *the life of Jesus* on earth. *Jesus was crucified at thirty-three years.* He spent over *three plus years in His ministry teaching the good news (the Gospel)* that *"the kingdom of God **is** come upon you"* (Luke 11:20), and *"**is** within you"* (Luke 17:21). Recall, *He suffered three hours dying on the cross, while* ***the sun*** *was darkened (a solar eclipse) during His crucifixion,* as prophesized in Isaiah 10:13. Recall, *He spent three days and nights in the belly of the earth,* as was foreshadowed by the prophet Jonah in the belly of the whale, before *He resurrected* according to the New Testament Gospels. Curiously, I was informed by a *priest* visiting *the Vatican* that to reach the top of the Dome of St. Peter's Cathedral in Rome, Italy, one must climb *three hundred thirty-three steps.* Is this another *coincidence* or another *God-incidence?* Can you imagine? On a trektheworld.com TV show a traveler was planning a climb to reach the top of Mount Sinai, and learned that it will take 3,330 steps to reach the top. God really has a *sense of humor.*

In September of 1995 a retired Archbishop Genaro Prata in Rome, Italy, who had taught *Canon Law* in Rome, invited me to *the Vatican* in Rome to give a talk to *Cardinal Ratzinger's Office* concerning the medical and scientific studies on Nancy Fowler, the seminarian and Patricia Talbot (Pachi). This same Archbishop attended the appointed testing of June 13th, 1993 in Conyers and was convinced of Nancy's authenticity by his own personal observations and experiences in Conyers, Ga. It was he who arranged the meeting with *Cardinal Ratzinger's Office.*

Then Archbishop Bertone (who is now – The Secretary of State of the Vatican, Tarcisio Cardinal Bertone), representing *Cardinal Ratzinger (now Pope Benedict XVI),* in our Meeting at *the Vatican* seemed to be delighted with our medical and scientific investigations and results, though I must admit, I fully did not understand all the *new data* - at that time. Archbishop Prata said he would call me in about two months, after he had time to review and discuss the *new data* with *the Vatican.* Two months after our meeting in *the Vatican,* Archbishop Prata paged me. This was a moment I will never forget.

It was my day off work, the day after *Thanksgiving* after 3:00 p.m., and I had just come back from the gym. I started to shower and my digital pager began beeping. My wife picked up my beeper and said I was receiving a telephone page from the Archbishop in Rome. While I was still in the shower she said, "Honey, you are getting paged from Rome, Italy." I turned off the shower immediately and asked, *"What* did you say?" She repeated what she had just said. So, I quickly dried off then picked up my beeper and looked at the digital printout which read, *"Please call* Archbishop Prata in Rome, Italy."

I could not believe I was being paged about *the Vatican's review?* The time of this page on the digital display was **3:33 p.m.!** As I had been so deeply pondering the true significance of the number 333, I could only in awe quickly look up towards the heavens and say to our Almighty God, *"Wow! You don't miss a beat."* While any hardened skeptic *(like me)* might surely claim this incident to be a pure *coincidence,* the uncanny nature of this incident like many, many others has caused me to adopt the new term, *God-incidence.* The *journey science to faith* continues...

REFLECTIONS ON LIGHT

In reviewing all of Nancy's reported visions or apparitions, and the vocabulary she uses to describe them, it seems apparent that ***light*** *plays a major role.* We asked Nancy and pondered why does *light* play such a major role in the *visions or apparitions of Conyers.* Why do some people claim to see *light* and others do not? I for one witnessed no unusual or unexplained light of any kind during the apparitions that day. However, a quick even skeptical peek at the photographs of the chimney façade taken by the radiation research team clearly demonstrates a definite *increase in* ***the light*** or ***light energy*** *reflected on the chimney and outside façade the farm house during the apparitions* that was *not present before* or *after the apparitions.* Many years after our medical and scientific tests of June 13th, 1993, I had the opportunity to go back and reflect on all the studies conducted along with all the *new data* and results the entire research team obtained that day. In reading some of *the messages given to Nancy,* as well as reviewing many Biblical references and citations related to the topic of *light,* several things became clearer and clearer from an overall perspective which when first analyzed merely medically or scientifically was quite confusing and somewhat nebulous.

The following excerpts may hopefully *shed some* ***light*** on this topic. At the very least, these passages were *food for thought* to a group of very hungry medical scientists desperately trying to explain something their *good science* could not. In the New Testament in John 8:12: *"Again Jesus spoke* to them*, saying, I am the light of the world; he who follows me will not walk in darkness, but will have the light of life."* In the Old Testament, Psalm 27:1 reads, *"The Lord God is my light and salvation."* Isaiah 51:4 says, *"... the light of the people,"* and Isaiah 60:20, *"the Lord is everlasting light"* and Micah 7:8, *"the Lord is my light."*

On September 1st, 1989, Jesus said to Nancy, *"I am light, my dearest daughter. Why do you read in poor light?"* Nancy replied, *"My Lord,* there is no light here in this church.*"*

Jesus then said, *"I am your light. In my light you will find all truth, all knowledge, all love and wisdom. Seek my light and you will have everything that you seek. Do not be troubled by men. Your foes will not harm you. I have told you: you will not be defeated. Dearest daughter, no one can defeat you because I cannot be defeated. Know that I reveal the truth to you. That is all I need you to write at this time. Remember, I am the fountain of all truth. Truth cannot be taken from you. I cannot be taken from you. Be comforted by my words."* On January 31st, 1990, Nancy was praying before *the Most Holy Blessed Sacrament* and *Jesus* said, *"Be at peace. Look to the light and you will find the truth."*

On December 13th, 1992 the Blessed Mother explained to Nancy that she wanted Jesus to live in each of us and said, *"When Jesus lives in you, you emit rays of his light. I desire the world to give birth anew to my Son, emitting rays of light from each temple (our bodies)."* Nancy thought of *the rays of light* that she sometimes sees coming from people's hearts. Nancy has seen *the light* around some people so, so bright that the person disappears and all that she can actually see is *the light.*

On December 29th, 1992, *Jesus* said to Nancy, *"Can you figure out my light?"* Nancy replied, *"No."* She said *Jesus* was showing her what *He* could do with the *mystical light that she sees.* Nancy saw *the light flashing* on the ceiling, then on the corpus on the crucifix and then on the wall. *The light* continued to flash as *He* moved it around. *Jesus* said, *"I am the source of all light. I am light itself."* Nancy asked George, "Does that make sense?" George Collins replied, "That is God, but I can't understand how He does it." Nancy then said to Jesus, *"You are really good." Jesus* replied, *"And you are really my daughter. Many people want to quiz you and test you. That is what they want to do to me. My children get confused when they try to figure me out. Remind them of this."* Nancy said, "This whole conversation is over my head." *Jesus* then replied, *"And blessed are you who know this. Bow your heads."*

On March 3rd, 1995, *Jesus* said to Nancy, *"You will know the Mass much more through the visions I show you."* Nancy asked, "What about your word?" *Jesus* said, *"I give you visions of light on my word, on the angels, on the people of God."* On January 19th, 1995, *Jesus* began to speak to Nancy as she was preparing a talk. *Jesus* said, *"Tell them...I am the true light and source of all light. Tell them I am helping them to grow in holiness in each moment they seek me in the depths of their hearts. True holiness is founded in obedience and humility and seeking My Will in selfless love. Pray each day that you may always live in the light of my love. I love you and bless you in more ways than you will ever know."* The next message is interesting and teaches us *(me)* a wonderful lesson.

On December 10th, 1990, Nancy had been doing some things on her own without letting Jesus lead. This independence was leading to a lack of *peace* and some frustration. She was letting what some people were saying take her focus off Jesus. *Jesus* appeared and again reminded her, *"Nancy, you are like the dog at the end of the chain. You are tugging and fighting. You are going to get very worn out. Please let the Master lead. Walk in harmony with the Master. The dog does not have greater intelligence than the Master. The dog must rely on the Master for his food, for his care. The dog learns to trust the Master. He knows the Master loves him. The dog knows the Master will not lead him astray. Walk in harmony with the Master. Walk in trust. If the Master takes care of the dog, how much greater care will I give to my dear children? Is there anyone on earth... is there anyone anywhere who can love you more than I do? Is there anyone, anywhere, who suffers like I do for you? Is there anyone, anywhere who has greater patience than*

I? My little child, come, come to me. I will mend your wounds. I will dry your tears. I will comfort you in sorrow. I will speak to you in silence. I am your light, and I will show you the way. You will never need to be afraid of the darkness. I will never abandon you, and my love is endless. In my love you will never be thirsty, and you will never hunger. You will never lack anything." Nancy said, "I am so unworthy to see your face." *Jesus* then said, *"My little child of mercy, my precious little girl, will you ever find a greater friend, a greater companion, a greater teacher, a greater physician? Will you ever find anyone greater? Will you ever find anyone more learned than I am? Will you ever find anyone who has greater riches to give you?"* Nancy said, "There is no one greater Lord... than you."

Jesus said, *"Then why, dear, dear, dear precious daughter, do you look to man before me? Do I place anyone before you? Please do not try to understand what you can never understand. I am beyond all human reason... logic... feelings. I am beyond time. I am beyond everything in the physical world of man. How I pour my love out to you and all of mankind. Weary am I to find no place to rest. When you rest, do you not want to rest for a while?"* Nancy said as she looked at *Jesus, "He* is crying." *Jesus* said, *"If only I could rest longer in you and all of mankind."* Nancy said, *"He* is radiant and *the light* is fluctuating and affecting my eyes because of the brightness. I see the crucified face of *Jesus. He* is worn out and exhausted."

The above messages given to Nancy concerning *light* are interestingly reminiscent of a very important quote from the Old Testament. One of the most revered prophets Isaiah relates *The Oracle on the Servant of the Lord* Isaiah 42:1-9 (*NJV)* in this way:

"Here is ***my servant*** *whom I uphold,* ***my chosen one*** *with whom I am pleased,* ***upon whom I have put my spirit; he shall bring forth justice to the nations,*** *of crying out, not shouting, not making his voice heard in the street. A bruised reed he shall not break, a smoldering wick he shall not quench, until he establishes justice on the earth; the coastlands will wait for his teaching.*

Thus says God, the Lord, who created the heavens and stretched them out, who spreads out the earth with its crops, Who gives breath to its people and spirit to those who walk on it: ***I, the Lord, have called you*** *for the* ***victory of justice.*** *I have grasped you by the hand; I have formed you,* ***and set you as a covenant of the people, a light for the nations, to open the eyes of the blind,*** *to bring out prisoners from confinement, and from the dungeon, those who live in darkness.* ***I am the Lord,*** *this is my name; my glory I give to no other, nor my praise to idols.* ***See, the earlier things come to pass, new ones I now foretell; Before they spring into being, I announce them to you."*** Then, see in Isaiah 42:13: ***"The Lord*** *shall go forth* ***as a mighty man..."***

In these two very important excerpts noted above, ***the word*** *of God* promises and *foretells* of His *suffering servant, His chosen one,* in whom *God* has *put His Spirit,* and *"he shall bring forth justice to nations."* The Lord God has indeed set Him before us, as *a covenant of the people, a new covenant,* and as ***a light for the nations***. It is then understood in *Messianic tradition,* that this *suffering servant* --- *"**my chosen one,**" and "**the light** of the Gentiles...**my salvation** even to the farthest part of the earth* (Isaiah 49:6)*"*--- **is** the *new covenant* for all people and all nations, including Jews and Gentiles alike. And this *suffering servant* **is** *the Messiah, the Christ* or *Christos* in Greek, which means *the Anointed One of God.* Now see how *the Lord shall go forth as a mighty man.* ***This prophecy of Isaiah I believe is fulfilled by Jesus, and confirmed by all our medical and scientific data documenting "the light"- in His Living Presence.***

In John 1:1-5, (thanks St. Jerome) the prologue reads: *"In the beginning was the Word, and the Word was with God, and the Word was God. He was in the beginning with God. All things came to be through Him, and without Him nothing came to be. What came to be through Him was life, and this life was **the light** of the human race; **the light** shines in the darkness, and the darkness has not overcome it."* We have already seen how the new medical and scientific results of our meticulous and sophisticated research data unequivocally demonstrated increased levels of ***the light*** energy which was present *only during the visions, heavenly visits or apparitions* to Nancy. These results combined with some of the above excerpts seem to suggest these remarkable conclusions; each person, however, must ultimately make his or her own interpretations. Please just look at all the astonishing *new medical and scientific data.*

MORE REFLECTIONS ON THE JUNE 13th, 1993 APPARITION ROOM TESTING

Years after the June 13th, 1993 testing, I discussed with Nancy the real *confusion* and astonishment which ran rampant among all members of our medical and scientific research team due to many unexplained results. I was shown a message Jesus had given Nancy on May 11th, 1993 just over one month before our testing: *"I will give a message for the United States: Who are men that think they know my ways? Who are you to question me? I have set Conyers apart. I tell you, scientists, doctors, theologians will be **confused** because they cannot figure me out. My way is not man's way."*

In an interview with one of the highest ranking neurologist and EEG expert in Australia, Dr. John Walsh of the Royal Prince Alfred Hospital in Sydney, the Australian film crew claim they discussed the results of our medical and scientific testing with Dr. Walsh, especially the unprecedented 3 Hz delta brain wave activity seen *only in the living presence of Jesus - in His Living Presence.* Dr. Walsh said these findings represented a *physiological impossibility.* Indeed, for someone to have 3 Hz delta brain wave activity with eyes open, awake, alert with focused attention and fully conscious was uncanny. The Aussie film crew also said to me, *"Dr. Walsh* had *never seen or heard of it ever happening and could not believe it had happened."* But as shown, not only did it happen once, but *five times* thus far.

This *physiological impossibility* Dr. Walsh mentions is an astonishing new finding of 3 Hz delta rhythms in a *deep sleep* topographic EEG pattern that was repeatedly recorded simultaneously with an awake, alert with focused attention and fully conscious subject. This can be demonstrated by the EEG patterns of *alert with focused attention* beta rhythms superimposed on the *deep sleep* delta rhythms. This amazing *new data* and *physiological impossibility* repeatedly occurred ***only** in His Living Presence,* much to the amazement and *confusion* of the most educated and highly trained and hardened skeptic members *(like me)* in our medical community.

Can you imagine? *Science* brought me to *faith.* Or rather did *God the Almighty, the Creator of all science* bring me to faith? I ponder. I am almost ashamed to admit that this journey was not an accident, but almost a requirement for my initial disbelief. I was a real super-doubting Thomas to the max. So, I will assume that of others too. Undoubtedly, this is a sad commentary on *me* and on our modern day *spiritual life in America.* Indeed, have we become a *faithless nation?* On September 2nd, 1990, the Blessed Virgin Mary's first message *echoing the words of Jesus* to our entire Nation, the United States of America was, *"There is too little faith here... I am very sad."*

Truly it seems that we need and even demand in today's technical world *hardcore science* to help us believe and/or to have any real faith in God, at least I certainly did. We (I) *want proof* of everything, *esp. what* we (I) *can not see* with our (my) very own eyes. We have become a society and a nation full of super-doubting Thomases to the max (just like me). Mingled with a strong *human will* and attitudes of rebellion against all types of authority, overwhelming complacency, rampant apathy and a genuine lack of trust in *God,* in *the word of God* and simple *faith;* yes my *dearest America, both you and I need a lot of help.* We need an immediate colossal IV (intravenous) injection bolus and a continuous daily infusion of *faith.*

I humbly, and almost shamefully, must admit that I was not initially content with the amazing and unprecedented results of the *baseline studies,* which revealed these very special EEG patterns. My hardened skepticism caused me to *hunger and thirst* for further *testing* because of **my lack of faith**. Unsure of what we were uncovering (discovering) or even by being unable to admit the sheer complexity of it all, I like a good scientist wanted **more data, more tests.** Though this very energetic drive for *more data* on my part is perhaps laudable from a scientific perspective, from a spiritual one I fully embodied and vocalized St. Thomas' own great doubt even in the splendor and magnificence of God's handiwork. At this point of my journey *science to faith,* some might conclude that I was a *near perfect scientist,* perhaps, but without any doubt a very *imperfect disciple of faith.*

The medical and scientific results we obtained undoubtedly tended ***to validate and authenticate** Nancy's* claims of *heavenly visits or apparitions, and* ***visions of***

light as Nancy likes to describe them, ***rather than disprove*** them. Our amazing *new data* helped to corroborate the many testimonies given by numerous priests, nuns, religious, pilgrims and even some reporters who claimed to have seen *the light* show *during the apparitions.* The scientific radiation team quantified, both visually and statistically, significant increases in *the sun light.* We actually recorded greater than 30-90% *more sun light* --- **only** *in His Living Presence* or *when the Blessed Virgin Mary brings her baby Jesus to us.*

This astonishing occurrence can and will be interpreted for its amazing Biblical significance since both *the New* and *Old Testaments* use the word *sun* in many references concerning the a*nointed one to be sent, the Messiah, the Orient,* the *Son of man* and the *living Son of God.* References like Rev 12:1-2: *"A woman clothed with the sun, and the moon under her feet...And being with child..."* Can you recall *Who* this *child* is? See Rev 12:5: *"And she brought forth a man child, who was to rule all nations with an iron rod: and her son was taken up to God, and to his throne."* Now read Psalm 2:6-9 to see just *Who* is this *child?* See Psalm 2:6: *"But I am appointed king by him over Sion his holy mountain, preaching his* (God's) *commandments.* ***The Lord hath said*** *to me:* ***Thou art my son, this day have I begotten thee****. Ask of me, and I will give thee the Gentiles for thy inheritance, and the utmost parts of the earth for thy possession. Thou shalt rule them with a rod of iron..."*

So, *Who* **is** the *begotten son of God; Who shall rule them* (the nations) *with a rod of iron; and Who* **is** *the son* of the *woman clothed with the sun?* The *sun* is also mentioned with the descriptions of the *transfiguration of Jesus* in Matthew 17:2: *"And he was transfigured before them. And his face did shine as* ***the sun:*** *and his garments became white as snow." The sun* is mentioned with descriptions of the *resurrected* and *glorified Christ Jesus* as seen in Rev 1:16: *"and his face was as the sun shineth in his power,"* and is also mentioned in many of the psalms. See Psalm 88:36-37: *"I will not lie unto David: his seed shall endure for ever. And his throne as* ***the sun*** *before me..."*

See other prophetic Holy Scriptures like Malachi 4:2: *"...****the Sun of justice*** *shall arise, and health in his wings..."* See Chapter 9 for a more complete study and review of many references concerning *the sun* in association with *the anointed one,* the chosen one of God, whom God the Father sent.

In *the light* of these astonishing results, some readers will choose to automatically and voluntarily make these amazing and unprecedented holy connections between medical science and holy scriptures; however, for the very hardened skeptics *(like me)...*

...the journey *science to faith* now gets exciting...

CHAPTER IV

"I AM ALIVE"

JUNE 13th, 1993 TESTING – "BEHOLD, JESUS IS ALIVE ON THE CROSS"

Though our initial *medical and scientific data* of the June 13th, 1993 testing had been overwhelming and unprecedented, the day was not yet over. Recall that in the apparition room during the initial testing that day, in one of the apparitions of Jesus to Nancy, Jesus said to Nancy that *He (Jesus)* would give a *special message* to the entire medical and scientific research team after the *Blessed Virgin Mary* was finished giving *her message from Jesus* for the United States and the world. After *Our Loving Mother's message* was delivered by Nancy to the public, we were then to go to Nancy's house where *Jesus* was to give us (the research team) a *special message.* This would provide us with a third opportunity to test Nancy in yet another different testing environment.

On hearing this startling news, I became quite excited and a little nervous. With the very large crowds present on this apparition day, I did not want to take all my equipment down and move it to Nancy's house. So, I asked permission if we could go somewhere else much closer to receive this *special message,* and for this additional testing opportunity, preferably near the farm house property. A *green light* was given to us to perform this additional testing in the *adjacent room to the apparition room* within the farm house. This was very welcome news to me. Now we did not have to carry all of our heavy equipment over to Nancy's house as was originally planned, especially with over 80,000 pilgrims present for these medical and scientific studies. After the *apparition room* testing was completed, we rapidly started setting up in the *adjacent room:* an average-size bedroom with a simple fireplace. The cameras had to be strategically placed, considering that approximately fifteen people from our entire team would be working in this room.

In the adjacent room the fireplace mantle was a beautiful, resin/hand-carved wood *crucifix - Jesus on the cross* on the wall, measuring 15 inches tall and 9 inches across. On the mantle were some statuettes of angels and one of the Blessed Virgin Mary. Immediately in front of the fireplace were two kneeling pews. Directly behind the kneeling pews, the scientists and medical team set up all their electronic equipment: the Geiger counters; the ambulatory audiovisual TV-EEG telemetry system; the EMG of La Fayette; the TV and video cameras; the picram oscilloscope, the photonic ionic cord probes and amplifier, etc. Members of the medical and scientific research team present for this 3rd round of tests included: Dr. G. Hogben; Dr. P. Callahan and his dear wife, Winnie; Dr. R. Castanon; Dr. H. Velasquez and the radiation team; myself, Dr. R. M. Sanchez, with my wife and my medical team, the video expert and the Australian film crew busy filming a documentary of the testing.

As the medical and scientific team walked into the room, I placed myself immediately behind Nancy, directly in front of the resin/wood crucifix on the wall, approximately five feet from the wall. Then Nancy, George Collins, a Catholic priest and nun entered the adjacent room and knelt down. The priest and nun knelt right next to Nancy, with George directly behind them. The rest of the medical team and scientists completed their equipment setup. Then when we were all ready, the door was closed and *the testing* began.

As Nancy began to pray...I remember a feeling of calm and peace in this adjacent room despite the noise and clamor of the different radiation detecting equipments and cameras assembled behind Nancy. All our equipment was set up directly behind Nancy *(by design),* so that, as she was kneeling in prayer and looking up towards the crucifix on the wall, Nancy would not be able to see any of the equipment's display screen monitors. Interestingly, as soon as Nancy started praying, I began to hear the sounds of the Geiger counters commence *"clicking."* I immediately turned my head towards one of the display screens next to me to my right and observed that the picram oscilloscope display screen was suddenly starting to record a tremendous initial surge of low ionizing radiation fields of light energy or essentially a surge of the *invisible light radiation energy fields (below the visible light radiation spectra)* in the room. On Dr. Callahan's picram oscilloscope display screen I could see the sudden increases in the amplitude intensity readings from 1mV to a high of 80mV, then later to 90mV with *the probe* in her hand recording Nancy's atmospheric-skin boundary radiation readings *(her aura).*

As the instruments started to record the sudden increases in the *invisible* light radiation energy fields within the adjacent room, Nancy excitedly said, *"I see light."* A short time passed. And afterwards, as the readings on the monitors recorded decreasing levels in *the light* energy intensity, Nancy began to say, *"The light is now dimming...it is fading... it is now gone."*

Moments later, Nancy again said with excitement and joy, *"I see lights again, much, much brighter."* Dr. Callahan took another recording probe and positioned it almost on the wall and asked Nancy to tell him where *the light* was, so that he could try to place this probe as close to *the light* as possible. As he drew nearer and nearer to *the light* source on the wall, Dr. Callahan's picram oscilloscope recorded astronomical increases in the amplitude intensity (mV) of the *invisible* light radiation energy fields - *the light* source - *Nancy was seeing* on the wall. At this precise moment in time, Dr. Callahan's probe documented a reading of the atmospheric-wall boundary radiation energy fields near the crucifix on the wall of **80-90 mV!**

Dr. Callahan later said these spectacular energy surges just measured are similar to the tremendous surges of electrical energy readings produced in nature only by *flashes, bolts or darts of lightning* from the sky directly striking very near the vicinity of an actual recording probe. Dr. Callahan had never recorded Soliton waves with an amplitude intensity of more than 25 mV anywhere else in the world. Can you imagine real *flashes, bolts or darts of lightning energy* actually being recorded inside the bedroom of a farm house on a hot, clear and very dry day? Wow! Can anyone please explain this *new data? What* does all this really mean?

I remember watching Dr. Callahan closely as he opened his mouth in genuine disbelief and amazement at these *new data* energy readings—of *Soliton waves* with amplitudes in the high 80-90 mV range. Wow! Now to place this *new data* in another perspective that would be sort of similar in today's modern world of science: the *new data* recorded by Dr. Callahan would be like a race car driver registering speeds of over 5,000 miles per hour or incredibly like a meteorologist predicting winter temperatures of over 300°F. Get the picture? This amazing reading of 80-90 mV is truly so outlandish and unbelievable; especially, when you realize this *new data* was measured inside a bedroom on a very dry beautiful day with bright clear blue skies and no electrical lightning storms in sight.

Basically Dr. Callahan measured *flashes* or *bolts* or *darts of* ***lightning*** **- light energy** in this adjacent room at the very moment Nancy said, *"Everybody*, please kneel! ***Jesus****... our Lord and Savior...***is alive** on the cross *(crucifix)."* Nancy later told us that she could *see* ***the light*** *of Jesus* ***pulsating*** in intensity *around the cross* and could *hear Jesus speak interiorly (His living words)* to her. This occurred while the *Soliton waves* mV amplitude intensity readings (recorded at the same time) remained amazingly in 80-90 mV range. Here we see that *Jesus - in His Living Presence* and *His living words - in the light (His light)* generated the same exact type of *light energy.* Thus, we recorded and documented astronomical surges of *invisible light radiation energy fields* similar to real *flashes, bolts or darts of lightning - light energy* in Nancy's *aura* and *in the room.* So now I ask, *"What* does *Jesus - in His Living Presence* or *Jesus speaking His living words – in the light (His* living *light)* and *flashes, bolts or darts of lightning - light energy* have in common*?"*

I vividly remember kneeling out of respect and immediately noticing around me that most of the medical team and scientists who were atheists, agnostics, Jewish or hardened Christian skeptics *(like me)* were not kneeling. So, I asked aloud for everyone to *please kneel* out of respect. As they started to kneel together in near unison, I recall hearing Nancy say, "Thank You... Jesus. Thank You, Jesus for being here. Praise You...*Jesus."* Nancy's *aura* - now also measured 80-90mV!

At that moment, Dr. Callahan quickly stood up and the professor asked him to place one of the probes on the hand/wrist area of the *resin/wood crucifix.* At that moment Nancy said, *"Jesus* **is** *alive* on *the cross."* Then, one of the probes was placed on the resin/wood crucifix - *hand/wrist area* (as our audiovisual TV-EEG telemetry shows) and Dr. Callahan's picram oscilloscope display monitor started to record and register biological-like electrical energy ***pulsations, a real bioelectrical living pulse!*** Can you imagine our *(my)* surprise and astonishment? Dr. Callahan then quickly moved the probe onto the *chest-heart area* of the resin *corpus of Jesus* on the wood cross *(crucifix)* on the wall. Once again, at the precise moment *the probe* was placed over the resin *chest-heart region,* the picram oscilloscope again clearly detected an even stronger *pulsating biological type of electrical energy*—this is unbelievable. Can you imagine a *living pulse* emitting from a resin model *of Jesus crucified on a wood cross* on the wall at the exact moment in time Nancy says, *"Jesus* **is** *alive* on the cross." Wow! I can honestly say I would never have believed this if I had not been an eye-witness to this extraordinary event myself. I am quite sure many of you will (no doubt) initially succumb to pure gross intellectual pride of the *doubting Thomas* quagmire kind (just like I did). But everyone in the room did eye-witness this astonishing *new fact.* After being totally in awe of all its implications, I finally had to sit down. *Just imagine?* The detection of a bioelectrical type of pulsating activity that is seen only with *alive* biological electrical organisms of the *adult human species* variety - was now being recorded from this *(dead) resin/wood crucifix* --- an inanimate and seemingly non-living object, on the wall.

This *new data* just recorded occurred *only* during the moments in time that Nancy said, *"Jesus* **is** *alive* on the cross;" and when *hearing Jesus speak (His living words)* to Nancy (*interiorly),* while *seeing the light of Jesus* on the cross *in three dimensions.* Interestingly, Nancy saw a *three dimensional - light energy source.* Wow! So, *Who* or *what* was this *three dimensional light* energy source? Can you imagine actually recording *a living pulse, a heart beat like type of bio-electrical pulsating activity emitting from a seemingly non-living, lifeless* (dead) *resin model of Jesus crucified* on a wood cross? Just imagine our *(my)* surprise with this *new data.*

With great wonder and excitement, and also being a neurologist, I quickly asked Dr. Callahan to place *the probe* on the resin model ***head*** *of Jesus* crowned with thorns on the wood cross. As Dr. Callahan quickly placed *the probe* over and on *top of the head* area, again we immediately recorded *biological type of electrical pulsations,* but with a much faster frequency than was initially documented over the chest area. Wow! Wow! Wow! Later, much later when Dr. Callahan re-analyzed the frequency rate in cycles per second, he found that the new recorded rate was in the *alpha-beta* range - with approximately a 12-20 Hz pulsation activity range detected!

The *alpha-beta* range *(mostly beta)* is typically seen in *normal adult human EEG recordings, while awake and alert with eyes open.* This exciting *new data* actually implies that *the probe* was placed on a *head* of a *living normal adult human brain,* rather than being placed on the (dead) *resin head of Jesus* on a *wood cross.* Recall, we are eye-*witnesses* to this extraordinary event. What a *contradiction.* Imagine, an *alive* and *dead resin/wood crucifix?* Where else in these studies have we seen this type of *contradiction* - of being *alive* and *dead* simultaneously?

Recall how Dr. Callahan's recording of the *Schumann waves* frequency readings very closely *mimicked* our *EEG brain wave activity* frequency readings. I immediately thought to myself, *"I wonder...* is it possible that *Jesus* **is** *really alive...*on the cross at this moment*?"* While my hardened skeptical mind begged for even more proof, I could not resist the feeling of tremendous excitement over these very *new* astonishing developments.

During the testing Dr. Callahan had placed another probe approximately 7-12 inches away from the crucifix and off the wall of the adjacent room. Throughout the amazing new discoveries this new probe was measuring the atmospheric low ionizing radiation energy field readings in the room. Just prior to getting started *before the apparitions,* he measured the baseline atmosphere in the adjacent room. He found low ionizing radiation energy fields in the North American Aviation Radio Band Spectrum or in the *radio wavelength* radiation energy range. He measured a reading of about 800-1,000 Hz before the apparitions.

During the apparition of Jesus - alive on the cross, as well as, when Nancy later *heard Jesus speak (interiorly)* and saw *His Living Presence in the light* on the cross, Dr. Callahan measured a range of 3,000-4,000 Hz in the low ionizing *radio light energy fields* region of radiation, averaging ~3,300 Hz for the majority of the time with very brief and quick surges shooting up to 4,700-4,900 Hz. These brief quick surges of energy bursts occurring several times *only* when Nancy said, *"the crucifix* **is** bursting *in light,"* were amazing. All the above measurements were documented, while he was simultaneously recording with the other probe coherent bursts of energy or m*aser-like infrared laser signals* actually *emitting from the cross* on the wall; and also recording a 3-4 fold increase in the atmospheric *radio light radiation* energy fields in the adjacent room *during the apparitions.*

Dr. Callahan found this *new data* very intriguing, since in the history of medicine and anesthesia back in the 1800's dentists used a particular range of low ionizing radiation energy fields, a region called *electrical anesthesia,* also known as the *anesthesia region* in the 2,000-4,000+ Hz range. It was termed *anesthesia,* because this *radio light energy* placed with *a very low voltage* was actually used to *anesthetize* people before dental procedures. He said: *"Wherever* this energy reading is strong in the atmosphere, like during the *heavenly visits* or *apparitions,* it has a *very relaxing, calming* and surrounding overall *peaceful* feeling *effect."* No wonder, we felt such an incredible *calm* and totally *relaxing feeling* and such a *profound peace* in the adjacent room *in His Living Presence* especially during the moments Nancy said, *"Everybody,* please kneel...*Jesus* ...Our Lord and Savior... **is** *alive* on the cross." Nancy said she could see *the light of Jesus* pulsating with intense brightness *on the cross* and could *hear Jesus speak (interiorly).* So, what does *peace* and *Jesus (in His Living Presence* and *His living words - in the light, His light)* have in common? Where have we seen this before, in our studies?

At one point during *the testing,* the noise and clamor of the instruments in the room suddenly increased in intensity, thus registering again a tremendous increase in *the light* energy radiation field of the room. The Geiger counters appeared to be clicking faster, click, click, click, click... I quickly looked over towards Nancy, as she gently and reverently raised her head up and lifted up both arms and hands slowly.

While still in an apparent *state of ecstasy* with the typical radiant glow on her face, Nancy shouted out in a soft, reverent yet exuberant voice, *"How beautiful...*the *crucifix* **is** bursting *in light."* Following this Nancy said, *"The light* fluctuates with intensity at this very moment." Indeed, at this precise moment in time, I could simultaneously hear Dr. Callahan *shout out* with great awe and vigor, *"Did you* see that? Did... You... See... that? I am getting bursts... I am getting **bursts of light**." He joyfully jumped up and down smiling over the *new data* he was collecting at that very moment, which coincided precisely with Nancy's comments. Following this, Nancy said, *"Thank You, Jesus.* Praise You, *Jesus. The light* is getting dimmer... now it is much dimmer... *Jesus* just said, *'That is all.'* Now it's gone *(the light is gone)."* Almost simultaneously with Nancy's last statement, Dr. Callahan concurred, "The signal *(of light)* has disappeared."

Nancy jumped up and excitedly said, *"Oh my* goodness, *at the same time as I said it.* Wow... *Jesus* just said, *'That is all.' ...Thank You Jesus."* She then added, *"My* goodness...that is fascinating," remarking on the fact that *Jesus* just said, *"That is all,"* at the precise moment in time that all the instrument signals - recording *the light* bursts of energy in the room - had just disappeared. Wow! As Nancy was getting up to sit down from the kneeling position, Dr. Callahan handed her *the probe* again and asked her to please kneel down once more and say a *Hail Mary prayer,* so he could get another reading from her. With that, *the testing in the adjacent room* before the crucifix was concluded. During the *Hail Mary* prayer, while Nancy was kneeing down praying, she saw a *light* and for a brief moment again Dr. Callahan measured a tremendous quick surge of *light energy bursts* in the adjacent room with approximately 4,000 Hz and a *Soliton wave* amplitude intensity of 40 mV! I pondered. *What* is this? What just happened?

Both Dr. Hogben and the professor then completed the *after the apparitions* examinations and clinical observations for the psychiatric evaluations and neuropsychophysiological studies, all of which yielded *normal results* once again. As for me, I could not wait to get back to my laboratory to download the digital magnetic tapes into the Oxford II Tower and print the ambulatory EEG telemetry system hard copy and *raw data* results on EEG paper, and then review the entire appointed June 13th day (6/13) of the medical and scientific testing. Once again, I pondered. What will this *new data* show? What will it reveal?

The soundtracks of our video monitors recorded our excited awe-struck conversations following *the testing before the crucifix.* Dr. Callahan was asked to explain how a *(dead)* resin/ wood crucifix could produce *alive* type bioelectrical energy pulsations, and explain the bursts of maser-like energy or infrared laser light energy recorded, while Nancy was simultaneously seeing the living presence of *Jesus alive* on the cross in the form of *"mystical light* or *the light (His light),"* and was also *hearing Jesus (interiorly)* saying: ***"I am here."***

Dr. Callahan later elaborated, *"I cannot explain how* that (dead) *resin/wood cross (crucifix)* hanging on that wall can be emitting *(alive; living biological type of) electrical energy.* I was also detecting from this resin/wood cross maser-like bursts or infrared laser bursts or rather powerful coherent bursts of energy, which are called maser-like infrared *laser signals.* They were in the ***radio frequency*** not in the *(visible) light frequency.* Being in the radio frequency, they are not visible. But there is no way that a *resin/wood cross (crucifix)* could be producing that. I could go into my laboratory and produce those sort-of waves by building an electronic oscillator, but I can't explain it coming from the *resin/wood cross.* The only possible way it could be happening, is that *God is focusing some of these waves from the atmosphere onto the cross. He (God)* is focusing *the light* onto the cross, except that it is not light, light (visible light), it is radio light (invisible light). It is as if *the crucifix (Jesus on the cross)* has become temporarily *alive* because *God* has put *(His) energy into it from the atmosphere.* Or to put it another way, *the crucifix* is emitting radiation that it could not emit unless it was absorbing that radiation from the atmosphere and throwing it back at us, which essentially means, that the (dead) resin/*wood crucifix (Jesus - on the cross)* **is** *breathing light... it is* **ALIVE!**"

Dr. Callahan was asked this question: "Could the *living* energy… that you were detecting…coming from the *crucifix (Jesus on the cross)* be explained in any other way—maybe as being a product of *mass hysteria* or the *power of the minds* of people present in the room, who were focusing their attention on the crucifix?" Quickly Dr. Callahan retorted, "*What* counts that out immediately as an explanation is that when I quickly moved my probe detector away from the crucifix several times, *the signal went flat* each time. We all saw that, yet, we were all still in the room watching *what* I was doing. *Mass hysteria?* No way. The *power of the minds,* I can truly say without a single doubt, absolutely… *played no role here.*"

In this brief and special moment of my life, the entire research team *(and I)* eye-witnessed an amazing series of unprecedented and astonishing *supernatural events* with *medical and scientific documentation* unfold.

RESULTS OF THE TESTING – "JESUS IS ALIVE ON THE CROSS"

Even more astonishing were the *new medical and scientific results* when considered all together as a total package with the study of the subject Nancy and her external environment simultaneously. The unprecedented results will now be reviewed in the order of *the experiment design* from the pure science of the external environment to the intensive neurophysiological medical science of the subject:

A) Professor (now retired) Philip Callahan, Ph.D.

Dr. Callahan recorded with his patented photonic ionic cord amplifier Nancy's atmospheric-skin boundary radiation energy field *(aura)* changes, which increased from 1mV to 80-90mV. As mentioned, Dr. Callahan has never recorded *Soliton waves* with an amplitude intensity of more than 25 mV anywhere else in the world. In the *apparition room* earlier in the day, when the Blessed Virgin Mary brings baby Jesus and speaks to Nancy, he recorded *lightning light* amplitudes of 25-40 mV range. In the *adjacent room before the crucifix,* when *the light* intensity increased even further as Nancy said, "it was much brighter", the amplitude intensity at that moment increased to astronomical amplitudes of 80-90 mV in the *lightning* light *energy* range. According to Dr. Callahan, the incredible and astronomical increases documented in amplitude intensity levels remained at this very high level of intensity during the entire time Nancy said, *"Jesus* **is** *alive* on the cross." Can you imagine, scientifically *Nancy's aura* was *truly lightning energy* being reflected *in His Living Presence* at that moment. What an awesome *power source of energy recorded: the light intensity* of *flashes or bolts or darts of lightning energy in the apparition room, the adjacent bedroom and in Nancy's aura.* So, *what* does *flashes or bolts or darts of lightning* have in *common with Jesus - in His Living Presence?*

His second probe placed 7 to12 inches away from the crucifix. This probe was strategically placed there essentially to measure any atmospheric radiation energy changes in the room. As Dr. Callahan measured the atmospheric radiation energy in the *adjacent room in His Living Presence,* a 3-4 fold increase was recorded that generated a very *relaxing, calm and peaceful light energy.* He also measured the atmospheric-skin boundary radiation changes in *Schumann waves* on Nancy which measured 3-4Hz *(similar to the brain waves of deep sleep),* while the *Soliton waves* amplitude intensity levels had amazingly increased from I mV to 80-90 mV. Thus, the surface area of Nancy's aura/atmospheric-skin boundary radiation energy fields actually recorded an amazing surge in the *lightning light* energy intensity range.

Now with the second probe *in His Living Presence,* Dr. Callahan recorded and documented --- low ionizing radiation energy field increases in the *radio wave* radiation energy *(invisible) light spectrum* from a baseline reading of 800-1000 Hz to a range of 3,000-4,000 Hz, which is a full 3-4 fold increase in energy from the original *baseline* range --- in the room. Interestingly, physicists and dentists often call this *radio wave frequency-light radiation energy* region in the range of 2,000-4,000+ Hz, the *electrical anesthesia range.* This range was *only generated* in both the apparition room and the adjacent room *in His Living Presence* or when *the Blessed Virgin Mary is bringing baby Jesus to us.* As mentioned before, this energy was used by dentists in the 1800's to help *calm and relax* their patients before performing dental procedures. No wonder, we all felt so incredibly *calm and relaxed* with a deep penetrating feeling of profound *peace and tranquility.* Thus, a truly relaxing and *peaceful light* is generated *in His Living Presence.* Dr. Callahan believes that this is just another example of *how God manipulates His Own created science* to ready or perhaps to prepare *His* adopted children as well as *His chosen souls* for being - *in His Living Presence.*

Neither the medical and scientific team nor I could adequately explain in words just how profound this penetrating feeling of *peace* and a sense of *total relaxation* was felt by all of us *(including me)* in the adjacent room. But, maybe now we have a scientific explanation. Thus, when Nancy said, *"Jesus* **is** *alive* on the cross*,"* we recorded and documented at that moment instantaneous *peace interiorly* with the delta *deep sleep* EEG pattern and *exteriorly* with a deeply relaxing and *peaceful light* called *electrical anesthesia*. So, *what* does *Jesus* and *peace* have in common?

We recorded all this exciting *new data* during the time that Nancy said*, "Jesus* **is** *alive* on the cross*,"* and was seeing *the light* and *in His Living Presence* in the form of a *mystical light* (explanation: *mystical light* is a light a *chosen soul* sees that others do not see, but thanks to modern technology we actually recorded and documented *the light* energy in our medical and scientific studies that is *invisible* to our eyes, but *visible* to the *chosen souls* and our research equipment). While Nancy was claiming to see *the light* on the cross and *hear Jesus - His living words interiorly,* Dr. Callahan amazingly detected biological-type electrical energy pulsations emitting from the *wrist area* and then later from the *chest/heart area* of the (dead) resin corpus of Jesus on the wood cross *(crucifix)* on the wall of the adjacent room. Dr. Callahan placed the probe, I had requested, on the resin *head of Jesus - crowned with thorns*. He again unbelievably detected (and we were all eyewitnesses to this fact) biological-type electrical pulsations, but now with a faster frequency. Can you imagine our utter astonishment and surprise with these *new* and unbelievably provocative scientific findings? Can you imagine my total awe and wonder at what Dr. Callahan was actually recording? Where these faster frequencies true bioelectrical brain wave activity pulsations?

Later, fully analyzed these bioelectrical pulsations recorded and documented were definitely found to be in the *alpha-beta* 12-20Hz frequency range *(mostly beta),* which is a typical frequency range for an alive, awake and alert normal - adult human brain with eyes open. But, how can this be possible? Since we all saw (I saw) *the probe* placed on top of the (dead) resin *head of Jesus* on the wood cross. How is it possible that we measured *living* bioelectrical type pulsations from a *(dead)* resin/wood crucifix? Did *Jesus* really *come* ***alive*** on the cross? Was *Jesus* really and truly *alive,* as Nancy said so many times *during the heavenly visitations?*

Then Nancy said*, "How beautiful...the crucifix* **is** now *bursting in light;"* and then said*, "The light* fluctuates in intensity at this very moment.*"* At this precise time, Dr. Callahan then detected from ***the cross*** maser-like *infrared* ***laser bursts*** or coherent bursts of light energy -- that are called *maser-like infrared* ***laser signals****.* Dr. Callahan explained that this was not light, light (visible light), but radio light energy (invisible light). Later, he explained to us that *the crucifix (Jesus on the cross)* was actually *emitting light radiation energy* that it could not possibly emit, unless it were absorbing that light radiation from the atmosphere and then throwing it back at us in the room. He felt this essentially meant that *the crucifix,* the (dead) resin/wood image of *Jesus* crucified on the cross (on the wall) was ***breathing light,*** and thus, the (dead) resin/wood model of *Jesus* crucified on the cross ---**is *alive!***

NOTE: All these amazing *new findings* occurred *only during the same, exact* and precise *times and moments* that Nancy said, *"Jesus* **is** *alive* on the cross*."*

Are you *speechless* yet?

As a hardened skeptic, thanks to my many years of professional medical and scientific training, I certainly had and have a lot of explaining to do with the new data and all the astonishing *new scientific hardcore facts.* Yes, I was speechless then and for a long while, but not now. According to these meticulously tested facts, our astonishing and wondrous *new medical and scientific data... Jesus* **is** *alive!* So, what does *Jesus - in His Living Presence* and *the light* have in common? What does *Jesus – in His Living Presence* and *the life* (living/alive) have in common? And what does *the light, the life (living/alive), the cross* and *Jesus – in His Living Presence* all have in common?

Please ponder this: *On the cross* we scientifically recorded *the light – Jesus - in His Living Presence,* so we can truly say ***the light*** *and* **Jesus on the cross are *one.*** This is a very, very special moment indeed when Nancy says, ***"Jesus* is *alive on the cross."*** Recall, we scientifically recorded and documented *living* type emissions of bioelectrical pulsations from *the light* on the cross and from *the light* of the cross on the wall. Thus, we can say *the light on the cross* and *of the cross* that **is** *living* and very much *alive* **is** *the life* --- that **is** *one with Jesus* --- the moment Nancy said, *"Jesus* **is** *alive* on the cross*."*

This is very exciting news... Dr. Callahan recorded *the light* energy in the range of low ionizing radiation energy *emitting* from the resin/wood *crucifix (Jesus on the cross)* on the wall in the form of maser-like coherent bursts or infrared laser bursts or signals. This is indeed very significant, as it supports and confirms Nancy's claims of actually seeing *bursts of light,* when literally saying, *"The crucifix* **is** *bursting in light."* Dr. Callahan summarized his observations by saying, ***"The crucifix... Jesus* on the cross... is breathing light... it is alive!**" Now, I will summarize Dr. Callahan's *new data:* The *glory of Jesus* on the cross – *in His Living Presence* **is** a *true Living Light. Thus,* ***the Living Light* on and of *the cross /in, with* and *through the cross and His Living Presence* is *one.*** Wow! This is deep.

B) Dr. Humberto Velasquez

Dr. Velasquez along with his radiation team recorded the actual visual evidence of low ionizing light radiation energy by accident or maybe by *coincidence (God-incidence). The light* energy could be actually seen on his video (the video that was used by the radiation team to document the Geiger counter display monitor readings). On the video, just behind the Geiger counter display monitors, you can definitely see *bursts of white light* as well as *increases in the intensity of the light,* during the same time Dr. Callahan was also recording *(maser-like, invisible)* infrared laser bursts of light *(radio light) emitting from the crucifix.* What the video actually recorded was *the visible light - coherent bursts of laser white light signals,* consisting of rather dense *coherent bursts of white light,* as seen *dancing on the wall.* As seen with and through our own human eyes, these dense *coherent bursts of white light* have a slight *silver white hue.* This slight *silver white hue color* change from *pure white light* is a well known physiological response of *the human retina* to dense coherent bursts of *white laser light.* Thus, what we recorded and literally eye-witnessed was *physiologically correct.* These abundant dense coherent bursts of laser white light signals *seen flashing on the wall* by most of the people in the room was also *filmed by chance* in the background of the radiation team's video, while the video was actively recording and documenting the Geiger counter's display monitor readings.

Dr. Velasquez and the radiation team's equipment in the adjacent room once again detected statistically *insignificant* changes in the *gamma* radiation energy fields. Thus the high ionizing *gamma* radiation detected *during the apparitions* was **not** statistically significant. Basically, there were no statistically significant changes in the amount of *gamma* radiation detected*: before, during and after the heavenly visits or apparitions.* Thus, the *gamma* radiation energy readings *did not change significantly* during these *heavenly visitations* or *apparitions* or *supernatural events.* Recall, Dr. Velasquez's Geiger counters were calibrated for recording only the high ionizing light radiation energy field changes and not the low ionizing light radiation energy field changes.

The amazing *white laser lights* recorded on video *by chance* documented *the light* energy changes seen in the 3% *visible light spectra range.* These low and extremely low light radiation energy field changes with all the amazing and astronomical increases were dramatically corroborated by Dr. Callahan's very specialized and patented equipment *only* while recording - *in His Living Presence.*

Recall, Dr. Callahan recorded these amazing statistically significant changes with the documented tremendous increases in the extremely low and low ionizing radiation energy fields in the form of *(maser-like) laser bursts or signals* and also by recording the increases of *radio light energy* in the atmosphere of the adjacent room from 800-1000 Hz to +3,000-4,000 Hz range called *electrical (magnetic) anesthesia.* This is a relaxing *peaceful light energy* that actually *generates* a profound calm and a very deep penetrating *peace* and relaxing atmosphere. Also, Dr. Callahan recorded astronomical increases in the *Soliton wave's* amplitude intensity from 1 mV to 80-90 mV simulating powerful *flashes or bolts or darts of lightning* light energy from Nancy's atmospheric-skin boundary radiation energy fields *(her aura)* in the adjacent bedroom. Imagine Nancy blazing in lightning.

Thus, *Nancy* with her intense *aura of lightning* **is** like a *dart of lightning.*

C) Professor R. Castanon, Ph.D.

The professor's clinical neuropsychological observations of Nancy were recorded and documented during the announcement, *"Jesus* **is** *alive* on the cross." He found Nancy to be *normal,* and basically in the same normal neuropsychological state that was documented earlier in the day in the previous apparition room as studied *during the heavenly visits.* However, the neuropsychophysiology studies performed using the EMG system from La Fayette once again recorded *during the heavenly visits* of *Jesus - in His Living Presence* an astonishing and unprecedented **0 micro-Volts.**

Recall, the measurement of 0 micro-Volts is *only* recorded when you are *dead.* But Nancy was obviously not dead, and she was and is very much *alive.* So, what does this mean? Nancy is once again recorded and documented by this instrument to be basically *as dead.* What a *contradiction of known physiological terms and principles.* How can you possibly be *alive and dead at the same time?* What a *contradiction.* Or is this what it means to be ***as dead?*** And just what does the phenomenon *as dead* have in common *with the living presence of Jesus?* The professor also had earlier completed a neuropsychological battery of Nancy and found the entire study to be *normal,* which demonstrated no psychotic, neurotic, affective, thought, mood, or personality disorders, and no clinical evidence of any malingering or lying or hysteria, and no epileptic behavior.

D) George Hogben, M.D., Psychiatrist

Dr. Hogben's psychiatric clinical observations after the apparitions were already previously discussed in the last chapter. Please see his entire report for a complete analysis and psychiatric assessment. To reiterate his psychiatric impression in a generalized form: Nancy was found to be *normal* from a psychiatric point of view *before, during and after both apparitions* of June 13th, 1993 in the apparition room and the adjacent room. It is very important to know from a medical and scientific perspective that Nancy has been meticulously examined from a psychiatric point of view repeatedly and found to be *normal with no psychiatric disturbance* in all of the many examinations performed by a very qualified New York Board Certified psychiatrist.

E) Ramon M. Sanchez, M.D., Neurology, Epileptology/ Neurophysiology

Nancy's brain waves before the visits of Jesus were similar to the EEG baseline studies. The EEG demonstrated *normal* alpha rhythms with mixed beta activity with eyes open in the posterior head regions. With eyes closed, more prominent alpha patterns were noted in the posterior head regions and with low amplitude beta activity seen over the anterior head regions. At the precise moment when Nancy announced that *Jesus* ***is*** *alive on the cross* — 3 Hz delta rhythms (*deep sleep* patterns- while awake) were again recorded. This unprecedented *new* brain wave activity was recorded up until the very moment Nancy says, *"Jesus* said, *'That is all.'"* And simultaneous with Nancy's announcement, Dr. Callahan said, *"All* the *(maser-like coherent bursts of infrared) laser signals* have now disappeared." At this moment in time, we could all hear the clamor and noise emanating from the monitoring equipment in the adjacent room suddenly become silent. Then, the same initial range of readings documented earlier in the *baseline studies* and *before the apparition testing* was again recorded from both the EEG and the different monitoring equipment in the room.

During the moment when Nancy said, *"Jesus* **is** *alive* on the cross," the sixteen channel intensive monitoring ambulatory audiovisual TV-EEG telemetry system recorded a sudden and profound increase in medium to higher amplitude *delta* rhythms with a brain wave frequency ranging from 2.5-3.5 Hz. There was a predominance of *3 Hz delta rhythms* recorded with no spikes, no sharp waves, no epileptic activity and no epileptic behavior. Can you imagine - 3 Hz delta rhythms were once again recorded forming the astonishing and unprecedented *new* EEG pattern of 333. On this very special occasion, however, the 333 EEG pattern was now being detected with a >30% higher amplitude than all the previous recordings. The 3 Hz delta rhythms formed a *deep sleep* topographic EEG pattern and at times even generalized over the entire brain, while Nancy was still awake, alert with intensely focused attention and eyes open. Wow!

The 3 Hz *delta rhythms* again were recorded on EEG predominantly over the frontal temporal central parietal regions, bilaterally, with no focal slow waves or sharp waves, no spikes or spike wave activity, no paroxysmal discharges, and no epileptic activity or epileptic behavior. Nancy's eyes were open with focused attention and markedly decreased blinking, typical for states of *ecstasy.* During this time you could actually see the *beta rhythms* actually *riding on top* of the 3 Hz *delta rhythms* in all channels with slight accentuation in the anterior regions bilaterally. The *beta rhythms* recorded on EEG were typical for a fully awake, alert normal adult brain with focused attention.

For the few brief moments when Nancy closed her eyes, most of the *beta activity* disappeared. Despite some anterior *beta* rhythms most of the brain wave activity recorded while awake with eyes closed was the 3 Hz *delta rhythms* of moderate to high amplitudes. Thus, on EEG Nancy's brain was in a *heavy sleep,* a *deep sleep,* while simultaneously *awake and alert* with a radiant glow seen on her face during this entire period of time. Nancy was in a state of *ecstasy.* Once again we were all eye-witnesses of this *oxymoron* and *pure contradiction* of physiological medical science. This *contradiction* was clearly visible and seen on the ambulatory audiovisual TV-EEG telemetry monitoring system and eye-witnessed by all those hardened skeptics in the room *(like me).* As soon as *Jesus* said to Nancy, *"That is all."* Nancy's brain waves returned almost instantaneously *(within milliseconds)* to her *baseline study* EEG brain wave activity patterns, which are all *normal.* At this point, we had now acquired a lot of *new data* on Nancy's brain wave activity EEG patterns, now encompassing many hours of EEG testing to compare with.

Of all the EEG studies documented to date on Nancy *in His Living Presence,* when *Jesus appears* to Nancy *alive* or when *Jesus speaks* to Nancy – *His living words* in *the light (His light)* or when Nancy sees *the light/Jesus in light/the living light/the living presence of Jesus in light,* Nancy's EEG electrical brain wave picture was the *most* unprecedented in the above studies. Recording an *alive pulsating light/living light/ or life giving light* from *the cross* as *God* declares the *(dead)* lifeless *resin/wood crucifix* on the wall *to come alive* with *Jesus on the cross* and Nancy sees *Jesus alive on the cross,* was just amazing. Just imagine all this astonishing *new data* is now *recorded by science* in the adjacent room. Is this what *Jesus foretold* to Nancy in the apparition room? Recall, *Jesus* said, *"Watch what I will do."*

Dr. John Walsh, a highly regarded neurologist and EEG expert of the Royal Prince Alfred Hospital in Sydney, Australia, claims that it is a *physiological impossibility* for any subject to have 3 Hz delta EEG brain wave activity and be awake, alert and conscious. Nonetheless, it was this *physiological impossibility* that we somehow repeatedly recorded and documented during all *the testing* of Nancy *in His Living Presence – in the living presence of Jesus.* Later, I privately asked Nancy how she felt *during the tests* kneeling before the crucifix. Nancy replied, *"In the presence of His light,* I experience *His Living Presence* and *His* all-embracing love, joy, mercy and *peace."*

Nancy's simple yet profound answer led me to seriously wonder, *"Had* we somehow measured *the peace of God...?"* Almost as soon as I considered it, however, I was deeply humbled at what must have surely been our good Lord's amusement over it. Are we so vain and prideful to even suggest that we could ever *measure His* true *peace* or even *His* immeasurable *love and mercy?* But for every bit of *new data* God allowed us to measure according to our meager human scientific standards, imagine how much more exists that no mere man could ever conceive or even calibrate.

In God's *Divine Will, He gives* us *so much with His charity, His* awesome unconditional *love*, unmatchable *self-sacrifice,* that is so generous and *always abundantly giving* to overflowing, and *His* unfathomable *Divine Mercy* towards us in *His* creation and magnificent handiwork, we (I) can only imagine we are measuring a mere *glimpse of God.* What an awesome glimpse! But in reality and in retrospect: *God was, is, and will be* always measuring us (me).

With all of God's Divine assistance, help, mercy, love, patience, blessings and graces how can we (I) possibly go wrong? O yeah, I almost forgot --- man's *human free will.*

Our *journey science to faith* continues...

REFLECTIONS ON THE TESTING – "JESUS IS ALIVE ON THE CROSS"

After reviewing the medical and scientific results of the repeatedly numerous and meticulous tests and clinical observations of Nancy during the testing before (in front of) the crucifix, I could not help but wonder about the true nature of *the light* that we had detected. Using very specialized instruments, Dr. Callahan detected the presence of significant increases of both extremely low and low ionizing radiation energy field changes which indeed represents *the essence of light energy.* Recall, Dr. Callahan recorded *maser-like infrared* coherent *laser bursts* in the form of *radio light,* while Dr. Velasquez's video by chance actually filmed *bursts of dense coherent white light laser signals* on the wall around the crucifix just behind the Geiger counter display monitors being filmed. Dr. Velasquez visually detected on video *by chance or by co-incidence* the tremendous increases of low ionizing radiation energy fields in the *visible light radiation spectra* by documenting these dense coherent bursts of *white light laser signals* with a *silver hue (as seen by the human retina)* near and around each different crucifix on the walls of both the apparition room and the adjacent room that was tested on this day *during the heavenly visitations or visions or apparitions.* Moreover the fact that Dr. Velasquez did not measure any statistically significant increases of *gamma* radiation energy fields *before, during or after the apparitions* really proves that *Nancy's visions, heavenly visits and apparitions* are indeed not fraught with any harmful radiation effects. God forbid.

In my journey science to faith, I soon painstakingly realized that we had somehow unbelievably, incredibly, amazingly, and in reality detected and documented *His Living Presence in* ***the light*** *(His light) on the cross* hanging on the wall of the adjacent room. Wow! Although this *new data* was indisputable from a medical and scientific perspective, in the beginning of my research I really did not understand all the potential *faith based implications* or the reality of what these *new hardcore facts (not fiction)* really meant. After reviewing all our meticulous tests, facts and figures pertaining to all the medical and scientific data collected and even after reaching my 49th birthday almost 10 years after all the studies were completed, I can say now without a doubt, that our collective and unprecedented *new data* was and **is** truly *a pure gift from God.* Our *new medical and scientific data* clearly *confirms* and amazingly shows that *God* **is** *alive* and really exists. Sorry atheists.

In awe of God's majestic unconditional tender love and *His Divine Mercy* towards all *His* created children, I can now begin to see a glimpse of *His Glory.* I can now see how again and again *God* is always demonstrating **His** awesome power repeatedly through *His Divine Will, His* merciful love, *His* charity and humility *on the cross* towards *us (me)* personally, our family, *the Church* and *all souls* in this world. I can now also see a glimpse of just how *jealous God* is of all our love for *Him;* especially, after generously placing on my lap all the *evidence* collected from our astonishing *new medical and scientific data,* which literally *proves* or *confirms* the real true *living presence* and *existence of God.* It shows us all incredulous medical scientists, intellectuals and hardened skeptics (like me), that this *new data* scientifically *confirms* the real true *living presence* and *existence of God.*

Atheists beware: C.S. Lewis is right; sorry Freud. Dr. Armand M. Nicholi, Jr. has a new book called *The Question of God?* Based on a popular course he taught at Harvard University for over 25 years where the question over the existence of God is fiercely debated by studying the teachings and writings of two historically giant intellectuals -Sigmund Freud *(a Jew turned atheist)* and C.S. Lewis *(an atheist turned Christian).* The principle *question* they ask is: *Does God really exist?* In this heated debate the two intellectuals virtually square off on the existence of God. So, for those who are still looking for the right answer, you need to look no further. I believe God has humbly in His awesome love, mercy and charity for us has given me (personally) and the entire medical and scientific team *the answer* to this very fundamental and central issue for all humanity. Based on our *new* collective medical and scientific research *data,* C.S. Lewis is *right on.* So, the debate is finally over. Sorry, Freud. ***The answer* is** (drum roll please): ***Yes! God really exists!*** Recall, our collective *data* finally gave me and all of us hardened skeptics something real, hardcore and truly *tangible* to sink our *(my)* teeth into. I can now see the real true medical and scientific *living proof* and *confirmation* of *His Living Presence,* as was repeatedly tested and documented in our studies. I can say *living proof* because we have documented our *new data* on video. Thus, where *faith alone* did not suffice – it is now literally in black and white (and in full color) for the whole world to see. But now we must decipher its total and true glorious meaning and significance. So, the *journey science to faith* continues...

In a message to Nancy dated December 12th, 1990, Jesus said, *"I use the crucifix to show you my light and my constant presence. You are to bear witness to my living presence and to show the world my love and mercy through the cross. I, the Risen Lord, appeared most in the light of the cross and I am one with the Holy Trinity of God. The light and the cross are one... believe and know I love you and help the world to know and believe I love them all equally. Remember to tell the world that this Light is Me."*

The imagery of Dr. Callahan's observations when he said, ***"I am getting light,"*** and later, ***"The crucifix (Jesus on the cross) is breathing light...it is alive,"*** while Nancy was seeing *the* living *light* of Jesus *in His Living Presence on the cross* and was simultaneously *hearing Jesus speak* to her *(interiorly),* was indeed very remarkable. Based on the unprecedented *new data* just obtained, we can medically and scientifically conclude, that the **dead** resin/wood crucifix , indeed, became **alive** and *came to life with living pulsations --- from the living light of Jesus,* when Nancy said, *"Everyone,* please kneel. *Jesus...* our Lord and savior... **is** *alive* on the cross..." This is truly amazing. Please feel free to shout it out along with me any time. All in one chorus, together now and please don't be shy: *"Holy, holy, holy, the Lord of hosts"* (Isaiah 6:3)! If another explanation exists for all the above findings, it has yet to be discovered by modern scientific techniques. So, *what* is the real message *God* is trying to give to us and especially me and the medical and scientific research team on this appointed and anointed day of (6/13) June 13th, 1993? And *why* is *God* trying so hard to reach us and give us these *urgent messages?* I pondered. *What* exactly is *Jesus* or *Our Loving Mother* trying to tell us faithless hardened skeptics *(like me)* and the entire world?

I now believe that *God (the Holy Trinity)* and *Our Loving Mother* are mercifully, lovingly and urgently trying to tell all of us through our medical and scientific testing that not only does *God* really exist, but *His Living Presence* **is** very much *alive, tangible, and approachable.* In my search for *the truth* concerning the *heavenly visitations* or *visions* or *apparitions,* I soon found out that *the Holy Bible* **is** *in harmony with* ***the truth.*** The Bible is an incredible source of revelation (especially when *connected* to our medical and scientific data) for all to see *the mystery of all mysteries: the Holy Trinity - One God, His Divine Will* and *His Living Presence* with *His signature* - 333! See Chapter 9. I soon realized *the Holy Spirit, the Bible* and *the Church* were going to be *my best sources of information* to hopefully answer all my very personal questions raised by the collective medical and scientific research on the *three chosen souls.* Interestingly, the word the B.i.b.l.e. some say stands for:

Basic **I**nstructions **B**efore **L**eaving **E**arth

What did *the Holy Bible* teach me in the past 10 years? I learned that *the heavenly Father sent His only begotten Son, Jesus,* (Psalm 2:7) *to visit His chosen people the Jews first and then the Gentiles* (Genesis 49:10; Psalm 2; Isaiah 26:21; 42:1-7; 49:5-13; 52:9-10; 56:5-8; 66:18-22; Micah 1:3; Zachariah 13:1-9) - in the early rains (Psalm 72:2-8;Isaiah 45:8; 55:10-11; Ezekiel 34:26; Hosea 6:3; Joel 2:23) as was prophesized to be *the prophet, the high priest,* and *the king* in the form of both the *Son of God* and the *Son of man* (Deuteronomy 18:15-18; Psalms 2, 8, 44, 72, and 110; Proverbs 30:4-5; Wisdom 2:12-13; Isaiah 9:6-8; Jeremiah 33:14-17; Ezekiel 37:22-24); *Jesus* the only true living *Messiah* was the anointed prophet (Deuteronomy 18:15-18); the anointed high priest in the *order of Melchisedech* and the anointed King of kings of the Jews (Genesis 49:10; Numbers 24:16-19; Psalms 2; 45:2-8; 68:12-13; 72:2-17; 89:27-30; 110:1-7; Isaiah 9:6-8; 11:1-5; 41:1-5; 49:5-13, 22-23; Jeremiah 33:14-17; Ezekiel 37:19-28; Zachariah 6:12-13; Rev 19:16) with the crown of thorns *He* willingly accepted death on a tree *on the cross,* see the passion of *the Christ* (Genesis 49:10-11; Psalm 22; Psalm 69:4-27; Wisdom 2:12-21; Isaiah 50: 6-7; 52:13-15; 53:1-12; 63:1-3; Zachariah 9:11-12) and the crucifixion (Genesis 49:10-11; Psalm 22; Wisdom 2:12-21; Isaiah 25:11; 49:16; 53:1-12; 63:1-3; Jeremiah 11:15-19; Zachariah 3:8-9; 12:10; 13:6-7); though *He* was sinless

(Wisdom 2:12-14; Isaiah 53:9-11; Jeremiah 11:15-19; Sophonias 3:5) *He* was offered because it was His own Will (Isaiah 53:7), so *He* could perfectly fulfill *His* Father's Divine Will by taking on all the sins of mankind for their salvation and redemption (Deuteronomy 49:10-11; Isaiah 53:1-12; Micah 7:18-20; Sophonias 3:14-17; Zachariah 9:9-17); the perfect *"sacrifice of praise"* (Psalms107:13-22;116:16); *the lamb of God Who* takes away the sins of the world (John 1:29-36; Rev 12:10-11; 19:6-13;21:22-27; 22:13-16) and through *His* resurrection (Psalms 3:4-6; 15:8-11; Isaiah 25:6-11; 26:19; Ezekiel 37:9; Hosea 6:3; 13:14; Amos 9:11; Jonas 2:7; Micah 7:7-8; Sophonias 3:7-9; Zachariah 9:13-14) and *His* ascension into heaven (Psalms 110:1; 67:5), so that anyone who believes in the *One Who He sent* (Deuteronomy 49:10) can be saved and *live eternally* forever in *His* Kingdom, the real true paradise! And he who keeps all of *His* commandments of love and receives *Him, He* will then dwell within you. *He* loved you so much, that *He* actually died for each and every one of you! First, *He* died for *His chosen people* the Jews and then for you and me and all of the Gentiles. Through *the life giving power of God's Holy Spirit, God* sends to me and you the *living waters of Baptism* (Ezekiel 36: 25-26; John 3:5) and later the *Baptism of fire* (3 Kings18:36-39;Luke 12:49) and *the spirit of grace* that is given freely to be *born again in spirit* and *in truth* (John 4:23-24). Now all of mankind (yes, you and *me*) has a true chance to receive *"the way, and the truth and the life"* (John 14:6); *"the life"* which **is** *eternal life.*

So, we can live in the *new heavenly Jerusalem* and enter into *God's circle* of love, circle of fire, circle of blessings, circle of power, and circle of *life. God invites you* now to His banquet and welcomes all of you prodigal sons and daughters into *His living circle* where *God* becomes a *living wall of fire* that destroys all your enemies round about you - Psalm 96(97), and is the *living flames of love – His Signature 333.* You can be saved from eternal damnation *(hell)* just by accepting, believing in and following the One Who He *(Father God)* sent – *Jesus* – the living Son of God, the *anointed one,* the Jewish *Messiah, the Cristos* or *the Christ,* the (living) word of God, the Incarnate Wisdom, the Prince of Peace, the light, the law, the Lord God of Israel – 6 1 3 - the Holy One of Israel, the Sun of Justice, lightning that lighteneth from under heaven, the Orient, the Angel of the Lord, the living bread which came down from heaven, the Prophet, the Highest Priest forever in the order of Melchisedech, and the victim (God's greatest Holocaust – *sin and peace offering*) – the bridegroom, the good shepherd, the door, the vine, right arm and right hand of God, the finger of God, a fiery law, the living Temple of God, the everlasting light, the everlasting peace, the first and the last, the beginning and the end, the Alpha and the Omega, the root and stock of David, the morning light, the bright and morning star, the desired of all nations, the covenant of peace, *the new everlasting covenant,* the only begotten Son of God, the beloved Son of God, the living Son of God, the Son of man, the way, the truth and the life, *the Holy Eucharist!* Holy, Holy, Holy, Lord God of Hosts, heaven and earth is full of Your Glory, *Hosanna in the*

Highest! Blessed is He who comes in the name of the Lord. Praise you Father God Almighty. Praise you Jesus. Praise you Holy Spirit. Praise you Holy Trinity – One God. So, come on now and please ask *Jesus* to come into your life, and through *His Precious Blood* receive *the Holy Spirit, the Spirit of Truth,* and receive *Jesus - the Truth* and be redeemed, justified, sanctified and *be converted to God,* be saved and be born again. Receive God's immeasurable love and mercy. Receive eternal salvation. So, choose *life* not death. Praise the Lord! Praise God the Almighty!

Inspirations from the Holy Spirit - a love letter to all Muslims

Attention to all beloved Muslims who worship *Allah* - Please take notice that your God – *Allah* - asks you, your sons and your daughters *(if you are willing)* to make the ultimate sacrifice --- to die in *Jihad* for the glory of Allah in order to assure yourselves a place in paradise (Heaven). Now please let me introduce you to the most loving, kind, gentle, merciful and awesome living God, Who sent *His* only begotten *Son - Jesus - to die for you,* your sons and your daughters; so that if *you* will believe in *the One He sent* - the only begotten and living Son of God - *Jesus* - all of you, including your sons and your daughters, can live eternally with God in paradise --- forever in peace, love, joy, and heavenly bliss, and *no Jihad* **is** needed! So, come taste and see the goodness of the Lord. Come and see *"the true light of the world."* See how your ancestors from Arabia, Saba and Tharsis found *Him - the light of the world* long ago (over 2,000 years) lying in a manger, in Bethlehem, in swaddling clothes, after following the *great new star* in the heavens, as was foretold over 3,300 years ago (Torah: Numbers 24:17). So, come now, believe, and follow *Jesus, "the bright and morning star"* (Rev 22:16). Come and see the awesome one true God, the Holy Trinity, the Three-fold Unity and mystery of the Three in One – God; no - not three Gods, but *One Triune God, One in substance and undivided, the Divine Will of God. Jesus, "the word of God (the Father)"/ "wisdom" incarnate (John 1:14) and "the bread of God" incarnate* (John 6:33-41) was sent to this world by Father God with the power of the Holy Spirit of God for you and for me. *Jesus* wants to heal you - *all of you* - including all your sons and daughters of *Abraham* and of *Islam.* Yes, *Jesus* wants to dry all of your tears and remove all your fears. So, please come taste and see the goodness of the Lord. Come to the *everlasting covenant of peace* (Isaiah 54:10 and Ezekiel 34:22-25) just like *your ancestors* did on a silent holy night. Amen.

Dear beloved Muslims, please remember your own rich history. See how *your ancestors,* the wise men, the kings of Saba, Arabia and Tharsis came looking for the newborn king of Israel 2,000 yrs. ago. They followed a great new *rising star* as it settled over the city of David, Bethlehem, in Judea; interestingly called *"the city of Bread."* They came to see and pay homage to the newborn king, as was foretold in the ancient Holy Scriptures, the *Torah - The word of God,* as written by Moses, a

Jew, raised as the son of the daughter of an Egyptian Pharaoh. The three middle-eastern Arab and Persian kings and wise men *(your ancestors)* came to offer gifts for the newborn *King of kings.* The Bible says they followed the *great new star* and found the *baby Jesus* in a manger wrapped in swaddling clothes. They *(your ancestors)* brought to the newborn king of Israel *(Jesus)* gold, frankincense and myrrh. And interestingly, please note that roughly ~ 610 years later *Muhammad, your prophet,* came onto the scene preaching *Islam,* and died by 632(633) A. D.; but, by the year 666 A.D. Muhammad's *new teachings* sparked the start of the Islamic movement against Judeo-Christians when it began attacking Sicily in Italy. So, in the year 666 A.D., interestingly, Islam's movement *against Christ, against the Jewish Messiah,* was born. Thus, *the very first major anti-Christ movement ever recorded in history was in the year 666 A.D.*

Please recall, the three kings and wise men *(your ancestors)* came following *the new rising star* after reading and hearing *the holy words of God* as it is written in the most ancient and holy scriptural writings found in the *Torah.* This was written by Moses well over 3,300 years ago, see Numbers 24:17*: "...a star shall rise out of Jacob and a septre (kingship or kingdom) shall spring up from Israel."* Now see your spiritual father Abraham, while he was still a Gentile called *Abram,* in Genesis12:3: *"...in thee* shall all the kindred be blessed*."* Also in Genesis 22:18: "And *in thy seed* shall all the nations of the earth be blessed, because thou hast obeyed my voice*."* These passages are very important since before the destruction of the Jerusalem Temple by the Romans in 70 AD, the genealogy of *Jesus* was historically recorded and documented in the Temple. *Jesus* can be perfectly traced back to *the seed of Abraham,* as it is written in Matthew 1:1-18, which clearly shows *the genealogy of Jesus* and fulfills the prophecy of Moses in Genesis -*"in thy seed (Jesus) shall all the nations of the earth be blessed."* Please see *the word of God* prophesized by David and beautifully written in Psalm 71, where all the verses tell us something about the coming of the Messiah, the Anointed One and *the Christ.* Psalm 71 foretells us about *the future kings and wise men (your ancestors)* and all the nations that shall come looking for *him* to serve and adore *him (Jesus),* and that shall offer presents and bring gifts, and they shall give *him (Jesus)* of the gold of Arabia, for *him (Jesus)* they shall always adore and bless *him* all the day, and before *him (Jesus)* the Ethiopians shall fall down and *his* enemies shall lick the ground. See Psalm 71: *"...*For *he* shall deliver the poor from the mighty and needy that had no helper. *He* shall spare the poor and needy: and *he* shall save the souls of the poor. *He* shall redeem their souls from usuries and iniquity: and their names shall be honorable in *his* sight.... For *him* they shall always adore: they shall bless *Him* all the day... Let *his* name be blessed for evermore: *His* name continueth before *the sun.* And *in him* shall the tribes of the earth be blessed: all nations shall magnify *him.* Blessed be the Lord, the God of Israel, *who* alone doth wonderful things*..." Who* are they talking about? *Who* is *he* that *shall save the souls of the poor* or *he* that *shall redeem their souls from usuries and iniquity?* Psalm 71, written by David, as well as in all the many other Messianic prophecies written in the Old Testament by Moses and the prophets, I now wholeheartedly believe they are talking about *Jesus*, the living Son of God, Who is One with His Father God and is One with the Holy Spirit of God – *One Triune God.*

Thus, I believe in *one God* - three persons - *one substance undivided, the Divine Will of God.* The 333 EEG signature pattern, we recorded in the science of *His Living Presence,* is indeed --- three cycles in one second. This is the true circumference of God's heavenly circle, *the circle of life.* **The fire** *round about* God's heavenly Jerusalem, as prophesized by Zachariah 2:1-5. This is revealed in the Book of Revelation Chapters 21 and 22. *The circle of life,* graciously and mercifully invites you – *yes you* - to enter into *God's living circle of love, mercy, fire, blessings and eternal life by just believing in the One whom He sent - Jesus,* the Son of man (Deut.18:18) and Son of God (Deut.18:15). And please remember my dear beloved Muslims, and all my dear brothers and sisters - *Gentiles* (like me) representing *all of mankind who are not Jews,* the chosen people, ***God loves you!*** Now please hear *the word of God* as prophesized by the great prophet Isaiah 60:1-6*:* "Arise, be enlightened, O Jerusalem: for *thy light is come* and *the glory of the Lord is risen upon thee.* For behold darkness shall cover the earth, and a mist the people: but the Lord shall arise upon thee, and His glory shall be seen upon thee. And the *Gentiles shall walk in thy light, and kings in the brightness of thy rising...* The multitude of camels shall cover thee, *the dromedaries of Madian and Epha: all they from Saba shall come, bringing gold and frankincense: and shewing forth praise to the Lord."* This sounds so familiar.

Please, beloved Muslims, recall again your own rich ancestral history. Has the above prophesized historical event ever occurred? Just remember the *Christmas stories* concerning *the birth of Jesus* as shown in many movies and TV shows during the Christmas holidays that many of you may have been exposed to. Remember how the wise men and the kings from Arabia and the kings from Saba and the kings from Tharsis and the Islands followed the bright *new rising star* that actually hovered over Juda in *the city of David,* named *Bethlehem (Ephrata).* And, as already mentioned above, recall the story of how these *wise men and kings* brought *gifts of gold, frankincense and myrrh* after finding the *new born infant* (the King of kings) with Mary and Joseph lying in a straw manger wrapped in swaddling clothes. *Your Arabian and Persian ancestors* actually found *Him (Jesus)* as written by Moses (Numbers 24:17: *"the star rising out of Jacob...")* thousands of years prior to this very *holy night* like in the song: *"Silent Night,"* where out of the darkness *thy light* is come. The prophet Micah also prophesized this very holy event correctly.... see Micah 5:1-5 especially verses 2 and part of 5: "And Thou, *Bethlehem Ephrata,* art a little one among the thousands of *Juda:* out of thee shall *he* come forth unto me that is to be the ruler in Israel: and *his going forth is from the beginning, from the days of eternity...* And *he shall stand, and feed in the strength of the Lord, in the height of the name of the Lord his God*: and they shall be converted, for now shall *he* be magnified even to the ends of the earth. ***And this man shall be our peace."*** *Who* is *he* - *this man* going forth from *the beginning* - *Who* shall be *our peace*? *Jesus.* Now, recall the *new medical and scientific data* as presented. Is *Jesus* truly *the God-man* as prophesized by Isaiah? See Isaiah 9:6*: "For* a *child is born to us,* and *a son is given to us,* and the government is upon *his* shoulder: and *his name* shall be called wonderful, counselor, the *God-man (God the Mighty),* the Father of the world to come, *the Prince of Peace."* Just look at the above verse again in Micah 5:1-5:*"...His going forth is from the beginning, from the days of eternity... he shall stand, and* ***feed*** *in the strength of the Lord."* Maybe now, this is all starting to make some sense to you.

In the New Testament Book of John 8:25, *Jesus* was asked by the Jews in the Temple: *"Who* art thou? *Jesus* said to them: *The beginning*; *who also speak unto you."* In this last verse I believe *Jesus* is saying that *He* **is** *the beginning* and One with God His Father and telling us, like Micah that *"His going forth is from* ***the beginning."*** All the above prophetic *words of God* were truly fulfilled perfectly by the birth of *Jesus.* In these troubled times we currently live in, with *terror running amuck,* the point I am trying to get across to all Gentiles, especially you my dear beloved Muslims - is that *your ancestors (wise men and kings)* now over 2,000 years ago – actually read or heard these prophetic *words of God* as prophesized over 1,300 years prior to the birth of Jesus and acted on them. These kings and wise men *(your ancestors)* after reading or hearing about *the Bible* prophecy - followed *the light.* They followed the ***prophecy of Balaam*** in Numbers 24:17: *"A star shall rise out of Jacob and a sceptre shall spring up from Israel."* This led *your ancestors* to the *King of kings and Lord of lords* (Rev 19:16) and to Micah 5:5: "*this man shall be our peace."* Now I invite you, your sons and your daughters, to please remember your rich history. Please, now go and honor *your ancestors* by imitating the Biblical wise men and great kings. Come taste and see the goodness of the Lord. Follow *the light, thy light* and *the true light of the world.* God is calling all of you, *dear Muslims,* again and again. God is inviting you - *yes you* - just like God had called and invited *your ancestors* over 2,000 years ago - to become *one with the light, the truth* and ***our peace*** *for this world.* Remember, *Jesus* died for you and your sons and your daughters. *Jesus* resurrected from death on Calvary in three days, as was prophesized about Him and as *He* Himself prophesized about Himself - *as the Son of God,* before willingly accepting and embracing death on a tree for all our sins and transgressions. Go see and visit the *empty tomb of Jesus!*

By just believing in *Jesus* (the One that God sent) you and I can resurrect our lives from the pit and resurrect our souls from sin and death - *with Jesus, in Jesus and through Jesus* - and safely reach *eternal life with God in paradise.* Now look at the *new* medical and scientific facts just presented to you. *Jesus* **is** *King of kings* *and Lord of lords - Jesus* **is** *the Eternal Word of God the Father made flesh (John 1:14). Jesus is the living bread, which came down from heaven. Jesus* **is** *pure Love, the living flames of love.* So, I again invite you to come to *thy light* – come to the one true God: The Father, Son and Holy Spirit -*One God, the Divine Will of God, the Most Holy Trinity.* I invite you to accept *Jesus,* as your *star,* your *true light, Lord and Savior* - sent by Father God for you and me. Be *born again - in spirit, in truth and in fire.* Ask God for forgiveness. Repent. Then, wash yourselves and be made pure in the baptismal living waters of the Holy Spirit. Wash yourselves of all your sins - in the Precious Blood of Jesus. Let *the living fire of Jesus and the Holy Spirit anoint you with all God's graces necessary for salvation and everlasting eternal life for you and all your children.* So, come taste and see the goodness of the Lord God *Our Father.* Come to the marriage supper of the *Lamb of God.* Fear not, do not be afraid or disbelieving any longer, but *believe* --- in the One whom He *(Father God)* sent --- **Jesus.** Amen.

* * *

Nancy received a private message from *Jesus* in the late evening hours after (unbeknownst to Nancy) I had just completed editing part of Chapter IV. I was speaking to Nancy on the phone when *Jesus* appeared to her and said, *"My children this is my work* (referring to this book). *I am alive. I am alive. Please tell my children,* ***I am alive."*** Then moments later, while Nancy was still praying, *Jesus* said, ***"I am light.*** *Without my light the world is in complete and total darkness. There is no other light.* ***I am light. My light and the cross are one."***

Now, please reflect on the title of Chapter IV: **I AM ALIVE**.
This is truly astonishing!

The journey *science to faith* is now starting to get really interesting...

And very intriguing indeed...It definitely *got* and still *gets* my attention...

I hope it *gets* yours...

CHAPTER V

PRESENCE OF "THE LIGHT"

THE TESTING OF JULY 13th, 1993

Members of the medical and scientific team were asked to submit a written report of their findings to *the Church.* This was not an easy task (especially for *me*) since our medical and scientific results were so unprecedented and astonishing. All the scientists (I) begged for more studies to increase our database and to further validate our individual spectacular findings. I especially felt we needed more testing before writing or publishing any reports, particularly a report concerning such new ground breaking data never before recorded in the adult and pediatric clinical neurophysiology literature.

Approximately one week before the July 13th, 1993 apparition, I received a phone call from Dr. Velasquez informing me that he had just received permission from Nancy to repeat his radiation studies. Dr. Velasquez requested that I be present for these repeat radiation studies, in order to assist him and be a witness to the testing. I quickly consented to this request, knowing it would provide me with another opportunity for more clinical observations of Nancy.

In preparation for the testing, I asked a dear friend, a most-respected female Jewish doctor, to assist me in the clinical observations of Nancy. This doctor in my opinion, is one of the most brilliant, insightful and analytical minds that I have ever had the pleasure of working with. (Her name has been omitted at her request, as she fears publicity would hurt her family and would also intrude upon their privacy; so, she respectfully asks all who know her to please politely respect her concerns and wishes). July 13th,, 1993 was another hot summer day in Conyers, involving another slow crawl to the farm house because of slow moving traffic. The crowds that day numbered approximately thirty thousand. The Sheriff's Officers of Rockdale County were so very efficient and effective in directing all the multitude of cars and buses. Pilgrims from all parts of the world congregated for the noontime *rosary prayers* and expected apparitions of *Jesus* and *Blessed Virgin Mary, Our Loving Mother*, and the heavenly court of God.

When the medical team arrived at the farm house, we met with the radiation team. Dr. Velasquez was busy setting up his Geiger counters and equipment. He then started arranging magnetic strips in the same identical geometric format used during the initial appointed testing day of June 13th, 1993. On this occasion, Dr. Velasquez had again brought videotaping equipment to record the Geiger counters' display monitor screens which were set up both in the apparition room and outside of the apparition room around the farm house. His goal was to monitor the high ionizing *gamma* radiation levels in these geometrical predetermined areas.

My medical team had the opportunity to meet once again with Nancy and to make further clinical observations. The members of my team observed Nancy from the right back corner of the apparition room, which allowed a diagonal view of Nancy from her right side while she was kneeling *during the apparition.* I placed myself on the opposite rear corner of the room, on Nancy's left side, to observe from another different angle.

Overall, it was an unexpectedly exciting day. The pilgrims were reverent in their prayers with joyous anticipation of what was allegedly expected to occur. Nancy came into the *apparition room* at noon and knelt in the prearranged pews in front of the triangular, tri-tiered, wooden shelves which contained the statues of *Our Loving Mother* and religious pictures previously described. Recall that this area was the site of the monthly (on the 13th of each month) public noontime *apparitions,* and was an exact replica of the original apparition site in Nancy's home, where the first apparitions occurred. As Nancy knelt, the noon prayers and the well-known *Fatima song* began to be sung.

Nancy remained very still and reverent in her prayers. I was again struck with the clinical similarities of our medical and neurological observations of that day in comparison with our previous testing. As soon as the Geiger counters clicking sounds commenced, it was announced over the loudspeakers, *"Our Blessed Mother is here."* The room filled with priests, nuns and religious seemed caught up in the emotion and awe of what was taking place. I could see streams of tears flowing down the cheeks of many pilgrims pouring forth from their eyes while kneeling in reverence.

The *rosary prayers* began, with the first part of each prayer said in the various native tongues of those present depending on who was leading the prayers, and the second part said in English. However throughout the recitation of the fifteen decades of the *rosary prayers,* Nancy was seeing *heavenly visions, apparitions* and receiving messages from the *Blessed Virgin Mary.* I could clearly hear the Geiger counter sounds penetrate the room. *"Click...click...click...click."* Both Dr. Velasquez and the entire radiation team were visibly excited over *the data* they were collecting.

After everyone prayed the glorious mysteries, and finished the fifteen decades of the *holy rosary prayers,* Nancy announced that the *Blessed Virgin Mary, Our Loving Mother* will now give her monthly message to the United States of America:

"My dear children... open your hearts to God and allow my Son Jesus to live within you. Surrender your will to His Will. When you do this, you will have peace and direction for your life. My Son desires to heal each one of you. Go to Him. As my Son loves you and forgives you, you are being called to love and forgive each other. Pray, little children, pray. Express your prayer in love, and in this way you will have a closer union with God.

As your Loving Mother, I bless you. Please make the sign of the cross as I depart and remember to thank my Son for permitting me to come. When you

make the sign of the cross, I will bless you and everything you have brought with you. Please know I have carried the petitions of your hearts to my Son."

As the Blessed Virgin Mary was departing, the Geiger counter's clicking sounds appeared to have intensified. At the same time many in the room cried with joyous excitement, while pointing in the same direction Nancy was seeing the *Blessed Virgin Mary* depart. They shouted out, *"Look at the lights,* look at the lights, *look at all the lights!"* While not everyone saw *the lights (like me),* it was obvious that many in the room were genuinely excited while witnessing this incredible phenomenon. Wow!

After the *Blessed Virgin Mary* departed and all the prayers were completed, Nancy stood up and went out front to give the pilgrims the *messages from heaven* which she had received. Nancy said *Our Loving Mother* had appeared as the *rosary prayer* began and said,

"My dear children, thank you for your journey of faith. At the end of the glorious mysteries, I will give the message for the United States. (See the above monthly message) ***I invite each of you, my dear children, to give your heart to God in prayer. My children, they test and they test and they test. Pray my dear children for the grace of a greater faith."***

Upon hearing the last portion of the above message, I could not help but momentarily cringe since I was part of the testing research team that day. Nancy then said that she saw a beautiful crown appear on *Our Loving Mother's* head, and then Our Lady continued to say,

"There is too little faith. There is too little faith. I ask that no more testing be done. I ask that my children come and pray. My children are going to suffer more because they have not returned to God. There is universal rejection of God all over the world."

Three times Nancy said she saw a dark substance that looked like blood come down *Our Loving Mother's* face.

"Please love God more. Please," *she said as* Nancy described that the Blessed Mother's tone was deeply serious and pleading. Then the *Blessed Virgin Mary* said,

"Do you pray from your heart or from your lips? Where are my sick children?" The *Blessed Virgin Mary* was *not* looking very pleased at this point and kept closing her eyes. Her eyes looked downward and sad. She said,

"My words are few. My children, you are not listening."

Nancy said that she saw a blood-like substance streaming down *Our Loving Mother's* face as she was saying these words. Then the *Blessed Virgin Mary* went on to say,

"My children who are here are consoling my heart."

Nancy reported that after this, *Our Loving Mother* burst in an all encompassing flash of dazzling bright light.

Nancy explained that as the recitation of *the rosary* continued, she was given a vision of a giant wave coming from one direction. *Our Loving Mother* then said,

"Water will wash on the land. You must be cleansed. Please children, amend your lives. Please."

Nancy then saw another dark substance come down from *Our Loving Mother's* face, and thought that it was perhaps *a teardrop of blood.* The *Blessed Virgin Mary* said,

"My children do not know God. If they knew Him, they would keep His commandments. If they knew Him, they would follow in His footsteps. Tell my priests, tell my priests, to remain obedient to the Holy Father, John Paul II. It is God who chooses the Pope, not man."

The *Blessed Virgin Mary* then spoke about *love* to Nancy, saying,

"The answer for the world is love, love. No matter what is said, no matter what is done, always love, always forgive."

Nancy again reported seeing a dark substance, possibly *a teardrop of blood,* coming down *Our Loving Mother's face* and then *saw a vision* of a great amount of water flooding the land. The land was flat, and more and more water kept rushing over it, coming at a brisk pace. *Our Loving Mother* then continued saying,

"Look at the land mass; look at the amount of water. Why do you children remain stubborn? Amend your life."

The *Blessed Virgin Mary* continued later to say,

"I have a message for all my priests: remain obedient. Hold fast to tradition and serve in selfless love."

St. Padre Pio appeared to Nancy as this last statement was said. St. Padre Pio again appeared, as *Our Loving Mother* continued,

"Celebrate each Mass as if it were your last with utmost reverence and in great faith. Be a witness for God." Nancy was given the understanding from heaven above that *Our Loving Mother* was speaking to everyone in the USA and the world, especially her beloved priests.

Our Loving Mother continued,

"Be holy as God is Holy,"

Then the *Blessed Virgin Mary* explained to Nancy that everyone who comes to the apparition site is given *special graces.* Heaven was allowing her *(Our Loving Mother)* to lavish *special graces* upon everyone, who sincerely desired to be there. The *Blessed Virgin Mary* then began to cry once again. Nancy again saw a dark substance flowing down her face and asked, *"Why* do you cry blood*?" Our Loving Mother* replied,

"Because children are being murdered at this very moment. Abortion is murder."

She was visibly very sad, and *then Jesus appeared* according to Nancy. *Our Loving Mother* then continued saying,

"My Son comforts me. He is with me. Children, you do not know how close you are to a very great, great suffering. You are bringing this suffering upon yourselves. I am the Mother of God and your Loving Mother, and my Son has sent me to help you."

The *Blessed Virgin Mary* then asked Nancy to replace a *scapular* that was missing from the statue of *Our Loving Mother* in the *apparition room.* She went on to explain about the *holy rosary* and *the scapular* saying,

"These are important sacramentals. Please teach my children."

The *Blessed Virgin Mary* also spoke about the scientific testing and said,

"Testing is an interruption in your offering to God."

Nancy once again saw *blood* come down *Our Loving Mother's* face and asked *what* would happen when *the apparitions* and the monthly messages for the United States came to an end. *Our Loving Mother* replied,

"My Son will continue to instruct you in His ways. I will be at His side. Only rarely will I speak as God permits. Your suffering is saving souls."

Still speaking in front of the farm house porch to many thousands of pilgrims, Nancy then recited the earlier *messages from Jesus* on the morning of July 13th, 1993. *Jesus* appearing earlier in Nancy's home said,

"My children's hearts need to be healed. After I have forgiven you, then forgive yourself and then go to others and forgive them. All over the world my children's hearts need to be healed. I am the healer; come to me. Take my mother's hand; she will bring you to me. I am Jesus, Son of the living God. I am He who speaks to you, dearest daughter. Go and proclaim my words."

Nancy saw *a cross of white light appear* suspended in the air and then disappear. That morning, just before noontime, Nancy was praying in the adjacent room to the apparition room in preparation for the *heavenly visits* or *apparitions* of the *Blessed Virgin Mary. Jesus* appeared again and said, *"There will be rosaries that will turn to a golden color today. There will be many healings."* Nancy said that she saw a very bright light and then *Jesus* continued saying, *"Padre Pio (now-St. Pio) will be here today. My children must pray. My children must pray. You do not know, what awaits you."* Many years after this message was delivered from the porch, the Capuchin priest-monk-*Padre Pio* was canonized as *Saint Pio of Pietrelcina* by Pope John Paul II.

Upon hearing these words, I realized Jesus was foretelling some of the things which were to actually occur in the future on that particular day. Padre Pio *(St. Pio)* apparently did appear to Nancy. Many pilgrims claimed with excitement and joy that their metal or silver rosaries, different religious medals and sacramentals had turned a *golden color* as foretold by Jesus. Many accounts of *healings,* both *spiritual* and *physical,* were reported to the volunteers by numerous pilgrims that visited that day. These individuals were later asked to submit their testimonies in writing to the Archbishop of Atlanta in the Archdiocese of Atlanta, Georgia. While it is still not certain how many pilgrims actually followed through on reporting their *special healings,* many of the volunteers reported that they had received literally hundreds of written testimonies and thousands of verbal testimonies. Again, Wow!

What occurred next both shocked me to my core and literally challenged my thoughts on religion, faith and my worldly priorities. As I was listening to Nancy relay these *messages* to the thousands of pilgrims present, I felt someone grab my right arm with great force. I turned my head and instantly saw a bewildered and greatly astonished expression on the face of my colleague, the female Jewish doctor whom I had asked to accompany me professionally to the *apparitions* to clinically observe Nancy. She stated flatly, "You need to put me on lithium."

Alarmed, I asked her, *"What?"*

She replied, "Yes, I think you need to put me on lithium or something stronger after what I just experienced... I have never ever taken any hallucinogens, LSD, cocaine, or smoked marijuana...I have never taken any mood-altering drugs. And I have never been diagnosed with schizophrenia, psychosis, delirium, epilepsy..."

I quickly interrupted her outright, saying, *"Stop*, wait a minute—why are you saying all this?"

Still grabbing my right arm, the brilliant Jewish doctor literally dragged me into one of the private rooms in the farm house and described her entire experience in great detail. Her story was shocking and quite unbelievable. If I had not known her previously to be an extremely sane, level-headed, logical, professional, ethical and highly-educated individual, I would have found her story even more *unbelievable.*

She explained, "As the prayers in the room had begun I was mindful and respectful of the prayers being said despite my religion *(Jewish).* I really did enjoy hearing all the different foreign languages spoken during *the rosary.* But with the repetition of the prayers, I became bored. So, I started to look out the window at the mass of humanity praying outside. Suddenly, I was inspired to pray Psalm 23, my favorite prayer. While reciting Psalm 23 *in Hebrew,* I looked over at Nancy (kneeling) and continued my clinical observations. Towards the front corner I saw a very large, dazzling like and luminous white wings in the direction where Nancy was looking. Immediately in front of Nancy, I saw the most beautiful young woman, dressed all in white with a white veil over her head. She was so beautiful. Her complexion appeared ageless. I could clearly see that this young woman was speaking with Nancy, since her lips were moving, while she was looking at Nancy... As I saw this, I could hear the loudspeakers announce: *"Our Blessed Mother* is here."

"I asked myself if this was a dream. So, I closed my eyes. And when I opened my eyes, I saw the beautiful woman, who I presume is the *Virgin Mary,* smile, gently nod her head, and turn slightly towards the right side of the room. Looking right at me, she *smiled and called me by my first name.* I clearly heard her pronounce my name. Then later, I saw these *older men appear* dressed in long robes. Most of

them had beards. Some were wearing these odd funny looking luminous-like hats, right in front of the fireplace area, and many were *appearing,* one after the other. Nancy was still kneeling, looking up at *Mary* and praying. Then, I saw this young handsome man, approximately thirty plus in years, gently walk around the room. *He* was dressed in a white, white linen robe with 'elephant' sleeves. *He* had caramel brownish hair down to his shoulders and a brown scraggly, but full beard. *For a moment... he* looked like *he suffered...* but his big *honey colored eyes* expressed the most tender love and compassion towards the priests, nuns, religious and pilgrims in the room. *He* slowly walked around the room *blessing them* and *all the pilgrims present.* Very bright, luminous white, whiter than white and bright golden light could be seen emitting from *his chest and hands* as *he* blessed all the people. *Rays of light* would literally radiate out from *him* towards the people, engulfing them totally within *a bright cloud of light.* I saw *brilliant rays of light pouring forth* and *zapping* each person *he* stood in front of, especially Monsignor Armando Jimenez-Rebollar of Maryland, who I had the pleasure to meet with earlier.*"* Many years later Mons. Armando corroborated this *experience* by telling *me,* that *while he was praying - during the apparitions* on this anointed day, he profoundly *felt the living presence of God.* After he retired, he privately admitted to actually *seeing Jesus.*

In partial disbelief, I cautiously asked the Jewish doctor, *"Who* is *'he'* that you are talking about?*"*

She replied, "You know, the one you all call *Jesus."*

As I heard these words, I literally had to sit down with my mouth wide open. Knowing this extremely analytical doctor to be of sound mind and logical thought, I wondered *why* in the world would this *(Jewish)* doctor concoct, dream up or make up such a story. Certainly, this was *not* for any *secondary gain.* I was genuinely and overwhelmingly, deeply perplexed at what I had just heard.

Moments later, Nancy walked back into the farmhouse kitchen where we were sitting. Before I had a chance to even speak, Nancy proclaimed, *"I prayed* and prayed to God for a *spiritual sister.* I asked the *Blessed Mother* to please ask her Son *(Jesus)* to give me a *spiritual sister, someone to help me with my visions* and *apparitions.* At that moment the *Blessed Mother* smiled, nodded her head and looked over to someone in the back right side of the room, smiled again and called out a female name. But, I do not know who she is.*"* Then Nancy explained that, sometimes, she is allowed somehow to see completely around like in a 360-degree vision movie theater in amusement parks. She does not know how *God* does this. But, Nancy will be looking straight ahead and be simultaneously seeing everything round about her. This type of *360-degree vision* occurred with today's July 13th, 1993 apparition. Nancy said she saw *Jesus* walking around the room bestowing many *blessings* and *showers of graces* on the religious and all pilgrims present.

I immediately realized that my colleague and professional friend's extraordinary experience had just been confirmed and corroborated by the *heavenly visits and apparitions* Nancy had just proclaimed to have had experienced on this day of testing. Nancy and the Jewish doctor had not seen nor spoken to each other before on this day, but yet the two of them individually relayed *identical descriptions of these apparitions,* while in the farmhouse kitchen. So, I introduced Nancy to her *new spiritual sister* - the *Jewish* doctor – as chosen by our *Jewish* Blessed Mother.

God *(Wisdom)* truly has a sense of humor. Now, I had more reasons to ponder a deeper meaning for the results of our *new data* and for all its phenomenal implications.

RESULTS OF THE JULY 13th, 1993 TESTING

A) Dr. Humberto Velasquez and Radiation team

Dr. Velasquez's data on this second series of *gamma* radiation testing at the apparition site essentially reproduced the same initial radiation measurements previously recorded on June 13th, 1993 in both the apparition room and the adjacent room. *The experiment design* called for a series of measurements of high ionizing radiation - *gamma* radiation field energy readings to be analyzed at three separate and different times *before, during and after the apparitions.* Dr. Velasquez again detected no significant increases in *gamma radiation before, during or after the apparitions.* He recorded and documented the *normal range* and amount of *gamma* radiation energy that is typically *measured in the natural environment,* which is indeed very minuscule and *not harmful* to anyone. These non-harmful levels of *gamma* radiation were the readings essentially found in all of his repeated tests.

Since we witnessed and heard the Geiger counter *clicking,* I initially incorrectly presumed the Geiger counters were indeed detecting changes in *the gamma radiation* of the room. The *clicking* thus falsely appeared to me at first to increase in intensity during the apparitions, which Nancy has described as *visions of* ***light.*** At times, Nancy says, these visions fade in and out changing in the intensity of light present. However, without a doubt Dr. Velasquez's repeated series of tests once again demonstrated --- clearly, that absolutely *no statistically significant changes or increases* in the high ionizing *gamma* radiation energy fields *before, during or after the apparitions.* Thus, *no harmful radiation was measured during the heavenly visits, visions* or *apparitions.*

Indeed, this is good news for all the pilgrims and especially very good news for Nancy. Now the pilgrims and Nancy do not have ever to worry about *glowing in the dark* from over *exposure* to deadly and harmful *gamma* radiation energy fields. The results reaffirmed Dr. Velasquez's initial speculation and data that *no statistically significant increases* in harmful *gamma* radiation energy fields were ever *detected* during the *heavenly visitations, visions* or *apparitions.*

Recall that all the Geiger counter devices used by Dr. Velasquez were calibrated only to measure *gamma* radiation in the high ionizing radiation energy field's detection range. Again *no statistically significant increases* or changes were recorded. These repeated experiments by Dr. Velasquez were modeled after those of radiation specialist Dr. Lipinski, who studied the *gamma* radiation energy fields surrounding the apparitions in Medjugorje, Bosnia-Hercegovina. Dr. Velasquez once again by chance, co-incidence or *God-incidence filmed on video actual multiple bursts of dense coherent white light laser signals* seen with a *silver hue,* as corrected by the *human retina,* on the walls of the apparition room. He noted a surge of *laser bursts of coherent white light* in the *visible light* radiation energy field spectra. This surge was recorded best during the moments, when Nancy said, *"Our Loving Mother with her baby Jesus* is now departing with the *heavenly court of angels and saints"* or at other specific moments when Nancy said, *"Jesus is here."*

Dr. Velasquez said the bursts of dense coherent *white light laser signals with a silver hue* were corroborated with some of the studies done by Dr. Callahan on June 13th, 1993.

Dr. Velasquez speculated and proposed that the major radiation energy changes recorded *during the apparitions* were in fact *in the 3% visible light spectra* and *in the low and extremely low ionizing radiation energy field ranges,* as Dr. Callahan had clearly demonstrated repeatedly in the previous chapters. Recall, the astronomical *visible light energy* increases demonstrated by the 30-90% increase in *sun light energy* that was recorded on the outside façade and chimney of the farm house, and Dr. Velasquez's bursts of dense coherent *white light laser signals* filmed inside the room *by chance on video.* Dr. Callahan incredibly measured astronomical increases of low ionizing radiation energy field changes, when multiple *invisible light (maser-like) coherent bursts* or *infrared laser signals* or *radio light signals* were recorded ---*only during the heavenly visitations, apparitions* or *supernatural events of Jesus – alive on the cross,* when Nancy said, *"How beautiful…the crucifix* **is** now *bursting in light."* Wow!

To summarize: The entire radiation energy field spectrum produces *light* energy within their respective energy fields, however, our human eye can only see 3% of all this light energy available in our atmosphere. Recall, the *visible light spectra* of radiation energy fields only represents *3% of all light energy present* in the atmosphere. This simply means, we humans can not and do not see the remaining *97% of invisible light radiation* energy fields surrounding us at all times, unless *God* permits and blesses a person like a *chosen soul - with this gift.* However, the medical and scientific studies clearly recorded and documented statistically significant increases in *the light* energy *only* during the heavenly visits, visions or apparitions in the *extremely low* and *low ionizing radiation* light energy fields all the way up to and including the *visible light spectrum.* Although the high ionizing *gamma* radiation energy *was detected, no statistically significantly increases were recorded* in the high ionizing *gamma* radiation energy fields: *before, during or after the heavenly visitations, visions or apparitions.*

B) Ramon M. Sanchez, M.D. and Medical Team

The clinical medical and neurological *observations* made that day once again clearly and repeatedly demonstrated Nancy to be entirely **normal.** Clinical examinations:

1) Medical and neurological examinations were completely *normal.*

2) Mental status examinations before, during and after were *normal.*

3) Clinical observations *during the visionary experiences* were *normal,* and are described as follows: Nancy appeared to be in a very prayerful state of *ecstasy.* She remained prayerfully reverent with a shy, humble and very genuine, innocent childlike quality. She was awake, alert and oriented, with *normal* higher cortical functioning and normal speech with a slight Bostonian accent. Her affect was normal and supple, appropriately changing with the types of *messages* and *visions* she was experiencing. Nancy maintained excellent *ego control* and *reality testing* throughout the entire period of time despite the apparent intensity of her *visions* and *heavenly visits.* Her train of thought was completely clear and logical. I noted absolutely no disturbance in her thinking and found no thought disorder. There was no evidence of confusion or any loss of contact with herself or the people around her. I saw no evidence of hysteria or affective disorder, and also no depression or mood disorder. There was no evidence of a personality disorder or hysterical personality and *definitely no evidence of any psychotic disturbances.* There was also no epileptic activity or epileptic behavior identified.

While Nancy was concentrating and keeping contact with the *visions,* she maintained the ability to relate to those around her especially to the transcriber George Collins in a very intelligent fashion. I saw *no evidence of a hypnotic trance.* As above, Nancy had a definite *normal* and steady affect which reacted appropriately to the thoughts she was expressing in conjunction with the type of *visions* she was seeing and experiencing.

Her mood was mostly joyful and with expressions of calmness and being at peace. When Nancy described *messages* or *visions* that were sad, she became appropriately sad without exaggeration. There was clearly no evidence of anomia, aphasia or apraxia. Her speech was fluent with no dysarthria and with normal content of speech. Nancy demonstrated normal immediate, short- term and long term memory skills. Once again Nancy's *entire cognitive mental status* was indeed *normal.* Nancy's *behavior during the visionary experience* was also *normal.* Finally, Nancy demonstrated no medical illnesses, no neurological or psychiatric mental status disturbances or disorders. Repeatedly, no mental status or cognitive pathology was ever identified.

These findings were indeed similar and identical to our initial *clinical observations* of Nancy *during the baseline studies* of June 11th and were also identical to *the testing results* of June 13th, 1993 done in the *apparition room* and later in the *adjacent room,* when *Jesus* gave us a *message* - the awesome *tangible new data* of *His Living Presence*. The *journey science to faith* continues onward ...

REFLECTIONS ON THE JULY 13th, 1993 TESTING

After repeating the scientific tests on July 13th, 1993, Dr. Humberto Velasquez realized he had documented very similar *data* on the two separate June 13th, 1993 tests completed in the farm house apparition room and later in the adjacent room. So, Dr. Velasquez recorded, documented, and has now repeatedly demonstrated that high ionizing *gamma* radiation energy field readings *do not significantly change* or increase *during, before, or after the apparitions*. This reaffirmed his initial first conclusions that *no harmful radiation* was *associated with the visions, heavenly visits* and *apparitions* of Nancy in Conyers. The Geiger counter sounds that appeared to simultaneously increase and decrease as with Nancy's *visions of light,* actually *did not* statistically demonstrate any significant changes in the *gamma radiation* energy fields. However*, by chance* or *co-incidence* or *God-incidence* as noted above, Dr. Velasquez captured on his video – actual flashes or *bursts of coherent white light* (with a slight *silver hue*) that was seen dancing on the walls of the *apparition room* on this day of July 13th,, 1993, during the time when Nancy claimed the *Blessed Virgin Mary* caressing her baby *Jesus* was seen departing with *the heavenly court* and at another time when Nancy said*, "Jesus is here."*

The filmed (on video) multiple dense bursts of *coherent white light laser signals* on the walls of the apparition room clearly corroborates with Dr. Callahan's astronomical increases in the intensity of *the light* energy measured in the low and extremely low ionizing radiation energy fields at the atmospheric-wall boundary radiation energy fields of the *apparition room* as well as the *adjacent room* during the *heavenly visits* or *apparitions*. Incredibly, the *repeated* meticulous *scientific tests measuring the presence of "the light" energy,* I now believe has definite ***Biblical significance*** and indeed very exciting implications. See the numerous references on *"the light"* in the Old and New Testament in Chapter IX.

Now read this short *message* given to Nancy on June 13th, 1993, concerning this issue of *the light* intensity. Nancy saw *a vision* of a globe as the *Blessed Virgin Mary* said, *"Stay close to my Son."* Then, the image of *Our Loving Mother* faded in and out several times. At one moment, Nancy could see the *Blessed Virgin Mary* just fine, and the next moment her image was very faint. There was a definite change in the intensity of *the light* during this apparition. The *Blessed Virgin Mary* then said, *"This is what happens when my children take their eyes off my Son. There is a change in the intensity of light in their soul."* In another *message* and *vision* given to Nancy on December 12th, 1992, the *Blessed Virgin Mary* appeared many times with the radiant *Jesus* as a child in her arms. To the right of the *Blessed Virgin Mary* there was an image of a huge, solid, black rectangle. Nancy later described the image as *darkness*. Then, as *Our Loving Mother* and her illuminating and radiant child *Jesus* moved towards the darkness, the darkness moved away. Nancy said that usually in her visions *Jesus* is a baby. In this peculiar vision, *Jesus* was a toddler, holding *His* head up on *His* own.

Nancy had seen this same *vision* repeated many times almost daily during the previous week beginning on December 2nd, 1999, the day President Bush and President-elect Clinton first met after the election. *Jesus* appeared to Nancy several times earlier on that day and said, *"The more man sins, the more you block out the light of God. More sins, more darkness, less light."*

Reflecting on this vision and message from *Jesus,* George Collins then said, *"It* keeps coming to me that in *the visions of the Blessed Virgin Mary with the child Jesus,* that Mary is offering her *Son, Jesus, the light of the world* to us and is thus moving back or moving away *the darkness* in the world.*"*

Reflecting on all the medical and scientific studies, which we had completed thus far, I was still left with the difficult task of writing as requested a medical report for the Archbishop of Atlanta, Ga. Since all the *new data* and *results* had now been repeatedly reproduced and documented, this *new data* became even more astonishing. As I had previously uncovered (or discovered) a series of stimulus specific evoked EEG brain wave patterns which were not only unprecedented but also considered by other EEG experts as *physiologically impossible,* we again reviewed all the *clinical observations* documented. Though no EEG tests were performed on the July 13th testing day, the medical team's clinical medical observations, during today's testing, were basically the same as our previous initial series of meticulous clinical observations and evaluations.

Now I was left to my own suppositions once again. So, I pondered. After successfully and repeatedly reproducing our test results on Nancy, I wondered whether *anyone else chosen by God* and *blessed to experience heavenly visits* or *visions* or *apparitions* might also develop the same stimulus specific evoked EEG brain wave patterns I recorded repeatedly with Nancy.

Question: Can the unparalleled 333 EEG pattern be observed in the brains of other *chosen souls*?

I really wanted to know. As inspirations with reoccurring thoughts of possibly making preparations for yet another round of tests, I recalled that the *Blessed Virgin Mary* had just said, *"I ask that no more testing be done."* Now, my interior struggle between *science* and *faith* intensified. On the one hand, I had uncovered (discovered) *new data* that incredibly authenticated Nancy's claims; nonetheless, my hardened skeptical, scientifically trained mind wanted (as usual) even more *data,* more *tests,* and much more proof to validate my findings. It was years before I learned that I already had more than enough *data* to validate Nancy's claims. I continued to be hounded by this simple question: *Will* being *in His Living Presence* produce (or evoke) the same topographic EEG brain wave patterns in other *visionaries* or *chosen souls,* as I had repeatedly reproduced with Nancy in the lab and in the field*, during the heavenly visits, visions* or *apparitions* of *Jesus?*

I thought if an EEG test could be performed on two or more *chosen souls* during *heavenly visits, visions* or *apparitions* of *Jesus,* what electrical EEG brain wave picture will we see or possibly find? Will we see the same identical and astonishing 3 Hz *delta rhythms* forming the unprecedented *pattern of 333* recorded *during the heavenly visits, visions* or *apparitions* of *Jesus?* Will we find the same identical 4 Hz *theta rhythms* like previously recorded in infants and small toddlers with *pleasure rhythms* in another adult brain *only during the heavenly visitations, visions* or *apparitions* of the *Blessed Virgin Mary bringing her baby Jesus* to us?

Note: Remember the *pediatric data* of the nine month-old infant girl being *kissed by her mother,* as documented in Dr. Maulsby's published case study of 1971. I pondered. Will we see and record *the same data?* These questions really hounded me. But, I feel I was being guided somehow in my desire and zeal to test and study Nancy again and again along with another *chosen soul.* Is it not the quest of all good scientists *to test* and *test* and then *re-test* again and again, until you get all your questions answered? But when it is a *matter of faith,* when do you stop testing? *Are we testing God? Or is God really testing us?*

The *journey... science to faith...*

...with all its bumps and bruises ...

...marches on ...

However, before we end Chapter V there are two crucial *messages for America that Jesus* gave to Nancy, on March 19th, 1991: *Jesus* said, ***"Let Me see this nation, this president, appreciate My mercy and My love. Put God back in this country. Put God back in your schools, in your government, in your leaders, in every man, woman and child. Then, and only then, will you be one great Nation under God. I abhor the murders in this land. You have murdered the unborn. You have murdered the word of God, removing it from your schools and your hearts. Put Me back where I belong."***

On March 21st, 1991, at the consecration of the Mass, *Jesus* said, ***"Unless the murders stop, I will send a punishment upon this Nation."***

So, *what* are we waiting for? Hello? **Wake up America!** I believe this is a true *Divine call* - for a real selfless love, mercy, faith, hope, and charity - type of action.

CHAPTER VI

IN SEARCH OF "THE TRUTH"

PREPARATION FOR THE AUGUST 20th, 1993 STUDIES (Including: the August 6th, 1993 testing in Puerto Rico)

I had researched the adult clinical neurophysiology literature for any and all data supporting our medical and scientific results relative to the specific brain wave patterns documented on Nancy Fowler's brain *during the heavenly visits* or *apparitions of Jesus and the Blessed Virgin Mary.* Initially I had not researched the pediatric neurophysiology literature, since we were testing adults. But, I soon discovered that it was only the pediatric medical and scientific literature that came even close to our findings. Interestingly, I found in the pediatric neurophysiology literature reports of *hedonic - pleasure rhythms* or 4 Hz theta rhythms that were seen *only in infants* or *very young children* (see Maulsby 1971 and Kugler and Laub 1971). Since I could not find any adult clinical neurophysiology/EEG literature that had ever reported such amazing unprecedented brain wave patterns as recorded and documented on Nancy, I strongly felt the need to test further - realizing I was headed into uncharted waters.

After reviewing the adult world neurophysiology literature and discussing my many questions with a score of prominent neurologists, clinical neuropsychologists, neurophysiologists and EEG experts (like me); I soon realized that *no one had the answer.* The very results themselves begged for more research and study. As a diligent scientist ***in search of the truth,*** I realized that *more testing* needed to be done for the purposes of validating our astonishing *new* and unprecedented *data.* But the *Blessed Virgin Mary* had just said to Nancy, in one of her messages on July 13th, 1993, *"I ask that no more testing be done."* So, I contacted Nancy to discuss many of the questions raised by the results of our medical and scientific research. I shared with Nancy my deep desire *to study and test* her further along with one or more subjects, who claim to experience *heavenly visitations* or *visions* or *apparitions* of *Jesus and the Blessed Virgin Mary.*

At the onset, Nancy said that the *Blessed Virgin Mary* wanted no more *testing* to be done. Again recall the message given on July 13th, 1993: *"I ask that no more testing be done."* However, *I insisted* that the unprecedented results of all our initial testing begged *for more studies* to be conducted ***to shed light*** on *what* exactly the stimulus specific evoked EEG brain wave patterns might really mean.

My proposed *experiment design* consisted of performing a *battery of baseline EEG studies* before the apparitions *on two or more chosen souls* and to conduct a complete neurological evaluation including mental status, psychiatric and neuropsychological examinations, as had been done with Nancy. These meticulous medical and scientific *studies would then be repeated* during the apparitions and after the apparitions were completed. With our ambulatory audiovisual TV-EEG telemetry oxford II system, we could essentially perform these tests anywhere including at that time our state of the art neurodiagnostic EEG laboratory. Nancy said she would *need to first ask permission from heaven* before she (Nancy) would consent to any further tests, since as above the *Blessed Virgin Mary* just recently had *asked* Nancy *"...that no more testing be done."*

Nancy mentioned to me that she knew of several persons *blessed with visions* that she would ask to participate in these new rounds of tests (I had requested), if given *permission from above.* Honestly at that time in my life, I was not used to this type of *getting permission from heaven* business. The hardened skeptic in me then pondered, *what* does all of this mean? One week after my blunt request, Nancy phoned. I will never forget the excitement in her voice when she said that while she was *in prayer* in her bedroom (last night) *the Blessed Virgin Mary* briefly appeared as *"Our Lady of Grace,"* and *agreed to appear for the additional testing* I had requested. However, the *Blessed Virgin Mary* now *asked* that *the testing* not be done at the farm in Conyers. The *Blessed Virgin Mary* in a *message* to Nancy said that further testing in Conyers especially on the 13th of the month would be a distraction for all the many pilgrims offering their prayers to God.

So, the *Blessed Virgin Mary* requested that *the tests* be done at the doctor's office *(specifically my office at St. Joseph's Hospital of Atlanta).* Upon hearing these words, I remember quickly taking out my pen and appointment book and asked Nancy matter-of-factly, *"When* does the *Blessed Virgin Mary want to come* and *appear for this testing?" "Oh* and... at *what time* of the day *does she want to come?"* Can you imagine? I could hardly believe it. I was unwittingly *making an appointment* with the *Blessed Virgin Mary to come to my office.* Later, I asked Nancy, *"Does she have co-pay?"* (USA doctor joke) *"So,* what time does she want?"

Nancy did not know *what time;* but, said any time we set up for the extra tests would be fine. We discussed *the tests* at length and decided on Friday afternoon, August 20th, 1993 for this special appointment. Nancy said there was a young seminarian, who she had in mind to be part of these additional tests. Nancy then said the *Blessed Virgin Mary* also *agreed to appear to this seminarian* for the tests, I had requested. I asked Nancy if there were any special requests in preparation for the additional testing. Nancy said she would prefer to have a *white sheet* or some type of white backboard behind the crucifix and behind a statue of *Our Loving Mother* as a backdrop. Nancy matter-of-factly said that when she sees *visions or apparitions,* the visions and the apparitions appear more vivid, more clearly distinct and with much more detail, when the background is white. It is similar with a projection screen in the movie theater. The whiter the screen background, the more vivid the colors with sharper definition you see a movie. Apparently, it is for this same reason that the crucifix over the fireplace in the farm house of the Conyers apparition room is mounted on a very large, white backboard.

Nancy said that for these additional medical and scientific studies requested by me, she would bring the crucifix from the farm house apparition room and also one of the statues of *Our Loving Mother* from where she (Nancy) has experienced many numerous visions and apparitions of the Blessed Virgin Mary.

I remember going shopping with my wife, to find white sheets in order to place one on my laboratory wall for this testing day. We deliberated over many options—satin, silk, polyester...? After giving it much thought, we decided on a simple white cotton sheet as the most appropriate linen for the testing. We did consider the fact we were living in the state of Georgia, where *cotton* is abundant.

One of the reasons *the testing* had to be conducted later in the month (August 20th) was because the young seminarian would be in town at that time. Furthermore, Nancy had already been invited in the early part of August 1993, to go to Puerto Rico for a series of talks. Nancy said she would return from Puerto Rico on the 11th of August, in preparation for the monthly apparitions of the *Blessed Virgin Mary* at the farm house (on the 13th). So, because of Nancy's numerous obligations surrounding apparition day, *the tests* had to be done the following week. Thus, the August 20^{th,} 1993 date was set.

On August 11^{th,} 1993, I received a telephone call from Nancy shortly after her return from Puerto Rico. Nancy was very happy and excited. She asked me to please contact Dr. Agosto and Dr. Dalmau, neuro-specialists from Puerto Rico, as soon as possible. So, I did. Dr. Teresa Dalmau is trained in adult clinical neuropsychology/neurophysiology and is an EEG specialist; while the neurologist Dr. Norma Agosto is Board Certified in EEG (electroencephalography) and is an Adjunct Professor of Neurology, University of Puerto Rico Medical School. When Nancy was in Puerto Rico, these two very well respected doctors independently asked Nancy to (please) *submit to more medical and scientific testing,* which would be conducted in their state-of-the-art laboratory in Puerto Rico. These fine doctors were at the time *not aware* of our unprecedented *new data* and results. After much prayer, Nancy finally agreed and humbly submitted to these additional tests.

Dr. Agosto's credentials are indeed very impressive, to say the least. She is a highly-skilled brilliant neuroscience specialist, who was trained at Columbia Presbyterian Neurological Institute in New York City, New York, USA. Dr. Agosto completed fellowship training in EEG and neurophysiology under the mentorship of Dr. Timothy Pedley of international epilepsy specialty fame. Then, without being able to provide any of the details concerning the medical and scientific data the doctors had just recorded and documented in Puerto Rico, Nancy said the results of their testing was indeed extraordinary, when *"Jesus appeared."*

With curious anticipation, I contacted Dr. Agosto, who said she had quite an amazing experience with Nancy's testing. By all accounts Dr. Agosto's laboratory most definitely is a state-of-the-art EEG/neurodiagnostic laboratory. During the time of the testing, Aug. 6th, 1993, Dr .Agosto's laboratory had been selected as one of 25 worldwide Columbia Presbyterian Neurological Institute's *beta sites* for computerized brain mapping quantitative EEG analysis. This is significant, because the *data bank* utilized for Nancy's quantitative EEG brain mapping comparative analysis was indeed the same *data bank* used in Columbia University's Neurological Institute, which holds literally thousands of patients/subjects quantitative EEG brain mapping comparative analysis data. It holds the quantitative EEG data – essentially all the electrical brain wave activity topographic picture data for both normal and abnormal quantitative EEG brain maps. These brain maps are utilized for comparative analysis of all the different types of neurological and psychiatric illnesses: Like dementia, delirium, manic-depression, bi-polar disease, schizophrenia, psychosis, anxiety, depression, stroke, epilepsy, migraine, multiple sclerosis, CNS demyelinating diseases, brain trauma, brain tumors, encephalitis, HIV, Parkinson's disease, degenerative brain disorders, and medication effects etc., *just to name a few.* We could *not* have dreamed up a better source for a *data bank,* with such a large comprehensive volume of mathematical, medical and scientific comparative analysis *data* already stored to be used for our comparative EEG analysis and neurological evaluations.

Dr. Teresa Dalmau then conducted a full clinical neuropsychology battery, which again proved to be entirely *normal* for Nancy's stated age of 45 yrs. The neurologist Dr. Agosto conducted the *baseline EEG studies,* which were again entirely *normal,* while awake with eyes open and eyes closed and also entirely *normal, during all sleep stages.* The baseline neurological and mental status examinations were *normal.* The quantitative EEG brain mapping comparative analysis record of Nancy demonstrated *a normal brain* for her stated age of 45 yrs., showing a predominantly mixed alpha-beta rhythms background brain wave activity that was seen symmetrically over the posterior head regions. No pathological patterns were identified, even when compared with the *data bank* from Columbia's Neurological Institute.

The quantitative EEG analysis recorded a *brief apparition* of the *Blessed Virgin Mary* in the Dr. Agosto's Puerto Rico laboratory. The EEG analysis demonstrated rare fast theta rhythms, but mostly early alpha rhythms in the 7-9 Hz range, with 8 Hz noted *with eyes open.* This *reflective* EEG pattern was recorded during the *brief experience* and *heavenly visit* or *apparition* of the *Blessed Virgin Mary—* described by Nancy at that moment - as a brief *silent appearance (no words).*

This predominant *alpha pattern* recorded is called a *reflective* or *relaxed* state. Note: The *Blessed Virgin Mary* did not speak and was not bringing baby *Jesus* during this *silent apparition.* This brief experience of seeing the *Blessed Virgin Mary* was similar to my initial EEG June 13th, 1993 recordings. When Nancy first saw *Our Loving Mother* appear briefly alone *not holding baby Jesus* or *speaking His words,* I recorded 8-9 Hz alpha activity, ~8.5Hz, *with eyes open,* a *reflective* or *relaxed* state.

Dr. Agosto said she did not expect nor even anticipate such extraordinary *supernatural events* would take place (especially) in her laboratory. The neurologist Dr. Agosto and Dr. Dalmau were both just merely trying to medically and scientifically evaluate Nancy via the quantitative EEG analysis method.

This mathematically derived *topographic electrical brain wave activity picture* for comparative analysis with such an incredible *data bank* available to them from the prestigious Columbia University's Neurological Institute in New York offered hopes of discovering whether there was any true pathology in Nancy's brain that could possibly produce any of her *heavenly visits* or *visions* or *apparitions.*

Basically Dr. Agosto was asking the same primary questions we were repeatedly asking ourselves here in Atlanta, Georgia, throughout all the medical and scientific studies: Questions like: Is Nancy's brain *sick* neurologically or psychiatrically or even *spiritually?* Are all these *supernatural events* real? Is it *fact or fiction?* We all wanted to know. I really wanted to know.

On the quantitative EEG analysis *data* during the *apparition of Jesus - in His Living Presence,* Dr. Agosto recorded a most extraordinary EEG brain wave change. As soon as Nancy said, *"Jesus is here,"* Dr. Agosto immediately saw the EEG quickly change to a different EEG frequency pattern. She incredibly documented the same amazing unprecedented EEG patterns I stumbled across in all our studies of Nancy to date. Dr. Agosto recorded the same unprecedented 3 Hz *delta rhythms* with a *deep sleep* stage-topographic pattern with no evidence of spikes, sharp waves, epileptic activity or behavior or any EEG pathology whatsoever. This rather *new* and astonishing EEG pattern of *deep sleep, while awake* was indeed recorded. At times the 3 Hz *delta rhythms* actually generalized and spread over the entire brain topography.

Incredibly, *this change* in Nancy's quantitative EEG brain mapping comparative analysis occurred instantly **within milliseconds** of the moment Nancy said, *"Jesus is here."* This change occurred at the precise moment in time Nancy said she experienced an *apparition* of *Jesus - in His Living Presence* during the quantitative EEG brain mapping comparative analysis testing. Dr. Agosto and Dr. Dalmau now have a very dramatic and extraordinary quantitative EEG analysis - topographic brain wave picture – and *raw EEG data* of Nancy's experience of *seeing Jesus - in His Living Presence.* Nancy was awake and alert with eyes open - in the *living presence of Jesus* - during this topographic picture. This amazing picture shows a quantitative EEG brain mapping color picture of *generalized 3 Hz delta rhythms* encompass Nancy's entire brain topography with one color/one frequency. Wow!

Later, during *the testing* when Nancy claimed that *Jesus spoke (His living words - in the light, His light)* to her, the same EEG pattern was again recorded demonstrating the same unprecedented 3 Hz *delta rhythms* with topography of a *deep sleep* pattern while Nancy (simultaneously) remained *awake.*

Once again the same astonishing 3 Hz *delta rhythms* typical of a *deep sleep*

EEG pattern, *but* while still *fully awake* was recorded and documented *only in His Living Presence* and when *Jesus speaks* to Nancy *(His living words - in His Light).*

Now to point out some amazing new observations, just look at the following:

1) Our original *data* and results of the *initial baseline studies* of June 11th, 1993 completed in my state-of-the-art laboratory in Atlanta, Ga., USA, St. Joseph's Hospital Center for Specialty Medicine.

2) The two separate out *in the field* studies done in the farm house completed in Conyers, Ga., USA, on the same appointed date of June 13th, 1993 that was recorded and documented in two different locations.

3) The clinical observations *in the field* during the testing of July 13th, 1993.

4) The *new studies* just completed above by Dr. Agosto and Dr. Dalmau on August 6th, 1993 in Las Piedras, Puerto Rico.

All the above medical and scientific research studies were completed on Nancy using different types of sophisticated EEG equipment in different locations by different certified and qualified EEG experts and technicians. This demonstrates that Nancy's *heavenly experiences of Jesus in light – in His Living Presence* and *Jesus speaking – His living words - in the light, His Light* --- using our strict medical and scientific criteria, repeatedly produced the same amazing and unprecedented *new medical and scientific data.* We can now say --- based on our combined research with the repeatedly reproduced identical *EEG data* from Nancy's *heavenly experiences of Jesus* as recorded and documented by different state-of-the-art neurodiagnostic laboratories in different countries – that *His Living Presence* and *His living words* are *one.*

Note: *His Living Presence* and *His living words* are indeed *one and the same.* One and the same experience*, heavenly visit of Jesus;* one and the same *stimulus specific living energy source;* one and the *same EEG patterns;* one and the same *medical science;* one and the same *EEG pattern and quantitative EEG brain wave mapping patterns* – and one and the same *mathematics;* one and the same *living presence;* one and the same *living words;* one and the same *living light;* one and the same *Jesus;* and one and the same *supernatural events.* When extrapolating all our combined medical and scientific research *new data* to date, we can conclude:

One and the same (living) *light.* One the same profound *peace.*
One and the same *harmony of truth.*

Dr. Agosto added that Nancy's quantitative EEG brain mapping topographic comparative analysis using the *data bank* from Columbia Presbyterian Neurological Institute in New York demonstrated no evidence of brain pathology: no schizophrenia, bipolar illness, depression, dementia, epilepsy, multiple sclerosis, stroke, toxic-metabolic encephalopathy, encephalitis, hydrocephalus, trauma etc.

Nancy's quantitative EEG brain mapping topographic comparative analysis matched with all *normal* brain maps for subjects/patients of 45 years old. The neurologist Dr. Agosto's clinical neurological evaluation of Nancy included a mental status examination that was entirely *normal.* Both distinguished doctors were very excited about the *new* astonishing *data,* as they had *never seen* any patient/subject actually develop 3 Hz delta rhythms in a *deep sleep pattern* during any EEG testing ever while the patient/subject remains simultaneously awake, alert with focused attention and totally conscious.

Remember, the 3 Hz delta rhythms in a typical *deep sleep* pattern was recorded while Nancy's eyes were open, *awake, alert with focused attention,* fully oriented and conscious. She clinically exhibited normal speech and content, normal affect and train of thinking and showed no evidence of psychotic or epileptic behavior. No EEG pathology was found in the meticulous medical and scientific examinations during the apparitions of the *Blessed Virgin Mary* and *Jesus.* Despite years of research experience and teaching in her field, Dr. Agosto had never before encountered such extraordinary and *unprecedented findings* as those which she recorded and documented on Nancy on August 6th, 1993 in her state-of-the-art EEG/Neurodiagnostic laboratory in Puerto Rico.

Dr. Agosto and Dr. Dalmau, much like my medical team in Atlanta, found Nancy's brain waves to be *normal* and healthy. Nancy maintained a *normal* mental status examination with eyes open during the moments she (Nancy) said, *"The Blessed Virgin Mary* appeared*" (briefly);* and then later, when she said, *"Jesus* is here.*"* Dr. Agosto emphatically stated that *no pathology* was ever *discovered in Nancy's brain* during an extensive quantitative EEG brain wave mapping comparative analysis study, while using the University of Columbia Presbyterian Neurological Institute's *data bank.*

Dr. Agosto stated that she recorded Nancy's **3 Hz delta rhythms with a deep sleep-topographic brain wave pattern, while awake, were seen (within milliseconds) only when Nancy said, *"Jesus* is here.*"*** These medical and scientific findings were extremely important and amazing. Dr. Agosto wrote in her medical report that no brain pathology could be found statistically on the brain mapping analysis done, and no epileptic activity or spike focus was ever found in the testing **before, during or after the apparitions of Jesus. Dr. Agosto also wrote, "These very unusual (EEG) activities seen with eyes open... should be considered as a normal variant."**

Note: A *normal variant* is an EEG term that identifies a particular EEG brain wave pattern seen in *normal subjects* in certain awake and sleep states that medical and scientific EEG research has noted as a normal variant pattern of EEG. As stated before, Dr. Agosto is a fully Board Certified EEG expert who has made these very keen, intelligent and respectable clinical EEG observations and medical scientific conclusions. I found Dr. Agosto's comments extremely insightful and helpful to me especially in trying to understand these *new* unprecedented stimulus specific evoked EEG brain wave patterns of *deep sleep,* while an *awake, alert with focused attention* EEG pattern is simultaneously superimposed and was recorded *only* in association with the *apparitions of Jesus* and whenever *Jesus speaks.* Most neurophysiologists would agree that it should be possible to reproduce a *normal variant* (if this classification is correct) in the brains of other individuals undergoing very similar experiences or conditions.

I was very excited to hear the news of Dr. Agosto and Dr. Dalmau's *new data.* Their collective *new data* corroborated and supported my medical and scientific testing done on both June 11th and June 13th, 1993, and my medical scientific clinical observations of July 13th, 1993. It was obviously also very important to me to have another witness and qualified expert in EEGs and neurophysiology *(like me)* to study Nancy using yet another different modality of EEG analysis (i.e. quantitative EEG brain mapping comparative analysis). These recorded and documented results were recorded in yet another state-of-the-art neurophysiology laboratory, in yet another country. Medically and scientifically this was and is very important, as it evidences the all-important criterion in medical science of showing **the great importance in the reproducibility of similar results in the testing to ensure the validity of the *new data* recorded.**

Thus, these *new* unprecedented stimulus specific evoked EEG brain wave patterns, that were recorded and documented on Nancy's brain mapping analysis during the *apparitions of Jesus - in His Living Presence,* yielded the same and unprecedented 3 Hz *delta rhythm* EEG brain wave patterns, I had repeatedly recorded and documented on all the *medical and scientific testing data* to date---but again *only - in His Living Presence* or when *Jesus, Who* **is** very much *alive,* speaks to Nancy *His life giving/living words of God - in the light, His light – the light of God.*

I called Dr. Agosto and invited her and Dr. Dalmau to come to the United States, to be part of my new medical and scientific research team *to test* and investigate Nancy again along with a young seminarian on Aug. 20th, 1993. At first, both doctors declined, saying that their schedules were so busy and that such a trip seemed impossible on such short notice. I nonetheless left an open invitation for them and asked them to please fax me a copy of their medical reports and scientific *raw data with Nancy's permission.* Within a few days, I received another unexpected phone call which heralded the good and wonderful news that despite their numerous commitments, both Dr. Agosto and Dr. Dalmau were able to somehow rearrange their busy schedules and come to Atlanta, Ga. They will now be present for the scheduled August 20th, 1993 medical and scientific testing.

So again, I called them in Puerto Rico and asked them to please bring all their EEG *raw data* for EEG comparisons with our *data* for a complete analysis. Now, I was definitely getting very excited at the glorious anticipation of what we would find in the *upcoming new tests.*

With *heaven agreeing to appear,* I was elated. Recall how the *Blessed Virgin Mary* lovingly caresses and brings her baby *Jesus, the light of the world,* to us. Can you imagine, O*ur Loving Mother* had just agreed - with permission from her *Son, Jesus* - to appear *(with Jesus)* ---- to Nancy and the young seminarian for the additional testing I had just requested. Wow!

Now with the doctors from Puerto Rico coming to be *witnesses for these supernatural events* in my EEG laboratory and to also have a chance to do more medical and scientific testing, I was indeed, very excited and ready to go to the next round of *more tests.* My true sentiments were now in full swing of a genuine anticipation, despite my initial hardened skepticism of the two months prior; plus an awe and wonder, as to *what* these *tests and more tests* would possibly reveal.

So, the *journey...science to faith...*now a true cliff hanger...
...with even more big bumps and bruises...*continues...*

But first, I want to plead **a strong defense for** *the greatest ever prayer* warrior and *miracle* ***intercessor*** *God gave us:* **Mary,** my Celestial Loving Mama, using *logic* from the *Holy Scriptures,* our amazing *new medical and scientific data* and *Mary's* most powerful, useful, yet *necessary* and *sublime lesson* for all of us – given *in the first miracle of Jesus* - during the *wedding of Cana.*

If you believe in *God,* Creator of Heaven and earth, *Who* created the entire universe with billions of galaxies, stars, moons, comets, meteors, suns and planets, the wind, the birds, the waters, the fish, the mammals and all the living creatures etc. and also the human race (us) with *His Creative Word, His Fiat - His Divine Will;* and believe *God* created *the holy angels,* the entire nine choirs in three tiers (3-3-3) with all their majesty and power; then you probably also believe that *"there is nothing impossible with God."* So, *Who* is the most powerful *Supreme Being* ever? I hope you answered: *God, the Almighty! God,* Who even created *the angel of light,* as it is written in Isaiah Chapter 14: Lucifer, also called Satan (the devil), who rebels against God and tries to set himself above *God, Who created him. Because of this rebellion,* he was cast down to earth with a third of the angels that followed him. So please, *do not* ever believe that Satan has more power than *God. God* forbid.

So, if *God creates man in His image and likeness* and *makes a covenant with man,* so be it. And if *God* makes *the plan for redemption* immediately after *the fall of man* with *the first sin,* when Adam and Eve *rebelled against His Divine Will,* so be it. If *God's plan for redemption of mankind* includes Gen 3:15:*"the woman... and her seed,"* prophetically *the innocent new Eve, "the virgin,"* Mary; and *her seed "the light of the world;" Isaiah 7:14: "Emmanuel," Jesus,* so be it. Recall the serpent's/Satan's (*"the father of lies," the master of all deceptions)* contribution to *the fall* of man (see

Gen 3:1-15), as *God* prophesized *His immeasurable love and mercy plan for redeeming man* using *"the woman,"* Mary and her *Son (the only begotten Son of God/Eternal Word of the Father).* So, do not be deceived by Satan any longer. The *prophetic vision* of the *Mother of God with child* given to Elijah on Mt. Carmel and *the prophetic words* given to Isaiah 9:6: *"For a child is born to us, and a son is given to us,"* **is** *part of God's plan for salvation.* So, if *God* wants *Mary* as *co-Redemptrix, since Mary gives us her Son,* **Jesus - the Savior** *and* **the Redeemer,** so be it.

Recall *the EEG pattern when Mary brings Jesus* is 444 and how this pattern of numbers is in *the gold* of *the Ark of the Covenant* and in *the number of buckets filled with water* poured over Elijah's holocaust. So, if *God* wants to show the world *the prophetic meaning of these numbers* discovered in the *medical and scientific studies on chosen souls* experiencing *the living presence of baby Jesus "given to us" by His loving Mother:* magnifying *Mary's fiat to God's Redemption plan,* so be it.

Recall, Moses wrote - *the Lord God "came...appeared from mount Pharan, and with him thousands of saints"* (Deuteronomy 33:2); and *in the transfiguration of Jesus* (demonstrating *His Divine nature* to Peter, James and John), *Moses and Elijah appeared as living saints* (Luke 9; Matthew 17). So, if *God* wants to show the world through our *medical and scientific studies* that when *Mary with her baby Jesus appears to the chosen souls,* it is *prophetically reminiscent* of John's *Book of Revelation* 11:19 and 12:1, with "*lightning,*" "*a great hail*" *("Hail, full of grace")* and *"A woman clothed with the sun,"* so be it. If *God* makes the word *"woman" prophetic* for the *most special relationship Mary enjoys with the Holy Trinity:* as the *beloved daughter* of *the Father*, the *spouse* of *the Holy Spirit* and *mother* of *Jesus, "the Son of God,"* (Luke 1:35), so be it. Now read Mary's 10 verses in Luke 1:46-55.

See how much *Jesus loves, honors* and *glorifies His Mother* by *including Mary's prayer* (from a loving mother's heart) for the wedding couple - whose feast ran out of wine - *to be in union with His first miracle* at Cana: constituting *Mary* as *Queen of miracles.* With great love for *His Mother Mary, Jesus* in fulfilling *God's everlasting new covenant with man* makes it a *family affair. God* is at the *Head,* we *His adopted children* are in the *body/sitting at the table around God,* and *Mary* is at the *neck of the body/*sitting at the table next to *God* as *His and Our Loving Mother.* So, if *God* wants to make - *His covenant with man* - a *family affair,* so be it.

Now see how *Mary* teaches us the most useful, yet necessary and sublime lesson ever at the *wedding of Cana.* With *the heart of a mother* and an imploring tone - knowing *her Son always wants to please her,* Mary asks *Jesus to help* when the wine ran out. *Jesus* says, *"Woman... my hour (for miracles) is not yet come."* Mary tells the waiters, *"Do whatsoever my Son tells you to do." So, Jesus blesses* the *water*-in six jars that *turns into* the most delicious *wine, as Mary asked/prayed.* Here - *Jesus* is saying, *"Do you need miracles? Come to my Mother,* for *I will not deny her."* Mary says, *"Do you want a miracle?* **Do** *the Divine Will of my Son, God."* So, *disciple* of Christ (John 19:27) **be not afraid** *to come to Mary for prayers.*

CHAPTER VII

"I AM!"

THE TESTING OF AUGUST 20th, 1993

It was another very exciting day, awaited with much, much curious anticipation. Both Dr. Agosto and Dr. Dalmau had arrived in Atlanta, Ga., a few days prior to the actual *testing* in order to compare their medical and scientific data with ours. We extensively reviewed all the EEG *raw data,* and were astonished to find the **same identical new unprecedented 3 Hz delta rhythms in a *deep sleep* pattern - while awake, with the same specific EEG pattern and morphology when Nancy says, "*Jesus* is here," as recorded from the laboratory in Rio Piedras, Puerto Rico**, that was previously repeatedly recorded and documented in our *baseline studies* in **Atlanta, Ga.,** and the two June 13th, 1993 *medical and scientific studies* completed in **Conyers, Ga.** This information was welcome news to us all. They had actually reproduced the same medical and scientific *data* I had discovered and arrived at similar conclusions in yet another state-of-the-art laboratory and in yet another location, the 4th location, but using different EEG equipment and different certified EEG technicians and EEG experts, as mentioned earlier in this book. Thus, the *reproducibility* of the *new* medical and scientific *data* supported the *validity* of our *new data.*

In preparing for the scheduled August 20th, 1993, medical and scientific testing, I performed *baseline studies* on the young seminarian. His identity is not revealed (at the time of this writing) due to his priestly vocation. The young religious has claimed very private experiences of *heavenly visits, visions* and *apparitions* to Nancy and a select few. This very special seminarian is today an active Roman Catholic priest. He wishes to remain anonymous and private with his gifts from heaven unless God, the Church or his religious order asks of him to do otherwise. Until that time comes, he remains actively serving in God's kingdom and full harvest.

THE BASELINE STUDIES ON THE SEMINARIAN

The neurological and psychiatric examinations were *normal,* and demonstrated a young gentleman in his mid-twenties with a totally *normal* cognitive mental status examination. Our medical examinations and scientific observations were as follows:

MENTAL STATUS: awake, alert, oriented x 3 with normal higher cortical functioning; normal speech and content, with no anomia, aphasia, or apraxia; normal train of thinking with excellent multi-tasking ability and no thought disorders identified. He has a normal affect with a supple mood. He is highly intelligent, animated, and speaks several foreign languages extremely well. Attention span was normal, and he has a normal immediate memory, short-term memory and long-term memory. There was no evidence of delusions, hallucinations, paranoid or psychotic behavior; and no evidence of anxiety, depression, or manic-depressive illness. Also no mood disorders identified, no hysterical or personality disorders were identified; and there was no evidence of malingering and no evidence of epileptic behavior.

NECK: supple with no evidence of meningeal irritation and a negative Kerning's, negative Brudzinski's sign, negative Forbes-Norris sign, and a negative L'hermitte's sign.

HEAD: Normal size without any deformities

SPINE: was without any deformities and normal range of motion.

CRANIAL NERVES I-XII: Normal sense of smell. He has normal pupils that were equally round and reactive bilaterally to light and accommodation with normal vision: OU 20/20 visual acuity. Normal corneal reflexes were noted bilaterally and the formal visual fields testing were normal. He has normal EOM's (extra-ocular movements) without nystagmus and a normal funduscopic examination with no evidence of papilledema OU (bilaterally). His face has a normal symmetrical smile with normal sensation. His uvula, palate and tongue were normal and midline with a normal gag reflex and normal bilateral shoulder shrugs.

MOTOR EXAM: No drift or fixation with normal 5/5 motor strength and good motor tone throughout all muscle groups tested. He has no tremors, twitches, tics, dystonia or myoclonus and no adventitious movements were noted. His muscles were normal and demonstrated no evidence of atrophy, fasciculations, myotonia, cramps or myokymia and with no evidence of spasticity or extra-pyramidal signs.

DEEP TENDON REFLEXES: Were 2+ symmetrically and bilaterally with no pathological spread of reflexes noted, no clonus noted bilaterally (sustained or unsustained), and no primitive reflexes were identified.

TOES: Normal downward pointing, bilaterally with a negative Babinski's sign.

POSTURE, STANCE and GAIT: Normal.

COORDINATION: No ataxia, no dysmetria, normal checking, and normal rapid alternating movements were noted bilaterally.

SENSORY EXAM: Normal primary and secondary modalities.

REFLEXES AND SIGNS: Normal abdominal reflexes; normal Romberg's sign; normal Wartenberg's sign; normal Schwartzman's sign; and negative primitive reflexes were identified.

Conclusion: The seminarian's neurological examination was entirely **normal** for his stated age.

The baseline EEG studies performed on the seminarian **were normal** in the awake, drowsy and sleep stages. *(In fact*, his EEG was *classic textbook normal for his age).*

The EEG evaluation and description is as follows: Rhythmic alpha activity was seen with eyes closed in the posterior head regions in the 10 -11 Hz range with faster beta activity seen in the anterior head regions and normal attenuation with eye opening, bilaterally. No pathological brain wave patterns were identified. No significant voltage asymmetry or focal slow activity was seen. No spikes, sharp waves or any epileptic discharges were recorded. No seizure activity was seen. Prolonged hyperventilation studies and photic stimulation studies using different filters were normal and failed to activate any pathological, paroxysmal or epileptic discharges or seizure activity. Sleep stages I and II were recorded with normal sleep spindles, vertex sharp waves, K-complexes, and no evidence of any pathology or seizure behavior identified.

Impression of the *baseline studies* on this day: **Normal.**

Dr. Agosto and Dr. Dalmau reviewed all EEGs and agreed with these findings. Dr. Agosto and Dr. Dalmau had the opportunity to clinically observe and fully examine the seminarian separately. They found the seminarian to be completely *normal,* in both of their extended neurological and neuropsychological examinations. The medical science and clinical observations of him were also *normal.* This is very important since two very qualified and expert neuroscience doctors had corroborated and supported all my *baseline studies* results of this young seminarian.

On the day of the testing August 20th, 1993, Nancy, George Collins and the young religious arrived at my medical office. Dr. Agosto and Dr. Dalmau had already arrived earlier in the morning and reviewed all my clinical data and *raw* EEG *data* on the two *chosen souls,* namely Nancy and the seminarian.

In order to avoid any sort of electrical contamination, we decided to use two different EEG systems for recording purposes. The young religious was recorded and filmed on the Oxford II ambulatory audiovisual TV-EEG telemetry monitoring system, while Nancy was recorded and monitored on the Nihon-Kohden, 21 Channel EEG, plus filmed by the same intensive monitoring audiovisual TV telemetry system. In this way, both of them could be audio visually monitored on the same TV video display screen, while their brain waves were simultaneously recorded on two separate and different EEG monitoring systems.

A camera was set up in the front right corner of the room to provide full head and trunk views of both *chosen souls.* Another hand-held camera recorded their actions and behaviors from the posterior view. The two cameras allowed full views of their eyes, faces, arms and trunks. The back sides of their heads and torsos as well as the religious objects in front of them were also now visible.

The crucifix from the farm house apparition room was mounted on the wall, which had been covered with a large white linen cotton sheet by my wife and medical staff. This large white linen cotton sheet was purchased to meet Nancy's request of a white background for this testing. A statue of the baby Jesus being caressed by the Blessed Virgin Mary (*Our Loving Mother statue*) was placed on a stack of EEG boxes also covered with another white linen cotton sheet. Two kneeling pews were borrowed from St. Joseph's Hospital of Atlanta's Chapel. We placed them in the room facing *the crucifix* nailed to the white linen cotton sheet dressed wall. Then, we asked the two *chosen souls* to please kneel for a moment to adjust all the cameras for optimum visual clarity.

Nancy and the seminarian were then taken individually into an adjacent room in my laboratory suite for the EEG scalp electrode hookup to the different EEG monitoring systems. At this time, we performed the *before-the-apparition* medical, neurological and psychiatric mental status examinations on each *chosen soul.* Present on this day were our two invited medical team guests just arriving from Puerto Rico, Dr. Agosto and Dr. Dalmau and my medical staff. As a surprise, Nancy's spiritual sister *(a Jewish doctor)* was kind enough to offer her services and participate in these clinical observations. Now if I had known that *she too* was going to have a *supernatural experience* on this testing day, I would have asked permission from my esteemed colleague to place EEG scalp electrodes on her head as well. No one could ever imagine nor concoct the incredible experience she was about to have.

Once Nancy and the seminarian had completed the medical, neurological, and neuropsychological examinations, the EEG scalp electrodes were placed on their heads and the EEG technicians completed their hookups - each to their respective separate EEG monitoring systems. Then, both were taken into the laboratory's audiovisual TV-EEG telemetry suite to start *the tests.*

Nancy knelt down to the right pew and the young seminarian knelt on the left pew beside her. As she looked around the room in the lab and saw the seminarian's garb and headset, Nancy proclaimed with excitement, *"George... George, my vision has just come true."* George later explained that Nancy had a vision that was documented and recorded in 1990, in which Nancy was kneeling in a small grayish-blue room *(like the room in my lab)* praying with this young religious seminarian and remembers remarking that he was wearing a very funny odd-looking hat *(the EEG headset).* She also recalled walking through a double door *(my lab's double door)* just prior to entering the room *(my EEG telemetry suite),* that Nancy thought in her vision was a chapel room, typically seen in many northern Catholic cathedral chapels. Later, George researched and confirmed Nancy's *prophetic vision was now fulfilled* in my lab. I found this quite extraordinary, because our very new St. Joseph's Doctor's Professional Building was not even constructed (basically did not exist) on the date of Nancy's vision.

Once Nancy and the seminarian were kneeling and the cameras were all rechecked to make sure everything was operational, we were ready to begin. I will never forget the contrasting feelings I felt in the room soon after the testing commenced. As the typical ambient temperature in the laboratory suite was drastically changed by a sudden cold, frigid air that literally swept throughout the room. I looked up immediately at our ceiling vents trying to ascertain *why* the air conditioning temperature had lowered so abruptly. As I looked up at the air conditioning vents, Nancy said*, "Ugh,* Satan is here*."* I recall a very uncomfortable and distinctly *eerie feeling.* I could not explain this deep gnawing feeling and sense of a strong disturbance associated with cold chills running up my spine. Nancy and the seminarian quickly initiated *prayers to God* commanding that "Satan be gone *in the name of Jesus."* In addition they recited the powerful prayers of *St. Michael the Archangel* and prayed for the *Precious Blood of Jesus* to be poured over the entire EEG testing suite and everyone present including me *(thank God).* Remarkably, upon *praying in the name of Jesus* within a few seconds -- the icy cold, eerie, disturbing *pure evil presence* was somehow completely gone and *vanished.*

Afterwards, as both Nancy and the seminarian continued to pray, the initial ambient temperature of the room returned. But within *six minutes,* I suddenly felt an even icier cold, frigid and even more *eerie disturbance* engulf the entire EEG testing room once again with even more intensity than the first encounter. Looking up at the ceiling air conditioning vents again I asked myself, *"How* could this air conditioning get so cold, so quickly...burr.*"* While still looking up and preparing to ask one of my EEG technicians to call one of the building's engineers and find out exactly what was going on with the buildings' air conditioning system, I again heard Nancy say*, "Ugh,* he is so vicious... Satan is back again... as a white serpent... over there on top of the crucifix at this very moment...Ugh.*"* I looked over towards Nancy and the seminarian as both started spraying *holy water* in the direction of *the evil one* and recited out loud the prayers of *St. Michael the Archangel.* Once again Nancy commanded the serpent to go away*, "In the name of Jesus,* Satan be gone!*"* Nancy and the seminarian then said *more prayers* asking God to pour the *Precious Blood of Jesus* over the entire EEG testing suite and all the people present in my medical office. Remarkably, moments later the eerie cold disturbing *evil presence* left the room *"in the name of Jesus."* Wow! I thought to myself at that moment, *what* awesome *authority the name of Jesus commands.* Both *chosen souls* continued to pray softly, but reverently for approximately fifteen minutes after this last encounter with *the evil one.* During the beginning moments of their prayers, the icy cold, eerie, disturbing and uncomfortable feeling in the laboratory suite drastically changed back to very comfortable, cozy ambient temperature and a peaceful good feeling was restored. The changes I felt in this room were both drastic and dramatic.

I pondered: *The name of* ***Jesus*** is and must be *the most powerful* and *awesome name ever.* Just recall the above experience in my EEG laboratory suite, and see the incredible **power and authority** *the name Jesus* has over *the evil one (Satan).* Moreover I pondered: *Why* does *the name Jesus* exert such power and authority over *evil dominions* and *principalities* and over Satan, *"the serpent?" Why?*

The young seminarian then began to sing songs, including the *Salve Regina* in Latin. If you can imagine what an angel sounds like singing, this would definitely be close. This was probably one of the most beautiful moments of the entire testing recorded and filmed. During the fifteen-minute period as the two *chosen souls* prayed, Nancy started reporting to see *light.* As they *praised God,* I remember the young religious saying, *"How beautiful...* this is un-be-lievable.*"* Then Nancy said, *"the light* is illuminating in *whiter than white light* from heaven as *holy angels* begin to appear and fill up this entire room. *St. Michael the Archangel* has just appeared.*"*

Then all of a sudden, both Nancy and the seminarian looked towards the statue of *Blessed Virgin Mary lovingly bringing her baby Jesus to us, Our Loving Mother* and Nancy declared *"Our Loving Mother (with baby Jesus)* is here.*"* It was at this exact moment in time that both audiovisual TV-EEG telemetry monitoring systems recorded the 4 Hz *theta rhythms* with the stimulus specific evoked brain wave pattern of **444!** This specific EEG pattern of 444 was previously seen ***only*** *during the testing of Nancy's brain* on June 13^{th,} 1993 in the apparition room at the Conyers farm house *when* Nancy claims that the *Blessed Virgin Mary bringing her baby Jesus to us* had just appeared or when *Our Loving Mother was speaking echoing the living words of her Son, Jesus.* After this, while the *Blessed Virgin Mary* was still holding *baby Jesus,* Nancy said, *"St. Joseph* just appeared holding a staff…now *many saints* are beginning to appear.*"* Nancy described, *"The saints* are appearing quickly one after the other… fast like flash cards... *praise You Lord."*

Nancy then said, *"Behold the Mother of God,* the *Blessed Virgin Mary* with her *baby Jesus.* Behold the *heavenly court of angels* and many *holy saints* are all here. This is truly awesome.*"* Suddenly, Nancy and the seminarian both simultaneously turned their heads to the right towards *the crucifix* hanging on the wall. Their in-sync symmetry can be clearly viewed and observed on both the audiovisual TV-EEG telemetry systems camera in the front of the room and the hand-held camera in the rear. Later, we (I) carefully reviewed the *front view* videotape. The expressions on both their faces were just priceless. Both *chosen souls* with open mouths were staring at the *heavenly vision* or *apparition of heaven* with a joyous and peaceful radiant glow of *ecstasy* on their faces, while also showcasing a genuine tender love with a humble, innocent childlike reverence.

Suddenly, Nancy said, *"Behold, the Risen Lord Jesus, Our Savior,* now appears in a glorified state. *Behold…our Lord Jesus."* Nancy said, *"Jesus* was full-size three-dimensional in an all white luminous *light."* On previous occasions Nancy has explained, *"The light I see* **is** *a light unlike any light on earth..."* She cannot describe this *light* as a singular visual experience. Nancy says, *"In the presence of*

His light and emanating from *His light,* I experience a profound deep *love, mercy, peace* and *joy* in my soul." Nancy says that it is her understanding that *she sees with the eyes of her soul, as God permits and guides.* Nancy could see *the crucifix* on the wall behind *Jesus.* She saw *Jesus* standing in front of her in an all *"dazzling, whiter than white luminous light."*

Later, after I interviewed and re-examined *the seminarian* in the experiment designed medical and neurological evaluations *after the apparitions,* I soon discovered that the seminarian had encountered a uniquely different visual mystical experience from Nancy's. The seminarian said to me, ***"I saw a light...brighter than the sun."*** I immediately said to myself, now where have I heard this phrase before? He went on further to explain that ***the light was so bright*** that it was actually causing his eyes to tear. He could barely make out *the silhouette of Jesus in light* because of the blinding brightness of *the light.* The seminarian then said, *"I could* clearly *hear His voice* (the voice of Jesus), *the voice of the Good Shepherd calling* to one of *His sheep*...so I follow and now serve *Him."*

Note: This *apparition of Jesus* to the seminarian remotely reminds me of what happened to Saul - now Paul – in his supernatural encounter with *Jesus as the Risen Lord* on the road to Damascus. Saul was ready to hunt down and take to prison any Jew that had become a Christian. This *supernatural event* and encounter experienced by Saul/Paul occurred *after Jesus had already died* by a Roman *crucifixion on the wood of the cross* on Calvary and had *ascended to heaven.* Saul's/St. Paul's experience with the *"Sun of justice"* (Malachi 4:2) is clearly shown in Acts 26:13: *"O king, I saw a light from the sky, brighter than the sun." ("I saw a light...brighter than the sun")*

According to their descriptions, it was obvious that Nancy and the seminarian were simultaneously having uniquely different experiences of *Jesus* and *His heavenly court.* At the precise moment that Nancy said, *"Behold, the Risen Lord...Jesus..,"* the two separate audiovisual TV-EEG telemetry systems recorded a dramatic and simultaneous unprecedented EEG brain wave change in both *chosen souls.* Amazingly, both Nancy and the seminarian's electrical brain pictures changed to the unprecedented 3 Hz *delta rhythms* forming the stimulus specific evoked brain wave pattern of 333. Since the young religious was in his mid-twenties, the 3 Hz *delta rhythms* were of slightly higher amplitude as would be expected, in comparison to the EEG of a mid-forty year-old person like Nancy. During the exact moments in time that *Jesus was present,* both Nancy and the seminarian demonstrated fairly rhythmic 3 Hz *delta rhythms with overriding beta activity.* Basically a topographic EEG *deep sleep* pattern and an *awake, alert with focused attention* EEG pattern superimposed or intermixed together. Indeed, I recorded a true *contradiction of pure physiological terms* and an *oxymoron.*

During *the testing,* both Nancy and the religious communicated with all of us in the room. They told us *what they were seeing* in a very intelligent, coherent, logical and sophisticated manner. On the audiovisual TV-EEG telemetry monitoring screen, one could see the typical radiant facial glow of *ecstasy* with a profound reverence, *love, joy and peace* and with *very little blinking* indeed. Objectively speaking, it is almost as if *eye blinking* somehow cuts down or cuts out time of the *visionary experience,* so the *chosen souls* keenly keep their eyes wide open and fixated on the *beatific vision.* This particular clinical observation was undoubtedly consistent with the numerous other clinical observations of Nancy in *states of ecstasy* during our prior testing. As *the apparitions* were ending, Nancy could be seen lifting up her hands and arms while looking upwards and saying, *"The Risen Lord... Jesus... His Blessed Mother...* and *His heavenly court...* are *now ascending* through the roof.*"* As the *visionary experience* ended, one could see - on both the respective audiovisual TV-EEG telemetry monitoring systems - the EEG recordings instantaneous return to the prior *normal baseline EEG patterns.* We then had the opportunity to clinically test and observe both *chosen souls* separately *after the apparitions* and *the visionary experiences* had ended. The medical, neurological, neuropsychological and psychiatric neuro-cognitive mental status examinations were entirely *normal for both chosen souls.* Dr. Agosto and Dr. Dalmau also reviewed all the *new data* and agreed with my medical and scientific evaluations.

It is important to note, that, albeit subjectively, while Nancy and the seminarian were seeing *visions of light*—they also proclaimed the *presence of angels,* particularly *St. Michael the Archangel.* They also saw *St. Joseph* and many *saints,* the *Blessed Virgin Mary* and her *Son, Jesus - in His Living Presence.* This *heavenly visit* absolutely produced a *drastically different feeling* in the room, *a joyful peace,* as compared to the evil one's cold disturbing eerie presence encountered earlier.

While the external environment was not measured in this study, I at least am a witness to feeling the same intensity of profound love, peace, joy, calm, cozy warm good feeling with this *heavenly visit* that was truly beyond any description. Words really do little or no justice in attempting to describe this wonderfully blessed feeling. This is the same exact *feeling* (I did feel) *during the heavenly visits* or *apparitions of Jesus, Blessed Virgin Mary* and the *Heavenly Court* previously recorded.

After Nancy and the seminarian stood up from their kneeling positions, they were brought into the adjacent room suite to remove the EEG scalp electrodes. George walked up to retrieve the statue of the *Blessed Virgin Mary with baby Jesus, Our Loving Mother,* and then removed *the crucifix* from the wall. As George passed by Nancy's spiritual sister *(the Jewish doctor),* she remarked, *"That's wrong."* I said, *"What* do you mean...that's wrong?*"* The Jewish doctor said, *"I saw* the letters, ***'I AM,'*** *all in white* on this letterhead.*"* She pointed to the black, lettered insignia, **INRI**, which refers to *Jesus of Nazareth King of the Jews.* I was very puzzled by her remarks. I then asked her again *privately* if she had an experience or had seen something during the testing.

In private the Jewish doctor humbly said to me, *"Yes.* I saw a tremendous bright white light... followed by a chorus of angels, all in a bright light. Then, I saw the most beautiful and magnificent Lady, I presume... *the Virgin Mary.* She was holding and caressing *her baby (Jesus).* Then, the light got even brighter and a man holding a staff appeared next to *Mary with her baby.* I heard Nancy say this was *St. Joseph.* Then, many more *people appeared all in light* and fast almost like *"flash cards"* or fast flashing pictures - similar to what Nancy was saying."

"Then, *the light* really turned super-bright and I saw... the shape of a man appear *Who* Nancy called *Jesus* - in the form of a bright white, white dazzling, brilliant light ... in three dimensions. *The light* was beautiful, awesome. I then *started seeing* ***a door*** appear right in front of the *heart/chest* area of the *corpus of Jesus on the cross...*on the wall behind the translucent white dazzling shape of *Jesus in light.* Then another brilliant, densely white luminous *cross of light* appeared just adjacent to *the crucifix* on the wall. But, I could not keep my eyes off *the door.* I really wanted to see... what was behind *the door... with such bright light pouring forth its entire outline.* I could see Nancy and the seminarian engaged in their experience, but like the TV game show... I wanted to see *what* was behind *"door No.1!"* Then, something happened...*the door* started to open."

"As *the door* opened widely, I was somehow *(in spirit?)* taken through *the door.* As I entered, I saw the most awesome and beautiful sight...the entire universe, galaxies, and *bright stars.* It was awesome ...and so beautiful. I was then taken somehow to a higher tier. Here, I saw tremendous *brighter white light* and *thousands upon thousands of beings*, all of them *in light.* Some had actual wings. Some had glowing type of head pieces? I somehow understood with almost *instant knowledge* that these *blessed beings* were *all very special* and unconditionally *loved by God."*

"Then, I was taken *somehow* to an even *much higher 3rd tier* of the greatest, *brightest light.* Here *I felt my soul deeply tremble,* as I ascended to this highest tier of the brightest *light* ever. I felt a series of awesome *powerful rumbles...*I then heard the *thundering sound* of *the Almighty Awesome Power!* ***My soul trembled*** as I saw *flashes of lightning.* I then saw what looked like a very large, giant, massive, very white, white beard lower face profile of an old, *ancient* looking man. Though I wanted to see *His* entire face, I could not... I could only see part the mouth and the lower face. But as I tried to see more of *His* face, *His* cheek bones instantly became like *giant towering cliffs!* Again, *my soul deeply trembled* and I heard yet more *powerful rumbles.* I saw more *flashes of lightning...* and I heard *thunder* again. Then, *the mouth* of the *ancient one* opened, and I heard *Him* say with *the greatest of authority - in thunderous all powerful voices,* "**I AM !**"

"Immediately after hearing these *words,* I was taken back *somehow* very quickly from where I had originally started, much like a videotape placed in quick

reverse mode. Descending from the third tier of *brightest light* to the second tier of *brighter light* with all the very, very special *beings in light,* I then descended to the first tier of all the galaxies, *bright stars* and planets. I saw ***the door*** again. It was now starting to close, as I passed through *the door.* I *somehow* saw myself exiting through *the door* at the *heart/chest area of the corpus of Jesus on the cross (the crucifix* on the wall*).* I passed through a *very brilliant light* and shape of *Jesus* in a *white dazzling luminous light,* as *Jesus* was literally standing in front of Nancy. Then, I found myself sitting *(within me)* exactly where I had originally started. I saw *the door* close slowly --- *on the heart/chest area of the corpus of Jesus on the cross (the crucifix* on the wall*).* Finally, I saw *3 densely bright-white luminous letters* all engulfed in a glorious brilliant light spelling the words --- I just heard**, "I AM."** I *could no longer see* the initials **INRI** *in black* on this headboard of the cross, but *only the 3 letters in bright white light. How* can you *explain* this? *What* does - this mean*?"*

Now, I was totally amazed, astonished and a little frightened by the statements just made by this brilliant and very analytical Jewish female doctor, my dear friend and professional colleague. What an incredibly awesome, insightful and yet *symbolic experience* she just described. Many priests to whom I have related this story to all remark at the *wonderful imagery* this story portrays; illustrating *how a soul goes to heaven* - **through *Jesus, the door!*** Recall, *Jesus* told *His disciples* in John 14:6**: *"I am the way and the truth and the life; no one comes to the Father except through me.*"** In the New Testament Book of John 10:10: *Jesus* said**, *"I am the door."*** Ponder these verses in *the light* of the *Jewish doctor's bi-location.*

Recall, *Jesus* said to Nancy, *"I am the living Son of God."* If *Jesus* **is** *one with His Father God,* this might help to explain *the new insignia* seen by the Jewish doctor on the headboard of the crucifix, which **matches the same words said** by *His* Almighty Father: ***" I AM ! "*** Indeed, this experience may also help clarify some of our initial misunderstandings of the *One God,* the Triune God, *the Holy Trinity,* and *Jesus,* the second person of the *Holy Trinity*—for all *Jews* and all *Gentiles* (who are basically all non-Jewish religions: Christians, Mormons, Muslims-Islam, Hindu, Buddhists etc.). This awesome *heavenly experience* of the female Jewish doctor, so vividly portrays to us all that - *the only way to God our Father in heaven* ***is*** truly and literally *through Jesus, with Jesus, and in Jesus.* Wow!

While I was still totally amazed and awestruck with the details of her story, as a medical scientist, I could not help but only ponder, how unfortunate indeed, that we did not have an actual EEG hooked up to the Jewish doctor during our testing just completed. Recall, she was *invited to help us evaluate* the two *chosen souls.*

The *journey science to faith* and true *peace...*

...continues...

RESULTS OF THE TESTING OF AUGUST 20th, 1993

The young seminarian's medical and neurological evaluations plus mental status examinations: before, during and after the apparitions were entirely *normal.* All of the EEG baseline studies before and after the apparitions were *normal.*

The EEG baseline studies performed on *the seminarian* were *normal.* Showing bilateral and symmetrical rhythmic 10-12 Hz alpha rhythms recorded with eyes closed, and mixed alpha-beta rhythms with beta activity at 20-25 Hz seen with eyes open. No pathological brain wave pattern or epileptic activity was recorded. Normal sleep stages I and II were recorded. All activation studies performed were *normal.*

The ambulatory audiovisual TV-EEG telemetry system recorded before the apparitions and after the apparitions was *normal,* and these studies were very similar and identical to our EEG baseline study, which was *normal.*

The ambulatory audiovisual TV-EEG telemetry monitoring system recordings *during the heavenly visits of Jesus* and the *Blessed Virgin Mary bringing baby Jesus* to us demonstrated the most dramatic EEG brain wave changes, while his mental status exam *during the heavenly visits* was *normal* with an awake, alert, oriented x3 and fully conscious state with *normal* higher cortical functioning. His speech was fluent with normal content and no dysarthria. He was able to articulate his experiences in the room to us in a sophisticated manner. No anomia, aphasia or apraxia was noted. He demonstrated a normal train of thought with evidence of logical thinking with an appropriate and animated affect during the entire visionary experience. No evidence of malingering or hysteria was noted. No mood, thought, affective or personality disorders were identified. No psychotic disturbances or epileptic behaviors were identified. I also recorded a seemingly deep reverence to God animated with a profound peace, love and joy. His face radiated with a glow of *ecstasy* as clearly seen on the TV video monitor *during the apparitions.*

The EEG changes recorded within milliseconds of the *Blessed Virgin Mary bringing baby Jesus appearing* demonstrated *rhythmic 4 Hz theta rhythms* primarily over the frontal, temporal and central head regions mixed with over-riding beta rhythms of low amplitude with an awake, alert with focused attention brain wave activity pattern (with no spike activity). Initially and frequently the *4 Hz theta rhythms* formed the unprecedented *EEG pattern of 444 - only* during this *specific apparition.*

The EEG changes recorded during the *heavenly visit* or *apparition of Jesus* demonstrated an immediate shift to *medium-to-high amplitude rhythmic 3 Hz delta rhythms* (with no spike activity) that initially and frequently formed the amazing and unprecedented *EEG pattern of* ***333 - in His Living Presence.***

Nancy's medical and neurological evaluations plus mental status examinations: before, during, and after the apparitions were (once again) all *normal.*

These findings were identical to *the testing* results during the *baseline studies* of June 11th and the out-on-the-field studies of June 13th, 1993 at Conyers, GA.

These *new findings* were also corroborated and supported by the medical clinical observations and all the quantitative EEG examinations and testing performed in the Las Piedras, Puerto Rico. In the neurophysiology laboratory of Dr. Norma Agosto, the clinical neuropsychological batteries and clinical psychological observations were performed by Dr. Teresa Dalmau of Puerto Rico. Nonetheless, both Dr. Agosto and Dr. Dalmau chose to repeat their medical clinical observations and examinations during this testing day of August 20th, 1993. *Their new data* and results agreed/*concurred with all our new data* and results. All our combined medical, neurological and clinical neuropsychological evaluations demonstrated that Nancy was indeed *normal.*

Nancy's audiovisual TV-EEG telemetry monitoring system recordings: before and after the apparitions were *normal for stated age*. Our data was again similar to all the *baseline studies:* of June 11th, 1993 in Atlanta, Ga., the two *appointed studies* of June 13th, 1993 in Conyers, Ga., and the *medical clinical observations* and radiation studies of July 13th, 1993 in Conyers, Ga., and *quantitative EEG studies* of August 6th, 1993 in Las Piedras, Puerto Rico, which were all *normal.*

Nancy's audiovisual TV-EEG telemetry monitoring system recorded changes that occurred *only during the heavenly visits* or *apparitions* were again dramatic:

a) During the appearance of the *Blessed Virgin Mary bringing her baby Jesus, Our Loving Mother*, Nancy's electrical brain wave picture dramatically changed to the characteristic *4 Hz theta rhythms* seen primarily over the bilateral frontal, temporal and central head regions with *posterior alpha activity* and low amplitude anterior beta activity seen overriding the rhythmic 4 Hz theta rhythms that initially and frequently forms the unprecedented *EEG pattern of 444.*

b) Nancy's EEG changes *during the apparition of Jesus* were likewise astounding. Instantaneous, quick changes within milliseconds to medium-to-high amplitude *rhythmic 3 Hz delta rhythms* was seen primarily over the bilateral frontal, temporal and central regions with *posterior alpha rhythms* and low amplitude *beta activity* seen over the anterior head regions superimposed or *overriding on the medium-to-high amplitude 3 Hz delta rhythms with eyes open.* The *3 Hz delta rhythms* initially and frequently form the specific EEG pattern recognized repeatedly with Nancy's *experience of Jesus* - producing the remarkable *EEG pattern of 333.*

Both *chosen souls* were studied with different audiovisual TV-EEG telemetry monitoring systems and incredibly had exactly the same type of drastic changes in their brain wave activity—*3 Hz delta rhythms with Jesus,* and *4 Hz theta rhythms with the Blessed Virgin Mary bringing her baby Jesus to us* - during the same EEG epochs (EEG time span). On occasions the 3 Hz delta rhythms that were seen in both Nancy and the religious *ranged from 2.5 to 3.5 Hz,* but the *3 Hz delta rhythms* dominated the *new data* results as observed in both *chosen souls* at the moments they proclaimed *the living presence of Jesus.*

Only during the two occasions that Nancy said Satan (the evil one) was present was there another sudden change in Nancy's brain wave pattern seen. On both of these *eerie occasions, 6 Hz theta rhythms* of low-to-medium amplitude were identified. The *6 Hz theta rhythms* frequently formed a pattern of *three single 6 Hz brain waves in succession,* forming an *EEG pattern of 666.* This specific EEG pattern was *never seen* in any of Nancy's brain wave activity studies *before, during, or after the apparitions,* at any time, on any date or in any of the testing locations.

It initially took a bit of deciphering to recognize the *666 pattern.* The first brain wave identified was a 3 Hz bifid wave, which represents two 6 Hz brain waves co-joined. However, after glancing at the 3 Hz bifid quickly, I was left with the impression of seeing one 3 Hz delta wave. This initially and momentarily confused me. So, I reflected and asked: *Why* were we seeing *a (single) 3 Hz delta wave* in the presence of Satan, when up to this point we had only recorded the 3 Hz delta waves *only in His Living Presence (the living presence of Jesus)?*

Upon further and closer inspection, however, the answer was very clear. We were not observing a single notched 3 Hz delta brain wave, but rather a *single notched 3 Hz bifid wave*, which in EEG terms actually represents *"two 6 Hz theta brain waves co-joined."* Following this single notched 3 Hz *bifid wave* was *a single 6 Hz theta brain wave,* thus forming the *pattern 666.* Also *successive 6 Hz theta rhythms in a pattern of three single 6 Hz theta waves* were recorded *only during Satan's presence* forming the *EEG pattern of 666.* This *EEG 666 pattern* dissipated quickly when Nancy's said to all of us in the EEG room that Satan was *cast out - in the name of Jesus.*

It is important to note that in the instances when Nancy said, *"Satan is here,"* the *seminarian did not demonstrate the same EEG brain wave pattern* as seen in Nancy. In a private interview later, the young religious explained to me that while he *did feel* and *experience the cold, eerie disturbance* in the room like the rest of us, *he did not see or recognize Satan's visible evil presence* like seeing the white serpent in the same tangible way as Nancy did. To explain this, some priests say the seminarian did not have the same *grace of discernment* given by God to see or experience Satan, as was given to Nancy at those two precise moments of time. So, the seminarian did not see Satan. This may help explain *why* the seminarian's EEG brain wave activity patterns *did not change* as Nancy's did. Thus, his real vivid level of God's given discernment during the testing towards *the old serpent* - Satan, was limited for him, just like the rest of us *(thank God)* in the EEG laboratory.

Of further intrigue and great interest was a phenomena captured on one of the videos. I do not know how to *explain* this. Although more recently*, the Holy Spirit* has given me a clue. So, I showed one of the videos of today's testing to a group of religious and a few doctors. None of them were told *what had happened* during the testing. This *video* came from the camera that was *focused on the crucifix during the testing* and was filmed behind the *two chosen souls* from the left side rear of the laboratory suite. When this video was shone to the religious and doctors present, they all made their personal comments and observations of the video, then one by one they left the room. However, shortly thereafter within minutes two doctors *(the only two doctors, who were Jewish)* came back to ask me a question. I was not prepared for their question. They asked*: "Why* was there a *white snake* on top of *the crucifix?"* I pondered. Can you imagine *what* these *two Jewish doctors* actually saw on this video? They somehow clearly and incredibly saw and described *exactly* what Nancy had *seen mystically* as Satan, when *the evil one* returned to the testing site for the second time in the form of *the old serpent* during the testing. *No one* can see the *white snake* or *white serpent* on this video, except these two Jewish doctors. *Why?* Why can the two *Jewish doctors see the old serpent (camouflaged in white)* on top of *the crucifix,* but *we can not (do not) see the white snake* on the same video? *Why?* I can only ponder. Recall Nancy said*, "Ugh,* he is so vicious... Satan is back again... as a *white serpent...* over there on top of *the crucifix..."*

The *journey science to faith* ***and peace...***
...with all its many twists and turns...
...continues...

REFLECTIONS ON THE TESTING OF AUGUST 20th, 1993

With the medical and scientific battery of tests completed on Nancy and the seminarian, we were now faced with *new data* even more astounding than ever before. We have clearly demonstrated that the different stimulus specific evoked EEG brain wave patterns recorded on Nancy earlier were not solely limited to her brain. But the same unprecedented EEG patterns can be produced or evoked in the brain of other individuals, who claim to have similar experiences like Nancy. We can now see that the other *chosen soul - the seminarian,* who privately receives *heavenly visitations, visions* or *apparitions of Jesus* and the *Blessed Virgin Mary* also produced the same astonishing EEG patterns.

Spiritual conclusions aside, the mere coincidences observed were uncanny. We now have two subjects of different ages and of different gender/sexes who are from two different countries*, sharing in common only the heavenly visitations* or *visions* or *apparitions.* Both *chosen souls* demonstrated the same EEG brain wave patterns of *3 Hz delta rhythms* with a *pattern of 333 in the living presence of Jesus* and *4 Hz theta rhythms* with *a pattern of 444 in the presence of the Blessed Virgin Mary bringing her baby Jesus to us,* at precisely the same time on the EEGs, while both were having the *supernatural events* or experiences *during the testing.* Also of interest, it should be noted that each *chosen soul* had a similar but uniquely different and personal experience associated with the *heavenly visits or apparitions.*

The fact that changes occurred instantaneously and simultaneously in both *chosen souls* was and still is a *medical and scientific enigma.* Indeed, observing the

EEG changes in only one of the subjects Nancy as seen earlier was significant enough and scientifically inexplicable, but recording the same EEG patterns in both subjects at once led squarely to one only conclusion: *something incredibly astonishing and scientifically unprecedented had really and truly occurred; something that might only be explained in the realm of the spiritual faith, but with medical science now in full assistance.* As mentioned, Nancy alone was apparently given this *special gift or grace to discern* the real presence of *the old serpent* Satan as in Genesis and Book of Revelation. Thus, it seems there is a logical consequence as to *why* we recorded in Nancy's brain waves the development of instantaneous rhythmic 6 Hz theta rhythms, forming another type of *stimulus specific evoked EEG brain wave pattern 666,* which *only* occurred *during the two occasions* Nancy claimed *that Satan was* now *present (recall: "Ugh, Satan is here").* The *"Ugh,"* I later discovered is Nancy's way of expressing *extreme disgust* and a deep personal feeling of something quite nauseating, horrific, horrible, bad or evil. Satan is all of the above and so much, much worse.

Satan is regularly termed *the father of lies, a murderer, the enemy, a thief, the devil, the evil one, the most proud one, the old serpent, the dragon, the beast or Lucifer, the deceiver & master of all deceptions.* While priests, nuns, monks, friars, rabbis, pastors, ministers, missionaries, chaplains, deacons, clerics and all preachers alike and even some theologians and religious educators repeatedly warn us of our modern day perils with our very complacent attitudes towards the devil's wily ways. Unfortunately, many people in our new society discount altogether *the enemy's* very real existence. They claim Satan's image is outdated, pure fiction and/or just a product of Hollywood. Sadly, many people in our modern day believe this lie. But now, *we have true medical and scientific confirmations that the evil one, Satan is alive and definitely up to his old tricks.* Satan is a very real, sinister and dangerous *enemy to each one of us,* as it is written in the Bible not pulp fiction.

I pondered: Does *Hell really exist?* If true, are you and I gambling with our *life?* Please see and read again the ancient Bible Book of Deuteronomy 30:15-20*:* "...I have set before thee this day *life and good* and on the other hand *death and evil....blessing and cursing...Choose therefore life that both thou and thy seed may live...*that thou mayst *love the Lord thy God,* and *obey His voice,* and *adhere to Him* (for *He is thy life, and the length of thy days..."*

Question: So, are **you** *gambling your life away?*

Can you imagine my astonishment and very big surprise, when I first recognized *the 666 pattern?* This eerie and evil number sequence, I earlier only recognized from the Hollywood movies. As was mentioned, the first brain wave identified in Nancy's brain during Satan's presence was a notched 3 Hz bifid wave. Once I realized that it was a notched 3 Hz delta wave and indeed not a true 3 Hz delta brain wave, but a notched 3 Hz bifid wave, ***actually two 6 Hz theta brain waves co-joined,*** which was followed by a single 6 Hz brain wave, the obvious conclusion was frightening as the succession of brain waves formed the pattern 666, a number commonly associated with *the arch enemy of God,* Satan. Was this single notched 3 Hz bifid wave just an EEG illusion or a real representation of Satan's masterful deception---and perhaps a diabolical attempt to lie, deceive and confuse *my new medical and scientific data* as well?

During the second encounter with Satan and only during the time Nancy was seeing the old serpent in white, did we repeatedly record and document a succession of three 6 Hz theta rhythms. Now a more obvious and precisely formed *new stimulus specific evoked EEG brain wave pattern of 666* was actually being *recorded only during the cold eerie presence of Satan.* I was definitely not ready for this *new data* and *new revelation. Hell exists and Satan,* the enemy, really *exists.*

Our medical and scientific research team after many hours of research was unable to locate any medical science or clinical neurophysiology precedent that had ever reported or recorded this unprecedented *new data* I had just obtained. This led most of us (especially me) in the research team to the utmost realm of curious speculation: *What* could this very specific mathematical and numerical stimulus specific EEG evoked brain wave *pattern of 666* possibly mean to us? After all my meticulous and arduous research, I now know that in medicine and science these specific patterns had absolutely no specific meanings per se. No medical or scientific data existed to my knowledge at the time of the testing that could help explain these astonishing phenomena I had recorded repeatedly. Again, while I am not a *numerologist or a theologian,* the lack of any available data or hard core explanations that were compatible with my medical and scientific training and background was definitely frustrating to say the least. As a natural consequence many years later, I began to gravitate towards *the Bible* for possible answers to my very personal questions raised by these studies, as I almost imperceptibly journeyed *science to faith.*

I know I was not spiritually prepared, nor completely ready for the abrupt changes which would soon come upon me personally and spiritually as the answers to my many private and professional questions were slowly revealed. Little by little, clues and new revelations came to light like tiny pieces of a very large puzzle. I became *hungry and thirsty* for *wisdom, knowledge* and the *holy presence of the living God.* So, I started to carefully read the Bible for the first time in my entire life (over these past ten years). I also read whatever related theological literature was available that could hopefully help me find any *further clues* concerning *the living presence of God* with the guidance of a good spiritual director along the way - my dearest friend and Catholic priest, Father Daniel Joseph McCormick. Other guides were St. Jerome's Concordance and the Latin Vulgate Bible; many educational tapes by Messianic Jewish Rabbi's, Dr. Scott Hahn and the Passionist's missions and educational talks; many other special writings by various doctors of the Church like St. Teresa *Sanchez* of Avila; authors Grant R. Jeffrey and Yacov Rambsel of the Hebrew Bible codes; volumes of writings by the early Christian Fathers and scholars of the Church like Pope John Paul II; I even watched educational shows on TV Cable Networks like TBN, EWTN, CBN for any clues, that may *shed light* on the *new medical and scientific data* discovered in our research and study of the *three chosen souls* tested. I especially want to thank again my spiritual director, Fr. Dan for all his help, prayers and especially all the Holy *Masses!* I want to thank Nancy, the seminarian and Patricia Talbot (Pachi) with my utmost gratitude for all their intercessory prayers. Thanks to all of them, I have received a plethora of *answered prayers* throughout the years of writing *this (His) book.* So, now with *the living fire burning deep within me,* I can proclaim with zeal*, "I am hungry and thirsty for the living presence of God."* Maybe this is what *Jesus* really means, when *He* says in Luke 12:49: *"I am come to cast fire on the earth..." Jesus* comes to cast a mighty and *holy fire deep within us, to* literally *set all our souls ablaze* with *fire, the living flames of love.* Now, we can be *living torches* of *His abundant light* and *life* dwelling deep within us: in our spirit, mind, heart, soul, and strength. *Jesus - "a fiery law"* (Deut 33:2*) with the Holy Spirit is* ***the fire of God*** *the Father* and *the true light of the world.*

To better understand what the above mathematical and numerical sequence of 666 might mean to us, it became crystal clear that the following verses found in the Book of Revelation in the New Testament was important in understanding what I had stumbled across and uncovered during the testing of the two *chosen souls,* see Rev 13:18 reads: *"Here is wisdom. He that hath understanding, let him count the number of the beast. For it is the number of a man: and the number of him is six hundred sixty six."* My utter astonishment was also joined by that of my medical and scientific colleagues soon upon our collective realization of what I had just recorded in my EEG laboratory. The newly discovered *stimulus specific evoked EEG brain wave pattern of 666* was recorded **only** during the moments that Nancy said*, "Ugh,* Satan is here*."*

This was indeed mind-boggling. It literally gave me and the research team a cold chill up our spines to contemplate the potential ramifications of these findings. I remember *praying to God* the night before *the testing*, something I had virtually stopped doing on a regular basis, except maybe in Church on Sunday's. I asked the Lord to show me where to look for the real significance and *wisdom* of these numbers - the 333 and the 444? I asked God*, "Lord,* if these *numbers* are important to *You,* please show me were to look, if it's Your *Divine Will?* On the very next day of the testing, I was faced with such an unexpected and blatant reply to my personal and professional query. Imagine finding the *number 666 EEG pattern, "the number of the beast"* (Rev 13:18) as it is written in the Bible, *only* in the presence of Satan. So, I *logically assumed* that the number 333 recorded *only* in the *living presence of Jesus* and the number 444 recorded *only* in the *living presence of Mary bringing us baby Jesus to us* should likewise also be found *in the Bible.* So,

I embarked upon a quest to locate scholarly biblical theologians, who might be able to assist me. But much to my chagrin, I initially came up empty-handed in this zealous endeavor until later, when little by little *clues* were given to me *(thank you Holy Spirit).* Five years after the testing, I accidentally stumbled upon a one of these very special clues. While on vacation in Key Biscayne, Florida, I happened to overhear a TV interview on the Trinity Broadcasting Network (TBN) cable channel, unknowingly switched-on by my daughters. I entered their room to hurry them for dinner and as I moved to turn off the TV, I was struck by the cover of a book being shown on the screen. The book, by Grant R. Jeffrey, was entitled *The Signature of God.* This title immediately grabbed my attention, since I had initially intended to title this book, *333: The Signature of God.* I quickly sat down in disbelief that someone else already had *my title* and continued to watch the show. I was even more amazed to discover that the title was chosen for mathematical and numerical reasons of a different kind, but yet similar to *why* I had initially considered it. Then one of the interviewers, Jan Crouch of TBN, asked both authors and Hebrew Biblical Scholars - Grant R. Jeffrey and Yacov Rambsel - while they were being interviewed: *"Is it true that both of you independently discovered three hundred and thirty-three #333 prophetic phrases that says or connects -* ***Jesus - the Messiah*** *in the Hebrew ELS Bible codes within the Torah, the Bible, the five Books of Moses?"*

Both enthusiastically answered, *"Yes!"* Upon hearing this, I quickly fell backwards on the bed with my mouth open. This is really *unbelievable!* Can you imagine - the same number of *3 Hz delta rhythms seen in triplets 333* - that we recorded *only during* or *in the living presence of Jesus -- in His Living Presence --* **is** the same number of times #333 - these scholars found prophetic phrases that say ***Jesus - the Messiah -*** encoded in the *Torah, the Jewish Holy Bible?* Is *Jesus* the true *savior of the Jews and the Gentiles as prophesied?* Recall, the name *Jesus* means *salvation* or *God saves.* If the name *Jesus* means *the savior, salvation* or *God saves,* then the following Old Testament Messianic *prophecy of redemption by the Christ* speaks volumes about *Who* and just *how Juda will be saved?* See Hosea 1:7: *"And I will have mercy on the house of Juda, and* ***I will save them by the Lord their God:*** *and* ***I will not save them by bow, nor by sword, nor by battle, nor by horses, nor by horsemen."*** So **is** *Jesus "the Lord their God," Who will save* them?

I was both astounded and thrilled. My initial intuition had proven to be correct. More accurately stated, the tremendous help and promptings of *the Holy Spirit* very early on led me to recognize that the *number 333 would* somehow, someday, somewhere *be found in the Bible,* directly related to *Jesus* and *God;* just as the stimulus specific evoked EEG brain wave pattern 333 was repeatedly recorded and documented in the *presence of Jesus – in His Living Presence.* Not having ever read the Bible at the time of these studies, I finally pushed myself into an arena of research that to me was indeed foreign and in very unfamiliar grounds: looking for *any solid biblical connection* between *His Living Presence* as portrayed in the Bible and *any of the new medical and scientific data.*

The proof provided by these two biblical scholars was significant and kept me firmly on the path towards *faith.* The fact that these **two Biblical Hebrew scholars had independently discovered three hundred thirty-three (333) encoded prophetic phrases within the Hebrew Torah that say --- *Jesus* (is) *- the Messiah -*** actually seemed much more like a ***God-incidence,*** than a *coincidence* to me. But whatever the label, their research had an impact on furthering the development of my spiritual life (thanks TBN, *praise* the Lord), since it helped confirm my medical and scientific research. Indeed, it confirmed that my research was much more than a fluke or a mere *coincidence.* The *new data* of the chosen souls --- truly correlates with the Bible. Can you imagine, now what this hardened-skeptic (I) was feeling? Just imagine finding out years after the studies were done, that *new data* from my research concerning *Jesus - in His Living Presence* was *encoded* (by God) literally thousands of years ago in the *Torah?*

Nancy has stated that she has no good explanations for the particular brain wave activity that she exhibits while in *ecstasy.* Both Nancy and the seminarian at times seem to be at a loss for words in telling us their full understanding of what they experience. In layman's terms, they claim that while they are *in the living presence of Jesus,* they feel an immense and indescribable profound peace, love and joy and a total detachment from all worldly concerns.

So now, we have recorded and documented in two chosen souls the 3 Hz delta rhythms forming the 333 pattern with the EEG topography of the most peaceful brain wave state ever, in the living presence of Jesus - *His Living Presence,* that is seen only during normal stages of deep sleep, while they were both fully awake, alert with focused attention and with eyes open.

Prior to thoroughly reviewing our results, Dr. John Walsh of the Royal Prince Alfred Hospital in Sydney, Australia, claimed that 3 Hz delta brain wave activity in an open-eyed, alert and conscious subject was *a physiological impossibility.* He had never seen nor heard of it. Once informed of our results, Dr. Walsh claimed that he could not believe it happened. But once verified and duplicated in multiple subjects via our testing, this *impossibility* seemed to require a new label. With great respect to Dr. John Walsh, our research studies confirmed the veracity of what was previously considered to be *physiologically impossible.* Reflecting on our findings, George Collins commented, *"When Nancy is in communion with Jesus* and is talking with Him, *she experiences His peace.* She has been told by *Jesus* that *prayer brings us before the living presence of God during which we obtain His peace. It is a peace that the world cannot give...* at times when I was troubled and things were weighing me down, I would go to *Mass* and find there that my *peace* would be restored. One day I told Nancy about how I obtained that peace. *Jesus* said to me through Nancy, *'That peace is me.'* This peace is the same peace I get when I go before the Blessed Sacrament and pray. If I pray before the Blessed

Sacrament (in His Living Presence), It changes me; It relaxes me profoundly. **As for the neurologists, we can only wonder if what they have captured on their EEG's is the actual peace of God or the signature of His peace.**"

Remember, the atmospheric radiation energy fields in the rooms increased 3-4 times the baseline measurements - *only in the living presence of Jesus* - reaching the energy range called *electrical* (magnetic) *anesthesia.* This energy is actually in the *low ionizing radiation energy fields* of the *radio wavelength spectrum* that was used by dentists in the 1800's for *relaxing* their subjects or patients before any major dental procedures. Wow!

Further illuminating this topic, I later found a New Testament scriptural writing from John 14:27, in which *Jesus* says to His disciples, *"Peace I leave with you, my peace I give unto you: Not as the world giveth, do I give unto you."* Clearly, then this *peace* Jesus refers to is precisely what the *chosen souls* attempt to describe, but are often unable to do so. Indeed, how could they be expected to describe something that is *given not as the world gives?* Could we then be so bold as to speculate that *God,* in His awesome humility and omnipotence, deigned to allow the **peace of Jesus** to be measured **on** our **EEG** tests? Are we being *so bold* as to proclaim that we are actually measuring *the peace of Jesus – "Prince of Peace," the peace of God?* Only if, in the same breath, we recognize that we could only do so because *God allowed it.* Ponder just how incredibly loving, merciful, generous and glorious **is** our God, the Almighty? Well, just think and contemplate on the concept of how merciful and loving God truly is: He (Father God) sent His only begotten living *Son, Jesus (the God-Man),* to live the human struggle without sin, while accepting all the sins of man unto Himself—then to suffer the passion and die on the cross – for you and me. So, the unblemished *Lamb of God* Who takes away the sins of the world—*the door* of heaven, *the Way* – can literally open *heaven* for you and me*; just by believing in the One He (Father God) sent—Jesus.*

As we follow *the way, the truth and the life,* see how *God* sends His glory and *His Holy Living Spirit (the spirit of Jesus and the Almighty Father)* to us in baptism, in all our daily trails and struggles and in our daily lives; if only we would just *ask God to come into our hearts.* So, we need not be orphans any longer, for *the Spirit of Life,* once invited to be within you and me, adopts us as God's very own, *God's children of the light.* See with awe and wonder just how loving, merciful, faithful, generous, compassionate, humble and *glorious God* is to all *His* created beings. Just ponder *His Divine Will, HIS LOVE* and *His Divine Mercy.*

George Collins and other religious people like him, regularly claim that their *peace* is restored by participating/praying at *Holy Mass* and in adoration/praying before the Most Holy Blessed Sacrament *(in His Living Presence).* Indeed, what other more *tangible* way of being *in His Living Presence* exists? Both proclaim *Jesus (in His Living Presence),* the living Son of God, as really and truly living and physically available - as *peace for us - to heal today's brokenness throughout the world. Jesus* – as prophesied in Micah 5:5: *"He shall be peace,"* **is** *truly present - Body, Blood, Soul and Divinity—***in** *the Eucharist,* **in** *the Holy Mass and* **in** *the Most Holy Blessed Sacrament. So, come and taste the true goodness of the Lord.* The traditional *Catholic* (which means *universal Christian*) *faith* teaches that when the unleavened *bread and wine* **is** *consecrated* during a Holy Mass, the *bread and wine* becomes *the Word of God, the true living presence of Jesus* (Luke 22:15-20).

The Christian Catholic faith also teaches *Jesus* **is** the living Son of God, **is** the Eternal Word, the Second Person of the Holy Trinity, and **is** thus *the Lord, thy God.* The *bread and wine* **is** true (meat) food and true drink – and true nourishment for our souls (John 6:56). Thus, *the living presence of Jesus—"the law," "the light," "the word of God"/ "the Word," " the Lord God of Israel," "wisdom incarnate," "Prince of Peace," "covenant of peace," "He shall be peace," and the "bread of God"* as it is written in John 6:33: *"For the bread of God is that which cometh down from heaven, and giveth life to the world"* - really enters *"in your bowels"* and God writes it *"in your hearts,"* Jeremiah 31:33. See how *God* can truly dwell *"within us."* Now please see Deuteronomy 8:3: *"...*not *in bread alone doth man live, but in every word that proceedeth from the mouth of God."* See Matthew 4:4 and Luke 4:4. To make sense of this last verse which is in two parts as it is written, I believe that in order for us *to* truly *live* according to God's *Divine Will* completely, we must all strive daily to live **in** *"the word of God"/ "the Word"* (*Jesus)* according to God's loving commandments. In other words **in** *"bread - of God"/ "the word - of God" doth man live;* the *life giving bread of God – Jesus* (John 6:54). See also James 1:17. In the following messages given to Nancy, *Jesus* reiterates that ***His Living Presence* is in** - *the Most Holy Blessed Sacrament* **--- and is ---** ***the Holy Eucharist!***

On February 4th, 1992 Jesus declared, *"I Am the one that gives you peace, and I Am the one present at the Mass."* On January 15th, 1993 Jesus said to Nancy, *"I Am Jesus, Son of the living God. I Am He Who is in this Sacred Host. Thank you for coming to be with Me here."* At the time of this *message,* Nancy was in church before the Blessed Sacrament. On May 4th, 1993 *Jesus* said to Nancy, *"My children need My sacrament of the Eucharist. I am the Healer. Receive My Body, My Blood, My Soul, My Divinity in the Consecrated Host. Receive Me in the state of grace and this way I will commune with you. I Am the Living Bread come down from heaven."* On July 17th, 1993 Nancy entered a church in Louisville, Kentucky. Though Nancy did not realize there would be a Mass and exposition of the Blessed Sacrament, *Jesus* welcomed her by saying, *"Look at My outstretched arms. I welcome you! I Am a Living Sacrifice of Love."* Nancy has been told many times by *Jesus, "The Mass is an ongoing sacrifice... and graces are endless at the Mass."* Indeed, even the late Pope John Paul II has confirmed this, declaring in his apostolic letter *Dominicae Cenae, "The Eucharist is above all else a sacrifice." The Eucharist* **is** *the "sacrifice of praise."* See Psalm 106:22.

The reality of *His Living Presence* in *the Eucharist* was vividly portrayed to

Nancy in a "frightening" vision on July 13th, 1992. On that morning, during the consecration of the Mass, Nancy experienced an *apparition* of a large, human-like creature with gorilla-like features. The creature came up from behind the altar and quickly snatched *a child* that was wrapped securely in a white blanket glowing in brilliant light. The creature began to run away with the child, which scared Nancy. She understood *the creature to be Satan* and *the child to be Jesus,* truly present in - *the Eucharist.* Satan was trying to snatch *Jesus* away from all His people by deceiving mankind into believing that *Jesus* is not really present in *the Eucharist.*

After the vision, Our Loving Mother said to Nancy, *"The world refuses to recognize the reality of Satan and his influences upon mankind. Please tell my children about the vision at the Mass this morning."* On November 19th, 1993 while Nancy was in Colombia, South America, *Jesus* appeared and said to her, *"Remain in my grace through the sacraments I have instituted for love of you. You are receiving special graces now. And at each and every Mass, you receive special graces."* In early 1990's undated messages, *Jesus* said to Nancy, *"I wait for you and I Am in every tabernacle of the world. I offer you all My love, all completely, totally to My Father. I offer Myself for love of you. Why do you stay away? Do you not know Me? Do you not know that I Am in every tabernacle? Come before Me. I will help you. I love you. I will heal you. See what gifts await you. Do I not always give more than I receive? Bring yourself to Me. I long for your presence. Will you not sacrifice yourself, your time, for your love of Me?"* **Jesus has told Nancy that He continues to offer and sacrifice Himself to the Father for our sins; He is the perpetual *"sacrifice of praise"*-- Jesus is a perpetual, ongoing, holy sacrifice to the Father - *for all our sins.*** In part of His message of November 19th, 1993 in Colombia, South America, *Jesus* said, *"My peace I give you; My peace I leave you. When you accept My peace and desire to live in My peace, My peace remains with you..."* The *words of Jesus* on February 4th, 1992: *"I Am the one that gives you peace and I Am the one present at the Mass."* Many people claim to experience *peace* upon attending *Holy Mass* or going before the *Most Holy Blessed Sacrament.* According to Nancy, *Jesus* Himself said, *"That peace is Me."*

Our *new data* has shown us tremendous manifestations of *His (God's) peace* in the testing, which undoubtedly corresponds to the measurable changes on EEG with the *deep sleep 333 EEG pattern.* This *new medical and scientific data* boldly invites us to extrapolate and conclude that *Jesus* **is** indeed *alive and* truly *present* in the Blessed Sacrament and that *Jesus* **is** indeed - *the Eucharist, the living bread of God.* So, have we medically and scientifically documented a true *connection* between a *profoundly physiological and tangible physical peace* and *the living presence of Jesus (in His Living Presence)* in the *Holy Mass* and the *Most Holy Blessed Sacrament - the Eucharist?* I believe so. Though our amazing conclusions reach way beyond the scope of *pure medicine and science,* they serve to complement the same.

The medical and scientific manifestations and reality that *Jesus* **is** truly *present in the consecrated bread and wine,* **is** the greatest, richest find and treasure ever uncovered in our medical and scientific studies --- *the purist and holiest gift from God.* As you will hopefully see in the next chapter which highlights a series of tests on yet another *chosen soul,* Patricia Talbot (Pachi), we discovered a marvelous and miraculous *supernatural event* hidden within a simple parcel of *bread and wine* that literally unfolds into an awesome heavenly cosmic blast of pure *living light* energy from the Almighty God. Our *new medical and scientific data* clearly shows that after the holy consecration of the *bread and wine* during the offering and celebration of the *Holy Mass, Jesus - His Living Presence* **is** *indeed the transubstantiated bread and wine, the Holy Eucharist - the true Body, Blood, Soul and Divinity of Jesus in this form,* which we can humbly receive and literally - *eat and drink. Wow!*

Maybe, that is *why* in the Gospel of John 6:51-59: ***Jesus*** says, ***"I am the living bread which came down from heaven. If any man eat of this bread, he shall live for ever; and the bread that I will give, is my flesh, for the life of the world.*** *...Amen, amen I say unto you:* ***Except you eat the flesh of the Son of man, and drink his blood, you shall not have life in you.*** **He that eateth my flesh,** and **drinketh my blood, hath everlasting life: and I will raise him up in the last day.** ***For my flesh is meat*** indeed *(true food):* **and my blood is** *(true)* **drink** indeed. ***He that eateth my flesh, and drinketh my blood, abideth in me, and I in him. As the living Father (God) hath sent me, and I live by the Father; so he that eateth me, the same also shall live by me. This is the bread that came down from heaven.*** **Not as your fathers did eat manna, and are** ***dead.*** **He that eateth this bread, shall live for ever."** *So, the Eucharist* **is** *the living bread which came (and daily comes) down from heaven* and has the ability to change us profoundly by transforming us all beyond description, into *God's children of the light,* as God graces us *in His Living Presence. The Eucharist* **is** the ultimate *gift of pure peace, love and joy* that **gives us** *the light, the way, the truth and the life (eternal life).*

The Church teaches that when you follow God's ways and *commandments of love,* confess your sins in reconciliation, *with a contrite heart,* and then receive *Him (Jesus – in His Living Presence)* in the form of *the Eucharist* during or after the Holy Communion of the Mass, *Jesus* will truly dwell *"in your bowels"/ "in your spirit"/ "within you."* Then, *Jesus* can manifest *His Living Presence* within your soul in many ways. Probably in more ways than we will ever know or can even fathom. I now believe that our *new medical and scientific findings* will clearly show you that one of the most prolonged, profound *peace (deep sleep) data* ever recorded in a human being was documented upon *receiving the Holy Eucharist.* This *data* is indeed incredibly similar and basically identical to the *new data* we recorded during the many other recorded manifestations of *Jesus - in His Living Presence,* I carefully described in the earlier chapters of this book. This prolonged and tremendously profound *state of peace* was recorded on EEG with Patricia Talbot's reception of *the Holy Eucharist* and is actually identical to our earlier EEG *deep sleep* patterns recorded during the many *supernatural events (with Jesus)* documented with the other *chosen souls, Nancy and the seminarian.* Therefore, this *new data* is indeed very, very *good news.*

We now have medical and scientific evidence to substantiate and confirm once and for all for the whole world to see that the actual *reception of the Eucharist* **is** indeed *a very special supernatural event of His Living Presence.* What a blazing cosmic blast of *fire!* Can you imagine, a literal time bomb of *eternal blessings (Jesus)* **is** actually stored up, *exists* and **is** *alive* in each and every consecrated unleavened wafer/*Holy Eucharistic Host --- the living bread, which came down from heaven?* Only heaven knows *what* this really means. Throughout the ages, the Catholic Church has documented many spectacular *miracles* that also confirm *the real presence of the Lord (Jesus) in the Eucharist.* These are called *Eucharistic miracles,* which are indeed sensational and beyond any real good scientific explanation. The following are a few examples of these incredible *miracles:*

1) The actual *spontaneous bleeding* of the *sacred Eucharistic Host* during the consecration of the unleavened *bread and wine* by an ordained Catholic priest, which has been filmed on videos and photographed in different countries throughout the world;

2) *The Eucharist bleeding* then *partly turning into actual human flesh* (heart muscle) that is currently still preserved in churches of Europe like *Lanciano* and *Ferrara,* Italy etc.;

3) *The Eucharist* turning into real *living flames without burning the priest* holding up the consecrated unleavened bread during a Catholic Mass in Jerusalem, Israel, in the beginning of this millennium. This Mass was held in the upper room, the place believed by some to be the possible location of the *last supper of Jesus.* So, *why* did the priest *not get burned?* The answer to this question may be in the Old Testament. Exodus 3:2: *"And the Lord appeared to him in a flame of fire out of the midst of a bush: and he saw that the bush was on fire and was not burnt;"* and then in Daniel 3: 20-24: "And he *(King Nabuchodonosor)* commanded the strongest men that were in his army, to bind the feet of *Sidrach, Misach, and Abdenago, and to cast them into the furnace of burning fire.* And immediately these men were bound and were cast into the furnace of burning fire, with their coats, and their caps, and their shoes, and their garments...and the furnace was heated exceedingly. And the flame of the fire slew those men that cast in Sidrach, Misach, and Abdenago. *But these three men, that is, Sidrach, Misach, and Abdenago, fell down bound in the midst of the furnace of burning fire. And they walked in the midst of the flame, praising God and blessing the Lord."* *How* did this happen? We then see in verse Daniel 3:92*: "He (Nabuchodonosor)...said: Behold I see four men loose, and walking in the midst of the fire, and there is no hurt in them, and the form of the fourth is like* ***the Son of God****."*

All the *new medical and scientific data* discovered above has indeed some awesome implications, especially since mankind throughout history has always tried to find better ways to get *closer to God.* Now there is a *very special way to get very, very, very close to God.* In Jeremiah 31:33 God says: *"...I will give my law in their bowels, and I will write it in their heart..."* If *Jesus* **is** *the word of God made flesh* (John 1:14), and *"the word of God on High* **is** *the fountain of all wisdom and her ways are everlasting commandments (the law)"* (Ecclesiasticus/Sirach 1:5), then *"my law,"* which **is** equal to *"wisdom"* and *"the (living) word of God,"* **is** indeed --- *Jesus personified!*

Question: So, just *how* does God *give* ***Jesus*** *-"my law"/God's law --- in their bowels? How* does God ***write*** *Jesus - "my law"/ "the word of God"--- in their heart?* (Recall, blood circulates throughout the body by means of the *heart, which* is a very powerful muscular pump with pulsating chambers)

Answer: *the Consecrated Bread and Wine of God. Jesus* **is** *God's gift/ "I will give my law," "a new covenant"* (Jeremiah 31:31), ***the Eucharist!*** *God* literally *writes with His Precious Blood - His law /Jesus in your heart,* read 2 Cor 3:3: *"not in tables of stone, but in the fleshly tables of the heart."* Please, ponder the above questions carefully as you read the next chapter. Remember, all the amazing and astonishing unprecedented *new data* we uncovered throughout these meticulous medical and scientific studies. Especially, recall the EEG *deep sleep patterns* recorded while awake *with the specific 333 EEG pattern,* that was *only* associated *with Jesus in His Living Presence.* Now that you are fully armed with these facts, that are indeed mind boggling and very significant, we can now begin to tell the story of our *last series of tests* conducted on yet *another special chosen soul.*

During the month of November 1994, in Cuenca, Ecuador, South America, the young and beautiful visionary - Patricia Talbot, nicknamed *Pachi* would be tested. The plan first involved a series of preliminary studies conducted by Prof. Castanon and after all neuropsychophysiological testing was completed, we planned to study Patricia by using an ambulatory EEG system for an entire day—nighttime and prayer time. With the *permission of the Archbishop* Luna of Cuenca, while in Ecuador by co-incidence or *God-incidence,* we even had the great opportunity *to test* Patricia *during the reception of the Holy Eucharist.* After a local Catholic Church's *Holy Mass* celebration, the local parish priest brought *the Eucharist to Pachi's home* for a private *Holy Communion* service. As a physician and skeptic scientist, I sensed in myself a most powerful desire and thirst to search diligently for *the truth* and for *true peace.* Indeed in my own personal *journey science to faith,* I soon found out that the following *final series of medical and scientific studies* completed in Chapter VIII, on yet another *chosen soul* and true *eyewitness,* really catapulted that quest. It confirmed to me the *true origins* of *"the light," and "the way, the truth, and the life,"* and showed me ***true peace*** **–** even in today's *war*-torn world, and *yes,* it actually showed me --- *the Peace of God* - I was seeking.

So, the *journey science to faith* continues...

CHAPTER VIII

THE PEACE OF GOD IN "THE LIVING BREAD"

STUDIES IN ECUADOR, SOUTH AMERICA JUNE 10th, AUGUST 12th AND NOVEMBER 17-19th, 1994

Almost one year after we completed the August 20th, 1993, testing of Nancy and the seminarian, I received another call from the professor informing me of the *International Symposium on Science and Faith* that was going to be held at the University of Cuenca, Ecuador, South America on November of 1994. The professor invited me to give a lecture presenting all the *new medical and scientific research studies and data* collected on the two *chosen souls* (Nancy and the seminarian) at this conference. He also asked that I be part of an investigational team to study yet another young visionary by the name of Patricia Talbot Borrero, a native of Ecuador. Her nickname is *Pachi.* I was then also asked to be one of the EEG interpreters and to help analyze these medical and scientific investigations of Patricia in South America.

Apparently from 1988 to 1990, Patricia Talbot (Pachi) had experienced a series of *visions, apparitions and heavenly visits* mostly from the *Blessed Virgin Mary* and on occasions *Jesus.* Because of my neurology medical practice constraints, I could not attend nor perform the actual medical and scientific testing of Patricia. I recommended Dr. Agosto and Dr. Dalmau, who had tested Nancy in Puerto Rico in early August 1993 and both had also assisted me in testing Nancy and the seminarian in my office on August 20th, 1993. So, in late August of 1994, the professor invited Dr. Norma Agosto and Dr. Teresa Dalmau to perform medical and scientific tests on the *chosen soul,* Patricia Talbot in her beautiful hometown of Cuenca, Ecuador, settled in the foothills of the Andes Mountains. Patricia is a beautiful young Ecuadorian, who says that she began to experience *heavenly visions* at the age of sixteen while working as a model. Soon, her *supernatural events* or experiences started to occur frequently and were dominated by *heavenly visits* or *visions* or *apparitions* from the *Blessed Virgin Mary.* In the *apparitions*— some private, and some in public places, the most recognized public location was high in the breathtaking Andes Mountains. Here in a garden-like grotto called *El Jardin Del Cajas* — the *Blessed Virgin Mary* referred to herself as the *Guardian of the Faith (La Guardiana de la Fe).* Patricia claims that the *heavenly visits* predominantly the *Blessed Virgin Mary* delivered a series of *messages* for all Ecuadorians as well as the whole world.

During the eighteen months of apparitions, the *Blessed Virgin Mary* appeared and spoke to Patricia over one hundred times. In addition, four apparitions took place in Mexico, and eighteen occurred in chapels and churches in Cuenca,

Ecuador. Still other *heavenly visits* or *apparitions* occurred in various other chapels throughout Ecuador. Eventually the Blessed Virgin Mary began to appear almost exclusively in *El Jardin Del Cajas,* and in her private home. On Oct. 30th, 2000 the active Archbishop of Cuenca, Monsignor Vicente Cisneros Duran, accepted a very handsome donation for the Catholic Archdiocese of Cuenca, Ecuador, for all the lands of *El Jardin Del Cajas.* Now the Catholic Archdiocese is planning to construct and actually build a *Holy Trinity Sanctuary* for religious acts at that location, which is to also be in conjunction with a Foundation developed for the *ministry* of *El Jardin Del Cajas.*

Much of the phenomena witnessed at other *Marian apparition sites* around the world were claimed to be experienced by the people of Ecuador as well. Many people made the long pilgrimage up high to the Andes Mountains just to be present for the *apparitions* of the *Blessed Virgin Mary.* Countless pilgrims reported seeing *bright lights in the sky* and *the sun spinning and dancing with different colors.* Others experienced smelling a wonderful *scent of roses,* seeing religious rosaries or medals turning into a *golden color* and many pilgrims had both their hands and faces sparkling with a golden glow from a glitter-like substance that the pilgrims claim literally fell from the sky like rain, which could not be rubbed off (but eventually disappeared). Thousands of people also reported *cloud formations with the image of the Blessed Virgin Mary in the sky,* and many, many incredible *healings* and *miracles* of all types took place during the *heavenly visits.* Most important, however, were the numerous *spiritual conversions* claimed by many of the pilgrims, who were eye-witnesses and present for the *heavenly visits* or *apparitions* of the *Blessed Virgin Mary, La Guardiana de la Fe in El Cajas,* near Cuenca, Ecuador, South America.

Prof. R. Castanon, Ph. D., from La Paz, Bolivia was asked by certain Catholic religious groups in Ecuador to consider studying Patricia Talbot. So, he first made a series of visits to the old picturesque city of Cuenca, Ecuador. The first visit occurred on June 10th, 1994. At that time, he interviewed Patricia and performed a full clinical neuropsychological battery of tests, which determined that Patricia was *normal.* He found no evidence of psychological pathology: no emotional imbalance or mood disorders; no anxiety or depression; no personality disorders, no thought disorders; no evidence of malingering or lying; and no psychotic disturbances or epileptic behaviors were found. The professor had an opportunity to investigate the history of Patricia's *heavenly visits* or *visions* or *apparitions.* Also as an aside of special interest to the professor, he performed a sociological study on the city of Cuenca's religious groups and the political makeup. Since one of the professor's many reported activities and expertise was in advising political campaign groups in Bolivia. During his second visit to Cuenca on August 12th,, 1994, the professor again performed a second battery of clinical neuropsychological tests plus neuropsychophysiology studies using the EMG system from La Fayette. These *baseline studies* were similar to those performed on Nancy (as seen earlier). He observed that Patricia's cutaneous/skin resistance and neurobioelectrical discharges emanating from her pre-frontal region muscle fibers actually registered an average range of 1.0 to 1.2 micro-Volts, which is in the *normal range* for the majority of the time that she was studied.

The professor also studied Patricia during prayerful moments. He noted that during the recitation of the *rosary prayer* some significant variations in her cutaneous/skin resistance and pre-frontal region muscle fiber neurobioelectrical discharges were detected. Much to his surprise and amazement, while Patricia was praying the *"Hail Mary" prayer,* certain astonishing and significant changes occurred:

1) During the very beginning of the prayer "Hail Mary, full of grace"- the display monitor registered measurements that dropped from the normal range of 1.2 micro-Volts to a completely relaxed range of 0.4 micro-Volts instantly, when Patricia pronounced the word Mary. Of interest, Patricia remained in the range of 0.4 micro-Volts until she began the second half of the prayer, "Holy Mary, Mother of God (mother of the Son of man, Jesus - the only begotten Son of God) ..."

2) Then upon pronouncing the word God, the display monitor instantly registered a drop to 0.3 micro-Volts. These significant drops in Patricia's cutaneous/skin resistance and pre-frontal region muscle fiber neurobioelectrical discharges were recorded and repeatedly documented. These precise and dramatic reoccurring drops were seen throughout the entire recitation of a full decade of the rosary prayer (ten Hail Mary prayers), whenever she said the word God.

In summary: Every time Patricia mentioned the Blessed Virgin's name Mary the display monitor recording registered 0.4 micro-Volts. Every time she said the words "Mother of God" referring to the "Mother of Jesus," the display monitor recording this event registered 0.3 micro-Volts.

Remember the significance of the number 3 (already mentioned in this book) in reference to *Jesus - in His Living Presence* and to *the Holy Trinity,* the One Triune God; and recall, the significance of *the number 4* (also already mentioned) in reference to the *Blessed Virgin Mary* lovingly *bringing* her baby *Jesus to us* or *speaking/echoing His living words to us* --- with the messages of her Son, *Jesus.* Now ponder this: in the picture of *Our Loving Mother,* the Blessed Virgin Mary is carrying her baby, *Jesus.* If you apply simple mathematics: *Our Loving Mother* --- bringing baby *Jesus* (4) + (plus) *Jesus*---bringing *the Holy Trinity* (3) = 7, *the perfect number* according to the ancient Hebrew Bible, *the Torah.*

The actual *Hail Mary* prayer basically comes from *four* Bible verses that are literally taken from the New Testament Gospel of Luke 1:28-42-30-35 *(4 verses),* and finishes with simply asking Mary to *pray for us sinners.* The Blessed Virgin Mary, with her very special relationship with God, is asked *to pray for us* - to pray to her Son, *Jesus,* and *to intercede for us before the throne of God: Father, Son and*

Holy Spirit. These *four verses* in Luke Chapter 1 clearly describe Mary's wonderful and powerful role and unique relationship with the *Holy Trinity.* In these four verses *Mary* is the most *blessed and* graced daughter of *God the Father,* spouse of the *Holy Spirit* and earthly Mother of the *living Son of God, the Eternal Word of the Father, savior of the world, Jesus.* Wow! *What a triangle of pure love. Mary, "the woman"* in Gen 3:15 & Jeremiah 31:22, **is** so *uniquely immersed in* and *lovingly intertwined with – the Holy Trinity of God.* This is probably *why* God calls Mary, *"the woman,"* since *God is all Three in One:* a Father, a Spouse and a Son - *to Mary;* so correctly, *God* calls *Mary – **"woman."*** In this title *God* describes ***all*** *of Mary's* **three** very special ***roles*** *with the Holy Trinity of God* as - *a daughter, a wife and a mother – three specific, different and equally important roles, all three* **in one.**

Luke 1:28-42 describes ***the Incarnation*** of the *only begotten living Son of God* ***through the power of the Most High God, the Holy Spirit,*** **Who *overshadows* Mary.** *This is the first time in Bible history, where the Holy Spirit overshadows a person (Mary)!* Prior to this glorious cosmic event, *the Holy Spirit of God only* overshadowed *masses of waters* or *things like - the Ark of the Covenant (Ark of the Testament). A*s it is written in the ancient Holy Scriptures, *the Bible: in the beginning* of time, *the Holy Spirit of God "moved over the waters"* (Genesis 1:2) *overshadowing* it, *overshadowing the waters.*

Biblically, *the Incarnation event* is definitely by far the most historic, majestic, merciful, and self-sacrificing *love event* ever recorded *in human history. God the Father* truly redeems mankind by sending *His only begotten Son.* This world changing event produced the utmost infinite cosmic glory of epic-like proportions for all mankind, the heavens and for all eternity. Now, *for the first time ever - the Holy Spirit of God* ***overshadows a human person*** - ***Mary,*** *the Blessed Virgin Mary.* The *Incarnation of the Eternal Word of God,* the *Incarnate Wisdom - "the Living Bread which came down from heaven"* is by far the most spectacular *supernatural event* ever recorded in the history of man. This most glorious event lead to the *fulfillment of 456 Bible prophecies* - concerning the birth, life, ministry of the *Good News,* betrayal, the passion, crucifixion, death, resurrection, and ascension of the *Son of man* and *the living Son of God, Jesus.* See the prophecies written in Gen 3:15; 12:3; 22:18; 49:10; Numbers 24:17; Deuteronomy 18:15-18; 2 Kings 7:11-16 and 25-29; Psalms 2:7; 8:3-8; 18:2-10; 45:2-10; 72:2-11; 110:1-7;Isaiah 7:14; 9:6-8: 11:1-5; Jeremiah 31:22-23; 33:14-16; Baruch 4:36-37; Ezekiel 34:23-26; 37:19-28; Joel 2:23: Micah 5:2-5; Aggeus 2:6-10; Zachariah 2:10-13; 3:8; 6:12-13; and Malachi 4:2, just to name a few. *Mary,* ***the living*** *ark of the new covenant* (See Rev 11:19 and 12:1), literally brings us *Jesus, "Emmanuel"* (Isaiah 7:14) --- which means: *"God is with us;" Jesus, Who* **is** *"the light of the world"* (John 8:12).

It was astonishing and indeed **unbelievable** that on yet another scientific monitoring device, here the EMG of La Fayette and on yet another *chosen soul,* in this case Patricia Talbot, the measurements yielded the same identical numbers.

These numbers coincided perfectly with the same mathematical and numerical patterns; we had previously recorded on Nancy and the seminarian. These two *chosen souls* were intensely and meticulously studied, as was already described earlier in this book, *during the heavenly visits* or *apparitions of Jesus* and *the Blessed Virgin Mary bringing her baby Jesus* to us. As the professor continued to test after the *rosary prayers* were completed, Patricia's cutaneous/skin resistance and pre-frontal region muscle fiber neurobioelectrical discharges rapidly returned to her baseline studies normal range of 1.0 to 1.2 micro-Volts. He was very surprised by these unprecedented findings. The professor claims has never seen the EMG of La Fayette readings drop so rapidly and so instantaneously at the mere mention of a *specific word* or a *specific name*. He indicated that while *words* can sometimes influence or induce neuropsychophysiological responses and changes; these changes usually take some time to develop. In his experience of over 25 years in this field, responses to words - simply **do not** change so rapidly or instantaneously to a specific number measurement, as he repeatedly recorded during these studies on Patricia. To his knowledge, this amazing rapid drop to a specific number measurement has never been recorded. So, after an extensive review of his initial *baseline tests,* the professor realized that further neurophysiology studies (i.e. EEG) should be conducted, in an attempt to either validate or negate Patricia's claims of *heavenly visits, visions* or *apparitions*.

Since the professor was already attending the *International Symposium on Science and Faith* in Cuenca, Ecuador during the third week of November 1994, he considered it timely to solicit my assistance in studying Patricia Talbot. However, because of my very busy medical practice work schedule and neurology on-call duty constraints in Atlanta, Ga., I was not able to attend the actual EEG testing of Patricia. I did, however, participate in the ambulatory audiovisual EEG-TV telemetry monitoring system review of the *raw data,* reading and interpretation analysis of the EEG testing along with my own clinical neurological observations from my several interviews on the third *chosen soul,* Patricia Talbot. Dr. Norma Agosto and Dr. Teresa Dalmau performed the actual intensive ambulatory EEG studies and neurological examinations on Patricia. The professor then performed complete neuropsychology batteries and neuropsychophysiology examinations. These medical and scientific studies were done to determine whether Patricia Talbot was normal and of sound mind. These medical and scientific studies were conducted on November 17-19th 1994 in Cuenca, Ecuador.

The experiment design was to study Patricia's *baseline EEG* during both the awake and alert state during all her daily activities including moments of *prayer and meditation;* and to study Patricia, while she was sleeping during all the stages of sleep. Another very interesting and surprising endeavor was to study Patricia's EEG/brain wave activity *during the actual reception of the Eucharist* at a *Holy Communion* service after a *Roman Catholic Mass* celebration, in Cuenca, Ecuador.

The Holy Mass **is** a *worship celebration* wherein - the Church teaches - ***"the living bread** which came down from heaven"* (John 6:41) **is *the living Son of God,*** *Jesus,* of whom John the Baptist said: *"Behold* **the Lamb of God,** *behold him who taketh away the sin of the world"* (John 1:29) and David prophesized in psalms as the perpetual ***"sacrifice of praise"*** (Psalm 106:22) --- **is** actually ***consumed.*** So, with the *"bread of life"* (John 6:35), *God* can literally *fill every hungry soul* and *inebriate the (thirsty) weary soul* (Jeremiah 31:25). *God* can *dwell deep within us* - becoming *one with us, His children. Don't* some people say, *"You* are *what* you *eat?"* Just imagine *what would happen if you - eat and drink – God/true peace?*

Moses even wrote in Exodus 16:35: *"And the children of Israel ate* ***manna*** *forty years, till they came to a habitable land:* **with this meat were they fed,** *until they reached the borders of the land of Chanaan."* Moses in this verse actually equates ***manna*** (the heavenly bread) with ***meat*** (another word for *flesh*). Interestingly, within the verses of Jeremiah 11:15-19 the words *holy flesh* is also equated with *bread: "...shall the* **holy flesh** *take away from thee thy crimes, in which thou hast boasted? ...*And I was as a ***meek lamb,*** that is carried to be ***a victim:*** and I knew not that they had devised counsels against me, saying: *Let us put* **wood** (the cross) *on his* **bread** (his *holy flesh* or *meat), and cut him off from the land of the living..."* *Jesus* clarifies this connection between *His bread, His flesh* or *meat* (food) as it is written by Moses and the prophet Jeremiah noted above in John 6:51-56: ***"I am the living bread*** *which came down from heaven. If any man eat of this bread, he shall live for ever*; and **the *bread* that *I will give, is my flesh, for the life of the world*...** For ***my flesh is meat*** (food) indeed: and ***my blood is drink*** indeed." Read John 6:31-59 for a better and more complete understanding.

We have now come to a fuller understanding of *Jesus: His Living Presence* and *His living words (in His light)* via our medical and scientific testing on Nancy and the seminarian (who is now an active Roman Catholic priest). But, it was Dr. Dalmau who brilliantly thought of and first considered that it would be very interesting indeed to see *what would happen to Patricia Talbot's EEG* (the electrical brain wave activity topographic picture) *during the reception of the Eucharist,* especially at the moment Patricia actually - eats and drinks - *the bread and wine of life?* Dr. Agosto and Dr. Dalmau brought their advanced computerized digital Oxford II PMD-12 lead ambulatory EEG telemetry monitoring system and the Oxford II Tower for the medical and scientific testing of Patricia Talbot. Also, the same Australian film crew that filmed Nancy had agreed to film and document part of Patricia's testing.

The Aussie crew recorded Patricia while she was praying, meditating and *receiving Holy Communion, the Eucharist,* during a private Communion service in her home. *The Eucharist* was given to Pachi by the local parish priest after a Holy Mass celebration *with the permission* of Archbishop Luis Alberto Luna of Cuenca for the sake of prudence and in order not to disturb or interfere with the *worship of God* during *the Mass celebration,* especially with all the scientific equipment and the

TV- video cameras etc. So, Pachi was *given permission to receive the Eucharist* in her private oratory/prayer room *at her home for this extra special testing.* Just like the Catholic priests who bring *the Holy Eucharist* to the sick, lame, or crippled - in their homes or hospital beds etc., Pachi received *the Holy Eucharist* at her home.

For *the testing,* Dr. Agosto's ambulatory EEG telemetry monitoring system was brilliantly combined with the Aussie film crew's audiovisual TV monitoring system for recording and documenting all the medical and scientific studies on Patricia. The nighttime sleep recordings were not filmed for reasons of privacy, but the EEG was recorded on the Oxford II ambulatory EEG telemetry monitoring system. All the EEG studies were thoroughly reviewed. For approximately twelve hours and twenty-five minutes of recorded EEG tracings, the initial *data* was found to be technically free of artifacts.

Once the ambulatory EEG information was retrieved from the Oxford II Tower and analyzed, all the *baseline studies* reviewed during the alert and wakeful states revealed results which were completely *normal* for Patricia's stated age of 22 yrs. Normal rhythmic alpha rhythms of 10 Hz activity was recorded in the posterior head regions, which could be seen bilaterally in the posterior temporal and occipital regions with eyes closed. All the *sleep stages* - EEG recordings showed *normal* stages of sleep with no pathological rhythms or patterns noted. No epileptic activity or epileptic behavior was identified. Thus, the *baseline awake and asleep EEG patterns* recorded *were all normal* with no epileptic foci or seizure activity identified.

During *prayer* and *meditation,* Patricia remained awake and alert with eyes open, and developed *normal beta rhythms* seen in the 18-20 Hz range bilaterally. After a *Holy Mass* celebration, the local parish Catholic priest brought *the consecrated Eucharistic Host* to Patricia's home (thanks to Archbishop Luna). Amazingly, while Patricia was *receiving Holy Communion* in her private oratory/prayer room --- at the very instant - *the Holy Eucharist (the bread) touched her tongue* --- a dramatic change occurred on the EEG. The *3 Hz delta rhythms* (*deep sleep* patterns) forming the astonishing unprecedented specific EEG brain wave activity *pattern 333* was *again recorded!* The *3 Hz delta rhythms* were also recorded simultaneously with slightly accentuated beta activity that was seen overriding most channels, but predominantly the frontal temporal head regions bilaterally with eyes open. With eyes closed, *the delta activity* recorded was just like a *deep sleep.* The *overriding accentuated beta activity with eyes open* is significant, because it supports the fact that *Patricia was* indeed *awake, alert with focused attention,* oriented and conscious *during the reception of - the Eucharist.*

This obvious *contradiction of physiological terms* was documented on the ambulatory EEG telemetry monitoring system and seen on the audiovisual TV video display monitor. The *3 Hz delta rhythms* (*deep sleep* patterns) that were recorded *simultaneously with* the slightly accentuated *overriding beta activity with eyes open,* suggested to us that *Patricia was* simultaneously *both awake, alert with focused attention and in a deep sleep,* since the predominant high amplitude EEG brain wave activity and topographic picture demonstrated a pattern typical of normal *deep sleep stages.* What *a contradiction – awake, alert* and *in deep sleep.* This *new data* is again not only very astonishing, but also definitely unprecedented.

Can you imagine - a presumed *physiologically impossible* EEG brain wave activity pattern that was recorded repeatedly in our previous studies - *only in His Living Presence,* is now recorded again - *during the reception of the Eucharist?* Patricia was both *awake, alert with focused attention* and *in a deep sleep* - simultaneously. Once again we see --- *what* an oxymoron *(a contradiction)* of known physiological terms and principles.

Where have we already seen this peculiar EEG pattern, *"a sign which shall be contradicted"* (Luke 2:34)? This is just like the results I recorded earlier with Nancy and the seminarian in Atlanta and Conyers, USA. This once presumed *impossible EEG pattern* is again incredibly being produced and evoked by *His Living Presence;* but, now in the form of *the living "bread of life"* (John 6:35). Or else, *how* can we possibly explain the amazing phenomena just recorded? *How* can Patricia (Pachi) be simultaneously *awake, alert with focused attention* and *in a deep sleep?* This is *a contradiction.* Wow! Now please, just ponder *God's peace* and magnificence.

After presenting my lecture on *"the testing of Nancy and the seminarian"* at the *International Symposium on Science and Faith* in the University of Cuenca, Ecuador, South America, I retreated to my hotel room with my wife. How romantic. There after spending some quality time with my wife discussing the events of the day, I had the opportunity to review and study all the *raw ambulatory EEG telemetry data* and audiovisual TV video monitoring system results obtained *during the baseline studies* on Patricia Talbot (Pachi). At the hotel I reviewed all the *new data* with Dr. Norma Agosto - including Patricia's moments of *prayer, meditation* and attendance at a private Roman Catholic *Holy Communion service* in her private oratory/prayer room at home, after a *Holy Mass* (worship) *celebration,* that documented Pachi's very special reception of *the Holy Eucharist.*

The Holy Eucharist is the *sacred unleavened bread wafer* that both Roman Catholic and Orthodox traditional sacramental priests daily consecrate on holy altars all around the world. The Roman Catholic and Orthodox traditional churches claim they are fulfilling Jeremiah's prophecy, as it is written in Jeremiah 33:14-18: *"Behold* the days come, saith *the Lord,* that I will perform the *good word (the good news/the gospel truth)* that I have spoken to the house of Israel, and to the house of Juda *(Jesus is from the lineage of Juda, Matthew 1:1-18).* In those days, and at that time, I will make ***the bud of justice*** *(Jesus) to spring forth unto David, and he shall do judgment and justice in the earth. In those days shall Juda be saved, and Jerusalem shall dwell securely:* and *this is the name that they shall call him,* ***The Lord our just one.*** For thus saith *the Lord: There shall not be cut off from David* ***a man*** *(Jesus)* ***to sit upon the throne of the house of Israel.*** *Neither shall there be* *cut off from* ***the priests*** *and Levites a man before my face* ***to offer holocausts,*** *and to burn* ***sacrifices,*** *and to kill* ***victims continually."***

This *promise* to Jeremiah, I believe obviously *relates prophetically to the traditional Christian priesthood – "for ever according to the order of Melchisedech* (see Psalm 109(110):1-4)*"* - that ***continually offers – Jesus, "the bread of life,"*** **as a *holocaust, a sacrifice* and a *victim-*** *in the daily "sacrifice of praise."*

Since the terrible, total destruction of the Jerusalem Temple in 70 AD, just *who indeed* is fulfilling this ancient prophecy - *"to offer holocausts...sacrifices...victims continually"* today? Catholic and Orthodox traditional churches still proclaim that *the unleavened bread, after the consecration by a priest, becomes - the bread of life,* the Lamb's Supper - *Jesus.* Yes, *Jesus* - the sinless unblemished *Lamb of God, Who takes away the sins of the world, the victim* and *the highest priest, the "sacrifice of praise"* - **is** truly *in His Living Presence - the Holy Eucharist.* OK now, can this be *true?*

Can you imagine *a wafer of unleavened bread* that actually changes at every *Holy Mass* consecration by a Catholic *priest* into *the Most Holy Sacred Body and Precious Blood, Soul and Divinity of Jesus, the Christ, the living Son of God,* the Son of the living God, *the Eternal Word of God and "the Bread of God"* (John 6:33) *made flesh - Incarnate* (John 1:14; 6:51-52), *the Son of man* and *the Lord-God Himself?* Can you imagine a *consecrated* wafer of unleavened *bread* **is** now the true *body, blood, soul and divinity of Christ Jesus, the living Son of the living God?* Is this *true?* Or is this just some sort of *bread-wafer- pagan-idol worship?*

Needless to say, I was again thrust into an immediate state of shock. I was completely astounded by the amazing and very dramatic results, which had occurred instantly upon Patricia's *reception of the consecrated Holy Eucharist.* In my private interview, Patricia said that at the very moment she *receives the Eucharist,* she interiorly and deeply feels *His Living Presence, the living presence of God.* Patricia also claims she frequently feels *totally encircled* or *surrounded,* and *completely encompassed* and *interiorly immersed* in God's most awesome *peace, love and mercy* --- during the entire *Holy Communion service* and celebration. So, guess *what* we found? Just as with the other two *chosen souls* seen the in earlier chapters of this *(His)* book, the same astonishing and *unprecedented 3 Hz delta rhythms (deep sleep* patterns*)* were again recorded, forming the *stimulus specific evoked brain wave pattern 333.* Wow!

The *333 EEG pattern* was again amazingly recorded - the very moment Patricia received *the consecrated Holy Eucharist* upon her tongue and consumed *"the bread of life"* (John 6:35, 48). This is the same exact instant and moment *the Holy Eucharist --- Jesus - in His Living Presence* really and truly dwells within Patricia. This is – *what* and *just as* - the Holy Catholic Church still teaches. Can you imagine the huge implications of *what* this awesome *gift from God* really means? *God* **is** truly *alive "within our midst"* literally and *can be alive "within us"* literally in the form of the *"living bread which came down from heaven"* (John 6:41), *"for my flesh is meat* (food) *indeed: and my blood is drink indeed"* (John 6:56), so that *"the bread that I will give, is my flesh, for the life of the world"* (John 6:52). Some of the songs I remember hearing, while attending *the Holy Mass* as a child, are finally starting to make some sense to me now. Just like *the songs: "Yahweh, I know you are near..."* or *"Taste and see." Wow! God* wants to be truly near to us and can be so very much more *near to us, in a very, very special way. Taste and see.*

We really do have a *very reachable* and *approachable living God.* Remember as was prophesized, *Jesus* came to us as a baby *born to a virgin* (Isaiah 7:14) in a manger in *Bethlehem* (Micah 5:2-4), which by *coincidence* or *God-incidence* is called *the city of bread* or *the city of David.* Mary *"wrapped him up in swaddling clothes"* (Luke 2:7). So just *how near,* approachable and reachable *is Jesus, the Son of the living God?* Can you imagine *God sent* ***His only begotten Son*** (Psalm 2:7) and *"the Lord said to* ***my Lord****: Sit thou at my right hand"* (Psalm 110:1) **to be** a totally defenseless *human baby,* ***"a child is born to us, and a son is given to us"*** (Isaiah 9:6) ***and be*** *the most approachable* **King of Kings and Lord of Lords** ever (Rev 19:16). Taste and see.

The *Savior* of mankind *the Eternal Word of God* and *Wisdom Incarnate - Divinely Wills* to be *Incarnate* in the form of *a human baby boy, Emmanuel (Jesus),* and **is** *born to a virgin (Mary) of the House of David,* as prophesized in Isaiah 7:14. Remember, the name *Emmanuel means "God is with us." He* actually *came, comes and will come to visit His people,* as prophesized. Thus, *God* fulfills *His* promises to *His* beloved *chosen people, the Jews,* and then later, to *the Gentiles;* as it is written in Isaiah 42:6 and 49:6. *God* brings us *the light of salvation - in Jesus, with Jesus, and through Jesus.* Please read the following Holy Scriptures and you will get a sampling glimpse of the promises that were fulfilled by *the birth, life, death, and resurrection of Jesus:* Deuteronomy 18:15-18; Genesis 3:15; 12:3; 49:10; 2 Kings 7:12-16, 25-28; Psalms 2:7-9; 8:2-5; 40:7-11; 45:7-8; 72:2-11; 89: 25-30, 38; 110:1-7 and Isaiah 7:14; 9:18: 11:1-5; 40:1-5,9-11; 42:1-8; 49:6-11: 59:16-17, 20-21; 60:1-7,19-20; 62:11; Jeremiah 23:5-9; 31:22-25; 33:14-17; Baruch 3:29-38; Ezekiel 34:9-16, 23-31; 37:19-28; Daniel 9:24-27; Hosea 1:7; 6:1-3; 13:14; Joel 2:19, 21-27; Amos 9: 9-11;Micah 5:2-4; 7:7-8; Nahum 1:15; Habakkuk 1:5; Sophonias 3: 5-17; Aggeus 2:6-10; Zachariah 2:10-13; 3:8-9; 6:12-13; 9:9-17; Malachi 1:11; 4:2-6 just to name a few verses of the ancient *Holy Scriptures* that is available in the *Holy Bible* on this special and specific topic: prophecy of *the coming* Jewish Messiah.

God *in, with and through the power of His Holy Spirit* comes to us and visits us in many special ways. Our loving *God* is so very, very near, approachable and reachable to us all everyday. But, just how near, approachable and reachable is *God, really?* Based on our *new medical and scientific data, God* is just as near, approachable and reachable as the very next visit to the *Holy Mass (worship) celebration service* nearest to you; or the very next visit to a *Holy Eucharist*

Tabernacle were *the Most Holy Blessed Sacrament, "the bread of God"* (John 6:33) is located. Actually, in the form of *the Most Holy Blessed Sacrament – His Living Presence* **is** in any *Catholic traditional church* nearest to you. So, go spend some time with *Him, the Lord God. Taste and see.*

Now I can better understand *why* the Church calls this wafer, *the Eucharist.* The word *Eucharist* comes from the *Greek word* that means *to give thanks and praise; also Eu = "true or good"* and *charist* = from *charism* meaning *"gift, a spiritual gift, divinely granted."* This is exactly what *Jesus* did during the Last Supper's 3rd cup, *the cup of blessing,* the third cup of the Holy Passover Seder *(Pasch)* meal, as written in the Holy Scriptures. Can you imagine *(eating and drinking)* feeding on the sinless *Lamb of God, Who takes away the sins of the world,* and simultaneously becoming immersed with the indwelling of *His Living Presence and true peace?*

We need to ponder these newly uncovered, unprecedented, medical and scientific *new facts. Our God* **is** indeed truly approachable and very reachable. The Lord willingly and literally wants *to quench the thirst of our souls.* The Lord, in Jeremiah 31:25, has: *"inebriated the weary (thirsty) soul...filled every hungry soul." Why?* To satisfy and nourish our weary, thirsty and hungry souls; so, that you and I can become *one with God, the Almighty.* Our merciful and loving *God* literally *wants to dwell deep "within you."* See Jeremiah 31:33:*"in your bowels."* God **is** indeed very near, approachable and reachable for us all. *God* **is** indeed *the Almighty One* **present** *when you receive Him* **in** *the Holy Eucharist.*

Recall, this *new* unprecedented *data* is identical and the same as the *new data* we recorded when *Jesus* manifests *His Living Presence in tangible medical and scientific evidence that proclaims He is alive* in the many *heavenly visits, visions* or *apparitions* when we tested Nancy and the young seminarian. In all our meticulous and intensive medical and scientific studies, we see that the *333 EEG brain wave pattern* is repeatedly *recorded* and documented *only in His Living Presence.* Since these *heavenly visitation experiences* are truly *holy supernatural events,* then *what* does *the reception of this consecrated unleavened bread wafer, the Eucharist,* and our medical science *new data* with the 333 EEG pattern *really have in common?*

If this 333 EEG brain wave pattern is *only* recorded during the experiences of being *in His Living Presence,* which are obviously *holy supernatural events,* then *what* kind of experience or event is this *new event* that we recorded with Patricia's *reception of the consecrated Holy Eucharistic Host?* Now with our *new data,* I believe that *the 333 EEG pattern,* we recorded at the precise moment in time Patricia received *the Holy Eucharist, is indeed a medical and scientific documentation of an event* that must be *labeled* **as,** and *truly* **is,** *a holy supernatural event.* So, armed with this *new medical and scientific data,* I ask: *What* does this *new information* mean for us?

Another *new finding* was also recorded ~ just moments after Patricia had received *the Holy Eucharist.* The 333 EEG pattern was again recorded with higher amplitude for a few EEG epochs (moments of time). This definite increase in the EEG amplitude was keenly observed on the video playback exactly when Pachi slightly and gently moved her ***left shoulder*** downward. This was a noticeably odd and sort of an unnatural shift, which made me quite eager to interview Pachi and find out *what* she had possibly seen or heard or even felt at that very moment. Recall, all the *new data* up to this point in time had clearly demonstrated the unprecedented 3 Hz EEG patterns *only **in** the living presence of Jesus in light, His living words in the light and His living pulsating light.* Now with Pachi's --- *reception of the consecrated Holy Eucharistic Host and at the moment her left shoulder moved downward* --- the same high amplitude and identical *3 Hz delta rhythms, the unprecedented 333 EEG pattern* was again recorded. So, *what* does this mean for us? And *what* did Patricia actually see or hear or feel? Did she - see *the light* of *Jesus? What* happened to Patricia the moment her left shoulder gently moved downward? So, *what* does *Jesus - in His Living Presence* and *the Holy Eucharist* have in common?

Much later, after my lecture at the conference in the early evening hours, my wife and I were invited to visit Patricia and her family at her home in Cuenca. We met with her husband, Andres, her parents and friends; including a number of volunteers, who support Pachi's mission in Ecuador. The group leader of the *Guardian of the Faith* Foundation was Sr. Gaston Ramirez, who kindly treated us with gracious hospitality. Earlier in the day it was Gaston, who drove us around the beautiful old city of Cuenca, Ecuador, and introduced us to Patricia Talbot's devoted support and prayer group. All the while in her home though, I could not wait to ask Patricia privately what she actually saw, heard or even felt during her *reception of Holy Communion,* since her EEG brain wave activity changed so dramatically to the same 3 Hz delta rhythms. Recall, this is the same 3 Hz delta *deep sleep* activity with the same *unprecedented 333 EEG pattern* seen and recorded previously with the two other *chosen souls,* Nancy and the seminarian, *only in His Living Presence.*

When I finally had the opportunity to privately interview Patricia, I was shocked to discover that ***she did not see or hear Jesus nor even see His light*** *while receiving the Holy Eucharist.* Recall, up to this point in our long series of medical and scientific studies on the *chosen souls* and with the experiences of the *heavenly visits* we had already studied, our *new data* was always associated with either a *supernatural event* of a visual stimuli or auditory stimuli (audibly or interiorly) or both stimuli combined. This was in concert with an interior feeling of profound peace, love and joy - as was experienced by the *two chosen souls:* Nancy and the seminarian. Thus, it was my obvious assumption that the *chosen souls* either had to **see or hear** (audibly or interiorly) *Jesus - in a holy supernatural event, while experiencing an interior feeling of profound peace, love and joy,* in order to be able to produce the stimulus specific 3 Hz EEG brain wave activity pattern of 333 in a *deep sleep* topography – as previously recorded **only** *in His Living Presence.*

Therefore, Patricia's information was once again unbelievably stunning to us *(to me),* as it seemed to introduce an entirely *new variable* into our equation for these *heavenly visits, visions, apparitions, supernatural events and holy experiences.* Patricia declares that when she receives *the Holy Eucharist,* she experiences a deep interior *feeling of profound peace, love and joy* that typically lasts ~ 15 minutes. Can you imagine the *deep sleep* EEG pattern of *3 Hz delta rhythms* forming the same *stimulus specific EEG pattern of 333* - is now once again being recorded and documented, the very moment Patricia receives *Jesus – in His Living Presence* in the form of *the consecrated Holy Eucharist.* Wow!

Digging a little deeper, I soon learned that when Patricia lowered her left shoulder moments after receiving *the Eucharist* in the *Holy Communion service,* it was indeed very significant. Patricia indicated that at that precise time and at the very moment she lowered of her left shoulder, she experienced and felt *the fatherly Living Presence of Jesus with tender love place His hand on her left shoulder.* For a brief moment Patricia ***also felt*** *His Living Presence standing close to her (almost like a quick cameo appearance).* This may help explain the brief increase seen and recorded in the higher amplitude of the 3 Hz delta activity for that particular moment in time. But, Patricia says that to a much greater extent and in an even more profound way, when she receives *the Holy Eucharist, she feels Jesus - in His Living Presence - deep within her very core (interiorly).* Pachi says she *feels His profound peace, love and joy* from very the moment *the Holy Eucharist touches her tongue and is consumed.* Pachi says that she *experiences - the peace of God* - in this profound way, whenever she receives *the Holy Eucharist.* Pachi says - *the peace of God* - she *experiences* usually lasts for ~ a quarter of an hour. But, on this occasion during the medical and scientific testing, the very holy *- peace of God - experience* upon receiving - *the Eucharist* - actually lasted ~ 20 minutes, as recorded on Dr. Agosto's ambulatory EEG telemetry system.

I reviewed the ambulatory EEG telemetry and the TV audiovisual video monitor display recordings of the entire private *Holy Communion service* in Pachi's home after the *Holy Mass* celebration by the local parish Catholic priest. After closely reviewing *the gentle downward movement of Pachi's left shoulder,* it does indeed appear as if Patricia is truly being given a *gentle loving touch* by someone, to help explain the downward shift of her left shoulder. Now we see that both *the reception of the consecrated Holy Eucharist* and moments later *the tender loving touch of Jesus* actually do provide *a tactile (touch) type* of specific *new stimuli of Jesus - in His Living Presence.* Patricia claims and ***feels*** *His touch* and *His heavenly visits – in His Living Presence* are almost *just like the experience of receiving the Holy Eucharist.* Thus, these *holy tactile stimuli* produce a plethora of *deep* feelings, especially a profound interior *peace, love and joy.* These *holy tactile experiences* also produce a pleasurable state of *ecstasy.*

Amazingly, Patricia's deep feelings concerning her *heavenly visits, visions or apparitions* were very similar to Nancy and the young seminarian's feelings, the two other *chosen souls* we previously tested. So once again, I see this astonishing *deep sleep 333 EEG pattern* while *the subject is awake, alert with focused attention* and the subject Patricia also feels a very profound interior *peace, love and joy* --- only *in His Living Presence*--- that was reproducibly measured on our EEG tests. Wow!

Now the astonishing and unprecedented 333 pattern and 3Hz delta rhythms (seen in the typical EEG *deep sleep* pattern-brain wave topography) are once again recorded and documented *in His Living Presence* upon the *reception of the consecrated Holy Eucharist* and moments later with the noted increase in amplitude upon the brief and gentle loving and tender *touch of Jesus.* Again *wow!* The total amount of time, that the *deep sleep pattern* was recorded on the EEG *while* Patricia was clinically observed to be *awake, alert with focused attention* with eyes open and the EEG beta activity was seen intermixed that attenuates with eyes closed during the time Pachi was praying fervently – after *receiving the Holy Eucharist* - actually lasted *~20 minutes long.* The entire ~ 20 minutes recorded, with the 3 Hz EEG brain wave activity and the occasional 3-4 Hz brain wave activity range intermixed in a *deep sleep topographic pattern - while awake and alert,* actually started at *the beginning* upon the *reception of the Holy Eucharist.* This ~ 20 minutes of EEG tracing also included the early recording of the - brief, gentle and tender *loving touch by the hand of Jesus* on Patricia's left shoulder.

Patricia continued to explain and readily confessed that *the living presence of Jesus* totally overwhelms her. She said, *"Jesus* gently touched me by placing His tender loving hand on my left shoulder for a brief moment.*"* Patricia indicated that she did not see or hear *Jesus.* But rather, she *feels - the living presence of God (a very holy tactile stimulus).* Patricia said this entire - very tangible *holy experience* was indeed accompanied by an immense, penetrating, interiorly profound *peace, love and joy* - upon *receiving the consecrated Holy Eucharistic Host* during her private Holy Communion service at home (with the *permission* of Archbishop Luna) after a sacred Catholic *Holy Mass celebration* in Cuenca, Ecuador.

Patricia further added that she experiences a deep interior *peace* similar to what George Collins feels (see Chapter 7). She also feels this same profound, deep and immense indescribable *peace* whenever she visits *Jesus - His Living Presence in the Most Holy Blessed Sacrament* in the tabernacle of a Catholic Church or whenever she *receives Jesus in* (the form of) *the consecrated Holy Eucharist* during or after the *Holy Mass.* Patricia says and proclaims that ***the Eucharist*** is one of the greatest, *most awesome gifts of God.* Imagine - *God can* literally *dwell within you.* Ponder this. God wants *to touch you,* to deeply dwell and *commune* with you.

So again, we were left with the same questions. Due to same identical results obtained from the different *visionary experiences:* is it possible that this *new data* is the real true brain wave activity- EEG pattern measurements of the **peace of Jesus**

in His Living Presence, **the peace of God? Could we be so bold as to presume this? Perhaps we could, but only if we simultaneously recognize the great humility shown by our awesome Almighty God, the Creator, in allowing it.**

Once again, our medical and scientific team was left scientifically baffled and personally fascinated, as a third visionary - *chosen soul* from another country, with yet a completely unique and new experience of *Jesus - in His Living Presence,* exhibited the same identical and *unprecedented EEG pattern of 333* as we had previously recorded.

The *journey* now skyrockets from *science to faith...*

...it truly does...

...just watch...

RESULTS OF THE SOUTH AMERICAN STUDIES

The neurological evaluations and mental status examinations on Patricia Talbot Borrero (Pachi) were both considered *normal* for her stated age.

The neuropsychological battery conducted by Prof. Castanon, Ph. D., on June10^{th,} 1994 - was entirely *normal.* There was no evidence of psychological disturbance or emotional imbalance, no depression or anxiety disorder, no personality disorders, no mood, thought, or affective disorder, no evidence of hysteria or malingering or lying, no evidence of psychological pathology and no psychotic disturbances were identified.

Neuropsychophysiology studies conducted by the professor on August 12^{th,} 1994 had revealed fascinating and significant changes in the EMG of La Fayette monitoring system display readings during the *Hail Mary* prayer. The *baseline studies* neurobioelectrical discharges emanating from Patricia's pre-frontal region muscle fibers registered a range of 1.0 to 1.2 micro-Volts (a normal range). As soon as Patricia pronounced the words *"Hail Mary,"* the readings dropped immediately to 0.4 micro-Volts. Later in the prayer, when she recited the words *"Mother of God,"* the readings dropped further to 0.3 micro-Volts upon pronouncement of the word *God.* The professor had no logical or scientific explanations for these unprecedented findings.

The EEG's recorded on November 17-19^{th,} 1994 using the Oxford PMD-12 ambulatory EEG system - *the baseline studies:* The awake and sleep recordings were *normal:* rhythmic 10 Hz alpha activity was recorded over the posterior head regions with eyes closed with low amplitude beta activity seen in the anterior regions bilaterally. *Normal sleep stages* were noted with no epileptic activity, no epileptic behavior, and no pathology identified.

After the celebration of the *Holy Mass* and particularly during a period of approximately 20 minutes after *Holy Communion* was given to Patricia at her home by a local Catholic priest with the permission of the Archbishop of Cuenca, she remained in reverent prayer upon *receiving the Eucharist.* At the precise moment that Patricia received *the Eucharist,* Patricia's brain waves dramatically changed and developed medium to high amplitude consistently rhythmic and predominate *3 Hz delta rhythms* with occasional *3-4 Hz rhythms intermixed,* seen best over the frontal, temporal and central head regions with some spread to the parietal and rare occipital head regions bilaterally; basically a *deep sleep* topographic brain wave activity pattern was identified, *while Patricia was awake.* She was *awake and alert with a focused attention pattern* that was featured by the low amplitude *overriding beta activity* seen throughout most channels with eyes open, especially over the bilateral frontal head regions. Thus, confirming the eye witnessed and audiovisual documentation of Patricia's *awake and alert status, while in deep sleep.* At times the *3 Hz delta rhythms* of high amplitude were recorded every 3-5 seconds with no spikes or sharp wave discharges, no evidence of epileptic activity or epileptic behavior, no FIRDA or PLEDS, no paroxysms or evidence of EEG pathology identified. What an *oxymoron* and *a contradiction* of EEG principles.

Initially and throughout the twenty minutes after Patricia received *Holy Communion,* Patricia's brain waves recorded on EEG amazing and unprecedented *3 Hz delta rhythms* forming the *stimulus specific evoked brain wave pattern of 333.* No EEG pathology was recorded. This is the same EEG patterns we had previously and repeatedly recorded with our medical and scientific testing of Nancy and the seminarian in Atlanta and in the testing of Nancy in Atlanta and Conyers, Georgia, USA, and in Puerto Rico, while *only in the living presence of Jesus – in His Living Presence.* Can you imagine *what* dramatic changes we just recorded on EEG? The emergence of *3 Hz delta rhythms* in a *deep sleep pattern mixed with beta* (an awake, alert with focused attention pattern) that showcases the now famous *333 pattern.* This is the same EEG pattern that was repeatedly recorded with Nancy and the seminarian when they *see, hear and experience Jesus - in His Living Presence.*

This is also the same EEG pattern recorded *in His Living Presence* when the scientists recorded 30-90% more *sun light;* and when we documented the astronomical increases in *the light* energy; and when we recorded *the living light (alive) pulsations* from the resin model of *Jesus on a wood cross (the crucifix);* and we also recorded *flashes or bolts or darts of lightning* energy in the rooms. Yes, these same *3 Hz delta rhythms, 333 EEG pattern,* was also recorded at the very precise moment in time the *Holy Eucharist* touches Patricia's tongue, as she receives *Holy Communion* from a local Catholic priest in Ecuador, while remaining in reverent prayer. This *new data* and *unprecedented 3 Hz EEG pattern* was again recorded lasting *~20 minutes* after Patricia received *Holy Communion.* This *new data* includes the brief *touch by Jesus* on Patricia's left shoulder that we recorded: generating and evoking briefly much higher amplitudes of the same identical *3 Hz delta rhythms* and the *EEG pattern of 333.* Wow!

PRELIMINARY REFLECTIONS ON THE SOUTH AMERICAN STUDIES

Now with all the *new medical and scientific data* we recorded and documented, I know that *God* truly has given us - the most awesome loving, generous and tremendous *gift* ever - *the living bread from heaven - Jesus. His* real true *living presence* **is in** and **is** the *Holy Eucharist,* that is *prepared for us daily* as the *"sacrifice of praise"* during the *Holy Mass.* St. Pio is absolutely correct about *the Eucharist* and *the Mass* as he said in one of his famous prayers after *Holy Communion: "Let* me recognize you *Lord* as your disciples did at the breaking of bread, so that *the Eucharistic Communion* be *the light* which disperses the darkness, the force which sustains me, the unique joy of my heart.*"* St. Pio said, "The world could exist more easily without *the sun* than without *the Mass."*

Just imagine in the *Holy Mass* celebration the *unleavened bread* is consecrated and becomes the true ***living bread of life,*** *the true light of the world,* the true *living presence of God.* The Lord wants to nourish our souls and give us all the mercy, graces and blessings needed to reach and enter *"the door." The Lord* wants us to enjoy *eternal life - with God, in God and through God.* Yes, *God* is taking us in *a circle of eternal life.* God is taking us into *His circle of light - in His Living Presence.*

Jesus, the ***living*** *word of God* and *the* ***living*** *bread which came down from heaven,* actually *became flesh (Incarnate)* within the womb of the Blessed Virgin Mary (the ark of the *new* covenant) *first to visit His chosen people* and *then the Gentiles* as foretold by the prophet Isaiah 7:14, 42:1-10, 49:5-13. The true *Lamb of God, Who takes away the sins of the world, Jesus* accepts death on a *tree (a cross) for all the sins of mankind* for *Jews and Gentiles* alike throughout history (past, present and future). Later, as prophesized by the prophets (Sophonias 3:5-17, esp. verse 8 and Hosea 6:3) on the 3rd day --- *the Lord resurrects in glory. Jesus ascends up to heaven* to the *right hand* of the *Father, God* (Psalm 110). *Jesus* takes the *keys of life and death* and becomes *the door of heaven,* as *Father God* promised. *God sends His Holy Spirit* to adopt us all, who accept *Jesus* as *the Messiah, the One Who He sent;* and invites our souls into the *baptism of water, spirit and fire. God* prepares our souls to be forever nourished with true food/meat and true drink, and *to eat* the *new covenant meal* and *drink of God. The Eucharist, "the living bread which came down from of heaven," and the Consecrated wine, "the blood of the grape,"* **is** indeed the *holy flesh* and *the Precious Blood of Jesus.* Both are *offered up to God* during the *Holy Mass* as *"the sacrifice of praise"*, a *perpetual* ongoing *daily sacrifice* for all the sins of man (Jeremiah 33:18). *The circle of* ***the life*** *becomes complete only when you do your part - to fulfill the new covenant of God.* So, *eat the Lamb of God!* Eat the *unblemished Lamb, Who takes away the sins of the world.* Recall what *Jesus* says after he drinks the 4th Pasch *cup of consummation.* John 19:28-30: *"I thirst...*when *he (Jesus)* had taken *the vinegar (old wine),* said: *"It is consummated." Or "It is finished."* We need *to consume* or *finish our part* to be **in** the *new covenant of God,* Jeremiah 31:33. So, *eat and drink the new covenant meal,* the Holy Communion *bread and wine - the Lamb of God.*

Thus, the true *living bread - Jesus Incarnates within the virginal womb of Mary* just like the true *living word of God - Jesus Incarnates within the virginal womb of Mary.* Later on, *Jesus - in His Living Presence* really and truly returns to us in *the Eucharist! He* returns to us through *His living words* in the Bible and *His living words given to chosen messengers* like *His loving Mother Mary, holy saints, holy angels* and the *chosen souls* we were most fortunate to test like Nancy, the seminarian, and Patricia. Also through many other *chosen souls* the Church has tested throughout its history and is currently investigating. I recall Patricia saying, *"I* experience *Jesus* as the most awesome unconditional and tender love. A gentle all embracing love that totally surrounds me with a deep profound joy and peace. The moment I receive *Jesus* **in** the *consecrated Holy Eucharist, His fire, the flames of His living presence dwells deep inside me."* At this precise moment in time Patricia says, *"I feel His Living Presence, the living presence of Jesus, the living presence of God." In His Living Presence,* Patricia **feels** immense love and a profound joy and peace, which she initially had some difficulty explaining because it is such an awesome feeling. After reception of *Holy Communion, the Eucharist,* Patricia was in a *state of ecstasy* with a radiant glow for *twenty minutes,* while praying on her knees with good muscular tone, awake, alert and conscious.

Why 20 minutes? This really intrigued me. Many years later, I believe I found the answer in lesson #374 of *The New St. Joseph Baltimore Catechism:* **"The 15 or 20 minutes that Our Lord is in us bodily after Communion is the best time of the whole day for prayer."** Also, recall during the period of time a brief *touch of Jesus* on Patricia's left shoulder was recorded - the EEG demonstrated a 3 Hz, ***deep sleep,*** 333 EEG pattern mixed with an overriding *beta,* awake and alert with focused attention EEG pattern. What *a contradiction.* These *new* findings were indeed distinctly unprecedented and challenging to our medical team and scientists.

MORE REFLECTIONS ON THE SOUTH AMERICAN STUDIES

The collaboration among the fine and respected doctors on our medical research teams along with the assistance of the Australian film crew once again recorded extraordinary *new medical and scientific data.* But with no medical or scientific precedent to explain these amazing results, we were left with the obvious conclusions: that the inexplicable *heavenly supernatural events were occurring* in Patricia's life, although we could not thoroughly verify it. **Those around Pachi of non-medical backgrounds could logically and in good faith take these astonishing results to validate and promote the authenticity of Patricia Talbot Borrero's claims of heavenly visits, visions or apparitions. And we would have no basis by which to refute her claims.**

Again a distinctly different scientific monitoring device, the EMG of Lafayette interestingly, also measured the same identical mathematical and numerical patterns that were previously recorded with the other *two chosen souls* in our medical and scientific studies of Nancy and the seminarian in the early chapters.

The number four (4) appears to be important in relation to the Blessed Virgin Mary bringing Jesus to us, as this number occurred repeatedly throughout all the studies on all *three visionaries.* Remember with Nancy and the seminarian the *4 Hz theta rhythms* were seen repeatedly *only in the presence of the Blessed Virgin Mary bringing her baby Jesus to us,* forming an *unprecedented EEG pattern of 444.* When Dr. Callahan's photonic ionic cord amplifier measured *Schumann waves* (extremely low radiation) at the atmospheric-skin boundary on Nancy that immediately changed from 14 Hz with 1 mV amplitude to 4 Hz with 40 mV amplitude intensity suddenly increasing the surface area of Nancy's atmospheric-skin boundary radiation light energy fields *(her aura)* tremendously whenever the *Blessed Virgin Mary* was caressing and *bringing her baby Jesus to us* and/or *was speaking (echoing) His living words to us.* Also during this experience, the other probe measured the atmospheric radiation energy fields in the two rooms that surged upwards from 800-1000 Hz to +3,000-4,400 Hz (with an average of approximately 4,000Hz). Remember the *electrical (magnetic) anesthesia* region, which generates a *peace*ful *light energy* and has a *very calming and relaxing effect* on people, **is** in the radiation energy fields region of the low ionizing radiation - *radio wavelength spectrum;* and recall, this *very relaxing and peaceful light energy* was actually used by dentists for performing different dental procedures in the 1800's.

Now with the studies of Patricia Talbot completed, using yet a fourth scientific monitoring device - the EMG of La Fayette, we measured 0.4 micro-Volts, whenever the *Blessed Virgin's* name *Mary* was merely mentioned during the *Hail Mary prayer.* Again the *number 4* was recorded. Four completely different medical and scientific monitoring devices, each designed to measure completely different types of energy fields— from EEG brain wave activity changes, to atmospheric-skin boundary radiation energy field changes (the aura) and to the atmospheric radiation energy field changes of the external environment, to the EMG of La Fayette cutaneous/skin resistance and the neurobioelectrical discharges emanating from the pre-frontal region muscle fibers changes—yet on all the distinctly different energy readings the changes recorded and documented on the distinctly four different devices had the number 4 – somehow associated with all of them whenever the *Blessed Virgin Mary was bringing baby Jesus to us* or was *speaking (echoing) the words of Jesus* also when the name of *Mary* was mentioned in the *Hail Mary* prayer that highlights *the Incarnation* - Mary bringing *"the light of the world," the light of paradise* back to us, *Jesus – "blessed is the fruit of thy (Mary's) womb."* Thus, we recorded and documented some astonishing results with even more astonishing interpretations, some of which we have to carefully decipher.

The name *Jesus* was always associated in our medical and scientific studies with the number three --- 3. In the studies on Patricia whenever she merely pronounced the words *Mother of God,* referring to *Mary as the Mother of Jesus,* a reading of 0.3 micro-Volts was recorded every time *the word God* was said. Remember, in our medical and scientific studies we repeatedly recorded and documented the number 3 --- especially the *3 Hz delta rhythms* and the astonishing *stimulus specific evoked EEG brain wave pattern of 333* - only *in His Living Presence* in 5 different forms as follows:

1) *The (living) light* as was recorded with the *living (alive) - light pulsations* that we actually measured from the resin model/wood crucifix *(Jesus on the cross).*

2) *His living words* – as was recorded whenever *Jesus speaks in the light* and the same medical science *data* was documented. So, *new data in His Living Presence* was found to be associated both with *the sound of His voice* of *His spoken words* as well as with *His spoken words* somehow literally and clearly heard *interiorly* in their brains. Although this last method of communication, *hearing interiorly* is still not fully understood scientifically *how God does it;* I theorize quite simply that this is likely accomplished by ***God's living word* which is *light*** (Genesis 1:3) somehow ***is being directly beamed into the brains of the chosen souls via electromagnetic wavelengths. God's light speaks directly into the brain* by *stimulating the auditory and receptive cortex areas of the brain directly*** *for comprehension and communication. Thus, God can bypass (Passover) our external hearing apparatus* altogether. Recall, *sound and light travels in same electro-magnetic wavelengths.* A medical and scientific example of this specific type of stimulation used experimentally in medical practice is called an *electromagnetic coil stimulator* which I had the pleasure to work with at a Harvard Medical School neurophysiology workshop with Dr. Chappius. The coil stimulates motor evoked potentials for intra-operative spinal cord EP monitoring for spinal surgery (evoked potential) testing. Harvard's electromagnetic coil stimulator directs magnified electromagnetic waves or beams of low ionizing radiation energy directly into the human motor cortex area in order to stimulate the motor cortex and produce evoked motor potentials. At strong settings the coil evokes contra-lateral limb movements.

3) *The living presence of Jesus* in the *heavenly visits* or *visions* or *apparitions.*

4) *The living touch of Jesus* also produced and evoked the same *new data.*

5) *The living presence of Jesus* in the *reception of the Holy Eucharist, the* *consecrated unleavened bread & wine:* The *"living bread which came down from heaven"* (John 6:41) & the *"blood of the grape"* (Genesis 49:11) -*the blood of Jesus.*

Now ponder this amazing new medical and scientific fact: Patricia upon receiving *the Eucharist* during a private *Holy Communion Service* after a *Catholic Holy Mass* and moments later *the living touch of Jesus* both dramatically changed her feelings interiorly, changed the EEG brain wave patterns and changed her neurophysiology. Though Dr. Callahan was not part of this study, I suspect the atmosphere in the room must have also changed, since the rest of the *new data* collected and documented - was the same and identical - to all the *new data* just recorded and documented with Nancy and the seminarian, while *in His Living Presence.* Imagine the magnitude and full scope of implications this *new medical and scientific data* really means and then contemplate the following: the *reception of the Eucharist* actually *produces and evokes the same new medical and scientific data recorded in all our testing on Nancy and the young seminarian,* which was *only* documented *during the heavenly visits, visions or apparitions of Jesus.*

Thus, with the *new data* just presented *upon the reception of the Eucharist,* we can now medically and scientifically say that *Jesus - in His Living Presence* or *in His living power source* of energy truly *comes to dwell deep within us – in our bowels / in our spirit* to nourish us as it is written in Ezekiel 34:23: ***"he shall feed them;"*** and in Jeremiah 31:25: *"...for I inebriated the weary soul: and I have filled every hungry soul."* Therefore *in, with and through - a Catholic Mass celebration, Holy Communion* and *the reception of the Holy Eucharist: the Consecrated Bread and Wine* can now be truly *labeled as a real bonafide* medical, scientific and faithfully *confirmed supernatural event.* ***At the Mass heaven truly meets earth!*** Recall that upon *reception of the Eucharist,* Patricia produced the same astonishing and unprecedented *new medical and scientific data,* that was reported to occur *only during the heavenly visitations or apparitions of Jesus* as previously tested. This *new data* undoubtedly tells us that ***receiving the Holy Eucharist*** **is** *indeed* **a *tangible, supernatural event.*** The *Lamb's supper,* ***the Mass*** **is *heaven on earth.***

Measurements with *the Blessed Virgin Mary* ***bringing baby Jesus,*** Nancy's atmospheric-skin boundary radiation energy fields (Nancy's aura) changed 14 Hz and 1mV amplitude to approximately 3+ Hz (but fluctuating in the 3-4 Hz range) with over 25 to 40 mV amplitude (a predominant reading of 3+: with 3+ Hz and mostly 30+ mV average in the apparition room). In the adjacent room to the apparition room of the farm house in Conyers, Ga., USA, *in His Living Presence:* 3+ Hz and a reading of well over 80 to 90 mV amplitude was measured. Also, the atmospheric radiation energy in the rooms increased from 800-1,000 Hz to +3,000-4,000 Hz *in His Living Presence* with an average of 3,300 Hz, which is predominantly a 3+ fold increase. At one point briefly the energy increased up to ~4,900 Hz in the atmospheric radio radiation energy fields of the apparition rooms that were recorded only *in the living presence of Jesus in light - on the cross.*

Christianity teaches that *Jesus* **is** *the Messiah, the Anointed One, the Christ,* (the *Christos* - in Greek) the *God-Man,* the ***living Son of God*** or the *Son of the living God.* Christian theology teaches there is only One God of One Substance Undivided, yet Three Divine Beings of the One God-Head, *the Holy Trinity.*

This is what the Jewish *Shema* entertains as it is interpreted in the *Zohar* by Rabbi Simon ben Jochai and his son Rabbi Eliezer in the years following the Roman Army's destruction of the Jewish Temple in Jerusalem in 70 A.D. This concept of a Triune God is also entertained in the Jerusalem Targums as written by Jonathan ben Uziel, a famous scholar and student of the great Jewish scholar Hillel the Great. The Targum of Jonathan and the Targum of Onkelos, interestingly, were written decades *before the birth of Jesus* and further provide us with precious and valuable insights into the understanding of *the Holy Trinity – the One God* as taught by celebrated Jewish sages.

Recall, some of these sages lived *before the birth of Jesus* while others mentioned lived *around the time of the death of Jesus on the cross* and *resurrection* in Jerusalem. **Is** *Jesus* the *Second Person of the Holy Trinity?* As the New Testament Gospel in Holy Scriptures proclaims: *Jesus is the God-man, the living Son of God!* See the Prologue of John 1:1-15. *Jesus* is the *Son of man,* the *God-Man* as was prophesied in Isaiah 9:6. *Jesus* fulfilled *His Father's plan of salvation for the sins of the world* by His birth, life, passion, crucifixion, death, resurrection and ascension to the seat at the right hand of God the Father, as was foretold by David in Psalm 2:7, 2:9, 110:1-4 and 98:1-2, to mention just a few. Just as amazing as the repetition of the *number 4* seen in association with *the Blessed Virgin Mary bringing Jesus to us,* was the repetition of the *number 3* seen in association with *Jesus.* Interestingly, this *new data* was collected and repeatedly measured on all our (3) three different scientific monitoring devices in all (3) *three chosen souls* that came from (3) three different countries - *only with Jesus (in His Living Presence) or* just by merely *mentioning His name as – God (as seen with Pachi).* Such a result was not only unexpected, but would have been impossible to concoct.

In the Old Testament (see Leviticus) *peace offerings* actually meant more exactly *fulfillment sacrifice* offered up in fulfillment of a vow, and *sin offerings* meant more exactly *sacrifice for remitting sin. God* promised and vowed *He would save* and *redeem His people and all the nations through the new covenant for all the sins of mankind.* See one of the greatest prophets Isaiah 42:1-9; 49: 5-7; 51:4-5; 53:1-12; 55:3-12; 59:1, also 12-21; and 7:14; 9:1-6; 28:16-18, 60:1-6, 12-20 and finally 61:1-2. *Jesus, the Lamb of God,* is the ultimate perpetual on-going eternal and perfect *peace and sin offering* and is the perfect *"sacrifice of praise"*- given freely to us by the most awesome, loving and merciful *Father God the Almighty Creator;* and this very special *peace* was even *foretold to us by Jesus Himself,* see John 14:27.

If 333 ***is*** indeed associated with *the Divine Trinity* and *Jesus, Who* **is peace personified** as foretold by David in Psalm 85:9, 11: *"the Lord will proclaim peace"* and *"justice and peace will kiss,"* in Isaiah 9:6: *"the Prince of Peace"* and in Micah 5:5: *"And this man (he) shall be our peace,"* then *Jesus* **is** *the second person of the Holy Trinity - One God. Jesus (in His Living Presence)* **is** then the actual **specific stimulus that evokes the EEG deep sleep brain wave pattern of 333** recorded in all three *chosen souls* and in some way **represents the most immensely profound *Peace of God* ever measured and documented.** See John 14:27: *"Peace I leave with you, my peace I give unto you: not as the world giveth, do I give to you..."* With tremendous awe we must then boldly speculate: Have we truly measured *the peace of God, the peace of Jesus*...the *Prince of Peace?* If so, we must again add without reservation that our doing so was only made possible by God's great humility.

Can you imagine, we now have medical and scientific proof of **three** *chosen souls* tested from **three** different countries, with **three** uniquely different *experiences of Jesus* yielding an identical *3 Hz delta rhythms - deep sleep pattern, 333,* while remaining awake, alert with focused attention and fully conscious—data previously considered *physiologically impossible.* While the details of their various encounters differed, they all claimed to experience *the most profound peace, love and joy* while deeply immersed in a *pleasurable state of visionary bliss,* often referred to as *ecstasy.*

It is my professional and much researched opinion, which is now supported by many of my medical and scientific colleagues that our *medical and scientific new data* overwhelmingly supports the fact that I have uncovered (discovered) a *new* form of *stimulus specific evoked EEG brain wave patterns* that were *previously considered to be physiologically impossible.* This *new data* has been clearly corroborated and reproduced by Dr. Norma Agosto's *initial EEG data* on Nancy and now on Patricia. These unprecedented EEG patterns can now be recorded and reproduced in other normal subjects, referred to in religious circles as *chosen souls,* who claim to experience the real true holy visible- audible- physical- tangible- heavenly *supernatural events of His Living Presence* in the many forms uncovered during our tests such as: visual and auditory *apparitions of Jesus* - in His Living Presence; His Living Presence in *the light ;* His Living Presence in *His living words;* His Living Presence in *His touch;* the interior peace, love, joy and a deep dwelling feeling of *His Living Presence* when eating and drinking *His consecrated Living Bread and Wine -- the Eucharist* and *the Sacred Wine (the Lamb of God's Flesh and Precious Blood – the blood of the grape).* Yes, we do indeed have a *very reachable and approachable God, Who* in this form can really and truly *dwell deep within us* (literally) in a very powerful way and *nourish our souls.* So, *after you receive Jesus, the kingdom of God* **is** *(truly) within you.*

Thus, *the Lamb's supper* **is** truly *a Holy Communion feast* and one of the greatest gifts ever given freely to mankind. Can you imagine the incredible privilege *God* has given to us? **A *tangible supernatural event* is *truly what occurs***

whenever we receive the Holy Eucharist. Everyone is invited to this *holy banquet*. Now I understand, why so many pastors, preachers and priests indeed so often say ---*"Repent...* repent, be made clean with *the Blood of the Lamb* by washing away all your sins in the Lamb of God's most *Precious Blood.* So, please invite *Jesus* into your life and into your heart right now." *Father God* sent *Him (Jesus)* to the Jews (first), then to us - the Gentiles. I now pray that *the Holy Spirit of God* will anoint you and guide you always in *the ways of God.* I pray you will always follow and *live in God's Holy Divine Will* and purpose for your life. Now just go to *"the house of God, which is the Church of the living God, the pillar and ground (foundation) of the truth* (1 Tim 3:15)." Recall, that our *three chosen souls* repeatedly reported a feeling of immense *love,* a profound *peace* and *joy* during each of the *heavenly experiences of Jesus* and recorded EEG *deep sleep* and *awake, alert patterns.* All the clinical observations recorded them to be awake, alert with focused attention and fully conscious. The unprecedented and reproducible *3 Hz delta rhythms* recorded, previously seen *only* in stages of *deep sleep* in normal adult subjects, seems to validate one of our conclusions: that we have possibly discovered a *new EEG normal variant,* as was proposed by Dr. Norma Agosto, a Board Certified EEG/ neurologist. I propose that we have discovered a *new stimulus specific evoked EEG brain wave pattern response.* I believe this is the most likely mechanism, since the evoked brain wave activity or evoked potential brain wave activity response occur within milliseconds of the stimulus specific *supernatural event* as recorded repeatedly in our studies.

Thus, the *stimulus specific supernatural event of Jesus* evokes the *3 Hz delta rhythms* (with a *deep sleep* topographic pattern) forming a *stimulus specific evoked EEG pattern of 333.* The *stimulus specific event of the Blessed Virgin Mary* caressing and lovingly *bringing baby Jesus to us and/or speaking the words of her Son, Jesus (His living words), to us* evokes the *4 Hz theta rhythms (pleasure rhythms)* forming a *stimulus specific evoked EEG pattern of 444.* Interestingly, the (*eerie) stimulus specific event of Satan* evoked the *6 Hz theta rhythms* forming a *stimulus specific evoked EEG pattern of 666.* This well known Biblical number of *the serpent* in Genesis 3:1-15 is *the number of the beast* or *the number of his name* (in Hebrew) as it is written in Rev 13:18.

Can you imagine, *the Peace of God - a deep sleep while awake, the most profound peace* ever that - *the 3 chosen souls* experience - *in His Living Presence? The peace of Jesus, the living Son of God* and *the Son of the living God,* **is** actually *measurable* (only by the grace of God) on EEG, as well as in the surrounding external environment and atmosphere. This is really unbelievable... unbelievable... unbelievable! Can you image, my utmost surprise and complete *astonishment* by these awesome works of *Jesus?* I felt just like Peter did in Luke 5:1-11.

In a message by *Our Living Mother*, in Conyers, Georgia, USA, Nancy was told that Conyers is *directly linked to Fatima. Messages* from Fatima, Portugal and

Conyers, Georgia say that *the **Blessed Virgin Mary has been entrusted to bring peace to the world**.* Now before you react adversely to this last statement, please first *reflect on the words* of this message. If the *Blessed Virgin Mary* has been entrusted to bring *peace* to the world, and ***peace*** (as seen in our studies) **is** *personified* and *equated with Jesus – in His Living Presence;* then the *Blessed Virgin Mary, Our Loving Mother, has* obviously *been entrusted* by *Father God to bring* ***Jesus (peace*** - **personified***) to the world.* Now after the 9/11 Twin Tower NYC terror and horror in our ever increasingly dangerous world *at war* with so many of its neighbors, we are in a most desperate need of *Jesus ("our peace,"* Micah 5:5*).* This may help explain *why* the *Blessed Virgin Mary* during the past twentieth century has increasingly appeared all over the world as never before in the history of mankind – *crying!* She is *crying* because *her children* all over the world *are seeking a false peace and* not the real *true peace – of her Son, Jesus.* So, *what* is the *Blessed Virgin Mary* trying to tell us? *What* is so urgent? *What* is so important? One of the most consistent *urgent messages* Nancy repeatedly received from the *Blessed Virgin Mary, Our Loving Mother*, is ***"children pray, pray, pray...take my heart, take my hand and let me lead you to my Son, Jesus."*** The *Blessed Virgin Mary* desperately *wants all of God's children to "repent and turn back to God now before it is too late."*

Her *Son, Jesus, the living Son of God,* and the *second person* of *the Holy Trinity - One God,* is calling you and is now extending His awesome *immeasurable* and unfathomable *love and divine* ocean of *mercy* to you and the whole world *in His Divine Will.* The *Blessed Virgin Mary* repeatedly says her *Son, Jesus,* is the *only* true answer and real solution for any real *true peace* in this world. So, ponder this: If *Jesus is peace* - as our medical and scientific *new data* convincingly shows, then whenever anyone, anywhere, anytime *prays for peace to come* into our world, our country/community/work-place, our schools, our home or even into our hearts, then you are actually *praying for Jesus to come,* since *Jesus* **is** *"our peace"* (Micah 5:5).

Our *journey science to faith* may never be over. Indeed, as *new medical and scientific data--* becomes available, it seems to bring with it an ever increasing *revelation and truth* of the mystery which overwhelmingly points to the real living existence of God, and the reality of the afterlife. Psalm 14:1 correctly says, *"The fool hath said in his heart, there is no God."* Sorry atheists. David did not have the advantages of all our astonishing *new data,* medical and scientific results; yet, David still really understood and proclaimed *the truth. Faith* **is** truly an *awesome gift from God.* Psalm 100:3 so correctly says: *"Know ye that the Lord He is God: it is He that hath made us, and not we ourselves; we are his people, and the sheep of His pasture." Jesus* **is** *the "one (Good) shepherd" - Father God* has *promised to send to his people,* as it is written in Ezekiel 34:10-11 and 23-25 -- and also written in David's famous Psalm 22 (23).

Ezekiel 34:11 says: *"For thus saith the Lord God: Behold, I myself will seek my sheep, and will visit them."* Read that verse again. The *Lord God* is saying that *He will seek His sheep* and *will visit them. Who* then are *them? They are His sheep who hear His voice* and *follow Him everywhere He goes* -- the one *(Good) shepherd.* Now see in Ezekiel 34:23-25 which says, "And *I will set up one shepherd over them, and he shall feed them, even my servant David: he shall feed them, and he shall be their shepherd...* And I the Lord will be their God: and my servant David the prince in the midst of them: I the Lord have spoken it. And I will make *a covenant of peace* with them*..."* In this last passage, not only is *he* the *Anointed One,* the *one (Good) shepherd* from David's stock *who shall feed them,* but *he* is also the *covenant of peace.* And *he shall feed them what? Who* is *he?* In this *messianic* passage *he,* I believe **is** referring to *Jesus.* Thus, *he (Jesus)* - their *shepherd is the Lord. Jesus* in *His humanity* will be *God's servant: "I the Lord will be their God and my servant David the prince (Jesus, son of David, Matthew 1:1-18) in the midst of them."* Notice *"my servant David" will also be their God.* Read the last verse Ezekiel 34:24. And *"he (Jesus) shall feed them" what?* **Answer:** *His living words* and *His living bread* (John 6:51); and *he shall be their shepherd. So, are you hungry* for God? Are you *thirsty* for God?

Author and Pastor Tommy Tenney, well known for his ministry work and recent book titled *God Chasers,* on his TBN show frequently challenges young Christians with these questions. When I heard him ask these questions on TV, I quickly shouted out to the TV (as if he could hear me): *"Come eat and feast* on the holiest banquet ever, *the Lamb of God, Who* takes away the sins of the world, *the Holy Eucharist!* Come drink *His Precious - Blood the blood of the grape!* Come and feast on *the living bread which came down from heaven.* Come and *feast on His living words.* In the *order of Melchisedech, Jesus* the *Lord Who* brings forth *His living bread and wine* for us, blesses us much like Abram was blessed by the *High priest and King Melchisedech* - before Abram became Abraham (Genesis 14:18-20). This same faithful and merciful loving Lord *Jesus* is really and *truly present* here for us all in the *most approachable form* ever possible, *the bread and wine.* So, if you are really *hungry and thirsty for God, come eat and drink!* For *His flesh* is *true meat (food) of the Lord, God;* and *His blood* is *true drink* of *the Lord thy God."* See and carefully re-read John 6:48-59. Just imagine what this *new data* really means for us all, who do not have the *faith to believe in the real presence of the Lord - in the Eucharist?* This is truly the greatest discovery and treasure ever. Yes, *Jesus* **is** *alive and* **is** *presently living in* a *consecrated Holy Eucharistic Host, the Most Holy Blessed Sacrament, closest to you or your home.* So please, come *eat and drink, taste and see* --- the goodness and full richness of *our Lord, thy God.*

Incredibly, we now have a *tangible medical and scientific confirmation of His Living Presence - in the Holy Eucharist.* Wow! So, *Heaven and earth really do merge at the Holy Mass.* What a gift. Sorry atheists and agnostics. Sorry all non-Judeo-Christian faith based religions... sorry to all my beloved brothers and sisters in Christ, especially the many *sincerely deceived* or disgruntled fallen away Catholic and traditional Christians. Sorry to all my many beloved anti-Catholic Protestant Christians, *who do not believe in the real true living presence of Jesus - in the Holy Eucharist.* Now, *rejoice and be glad* for *with the grace of Almighty God,* we truly have definitive *new medical and scientific data* that *confirms His Living Presence - in the Eucharist. Wow!* So, please let me be the first one to introduce you to the real true *Triune God* –in *His Living Presence, the Eucharist - Jesus,* the most awesome and unconditionally loving *"father of the world to come"* (Isaiah 9:6), my brother, my best friend, my personal *savior* and *yes - my Lord. Jesus, Who is One with God: the redeemer, the justifier and the sanctifier: the Holy Trinity.* Recall, *God's signature: His signature – 333. The Father, the Son and the Holy Spirit: the One Triune God.*

When you receive *Jesus in the Holy Eucharist,* you are simultaneously receiving *Father God and the Holy Spirit gloriously all at once.* All in one simple, very approachable awesome little package - *"the bread of life"* (John 6:48), since *the Holy Trinity* **is** *the Holy One -Three-fold Unity – God.* So now, ask *God* to *open the eyes of your heart* and reveal *the truth* about *His greatest gift to us, the mystery of all mysteries!* Ask God to give you all the graces and blessings needed to really believe, love, honor, glorify and worship *the true living Son of God, Jesus – "the Word of God"* (Rev 19:13) **in** *the Bible* and **in** *the Eucharist, "the living bread"* (John 6:41, 51). So, come taste and see *the Eternal Word of the Father - the Bread of Life* - our most awesome merciful and loving *Lord.*

In tracing my roots back from Cuba to Spain, it very was interesting and enlightening to me to find out that over 500 years ago in Northern Spain, in the region where my father's family came from, many of my ancestors were Jewish. My last name is *Sanchez.* This is an apparently prestigious *Spanish surname,* that is originally derived from the Latin name *Sanctius,* a derivative of *Sanctus,* which means *holy.* The name *Sanchez* in two parts means: *holy* = San and *family* = che; this was apparently a very prominent name among some of the noble merchant Jews in that region of Spain, during that time period. Just like St. Teresa *Sanchez* of Avila (*my cousin - far removed* and one of my family's *patron saints),* whose father and grandfather were both noble merchant Jews with the last name *Sanchez,* during the time just before the Spanish Inquisition.

Of interest, testing done on a Catholic priest named *Sanchez,* who has a very similar history to mine with Jewish customs at home - I also thought were Spanish, was performed at the Family Tree DNA in Houston, Texas, and revealed a >80% positive genetic markers for the *Cohanim family, (See TIME: July 11th, 2005, pg.52). The Cohanim* is *the family* of *Jewish high priests directly descended from Moses' brother Aaron.* My dear Jewish brothers and sisters please forgive me and all who dare to call ourselves *Christians* and may have mistreated you *in the name of the Christ Jesus, a Jew* of the House of David. In Luke 24:34 *while dying* **on the cross** *Jesus said, "Father, forgive them, for they know not what they do."*

Jesus, the Christ (the Jewish Messiah) came down from heaven *(sent by God the Father)* first for all Jews, and then for all Gentiles. God has genuinely placed in my heart a deep tremendous love and affection and respect for all Jews ever since I was a small child growing up in a predominant New York Jewish neighborhood in Miami, Florida, USA. One of my favorite all-time special breakfast meals today is still toasted bagels, cream cheese, soft poached eggs, onions, capers and nova (I wonder why?). Even my dear wife is Jewish. So, please try to understand my true intentions from my heart are good. I am not attempting to try to change your heritage or even your ancient and most holy religion of the chosen people of God. *Who* would dare? God forbid. But, I will definitely like to share with you a most tremendous gift and blessing God gave to me and to you 2,000 years ago. A gift that is so wonderful and so truly great for all our souls. *The gift of salvation!* Exactly *what Moses* and *the prophets foretold.* See how our awesome heavenly Father God today continues to graciously give us this great gift daily and offers it perpetually everyday for you and me, *Jew* and *Gentile* alike.

This great *gift* **is** *"the way, the truth and the life",* eternal life. This free gift from your Almighty Creator God has been given to me and you, *yes you!* This precious gift of *"the life" (eternal life)* I believe is *Jesus* --- Your true *Jewish Messiah, the seed of David* and *the seed of Abraham, Isaac and Jacob;* please, see the genealogy of *Jesus* in Matthew 1:1-18*, the* true *Anointed One, the* true *Prophet, the High Priest* according to *the order of Melchisedech, the only begotten Son of God, the King of Kings and the Lord of Lords, the Good Shepherd,* and *the Lamb of God Who takes away the sins of the world.* So worthy is *the Lamb of God!* So worthy is *the Lamb!* In John 4:22*, Jesus* said to the Samaritan woman: *"You adore that which you know not: we adore that which we know; for salvation* (Jesus) *is of the Jews."*

Salvation - Father God made possible for us all by willing the shedding of the most *Precious Blood* of *His only begotten Son* (Psalm 2:7) *Jesus,* a Jew born in Bethlehem (Micah 5:2) with the *rising* of a *new star* (Numbers 24:17), *the Star of David, rising* over the *City of David* (called the *City of Bread*) to *the virgin* (Isaiah 7:14) *Mary* and *Joseph from the House of David;* and *Mary,* who is also *of the daughters of Aaron* like her kin Elizabeth. Now *in the name of Jesus, whose name* in Hebrew *means God saves* or *salvation,* and *the name that is above all names,* we *Jews and Gentiles* alike *can all receive salvation by believing in the One (Jesus) Whom He (Father God) sent. Jesus* says in John 10:10: *"I am* come that they may have *life,* and may have it *more abundantly". So,* what kind of *life - more abundantly* does *Jesus* mean? I believe *Jesus* means for all of us to have *eternal life with the God of Abraham, Isaac, and Jacob.*

The *journey science to faith* continues...

Review of two messages given to the Jewish doctor - October 13th, 1993

Recall, the Jewish doctor whose name was called by the *Blessed Virgin Mary* on July 13th, 1993 (Chapter 5). For the following years on the 13th of every month whenever *Our Loving Mother with baby Jesus* or *Jesus Himself appeared* to Nancy this dear brilliant medical colleague somehow knew she had to be present for these *apparitions* as an *eye-witness* of these *supernatural events.* This Jewish doctor could not explain *why.* So, every time Nancy was to receive *heavenly visitations* or *apparitions* on the 13th of every month, she instinctively knew she had to be present. *Why?* To this day she still does not know. But, I believe the answer to this question must be searched for *in the holy fields of God* and *in God's mercy* and *love for His chosen* people *the Jews.* We can maybe get a hint as to *why?* From *two* deeply profound *messages* this same *Jewish doctor received* on October 13th 1993. Of interest Father Rene Laurentin the famous French Mariologist, who I had the great pleasure of meeting in early July of 1995 and 1999 in a Virginia suburb near Washington D.C., was indeed fascinated with the *two messages* given to this Jewish doctor, that expresses *God's* utmost love, charity and deep concern for all *His chosen* Jews. During the October 13th, 1993 *apparitions,* the doctor claims she clearly saw the following white luminous numbers *3:18* appear over the vicinity or area where usually the *Blessed Virgin Mary, Our loving Mother,* appears. And simultaneously she *heard a voice from above clearly say, "Luke."*

Shortly after, the doctor *saw* another set of *numbers made up of white light 5:38* suspended in the air again, just over the area where the *Blessed Virgin Mary* usually appears. Simultaneously, she then heard *a distinct voice from above* saying *a word in Hebrew* that refers to *shoes* or *sandals.* The doctor recalled a poem or verse from Holy Scripture, that she learned in grade school about how *John* did not think of himself as worthy enough to even untie the sandals of *Jesus* (John 1:27). So, she thought *John.* After looking up these two verses in *the Bible,* I clearly see *why* these *two messages* were *given* for all my beloved Jews, just as it is written ~2,000 years ago. Please read the *two messages* slowly:

Luke 3:18: **"In many different ways *John*** *(the Baptist; a Jew)* **preached *the good news* to the people and urged them to change their ways."**

John 5:38: Jesus said, **"And you do not keep *his*** (*Father* God's) ***messages* in your hearts, for *you do not believe in the one*** *(Jesus)* ***whom he*** *(God)* ***sent.*"**

NOTE: The last part of the first verse above reminds me of what *Jonas* (Jonah) did in Nineveh. The entire second verse was often a *message* given by *John* to all Jews, who do not believe in *the one whom he sent (namely Jesus),* and reminds me of the famous prophetic *Messianic verse* given to *Moses* in Genesis 49:10: **"The septre shall not be taken away from Juda, nor a ruler from his thigh, *till he come that is to be sent,* and *he shall be the expectation of nations.*"**

Interestingly, when *Jesus* was born *the septre of Juda* was indeed already taken away by the Roman captivity. So **is** *Jesus - the true Jewish Messiah, the Anointed One, the Cristos, the Christ and the One whom He (Father God) sent?*

Inspirations from the Holy Spirit – a personal love letter to all Jews

To my dear Jewish family, my beloved beautiful and faithful wife, all our dear Jewish relatives, the *remnant of Israel* all over the world and to all my beloved Jewish friends here in America: Please just take a peek and look at the wonderful ancient teachings found in the Jewish *Zohar.* The *Zohar* illustrates and clearly explores the origins of the *One Triune God (the Trinity).* This great Jewish rabbinical work actually probes into the *greatest mystery of all mysteries* and into a deeper meaning and *understanding of G-d,* as the enlightened Jewish sages discovered ~2,000 years ago, while reviewing the *Torah's* Deuteronomy 6:4 *The Shema.* (Thanks Grant R. Jeffrey for *The Handwriting of God;* some of the following excerpts are taken directly from pp96-104, in this valuable and informative source)

The Shema -- *the prayer* - which the observant religious Jew recites as a daily affirmation of their Jewish faith:

"Hear, O Israel: The Lord our God is One Lord."

The *Zohar* was written by two very brilliant Jewish sages, Rabbi Simon ben Jochai and his son Rabbi Eliezer (as mentioned earlier), and teaches the following: *"We* have said in many places, that this daily form of prayer *(the Shema)* is one of those passages concerning *the unity,* which is taught in the *Holy Scriptures.* In Deuteronomy 6:4, we read first *Jehovah,* then our God *(Elohim),* and again *Jehovah,* which taken *together make one unity.* But how can three names *(three beings)* be one? Are they verily one, because we call them one? How three can be one *can only be known through the revelation of the Holy Spirit,* and, in fact, with closed eyes. This is also *the mystery of the voice. The voice* is heard only as *one sound,* yet it consists of *three substances, fire, wind, and water,* but *all three are one,* as indicated through *the mystery of the voice*. Thus, are Deut. 6:4: *"The Lord, our God, the Lord,"* but *One Unity, Three Substantive Beings which are One,* and this is indicated by the voice which are one; and this is indicated by the voice which a person uses in reading the words, *"Hear, O Israel,"* thereby comprehending with the understanding the most perfect unity of Him Who is infinite; because all three *(Jehovah, Elohim, Jehovah)* are read with one voice, which *indicates a Trinity."*

Recall, this was written by two *Jewish rabbis.* Now, could you have ever imagined - that this material was written ~ 2,000 yrs. ago by Jewish rabbi's? No wonder so many Jews at ***the time of God's visitation*** *(Jesus on earth)* readily accepted the teachings of John the Baptist, born to Elizabeth *from the daughters of Aaron* and a high priest Zachary– (see Luke Chapter 1), and later accepted the profound teachings of *Jesus of Nazareth,* during the first century era. As the prophet Baruch so well prophesized - *His* (God's) *visitation on earth,* see Baruch 3:33-38:*"He* that sendeth forth light, and it goeth: and hath called it, and it obeyeth him with trembling... *This is our God, and there shall no other be...*He found out all the way of knowledge, and gave it to Jacob his servant, and to Israel his beloved. Afterwards *he* (God) *was seen upon earth, and conversed with men."* So, now we can see *the truth and wisdom* that is written in Psalm 25:14: *"The secret of the Lord is with them that fear Him."*

Another very brilliant Jewish Rabbi Menachem also wrote the following in his *Commentary on the Pentateuch* about Deuteronomy 6:4, the *Shema: "Hear, O Israel, the Lord our God is one Lord."* This verse is the root of our *(Jewish)* faith therefore Moses records it right after the *Ten Commandments.* The reason *(that there is said, Lord, our God, and Lord)* is, because the word *(in Hebrew)* does not signify *"Hear"* but *"to gather together, to unite,"* as in 1 Samuel 15:4: *"Saul* gathered together the people." The *meaning implied* is: *the Inherent-Ones* are so united together, *"one in the other without end;"* (they - *being the exalted God).* He *(Moses)* mentions the three names *mystically* to indicate: *"The Three exalted original Ones."* (Thanks again Grant R. Jeffrey)

Remember, this *commentary* was written by a Jewish rabbi and Hebrew scholar and *not by a Christian.* Inspired by *the Holy Spirit of God* I sincerely believe Rabbi Menachem wrote about the mystery of the *Trinity,* as the *threefold unity of the Godhead.* In his writings about *the mystery of the Trinity* he finally concluded, *"These are secrets which are revealed only to those who are reaping upon the holy field...,"* and *thus, only with the help of the Holy Spirit of God.* Again we see that these writings are from a *Jewish rabbi* and *not a Christian.*

Question: So, are you and I *"reaping upon the holy field?"*

Remember the cry of the Seraphims in Isaiah 6:3 as they sang: *"Holy, Holy, Holy; Lord God of Hosts! All the earth is full of His Glory!"* The Seraphims cry out to God three times: *"Holy, Holy, Holy..." Why?* Is it possible that these brilliant Jewish rabbi sages mentioned above were maybe on to something real big; big like possibly *the greatest mystery of God?* His real true *Tri-Unity* nature:

The threefold unity of the Godhead, the greatest mystery of all mysteries ---

The Holy Trinity – The Holy One and true God.

Pope John Paul II says, *"Only the Holy Trinity can save you."* As Biblical scholar Dr. Scott Hahn teaches in his excellent teaching tapes on *the mysteries of Holy Trinity:*

1) God the Father *redeemed us* by sending His only begotten Son *Jesus* of whom God is well pleased (Psalm 2:7: Luke 3:22).

2) *Jesus,* Who is *Wisdom Incarnate* and *the Word of God Incarnate, the truth,* justice and the judgment to come *personified,* as well as *the law (taught by Moses)* and *the word of God (as given to Elijah and all the prophets of God): justifies* us to the Father by following *the law* of His Father while on earth - completely sinless, thus, fulfilling all righteousness. He also *justifies us* by always following His Father's *Divine Will* perfectly till the very end, even accepting death on a cross *(on a tree) for the forgiveness of all sin; dying on the cross/shedding His Blood for* you and for me.

3) The Holy Spirit *sanctifies us* by making us *holy* in the eyes of God through the *baptism of living waters* and *the Holy Spirit of truth, the Spirit of Jesus and the Father - the fire - the living flames of love; the tongues of fire (the truth/the just)* that *rained down* during *the Feast of Pentacost* on the apostles and the Blessed Virgin Mary; and through this baptism of *living waters* and *fire* we are *born again into a spirit of life,* which is *eternal life.* So, praise You Lord God and bless You God Almighty... thank You, thank You, thank You for giving us *"Your only begotten Son"* (Psalm 2:7) and *the true Messiah - Jesus* – Who *Our Loving Mother* proclaims *is the living flame of love. Now just shout it out: "Holy, Holy, Holy..."* **Amen.**

Nonetheless in the pages of this *(His)* book, *it is the hope and prayer* of this hardened-skeptical-medical-scientist-turned-faithful-*on fire for God* –humble-servant (me) that *the gap between science and faith* has closed at least a bit for most of you (Jew and Gentile), so those *in search of:* ***"The way, the truth, and the life..."*** can take a *saving leap towards faith.* Let us be *children of God, children of the light* and *be not afraid* to take the hand of the *Blessed Virgin Mary, Our Loving Mother,* who lovingly and truly intercedes for us, prays for us, guides us and *only* seeks to bring us closer to her beloved Son, ***the living Son of the God, the Messiah, the Anointed One, the Cristos, the Christ – Jesus*** in *God's Divine Will,* our Lord God **is** indeed ONE: *The Father, the Son and the Holy Spirit!*

Now, please read *Our Loving Mother's last message* made public for the USA and the world by Nancy in Conyers, Georgia, USA, on October 13th, 1998. Then please, carefully and slowly, re-read it. *Our Loving Mother* (*echoing the words* of her *Son, Jesus)* says:

"My dear children, I have come to be with you today, and, as your Loving Mother, to instruct you.

"Children, please live your life in full union with God.

"It is most pleasing to God when you imitate Him and honor me.

"Seek the help and protection of my beloved spouse, Saint Joseph.

"Know of the help and blessings that you are able to receive by calling upon the souls in heaven.

"Pray for souls who are not yet united with God. They in turn will pray for you.

"Be ready for heaven.

"My Son has prepared a place for you. Follow Him. Avoid the temptations and ways of the world. You have the commandments of God.

"Children *[long pause]* ***obey.***

"Do not store worldly treasures. You will take with you the good that you

have done on earth, your love of God and neighbor.

"My requests remain the same as in Portugal** [Fatima] **in 1917.

"Please children, stop** [pause] **offending** [pause] **God. Please.

"God is** [pause} **the Creator and He is** [pause] **sovereign over all creation from the heavens above to the earth below. You have yet to see** [pause] **the forces of nature.

"No man is greater than God.

"No country is greater than God.

"If you choose to live apart from God, then you will fall and fall you will.

"Oh, my dear little children, God is all loving** [pause] **and you will reach Him by imitating Him.

"You are worried about the future but you do not attend to your daily duties.

"Please be attentive.

"My Son's heart is rich in mercy and love for you.

"When you are doing your best, do not worry. The future holds no concern to those who truly seek God, love Him** [Jesus] **and remain in His favor.

"The warnings have been given to you.

"Take seriously how you live your life.

"Pray, children, pray.

"On this day God presents to the world the title: "Our Loving Mother".

"Honor me under this title and graces will pour forth from heaven.

"From my motherly heart, I am giving you special graces this day.

"Please pray the Rosary for peace, please. Pray the Rosary for inner strength. Pray against the evils of this age. Keep prayer alive in your homes and wherever you go.

"Begin to live the messages of love and mercy.

"I ask you to make consecrations to the merciful loving Heart of my Son, Jesus, and to my Immaculate Heart. Make your home and rest in our hearts, dear children.

"As I depart, please make the Sign of the Cross and my Son, Jesus, will bless you. Remember to thank Him for permitting me to come.

"As your Loving Mother, I am gathering you together from East to West and all over the world in the one Body of my Son, Jesus. Be united. Be one.

"My Son and I do not leave you but remain with you.

"My parting words are:

"Be holy witnesses.

"Walk by faith.

"I love you, all my dear children."

Now our journey *(so blessed* and *graced by God)...*

...literally leaps from science to faith...

P.S. While working on this *(His)* book, I remember receiving encouraging *words from Our Lord* through Nancy. Though, I must admit that I can only truly call this book, *His book,* because of what *Jesus* said to Nancy one late evening at approximately 11:05 PM. I recall that I was on the phone with Nancy telling her about a new and exciting *revelation* that I believed *the Holy Spirit* had just led me to, when suddenly, Nancy started seeing *mystical white and bright golden lights* appear in her home near a picture of the *Sacred Heart of Jesus.* Then, after *casting out* ***in the name of Jesus*** *any demonic activity present* and/or *anything not of God,* Nancy said, *"the mystical light* around the *Sacred Heart of Jesus* picture has just intensified greatly...wait *...the Lord is appearing...* praise you *Jesus." Jesus appeared* to Nancy just in front of the *Sacred Heart* picture in her home and said, *"And watch what I will do with* ***my book."***

I now understand and believe that *this (His) book* **is** truly *His work* and *His meat (food).* And *His meat (food)* **is** *to do the Will of God, Our Father (John 4:34). So, His meat, His food, His flesh, "the living bread, which came down from heaven"* **is** also *His Divine Will - for you and me.*

I believe *"Our Loving Mother,"* the Blessed Virgin Mary with her *Beloved Son, Jesus,* the *anointing power of the Holy Spirit* and *the Divine Will of God the Father* has graciously guided *this (His) book* from its very conception in early October 1995. Thanks be to *our One God Thrice Holy --- Father, Son and Holy Spirit.*

Praise you and thank ***You, Lord!***

CHAPTER IX

WHAT IS TRUTH?

HIS SIGNATURE 333
THE WAY OF PEACE

The title of this chapter --- *"What is Truth?"* **is** appropriate here in this last Chapter IX because I am sure that many of you reading this book are right about now wondering: *What* is truth? This entire Chapter IX is an in depth and meticulous reflection on *the truth* in the last 8 chapters. It is also a summary of the *new medical and scientific data* our research team recorded that *with mostly the Holy Spirit's help* I gradually discovered very important *holy connections* to *the word of God* in the Holy Bible. Reviewing this *new data* I found even more surprising connections with the true Hebrew Bible ELS codes (not the *fictional Da Vinci codes).* As it is written in the Gospel of John 18:37-38 during *the passion of the Christ, the Messiah - the suffering servant:* Pilate asks Jesus a question: *"Art thou a king then? Jesus* answered: *Thou sayest that I am a king. For this was I born, and for this came I into the world; that I should give testimony to the truth. Every one that is of the truth, heareth my voice.* Pilate saith to him *(Jesus): What is truth?"*

This famous question posed by Pilate approximately 2,000 yrs. ago resounded within my entire being as I was writing *this book.* I pondered intensely about *the truth. So,* what is *truth?*

Is Jesus God? Is Jesus really the resurrected and glorified *Son of the living God?* Is *Jesus* truly *the Jewish Messiah, the anointed one of God, the Christ, the suffering servant of the Lord,* and *the Lamb of God, Who takes away the sins of the world?* Is *Jesus, the living Son of God* and *the son of man (the God-man), "God the Mighty"* (as it is written and prophesized in Isaiah 9:6)? I really wanted to know *the truth.* So, I struggled with the central and prime question presented in the title of this Chapter IX: *What is Truth?* I soon realized this is what it really boils down to. Either it's all *true* or it's all *false?* Anything in between with a mixture of truth and lie would be a deception. So, *what* is the *definition of truth?* What does the word *truth* really mean?

First, a look **in the dictionary** tells us that **truth** means:

1) Conformity to fact or actuality.

2) A statement proven or accepted as true.

3) Sincerity: integrity.

4) Fidelity to an original or standard.

5a) Reality: actuality.

5b) Often *truth* is that which is considered to be the supreme reality; and to have the ultimate meaning and value of existence.

Second, **in science truth** is sought out by very diligent research and meticulous recording of all the *data* and observations of a specific matter, finding or calculation that if repeatedly tested is reproducible and eventually in time becomes accepted as a *scientific fact* or *truth.* In search of *the truth,* and nothing but *the truth* (so help me God) is indeed exactly what I believe *the testing* by the entire medical and scientific research team accomplished in studying the *3 chosen souls* and in the testing of the surrounding atmosphere *during the supernatural events.*

Third, **in matters of faith truth** is attested to and confirmed by two or three witnesses. In faith, as we have just seen in the medical and scientific research above, *the truth* is basically confirmed as it is written in Deuteronomy 17:6 and 19:15: **"...by the mouth of two or three witnesses every word shall stand** *(as the truth)***."**

Interestingly, our medical and scientific research actually and unknowingly abided by all the above given *definitions of truth.* So, *the truth* about the testing *In His Living Presence* was sought out and confirmed not only in the fields of medicine and science, which was and is still our (my) duty, but was also confirmed by all the known *definitions of truth.* Initially, I thought these studies were all about the *chosen souls.* I thought it was all about Nancy, the seminarian, and Patricia's credibility and the truthfulness of their claims of *heavenly visits or visions or apparitions or supernatural events.* But I have to admit, I was wrong. These studies were all about *Jesus.* These tests were all about being *in His Living Presence - the living presence of Jesus.* I believe God utilized Nancy, the seminarian, and Patricia for a much greater purpose and grand plan. I believe *the Lord* wanted all of *His chosen soul s* and adopted children as well as the entire world to really and truly know more about *His Living Presence.*

Jesus Himself speaks of **the truth** in John 8:14-19, 23-40, 42-43, and 45-47:

"Although I give testimony of myself, my testimony is true: for I know whence I came, and wither I go: but you know not whence I come, or wither I go. You judge according to the flesh: I judge not any man. And if I do judge, my judgment is true: because I am not alone, but I and the Father that sent me. And in your law it is written, that the testimony of two men is true. I am one that give testimony of myself: and the Father that sent me giveth testimony of me. They said therefore to him: Where is thy Father? *Jesus* answered: *Neither me do you know, nor my Father: if you did know me, perhaps you would know my Father also."*

"...You are from beneath, I am from above. You are of this world, I am not of this world. Therefore I said to you, that you shall die in your sins. For if you believe not that I am he, you shall die in your sin. They said therefore to him: **Who art thou?** *Jesus* said to them: ***The beginning****, who also speak unto you. Many things I have to speak and to judge of you.* **But he that sent me, is true: and the things *I have heard of him, these same I speak in the world.*** And they understood not, that he called *God his Father. Jesus* therefore said to them: ***When you shall have***

lifted up the Son of man, then shall you know, that I am he, and that I do nothing of myself, but as the Father hath taught me, *these things I speak:* ***And he that sent me, is with me, and he hath not left me alone:*** *for I do always the things that please him.* When he spoke these things, many believed in him. Then *Jesus* said to those Jews, who believed him: ***If you continue in my word,*** *you shall be my disciples indeed. And* **you shall know the truth, and the truth shall *make you free."***

"They answered him: We are the seed of Abraham, and we have never been slaves to any man: how sayest thou: you shall be free?"

"Jesus answered them: *Amen, amen I say unto you: that whosoever committeth sin, is the servant of sin. Now the servant abideth not in the house for ever; but the son abideth for ever.* ***If therefore the son shall make you free, you shall be free indeed."***

"I know that you are the children of Abraham: but you seek to kill me, because my word hath no place in you. I speak that which I have seen with my Father: and you do the things that you have seen with your father."

"They answered, and said to him Abraham is our father."

"Jesus saith to them: *If you be the children of Abraham, do the works of Abraham. But now you seek to kill me, a man who have spoken the truth to you, which I have heard of God. This Abraham did not."*

"Jesus therefore said to them: *If God were your Father, you would love me.* ***For from God I proceeded, and came; for I came not of myself, but he sent me:*** *Why do you not know my speech? Because you cannot hear my word."*

"But if I say the truth, you believe me not."

"Which of you shall convince me of sin? If I say the truth to you, why do you not believe me? ***He that is of God heareth the words of God."*** Now please read the above verses again, slow and carefully. Or better yet read John 8:1-59.

Now, I ask you: Do you hear *the truth?* Do you hear *the words of God?* Yes, I am asking *you:* **Do you hear the truth?** Please ponder this question. I am sorry for getting so personal and for the long verses above. But I feel that both getting personal and reading the verses spoken by *Jesus Himself* (as it is written in the Bible) are indeed very appropriate for dealing with the true subject matter of being *in His Living Presence,* which is the essence and context and premise of *this book.* Now the meticulously tested and re-tested subject matter of being *in His Living Presence* in this book leads me and as it should hopefully lead you to the most important, personal and crucial life-saving question: **Is Jesus God?**

There are so many wonderful verses in the Bible that can also make this point, but I will only mention a few selected verses that really captured my attention. Before actually going on and *connecting the dots* for all to see (by the grace of God) what I discovered between science and faith, and also between our *new medical and scientific data* and the *Holy Scriptures* and even the *Hebrew Bible ELS codes.*

This will be a very special and definite eye opener for you, as it still is for me today. *What* a precious *gift from God* we received with *the new data.*

Really important are the series of *(holy)* connections I slowly learned about over the past ten years (especially the last 3 years), while deeply and diligently searching for *the truth* concerning *the living presence of God* in the different manifestations tested *in His Living Presence* and in the different ways *God* communicates with the *chosen souls* we had the incredible and great privilege *to test,* including the awesome reception of the *Holy Eucharist.* Also important are the many other *(holy)* connections I uncovered (discovered), possible only with the *graces and Divine assistance* of the *Holy Spirit of God* - Who *Jesus* Himself calls: in John 14:17**: "...the spirit of truth."**

See just some of the following *connections uncovered* below:

1) Whenever the *Blessed Virgin Mary* brings Jesus *the light (of paradise)* back to us, the *444 pattern* is recorded *on EEG;* and later, I find *the same mathematical sequence within the writings of Moses and Elijah* that symbolically describe the specific role and function of Mary as *"the handmaid of the Lord",* (Luke 1:38).

2) During the two eerie encounters with *the evil one* Satan, a *666 pattern* is recorded *on EEG;* and later, I find the same identical mathematical sequence is in ***The Apocalypse - Book of Revelation*** that relates this *specific numerical sequence of 666* to *the number of the beast (Satan)* and *foretells* the name of future *anti-Christ: "For it is the number of a man"* (Rev13-18).

3) One of our main scientific findings *in His Living Presence - the light* was literally *summed up in Hebrew* according to its inherent Hebrew letters and mathematical numbers *equaling a total of 613.* And later I find this is the same mathematical sum of other very *important phrases in Hebrew* that also equal 613 like *"the Lord God of Israel"* and *"Moses our teacher."* When I asked: *What* does *Moses teach?* I learn *Moses* ***is*** *"our teacher"* of *"the law."* The *Jewish prayer shawl, "the Tallit"* actually has *613 knots.* Each knot represents *the 613 laws, statues, decrees, precepts and commandments.* Thus, *613* is the total sum of *the law* God gave to Moses *(face to face)* as a *revelation* to the Jews. This was indeed so interesting and so very intriguing to then suddenly realize that *the appointed* and *anointed day* for our original *testing of Nancy* was on June 13th (613), the same day we recorded *the light – in His Living Presence.* Thus, 613 = *"the light"* = *"the law"* = *"the Lord God of Israel"* = *the appointed day of the testing June* 13th. Is this another coincidence or a *God-incidence?*

4) The deeply profound mysteries of *the way of peace, the Holy Trinity (One God)* and *the circle of God* are all interestingly associated with *His Signature 333* on multiple EEG recordings *in His Living Presence.* Then later, I find the same mathematical and numerical sequence is somehow intertwined with the Hebrew Bible ELS codes, the calculations of *pi (the constant of all circles), the circle of God*

(1 Kings 7:23) and possibly the sum total of 3 different coordinate *measuring lines* or *circles* (that possibly outlines *the sphere of God* round about the new Jerusalem (Zachariah 2:1-5; Rev 21:1-11, and 22-27).

5) The most important and astonishing *revelation* from all of our studies is the blessed realization and incredible confirmation that *His Living Presence* **is** *alive and living* **-** *through, with and in* **-** ***the Eucharist*** received ***where heaven meets earth - at the Mass or after the Mass at any Holy Communion or Adoration service.***

One of the early Christian writers St. Augustine (heralded as one of the greatest *Doctors of the Church*) wrote hundreds of years ago: *"The New Testament is concealed in the Old and the Old Testament is revealed in the New."* This profound statement by St. Augustine still rings true even today (as you will see) with my analysis of the *new medical and scientific data* gathered from our research and the *inspired Holy Spirit connections* already *set up by God from* **the beginning** in *the Old and New Bible*. For examples showing *"the New Testament is concealed in the Old Testament,"* please see Ezekiel 34:11, 22-29; 2 Kings 7:12-14; Psalm 2:7; Genesis 49:10-11; Isaiah 33:10; Baruch 3:36-38; Psalm 110:1; and Daniel 7:13-14. Then check out how *"the Old Testament is revealed in the New Testament"* in John 10:7-18, 23-38. Briefly we see in Ezekiel 34:11, 22-25: **"For thus saith the Lord God: Behold I myself will seek my sheep, and will visit them...I will save my flock,** and it shall be no more a spoil...**And I will set up one shepherd over them, and he shall feed them, even my servant David: he shall feed them**, and he shall be their shepherd. **And I the Lord will be their God: and my servant David** ***the prince*** **in the midst of them: I the Lord have spoken it. And I will make a** ***covenant of peace*** **with them..."**

Read the last verses carefully and see *what the Lord God* is really saying: *"And I the Lord will be their God: and (also)"* - I believe *(also)* is *implied* here – *"my servant David the prince in the midst of them..."* I believe -*"my servant David"* in this verse is *Jesus, Who "will be their God,"* since *Jesus* is *from the house of David*, and *King David* died long before the time of the prophet Ezekiel. *Jesus "the prince* of peace" (Isaiah 9:6) fulfills the prophecy and the *promise God makes to David:* that God *"will raise up thy seed after thee"* and *"will establish the throne of his kingdom for ever"* (2 Kings 7:12-13). Interestingly, the next verse in 2 Kings 7:14 declares prophetically *the relationship God has with David's seed:* **"I will be to him a father, and he shall be to me a son."** This verse foreshadows what *God the Father* so lovingly and willingly allowed *His Son, His only "begotten" Son, Jesus* (Psalm 2:7: **"The Lord hath said to me: Thou art my son, this day have I begotten thee"**) to endure for *His immeasurable love of man* and *His* unfathomable *Divine Mercy.* The latter part of this verse in 2 Kings 7:14 (see below) actually foretells *what* will happen to *God's Son Jesus,* as was fulfilled in *the passion of the Christ,* when *the sinless Jesus ("the just",* Wisdom 2:12-25) actually completes *His last supper Passover meal* on Calvary by so lovingly and willingly accepting *the 4th cup* or *the* *cup of consummation* (John 19:28-30), while still bleeding and dying on ***the cross,*** to fulfill the *Divine Will* of *His Father (God);* as *He, Jesus,* lovingly and mercifully takes on all the sins of mankind unto *Himself (a sin offering)* for all Jews and Gentiles alike. Recall, at *the Last Supper Jesus* only drinks *three of the four cups of wine* that is required by *God's law* to drink (Exodus 12:24) in order to complete the *Jewish Passover Meal.* After *the 3rd cup* or *the cup of blessing,* Jesus leaves *the Pasch* meal (without drinking *the 4th cup or the cup of consummation)* for Gethsemane at the Mount of Olives *to pray. Why?* It is very curious that *Jesus* did not finish the meal. It is as though *Jesus intended to do this on purpose. Why?*

Recall, *Jesus is sinless* and becomes *the unblemished Lamb of God.* So, now read and ponder again *what* is recorded in John 19:28-30 during *the last words of Jesus,* as is written by *His* beloved *disciple John,* a true historical eye witness to the actual crucifixion of Jesus: **"...Jesus knowing that all things were now accomplished, that the scripture might be fulfilled, said: I thirst. Now there was a vessel set there full of vinegar** *(old wine).* **And they, putting a sponge full of vinegar** *(old wine)* **about hyssop, put it to his mouth."** Here we see that *Jesus finally drinks the fourth (4th) cup of consummation. Jesus completes* or *ends His holy Passover meal, the Last Supper, on Calvary while dying* ***on the cross,*** and simultaneously *inaugurates Communion, the Lamb's supper meal and drink, the "sacrifice of praise"* offering, *the beginning* of *Holy Mass* on Calvary: *"new in the kingdom of my Father (God)"* (Matthew 26:29). Thanks EWTN and Dr. Scott Hahn. *Jesus* invites all of us *to drink* with *Him "the blood of the grape" (Gen 49:11), "this fruit of the vine"* (Matthew 26:29). And since *Jesus* is *"the vine"* (John 15:5) and *"the true vine"* (John 15:1), then *the Precious Blood of Jesus* that we literally *"drink"* (John 6:56) during *Holy Mass - the consecrated holy wine* is indeed *"this fruit of the vine"* that *Jesus (as God)* says *"I shall drink it with you - new in the kingdom of my Father (God)"* (Matthew 26:29). *Jesus, the Eucharist,* can now *dwell deep within you* when you receive *Jesus in His Living Presence -"the living bread which came down from heaven"* (John 6:41, 51). Recall, in the very first Passover meal, while the Jews were still in Egypt, *the unblemished* ***lamb's blood*** *was dipped* ***in hyssop,*** *then* ***sprinkled on top of the door*** *of each home* (Exodus 12:22-23) *to let the angel of death* ***pass over.*** So, in the New Testament: *Who is - the door?* See the answer to this question - below.

So, *why* is *Jesus* seemingly on purpose *uniting* the *Passover meal* so vividly with *the passion,* ***"the sacrifice of praise,"*** the sacrifice on Calvary, *the true unblemished Lamb of God, who takes away the sins of the world* and with *the Holy Eucharist* celebration and meal, *as* ***the daily*** *sacrifice of praise* (see Jeremiah 33:18; Psalm 115:16-17)*?* Now see how the latter part of this verse in 2 Kings 7:14 actually and indeed foretells *the passion of the Christ:* **"and if he** *(my Son)* **commit any iniquity I will correct him with the rod of men, and with the stripes of the children of men."** Speaking of ***the just*** *(the just one –Jesus)* as it is written in

Wisdom 2:13, we can clearly see the *relationship of God with David's seed* (in the genealogy of Jesus, Matthew 1:1-18). Now read Wisdom 2:13: **"He boasteth that he hath the knowledge of God, and calleth himself the son of God."** Is *the just (one) - Jesus* truly *the son of God?* The prophecy of *the sinless One* as *the Messiah* and *suffering just servant* accepting all of our sins, transgressions and iniquities as *an eternal* ***sin offering*** *to the Lord (for all mankind - past, present and future)* is best portrayed in Isaiah 53:4-5: **"Surely he hath borne our infirmities and carried our sorrows...But he was wounded for our iniquities, he was bruised for our sins: the chastisement of our peace was upon him, and by his bruises *(his stripes)* we are healed."**

Jesus accepted totally the *Divine Will* of His Father *(God)* for the redemption of all of man's souls. *Jesus* literally became *sin* itself *(see the brazen serpent),* so that *all sin* could be crushed and crucified forever, once and for all *on the cross* – especially for all of us who believe in *the One Who He sent* [*the One (Jesus) Who He (God the Father) sent*].

Father God willingly places *all of the sins of mankind* on *His sinless Son, Jesus.* This can be seen in Isaiah 53:6-12:**"All we like sheep have gone astray, every one hath turned aside into his own way: and the Lord hath laid upon him the iniquity of us all. He was offered because it was his own will,** and *he opened not his mouth: he shall be led as a sheep to the slaughter,* and shall be dumb as a lamb before his shearer, and *he shall not open his mouth."*

*"...***for the wickedness of my people have I struck him."**

*"...***because he hath done no iniquity,** neither was there deceit in his mouth.*"*

"And the Lord was pleased to bruise him in infirmity: if he shall lay down his life for sin, he shall see a long-lived seed, and the will of the Lord shall be prosperous in *his hand*. Because his soul hath laboured, he shall see and be filled: **by his knowledge shall this my just servant justify many, and he shall bear their iniquities.** Therefore will I distribute to him very many, and he shall divide the spoils of the strong, because **he hath delivered his soul unto death,** and was reputed with the wicked: and **he hath borne the sins of many, and hath prayed for the transgressors."**

Jesus is later prophesized in Ezekiel as the illustrious ***"bud of renown"*** (Ezekiel 34:29), *the bud of the house of David that will be renowned over all the earth.* As already seen in Genesis 49:10, the first Book of Moses, we can see in Jacob's prophetical blessings to his twelve sons that the tribe of Juda is clearly blessed and heralded to hold the sceptre (kingship/to be a ruler) and legislative powers, along with the blessings of great strength and fertility of Juda's inheritance, namely the seed of Jacob and later the seed of David, for it is *his seed* that will gloriously *bring forth the coming of the Messiah.* The God given ruling power*, the sceptre,* as foretold will not be taken away from Juda's race till about the time of the coming of *the Messiah, the Christ.* Of interest historically, the sceptre indeed had been utterly taken away from Juda by the Romans, before the birth of Jesus in Bethlehem 2,000 yrs. ago. Thus, the *Jewish Messiah* must have already come. See Genesis 49:10: **"The sceptre shall not be taken away from Juda, nor a ruler from his thigh, till he come that is to be sent, and he shall be the expectation of nations."** In Genesis 49:11, we see that he that shall be the *"expectation of nations"* and *"he...that is to be sent" is* also *foretold to suffer*: **"Tying his foal to the vineyard, and his ass, O my son, to the vine. He shall wash his robe in wine, and his garment in the blood of the grape."** This Messianic prophecy is fulfilled with *the passion and crucifixion of Jesus* --- just recall *the passion of the Christ.* Later, the Lord *(God)* actually even *foretells of His own innate Divine power to "rise up," "be exalted"* and *"now I will lift up myself,"* as it is written in Isaiah 33:10: **"Now will I rise up, saith the Lord: now will I be exalted, now will I lift up myself."**

Now please ponder the obvious question: *What* will the Lord *(God)* have to rise up - from or lift *Himself* up - from? To help answer this interesting question, please see Baruch 3:36-38: **"This is our God, and there shall no other be accounted of in comparison of him**. He found out all the way of knowledge, and gave it to Jacob his servant, and to Israel his beloved. **Afterwards he *(God)* was seen upon earth, and conversed with men."** Where in history has this happened? Is *Jesus* the Lord God? Now ponder, who is *"the Lord"* and who is *"my Lord"* in Psalm 110:1? *"The Lord* said to *my Lord*: Sit thou at *my right hand."* Is it *he* that *cometh in the name of the Lord?* See Psalm 117:26: *"Blessed be he who cometh in the name of the Lord."* And who is *he* who is at *the right hand* of the Lord and is *the right hand* of the Lord? See Psalm 117:16-17: *"The right hand of the Lord* hath wrought strength: *the right hand of the Lord* hath exalted me: *the right hand of the Lord* hath wrought strength. *I shall not die, but live:* and shall declare the works of the Lord.*"* Also in Isaiah 53:1: *"...*and to whom is *the arm* of *the Lord revealed?"* And later in Isaiah 53:10: *"...*if he shall lay down his life for sin, he shall see a long-lived seed, and the will of the Lord shall be prosperous in *his hand."* I now wholeheartedly believe *my Lord, he* who cometh in the name of the Lord, and *he* who is at *the right hand* of the Lord and is *the right hand* of the Lord, as well as *the arm* of the Lord and *his hand* is *Jesus personified* as *the truth, the life* and *the light* of the world. So, then *who* is *the Lord*? See Psalm 117:27: *"The Lord* is God, and *he hath shone upon us."* And what did *He shine? "He hath shone upon us" - the light (Jesus).* Recall, Genesis 1:3: *"And God said: Be* ***light*** *made (Light be made)..."* David may have said it best in Psalm 116:2: *"...*and *the truth* of the Lord remaineth for ever.*"*

Is *Jesus* also *"the son of man?"* See Daniel 7:13-14: *"...one* like *the son of man* came in the clouds of heaven, and he came even to *the Ancient of days:* and they presented him before him. And he gave him power, and glory, and a kingdom: and all peoples, tribes and tongues shall serve him: his power is an everlasting power that shall not be taken away: and his kingdom shall not be destroyed.*" Jesus* while referring to *Himself* actually answers this question in Matthew 24:30: *"...*and they shall see *the Son of man* coming in the clouds of heaven with much power and majesty." In Luke 17:24-25: *"For* as *the lightning* that lighteneth from under heaven, shineth unto the parts that are under heaven, so shall *the Son of man* be in his day. **But first he must suffer many things, and be rejected by this generation."** This is an obvious reference to *Jesus.* Now ponder all the above verses concerning *"the God-man"* (Isaiah 9:6) as we turn to the New Testament, which reveals the Old Testament above.

As we will see below in John 10:7-18, 23-38: *"Jesus* therefore said to them again: Amen, amen I say to you, **I am the door of the sheep**. All others, as many as have come, are thieves and robbers: and the sheep heard them not. **I am the door**. By me, if any man enter in, he shall be saved: and he shall go in, and go out, and shall find pastures. The thief cometh not, but for to steal, and to kill, and to destroy. ***I am come that they may have life, and may have it more abundantly.*** *I am* the ***good*** *shepherd.* The good shepherd giveth his life for his sheep. But the hireling, and he that is not the shepherd, whose own the sheep are not, seeth the wolf coming, and leaveth the sheep, and flieth: and the wolf catcheth, and scattereth the sheep: And the hireling flieth, because he is a hireling: and he hath no care for the sheep. **I am the good shepherd;** and I know mine, and mine know me. **As the Father knoweth me, and I know the Father: and I lay down my life for my sheep. And other sheep I have, that are not of this fold** *(a reference here to the Gentiles):* **them also I must bring, and they shall hear my voice, and there shall be one fold and one shepherd. Therefore doth the Father love me: because I lay down my life, that I may take it up again** *(reference to the resurrection of Jesus).* **No man taketh it away from me: but I lay it down myself, and I have the power to lay it down: and I have power take it up again. This commandment have I received of my Father** *(God)."* See how these last few New Testament verses of John 10:17-18 reveals the Old Testament as it is written in Isaiah 33:10, and the earlier verses of John 10:7-16 reveals Ezekiel 34:11, 22-29; 2 Kings 7:12-14; Genesis 49:10-11; Baruch 3:36-38; Psalm 110:1; and Daniel 7:13-14. So, St Augustine was right.

Now what really causes a lot of controversy among the Jews historically and even still today are some of the following verses as it is written in John 10:23-30: "And *Jesus* walked in the temple, in Solomon's porch. The Jews therefore came round about him, and said to him: How long dost thou hold our souls in suspense? If thou be *the Christ (the Messiah),* tell us plainly. *Jesus* answered them: *I speak to you, and you believe not: the works that I do in the name of my Father, they give testimony of me. But you do not believe, because you are not of my sheep. My sheep hear my voice: and I know them, and they follow me. And I give them life everlasting; and they shall not perish for ever, and no man shall pluck them out of my hand. That which my Father hath given me, is greater than all: and no one can snatch them out of the hand of my Father.* ***I and the Father are one."*** This last statement I believe is a true dividing litmus test for believers and non-believers. In fact after this statement we can see the strong angry reaction of the Jews ~2,000 yrs. ago that revels the reactions of so many non-believers in our day, as it is written in John 10:31-38: "The Jews then took up stones to stone him. *Jesus* answered them: Many *good works* I have shewed you from *my Father;* for which of those do you stone me?

The Jews answered him: For a good work we stone thee not, but for blasphemy; and because that thou, being a man, makest thyself God.

Jesus answered them: *Is it not written in your law: I said you are gods?* (Psalm 81:6) *If he called them gods, to whom the word of God was spoken, and the scripture cannot be broken; Do you say of him whom the Father hath sanctified and sent into the world: Thou blasphemest, because I said, I am the Son of God?* ***If I do not the works of my Father, believe me not. But if I do, though you will not believe me, believe the works: that you may know and believe that the Father is in me, and I in the Father."*** Now another very serious contention of controversy among many Jews and many other non-believers today that we can clearly see is written in John 11:25-27 below and occurs just before *Jesus raises Lazarus to life from his death* after being buried in his burial tomb for *four days:*

"Jesus saith to her *(Martha):* **I am *the resurrection* and *the life,* he that believeth in me, although he be dead, shall live: And every one that liveth, and believeth in me, shall not die for ever. Believest thou this?**

She *(Martha)* saith to him *(Jesus):* **Yea, Lord, I have believed that thou art Christ** *(the Messiah)* **the Son of the living God, who art come into this world."**

Just like Martha, above, now...approximately ~2,000 years later, *Nancy* has been asked by *Jesus* to be *a witness of His Living Presence* and to proclaim *Jesus is the Son of the living God,* the second person of *the Holy Trinity - One God.* In Hebrew *Elohim* refers to the plural noun *(Gods)* and is mentioned 500 times in *the Bible* with a singular verb. In Hebrew a plural noun with a singular verb is grammatically incorrect. So, *why* is this combination seen 500 times? Indeed, the plot thickens. The above scriptural examples though perhaps a bit lengthy, are given to provoke and hopefully inspire an avalanche of renewed interests and quests for *the truth* about *Jesus?* The verses above are indeed a source of *revelation* for all of us who read and study *the word of God* in the Bible. Especially for you (yes you), if you are still wondering: *Who* is this *Jesus?* Is *Jesus* the real true Messiah, *the Christ?* Is *Jesus* Lord? **Is Jesus God?**

In the verses just presented, we truly can see how in the Old Testament the New Testament was *concealed* and how clearly in the New Testament the Old Testament was *revealed as it is written in* John. So, St. Augustine was *right on* in his teachings after all. Later in this chapter, I will introduce an outline using a 3rd variable: the *new medical and scientific data* (first), then show the *Old Testament connections* (second), and then finish with the *New Testament connections* (third) where at times *Jesus* Himself *reveals* the Old Testament. Often *His words* amazingly connect with the *new medical and scientific data* directly and so beautifully. So, get ready for the amazing *holy connections* – coming up soon. *Connecting the dots* has never been more fun or fruitful. But first let me finish introducing *Jesus - the truth.*

In the Gospel of John 14:1-9 remember *Jesus* gave this discourse to his disciples after *the last supper:*

"Let not your heart be troubled. You believe in God, believe also in me. In my Father's house there are many mansions. If not, I would have told you: because I go to prepare a place for you."

Note: Jews will quickly recognize the meaning of this verse recalling the old traditional Jewish preparations that *the bridegroom* typically makes for his future *bride.* Many Biblical scholars today believe the *bride* **is** *us, the church of the Messiah, the Christ – Jesus.*

"And if I shall go, and prepare a place for you, I will come again, and will take you to myself; that where I am, you also may be. And whither I go you know, and ***the way*** *you know.*

"Thomas saith to him: Lord, we know not whither thou goest; and how can we know the way?

"Jesus saith to him: ***I am the way, and the truth, and the life. No man cometh to the Father, but by me.*** *If you had known me, you would without doubt have known my Father also: and from henceforth you shall know him, and you have seen him.*

"Philip saith to him: Lord, shew us the Father, and it is enough for us.

"Jesus saith to him: *Have I been so long a time with you; and have you not known me? Philip,* ***he that seeth me seeth the Father also..."*** *Jesus* clearly refers to *Himself* in the above verses as "*the way*, and *the truth,* and *the life."*

Upon further reflection on our medical and scientific research *in the living presence of Jesus,* we actually recorded *the light of the world.* Recall, the astronomical increases in *the light* energy and in the *sun light* energy. *The sun,* which is basically the most powerful blazing cosmic *fire* ball of *light* energy source available for our entire solar system emits *fire* for the heat and *the light* of our galaxy. Recall, we recorded *flashes or darts or bolts of lightning light* energy. We also recorded and documented the same identical medical and scientific *new data,* whenever *Jesus* speaks *His living words - in the light* to Nancy or to the young seminarian. Thus, if *Jesus* is ***the Word*** *of God "made flesh"* (John 1:14) and *the Bible* (as the *faithful* believe) **is** the *word of God,* then *the Holy Bible* or *the Word of God* **is** indeed *Jesus personified* - the true Eternal Word/*Wisdom Incarnate.* Thus, *faith* is truly an awesome merciful *gift from God.* We must continually ask *God* and pray everyday that we may all acquire and keep this great *gift of faith.* So, if *Jesus* is truly *the Word of God - "made flesh"* (John 1:14), then this may help explain *why Jesus (since His childhood)* so easily quotes from the *Old Testament Holy Scriptures.* If *Jesus* is *the Word of God made flesh, the Eternal Word/Wisdom Incarnate,* then *Jesus* **is** *the Living Word of God in all Holy Scriptures, the living Holy Bible.* Thus, *there is* ***life, eternal life - "the life"- in the Living Word of God.***

Now *"the way"* has a very special and *new* meaning for me through our *medical and scientific data. How* is that? Well first let me ask you a simple question: *What* do we *need to know* and to have in order *to find the way* or *the path* especially if you are in complete and total darkness? I will answer: Obviously, *you will need a good set of directions – a map and* also *a good source of light.* If you are totally blind you will need *a good source of sound* or *voice* to give you directions. Now can you imagine just *Who is* actually being recorded, if we are recording a true *living* map *the way* and *the light of God?* Is *the way* and *the light / "the Word of God"* (Rev 19:13) *"made flesh"* (John 1:14)? Recall, that the *new medical and scientific data* as recorded and documented *of Jesus in light in His Living Presence – speaking* to Nancy and later to the seminarian - were both identical. I believe we recorded the *living map* or *"the way" of God* as clearly shown in all the multiple tests meticulously repeated of Nancy and the seminarian, while receiving *the word of God* interiorly. I firmly believe that the *new medical and scientific data* shows that we recorded --- *the light of the world.* Recall, *how* we repeatedly recorded and documented astronomical increases of *the light* radiation energy in the atmosphere only *in His Living Presence, the living presence of Jesus.* So now given this *new data,* I believe I have a better understanding as to *why* John emphatically writes that *Jesus* **is** *the light, "the true light" of the world* (John 1:7-9). Recall, that *in His Living Presence* we amazingly recorded and documented astronomical increases in *the light* energy (from both the *visible light* and *invisible* low ionizing *light* radiation energy spectrum): the 30-90% more *sun light* (the fire ball from heaven) energy; the *flashes or bolts or darts of lightning light* energy; and the peaceful relaxing radio light energy in the 2,000-4,000+ Hz range called *electrical anesthesia.* If you sit back and really ponder what this all means, it is indeed mind-boggling.

With this *new data* I do believe we recorded *the true light of the world,* literally and scientifically speaking. Just think about what makes up all of our natural light in this world. As mentioned earlier, we humans can see only 3% of all light in the visible light spectrum that is produced by *the sun light* (heaven's bright cosmic fire ball planet, *"the day star"-* see Psalm 110:3) in the *day light or the morning light/star* or *the sun light reflects* its light on the *moon and stars* in the *night light.* We also see *visible light* energy produced by electrical thunder storms with *flashes or bolts or darts of lightning.* We know that the scorching heat from *the sun* or the tremendous heat produced from *a dart of lightning* is indeed strong enough to ignite a *fire or flames* in certain conditions. The *fire or flames* ignited can also produce *light* that is in the *visible light spectrum.* Science has shown us that most of us can not see the remaining 97% of light available in the *invisible* radiation spectra of light energy present in our atmosphere. The 97% of invisible light spectrum actually consists of all the high and low radiation energy fields (outside the 3% visible light spectrum) detected in the atmosphere of our planet, earth. Remember, that in our scientific studies we detected essentially all the energy fields in the *invisible light spectra:* the extremely low, the low, radio light, maser-like coherent bursts or infrared laser signals in the low radiation energy fields. We recorded all of these *invisible light* radiation energy fields with unprecedented increases never seen before and reaching to astronomical heights *only during the supernatural events – in His Living Presence, the living presence of Jesus.* We also detected and documented the other remaining *invisible light* energy in the *high radiation energy spectrum* available in the world. We are indeed very pleased to report that the *invisible light spectra* of high radiation energy, namely the *gamma* or high ionizing radiation energy fields *though detected did not significantly increase in value (thank God).* This was in retrospect a *good* thing. Indeed, a very good thing or else we may all be literally *glowing in the dark radioactively* whenever we are *in His Living Presence.* Thus, in John 8:12, it is *the truth* when *Jesus* says*: "...**I am the light*** **of the world: he that followeth me, walketh not in darkness, but shall have *the light of life.*"** If *Jesus* **is** *"the word of God"* (Rev 19:13)*, the living map* or directory from *God, "the way"* (John 14:6) or *"the* ***paths of justice****"* (Proverbs 2:8), then *Jesus is* also *"the light of the world"* (John 8:12) as it is written in the above verses. Thus, the above first sentence of this new paragraph is a true fact that is now clearly substantiated, corroborated and confirmed by our *new medical and scientific data.* We know *the Bible* **is** *the word of God* according to the *faithful.* That is indeed *what* both Jews and Christians preach. Thus, *the Bible* as *the word of God* **is** *the light* that pushes away the darkness from our world and also destroys all the darkness within our hearts. As mentioned before now I can better understand *why* in many religious circles *the Bible* is referred to as **B**asic **I**nstructions **B**efore **L**eaving **E**arth. *The Bible* is literally a road map or *the way* to find *life with God* and find *the way* to reach heaven *(paradise)* with *God* forever. If *His living words - in the light* during our tests *produced the same scientific data as recorded in His/God's Living Presence (like deep sleep),* then *"the word of God"* (Rev 19:13) in *the Bible* **is** *God* (John 1:1).

I now believe wholeheartedly and with strong convictions based on medical science that ***the Word*** *of God - in* ***the light*** *- in His living Presence* **is *God*,** just as it is written in John 1:1. So, St. John is right on. The following Bible verses may help you better understand the above statement: In Ecclesiasticus 1:1-9: *"All wisdom (the Word) is from the Lord God,* and hath been always with him, *and is before all time... The word of God* on high **is** *the fountain of wisdom,* and *her ways are everlasting commandments...*He *(God)* created her *(wisdom)* in the Holy Ghost *(Holy Spirit)..."* In the preaching of *wisdom,* see Proverbs 8:7-8: *"My mouth* shall *meditate truth... All my words are just...* " In Proverbs 8: 20-23, 34-35: *"I walk* in *the way of justice,* in the midst of *the paths of judgment...The Lord* possessed *me (wisdom) in the beginning* of *his ways,* before he made any thing *from the beginning. I was set up from eternity, and of old before the earth was made."* Finally in Proverbs 6:23: *"Because the commandment* **is** a *lamp*, and *the law* a *light,* and *reproofs of instruction* are *the way of life."* See how *"the light" and "the word of God on high is the fountain of wisdom" connect.* Please re-read these heavenly pearls.

The *new medical and scientific data* of *His living words in His Living Presence - the map* or ***"paths of justice"*** (Proverbs 2:8) and ***"the light of the world"*** (John 8:12) - that is confirmed by all of our *new data on **"the light,"*** can now be called ***"the way."*** Thus, *the word of God* and *the light of God* that we recorded and documented can literally show us *the way (in Him, with Him, and through Him).* See Jeremiah 17:15: *"Behold...Where* **is** *the word of the Lord? Let it come."* Now, let me finish introducing you to ***the Word** of the Lord, Jesus* – as *the truth.* While reading *the Bible* I saw an old Jewish phrase that was curious to me, namely: *"to do truth."* I soon discovered that *in Hebrew* this phrase actually means *to do what is just* or *righteous.* So, in Hebrew *"to do truth"* **is** *to do what is just or righteous.* Thus, *truth = justice = righteousness.* I must admit that reading *the Bible* now armed and equipped with all this *new* information was indeed for me very fruitful. A quick look at all *the Bible* prophecies of *the Messiah, the Christ, "till he come that is to be sent"* (Genesis 49:10) and you will be astounded by the many prophetic references of *Messiah* as *the just one* or as *the word, **justice:***

In Jeremiah, 11:20: ***"O lord of Sabaoth, who judgest justly;"*** 23:5-6: *"I will raise up to David **a just branch:** and a **king** shall reign, and shall be **wise**...In those days shall Juda be **saved,** and Israel shall dwell confidently* (with faith): *this is the name that they shall call him: **The Lord our just one;"*** 31:23: ***"the beauty of justice;"*** 33:15: ***"the bud of justice;"*** and again in 33:16: ***"The Lord our just one (Justice)."*** *In Isaiah,* 32:17:*"And **the work of justice** shall be peace;"* 41:2-3: *"Who hath raised up **the just one** from the east...he shall pass in peace;"* 41:10: *"...*and *the right hand* of ***my just one*** hath upheld thee;" 45:8: *"Drop down dew,* ye heavens, from above, and *let the clouds* rain ***the just:*** let the earth be opened, and *bud forth a saviour:* and *let **justice spring up*** together;" 45:23-24: *"I have sworn by myself, **the word of justice** shall go out of my mouth, and shall not return: For every knee shall be bowed to me, and every tongue shall swear."* There are many verses. In a prophecy depicting *the time Messiah is to come,* we see in Daniel 9:24: *"Seventy weeks* are shortened upon thy people, and upon thy holy city, that *transgression* may be *finished,* and *sin may have an end, and iniquity* may be *abolished;* and ***everlasting justice*** *may be brought; and **vision and prophecy may be fulfilled; and the saint of saints may be anointed."***

In Hebrew *seventy weeks* of years is equal to *seventy times seven* or 490 years, which are shortened. The time for *the Messiah to come* shall be no longer than 490 years. In verse Daniel 9:25, the time is shortened to actually sixty-nine weeks of years (which in Hebrew) = 483 years. In the actual best chronology of time as per the Hebrew calendar, this is the actual time of the *Baptism of Jesus,* when *Jesus* first began to preach *the good news* to all. In Hosea 10:12: *"...**but the time to seek the Lord is, when he shall come that shall teach you justice."*** In Joel 2:23: "And you, O children of Sion, rejoice, and be joyful in *the Lord your God:* because *he hath given you* ***a teacher of justice,*** and ***he will make the early*** and ***the latter rain to come down to you as in the beginning."*** And lastly we see *the truth* presented as *"the Sun of justice"* in Malachi 4:2:*"But unto you that fear my name, **the Sun of justice shall arise..."*** Psalm 50:21: ***"the sacrifice of justice..."***

NOTE: Now I hope you can better understand that *the Messiah* as prophesized in *the Holy Bible* and seen above is *"the Lord our just one"* or *"the Lord our justice"* which also means: the Lord our *truthful one,* the Lord *our truth, the bud of truth, the beauty of truth, the work of truth, the word of truth, everlasting truth, he shall come that will teach you* truth, *the teacher of truth* and finally *the Sun of truth* and *the sacrifice of truth.* Also *Jesus, the Messiah, the Christ* as the **wisdom incarnate** is prophesized as *"the truth, the way and the life."* In Ecclesiasticus 24:25:*"In me (wisdom)* is *all grace* of *the way* and of *the truth,* in me *(wisdom)* is *all hope* of *(the) life* and *of virtue."* I have attempted to show you in *this (His) book the way and the truth of God* as clearly shown above. Remember, both will lead you to *the life (eternal life),* which in the eyes of God is *good. The (good) life,* in the eyes of God which you choose, will lead you and all of us, who chose to follow *the wisdom of God, the word of God* - to paradise and to *eternal life.* Just like it is written in Ecclesiasticus 15:18: "**Before man is life and death, good and evil, that which he shall choose shall be given him.**"

Now I will finish in an *outline fashion,* what I alluded to earlier in this chapter:

A. To present the *new medical and scientific data* and ask provocative questions.

B. To connect **A.** with the Old Testament prophecies of *the Messiah, Jesus.*

C. To connect **A.** with the New Testament teachings of *Jesus* that reveals the Old Testament and shows us *how **Jesus** truly fulfills* a given *prophecy,* then declares and proclaims *how Jesus - in His Living Presence* **is** the actual *new data* we *recorded* and were allowed to document by the ***Divine Will*** *of God the Almighty.* Some *Reflections* were added when necessary.

The following o*utline* will cover 10 of the main *new medical and scientific discoveries of the testing* done - *in His Living Presence.* Interestingly, the number ten (10) *in Hebrew* refers to *salvation* like the *Ten Commandments* or *the Shema* (ten words).

THE OUTLINE CONNECTING MEDICINE AND SCIENCE TO FAITH WITH *"THE WORD OF GOD"*

The Ten (10) X Main Medical and Scientific Discoveries recorded and documented ---- *only in His Living Presence --- the living presence of Jesus:*

I. "The Sun" light:

A. On June 13th, 1993 at the farm in Conyers, Georgia, USA, approximately 30-90% more *sun light* was recorded and documented only *in His Living Presence* when a comparative study analysis was done on a *series of professional photographs* of the outside façade of the farm house/chimney area *taken before, during and after the heavenly visits or apparitions,* using advanced computerized digital photo-spectroscopy analysis (used in weather satellite forecasting analysis).

Question: What does Jesus and "the sun" light have in common?

B. In the Old Testament Holy Scriptures we can see as it is written in Gen 1:3: "**And God said: Be light made. And light was made.**" One of the greatest *lights of God* is indeed *the great ball of fire* planet *God created* for our galaxy called ***the sun.*** As David wrote in Psalm 18:6: ***"He** (Father God)* **hath set *his tabernacle*** *(Mary)* **in *the sun*** *(Jesus)*: **and he** *(Jesus)*, **as *a bridegroom* coming out of *his*** *(Holy Spirit's)* **bride chamber** *(Mary's womb)..."* I added the words in parenthesis *only* to show you *what I believe* David *prophetically* is trying to tell us.

Reflections on Mary as the first human tabernacle in "the sun"

Historically *Mary is the first human tabernacle for her son Jesus, "the Sun of justice"* (Malachi 4:2) and in this verse *Mary* indeed has a very unique relationship with God the Father. The perfect creation of God, God's *new Eve* or *"the woman"* (Genesis 3:15) is best written in the Canticle of Canticles or Song of Songs 6:8: *"One is my dove,* ***my perfect one is but one, she is the only one of her mother, the chosen of her that bore her. The daughters saw her, and declared her most blessed: the queens and concubines, and they praised her."*** I believe this verse in the canticle above plus a verse in Luke 1:28 describe some of the clearest *prophecies* ever written on the *Immaculate Conception of Mary* in the Bible. Especially with words like *"my perfect one is but one," "she is the only one,"* and *"declared her most blessed." Mary* **is** *the loving mother of Jesus* (Luke 1: 31) *and the spouse of the Holy Spirit* (Luke 1:35). *Mary* **is** *the handmaid of the Lord* (Luke 1:38) *and the most graced and favored daughter of God the Father* ever *created* - ***"full of grace"*** (Luke 1:28). *Mary* **is** unique in her relationship with *the Holy Trinity.*

We can see how *God the Father* in Psalm 18:6 sets up and creates *Mary* as the first perfect *living tabernacle, temple and church* with the *Incarnation of His Eternal Word* (John1:14) and as *the ark of the new covenant* (Rev 11:19) *in the sun (encompassed by and in Jesus).* And *"as the bridegroom coming out of his bride chamber"* probably means: *Jesus,* the *future bridegroom* with *his bride - the Church,* will come out of Mary's womb or *"bride chamber,"* since *Mary* **is** *the* very *first human temple or church* in history. As the *"the perfect one"* and *"most blessed"* daughter of *God the Father, Mary* **is** *the first living tabernacle,* as the *spouse of the Holy Spirit* and the *loving mother of Jesus.* ***Mary* is *the* very *first true Jewish Christian ever*** (Luke 1:31) as *mother of the Messiah* with a very special, glorious cosmic relationship with *the Holy Trinity: The Father, the Son and the Holy Spirit.*

Recall, in Luke 1:28: *"...Hail, full of grace,* the Lord is with thee: Blessed art thou among women.*"* If Mary had original sin, *why* did the *archangel Gabriel* greet her with this *great exaltation? "Hail, full of grace!" Mary* must be *sinless* in order to be *hailed* by the *great archangel Gabriel of God* as *"full of grace."* Recall, *nothing is impossible with God.* It is both logical and makes perfect sense to me that *God Who is perfect,* would want to create *a most perfect living tabernacle for Himself,* as I believe *He did* in the most blessed womb of Mary. Can you imagine the *baby Jesus* actually *created His loving mother Mary? Jesus* truly *loves His Mother Mary.* The Church teaches that *Mary was redeemed by her Son, Jesus,* before she was even born. This fact is confusing to many theologians. It is like trying to know what came first, the chicken or the egg. Now ponder the dilemma: *God* created *time,* so God is *outside of time.* We on the other hand are *held hostage to time.* We are locked in as *time travelers* each in our own private life journey on this planet earth. So, it's easy for us to be confused and rattled by all this. Essentially, God our Almighty Creator *always was, is and will be.* That is *why God is the Great* ***I Am!*** And *God* says to us that *He always existed,* presently exists and will always exist. *God is alive* all at once *in time* in the past, in the present and in the future; *and* simultaneously *outside of time. God in time* **is** *all Three in One* or *in all three times zones in one* (at once) or all *Three Divine Persons* of the *One God-Head* in all three time zones at once. Anyway you look at it - *"it's beginning to look a lot like Christmas"* with the best and *greatest gift* ever: Mary *bringing* Jesus - *the Holy Trinity – the One true God -- to us.*

I believe in *preservative grace,* which *preserves one from falling into sin* and saves one from harm or destruction. I believe the Almighty God's Divine *redemptive power* and *preservative graces* were both purchased for us by *the Precious Blood of the Lamb of God, Jesus* on Calvary, *Who takes away the sins of the world.* I believe *the preservative graces of Jesus* were indeed more than sufficient *to redeem Mary.* I also believe and now clearly understand that *Mary* was *redeemed and preserved from sin by Jesus* even before she was *created by Him,* when the most blessed and special *preservative and redemptive graces* gushed forth from the Almighty God *in the beginning;* as it is written in Solomon's Canticle of Canticles

6:8 and in Luke's 1:28. Thus, *Mary **"my** (God's) **perfect one,"*** truly came to us as **the *Immaculate Conception.*** Of interest, the incorrupt body of St. Bernadette of Lourdes is in Nevers, France, in a glass tomb. After over a hundred years *why* does her body still remain *incorrupt?* Even to this day, St. Bernadette looks like she is *sleeping.* The most special of her messages to the world from the *Blessed Virgin* is that *Mary **is** the Immaculate Conception as a special grace from God --- through the merits of her Son, Jesus.* So, now I ask you a simple question: Do you love your *mother?* I hope your answer is *yes.* Now, can you imagine or even fathom just how much *the Savior of this world* (the Son of the Living God, the second person of the Holy Trinity, God) loves *His Loving Mother, Mary,* who bore *Him, Jesus* on earth? God *created* Adam and Eve *perfect* in paradise, so *why not Mary?* Recall, how the *perfect Adam and Eve* listened to *a fallen angel (the serpent)* and brought us *sin,* responsible for corruption, disasters, diseases, pain, suffering and death. So, as part of God's master plan, I believe *God gave us* another *perfect man and woman,* who willingly listened to *the good angel of God (Gabriel)* in order to bring us mercy, redemption, salvation, resurrection and *"the life." Only* this *perfect man* was not to be just any man, but *the Son of man, "the Angel of the Lord," the Son of the living God,* God in *the second person of the Holy Trinity,* the *God-man* (Isaiah 9:6), *Jesus -"the word of God made flesh"* (John 1:14), *"the Lord shall go forth as a mighty man"* (Isaiah 42:13). *"That whosoever believeth in him, may not perish, but may have life everlasting* (John 3:16)."

* * *

B. (Continued) In two other Psalms written by David we see ***"the sun"*** in association with the *promise of **David's seed,** the Messiah,* and *his kingdom to come.* In Psalm 71:2-6, 17: "Give to the king thy judgment, O God: *and to the king's son thy justice:* To judge thy people with justice...*he shall save the children of the poor...**And he shall continue with the sun,*** and before the moon, throughout all generations. *He shall come down like the rain...**Let his name be blessed for evermore: his name continueth before the sun. And in him shall all the tribes of the earth be blessed: all nations shall magnify him."***

In Psalm 88:27-30, 35-38:*"**He shall cry out to me: Thou art my father; my God, and the support of my salvation. And I will make him my firstborn, high above the kings of the earth. I will keep my mercy for him for ever: and my covenant faithful to him. And I will make his seed to endure for evermore** (by his seed I believe God is saying that through David's seed Jesus and all who receive Jesus into their hearts will endure for evermore)**: and his throne as the days of heaven...the words that proceed from my mouth I will not make void. Once have I sworn by my holiness: I will not lie unto David: his seed** (David's seed is Jesus and all who believe in Jesus and follow Jesus) **shall endure for ever. And his throne as the sun before me: and as the moon perfect for ever, and a faithful witness in heaven."***

Again, I took liberty in adding some comments in parenthesis *only* throughout this section. These comments are just my thoughts on what I believe David is truly saying. Since *the sun* is considered by most scientists to be *a great light,* the famous verse in Isaiah 9:2 makes better sense to me now: ***"The people that walked in darkness, have seen a great light: to them that dwelt in the region of the shadow of death, light is risen."*** Later, in Isaiah 13:10: *"...**the sun shall be darkened in his rising**..."* Many scholars believe this *prophetic* statement was fulfilled by the *solar eclipse of the sun* that occurred when *Jesus (the Son of man)* was ***raised on the cross*** just outside the walls of Jerusalem during his crucifixion. I believe *the sun light* was darkened by God with the solar eclipse to show all of us that *the true light of the world Jesus* is more powerful than *the sun.* As *the* true *Son* is *raised on the cross* **– *the light is risen!*** *Jesus* **is** *the Incarnate Wisdom.* So, the Book of Wisdom 7:29 speaks of the excellence of wisdom**:** ***"For she** (wisdom) **is more beautiful than the sun, and above all the order of the stars: being compared with the light, she** (wisdom) **is found before it."*** Interestingly, if *wisdom* (the word of God) existed before the sun or moon or stars even before *the light of this world,* then *"the word of God"* or *wisdom* **is** *the beginning* - **is** with God and **is** God, just as it is written in *the prolog* of John 1:1-2. In Baruch 4:36**:** ***"Look about thee, O Jerusalem, towards the east** (to see "the sun" or "the Orient" or "the morning light")**, and behold the joy that cometh to thee from God."*** And in 5:5**:** ***"Arise, O Jerusalem, and stand on high: and look about towards the east, and behold thy children gathered together from the rising to the setting sun, by the word of the Holy One rejoicing in the remembrance of God."***

Another famous verse as it is written in Hosea 6:3 also describes ***the morning light*** which on our planet earth is ***the sun light*** and gives the prophecy of the resurrection of Jesus on the third day, that was fulfilled by Jesus, and Christians celebrate yearly on *Holy Easter Sunday.* This verse also prophesizes *the coming of Jesus* in the third millennium (as *"a day is as a thousand years"* to God) for all of us who believe in *Jesus* as *the Anointed One* He (Father God) sent: ***"He will revive us after two days: on the third day he will raise us up, and we shall live in his sight.** We shall know, and we shall follow on, that we may know the Lord. **His going forth is prepared as the morning light** (sun light)**, and he will come to us as the early and the latter rain to the earth."*** In Zachariah 3:8: *"... **for behold I will bring my servant the Orient."*** *Jesus, Who* according to *his humanity* as the *Son of man, the servant of God,* is called *the Orient - with His rising like* **the sun** *in the east - to bring light to the world.* Finally in the Old Testament, we see another one of the prophecies about *the anointed one* or *the Messiah to come* **is** also *associated with* **the sun**, see Malachi 4:2**:** ***"But unto you that fear my name, the Sun of justice* shall arise..."**

C. The New Testament can be clearly seen to reveal the Old Testament concerning the association between *Jesus and His followers/disciples* and *the sun (the sun light)* in the next few verses. In the *transfiguration of Jesus* as seen in Matthew 17:2:"**And he** *(Jesus)* was **transfigured before them. And his face did shine as *the sun:*** and his garments became white as snow." Later we see *what* really happens to the followers of *Jesus* in Matthew 13:43:***"Then the just shine as the sun, in the kingdom of their Father. He that hath ears to hear, let him hear."*** In the account Paul gives to King Agrippa (previously mentioned in this book), we see that in the Acts of the Apostles 26:13: ***"At midday, O king, I saw in the way a light from heaven above the brightness of the sun, shinning round about me, and them that were in company with me."*** This reminded me of what the young seminarian said after *the testing* of August 20th, 1993 in my medical office at St Joseph's Hospital of Atlanta, Georgia, *"The light of Jesus* was brighter than the most brilliant blazing fire ever, yet *a fire that does not burn.* ***The light of Jesus* was *brighter than the sun!*** *His light* was so powerful, so strong and so bright, that I could just barely make out the *silhouette of my Lord Jesus.* But, I could clearly *hear His voice.* As one of *His sheep, I hear the voice of my Master* and *my Lord,* my beloved *Jesus*, the G*ood Shepherd."*

In the final *Book of Revelation* or *The Apocalypse of St. John the Apostle,* we only need to look at the first and last chapters for revelations concerning *Jesus* and ***the sun***. In Chapter 1 in the Book of Revelation, *Jesus* says in verses 17-18: ***"Fear not. I am the First and the Last, And alive, and was dead, and behold I am living for ever and ever, and have the keys of death and of hell."*** Jesus appears to John in Rev 1:13-16: **"And in the midst of the *seven golden candlesticks, one like the Son of man,* clothed with a garment down to the feet, and girt about the paps with a golden girdle. And his head and his hairs were white, as white wool, and as snow, and *his eyes were as a flame of fire,* And *his feet like unto fine brass, as in a burning furnace.* And *his voice* as the *sound of many waters.* And he had in his right hand seven stars. And *from his mouth came out a sharp two edged sword:* and *his face* was *as the sun shineth in his power."*** Finally, in the last chapter of the Book of Revelation *Jesus Himself tells us* exactly *Who He is.* So, please read and re-read Rev 22:16:*"I Jesus* have sent my angel, to testify to you these things in the churches. ***I am the root and stock of David, the bright and morning star."*** In this last verse, *Jesus* actually connects *Himself* with the *science data* we detected *in His Living Presence.* Recall the 30-90% more *sun light* energy we recorded *only in His Living Presence. Jesus* in the above verse proclaims: *"I am…the bright and morning star."*

II. The "lightning" light:

A. When *Jesus – in His Living Presence* appeared to Nancy or when the *Blessed Virgin Mary appeared bringing baby Jesus* to us: *flashes or darts or bolts of lightning light energy* was recorded and documented. This tremendous *energy of* *light* was detected on June 13th, 1993 in Conyers, Georgia, USA, four times in the apparition room, and then again was later recorded with even more powerful *lightning* light energy recordings in the room adjacent to the apparition room.

Question: What does Jesus and *flashes or darts or bolts of lightning light* have in common?

B. In the Old Testament I will again start with Genesis 1:3*: "*And God said: *Be* ***light*** *made.* And *light* was made.*"* This is the first reference of *light.* And *lightning light* is a definite more powerful form of light energy. In Exodus 19:16 we see the first reference made of *flashes of lightning* in association with a powerful presence of God Almighty*: "And now* ***the third day*** *was come and the morning appeared (alludes to the morning light or the sun light):* and behold thunders began to be heard, and ***lightning to flash,*** **and a very thick cloud to cover the mount**, and the noise of the trumpet sounded exceedingly loud, and the people that was in the camp, feared.*"* In two of the David's Psalms the joyous reign of the glorious coming of *the Messiah, the Christ, Jesus* is described as being associated with the powerful *lightning* of God. See in Psalm 96(97):1-6:**"The Lord hath reigned, let the earth rejoice: let many islands be glad. Clouds and darkness are round about him: justice and judgment are the establishment of his throne. A *fire* shall go before him, and shall burn his enemies *round about.* *His lightnings* have shone forth to the world: the earth trembled. The mountains melted like wax, *at the presence of the Lord: at the presence of the Lord of all the earth.* The heavens declared his *justice:* and all people saw his *glory."*** In Psalm 143(144):5-6:**"Lord, bow down thy heavens and descend: touch the mountains, and they shall smoke. Send forth *lightning...*"** In the Book of Daniel 10:5-6*: "And I lifted up my eyes, and I saw: and behold a man clothed in linen, and his loins were girded with the finest gold: and his body was like the chrysolite,* ***and his face as the appearance of lightning, and his eyes as a burning lamp: and his arms, and all downward even to the feet, like in appearance to glittering brass:*** *and the voice of his word like the voice of a multitude."* The description of this powerful man by Daniel is very similar to the description John gives of *the Son of man, Jesus,* as it is written by John in Rev 1:13-18. In Zachariah Chapter 9 verses 9-17 are strong in its many Messianic prophecies, but for our purpose here please see verses in Zachariah 9-11,14*: "Rejoice* greatly, O daughter of Sion, shout for joy, O daughter of Jerusalem: *Behold thy king will come to thee,* ***the just*** and ***saviour:*** *he is poor,* and *riding upon an ass,* and *upon a colt the foal of an ass...he shall speak* ***peace*** *to the Gentiles,* and *his power shall be from sea to sea,* and from the rivers even to the end of the earth.*"* The next verse actually gives a *prophecy to the passion and death of Jesus,* Zachariah 9:11: *"Thou* also ***by the blood of thy testament*** hast ***sent forth thy prisoners out of the pit,*** *wherein is no water* *(reference to hell)."* I added the words in parenthesis. In Zachariah 9:14 *"thy king"* and *"the just and saviour"* **is** now declared *Lord God:* "**And the *Lord God* shall be seen over them, and *his dart* shall go forth as *lightning:*** *and* ***the Lord God will sound the trumpet,*** *and go in the whirlwind of the south."*

C. In the New Testament we will see where in the Gospels of Luke and Matthew, *Jesus Himself* refers to the *lightning light* - to be associated with *Himself as the coming of the Son of man.* In Matthew 24:27 *Jesus* said: "**For as *lightning* cometh out of the east, and appeareth even into the west: *so shall also the coming of the Son of man be."***

Luke says much of the same in 17:24, *Jesus* said: "**For as *the lightning* that lighteneth from under heaven, shineth unto the parts that are under heavens, *so shall the Son of man be in his day."*** In the next verse *Jesus* prophetically and correctly *foretells of His rejection* and even *His passion* in Luke 17:25: *"But* first *he must suffer many things,* and *be rejected* by this generation."

Reflections on *lightning* and *the Ark of the New Covenant*

I believe now we can better understand *why* whenever *Jesus* or the *Blessed Virgin Mary bringing her baby Jesus* to us appear to Nancy, we actually recorded and documented tremendous unprecedented bursts of *lightning light energy.* Remember how God *appeared to Moses* and *appeared to the children of Israel on Mount Sinai* in Horeb with *thunders and lightning to flash* and how the Psalms of David as well as the prophets also spoke of this *lightning of God* as noted above. I also believe that *Jesus,* the Son of the living God and the Son of man *(the God-man),* **is** the all powerful *energy source of* ***all light*** *(visible and invisible)* that makes up all *the flashes or darts or bolts of lightning and all* **the light** *energy in the world* we were able to detect and measure *in His Living Presence* (thanks be to God). So from our *new medical science data, Jesus* **is** *the true living light* and the *lightning of God personified.*

Another set of *lightnings* was also written about in the *Book of Revelation* in reference to *the ark of the testament* or *the ark of the (new) covenant* as clearly seen in Rev 11:19: ***"And the temple of God was opened in heaven: and the ark of his testament was seen in his temple, and there were lightnings, and voices, and an earthquake, and great hail."*** I believe *the ark of his testament* or *the ark of the new covenant* **is** *the Blessed Virgin Mary,* since in the very next verses in Rev 12:1-2, and 5, after John vividly describes *the ark of his testament,* he then describes the role of *a woman* and *Who* she gives birth to: *"And a great sign appeared in heaven:* ***A woman clothed with the sun,*** **and the moon under her feet, and on her head a crown of twelve stars:** ***And being with child,*** *she cried travailing in birth, and was in pain to be delivered...And* ***she brought forth***

a man child, who was to rule all nations with an iron rod: **and** ***her son was taken up to God,*** **and** ***to his throne."*** Recall, the prophetical Messianic Psalm 2:9: ***"Thou shalt rule them with a rod of iron, and shalt break them in pieces like a potter's vessel."*** Now, we can see the *fulfillment of prophecy* within Rev 12:5 as was clearly prophesized in the first verse of Psalm of David 109 (110): ***"The Lord said to my Lord: Sit thou at my right hand: Until I make thy enemies thy footstool."***

But, who is this *woman clothed with the sun?* I believe *the woman* **is** *Mary,* the true *ark of the new covenant/Jesus.* I also believe *Mary* ***is*** the prophesized *virgin mother of Emmanuel,* whose name means *"God with us"* (Isaiah 7:14). Thus, *Mary* ***is*** the *mother of the true Jewish Messiah* (Luke1:28-35). *The Son* of Mary, *the Messiah* shall rule all nations *"with a rod of iron"* (Psalm 2:9). Interestingly, during our scientific testing whenever *the Blessed Virgin Mary* appeared *bringing baby Jesus to us* we recorded 30-90% more *sun light surrounding* the outside façade of the farm house and chimney. So recall, *Our Loving Mother, the Blessed Virgin Mary* bringing *her baby Jesus* to us was indeed *dressed* or *clothed with* **the sun** literally speaking. Recall that inside the apparition room, we recorded simultaneously - a tremendous surge of *flashes, bolts or darts* of *lightning* - *light energy.* Now ponder what is written in Rev 11:19 and Rev 12:1. See how John's description of *the ark of his testament was seen in his (God's) temple* with ***lightnings*** *and great hail (Hail Mary)* actually fits our *new medical and scientific data* and portrait of *Our Loving Mother bringing Jesus to us* **clothed with the sun** and with *lightnings.* Imagine this is *what we recorded* in these *heavenly visits.* Nancy in private, says she often sees *mystical flashes or bolts or darts of lightning like light* whenever *Jesus* or *Our Loving Mother bringing baby Jesus to us* appear to her. Thus, with all the science documented we can now *see* how *Our Loving Mother* in Conyers, Georgia, USA, is vividly portrayed in Rev 11:19; 12:1. I believe this is just like *Our Loving Mother. "And great hail"* (Rev 11:19) I believe is a *heavenly chorus singing: "Hail Mary!"*

Please ponder this image. See - how the *baby Jesus* with eyes closed just so *sweetly sleeps* in the loving arms of *His mother Mary* and *how the living Son of God rests so sweetly in Mary's arms* for comfort, love and peace. *God the Son* created *His earthly mother Mary* as *His* own private *perfect living tabernacle* and *resting place on earth* as prophesized in Psalm 18:6: *"He hath set his tabernacle (Mary)* ***in the sun:*** *and he...coming out of... bride chamber;"* and Song of Songs 6:8-9: *"my perfect one (Mary) is but one, she is the only of her mother (Ann), the chosen of her that bore her. The daughters saw her, and declared her* ***most blessed:*** the queens and concubines, and they praised her. *Who is she* that cometh forth *as the morning rising,* ***fair as the moon, bright as the sun,*** *terrible as an army set in array?"* This is truly an *eye opener* for those *who still wonder* whether *Mary* ***is*** the *Immaculate Conception.* I believe that in the great master plan of mercy and salvation, *the Almighty I AM* with absolutely *no time constraints,* since *God created time and God* *is totally outside of time,* uses the *Precious Blood of His only begotten Son* (Psalm 2:7) *Jesus - to redeem, wash pure and make perfect - His Blessed Mother* before or at the moment of *Mary's conception.* So, His *new creation upon the earth, (my perfect one) a woman Mary;* see Jeremiah 31:22: *"...for* ***the Lord hath created a new thing upon the earth:*** A WOMAN SHALL COMPASS A MAN.*"* If *Mary* **is** *God's new creation* upon the earth made whole *without spot from conception, sinless, unblemished and full of grace,* maybe this is *why* in the of Gospel of Luke 1:28 the *archangel Gabriel* salutes *Mary* with a most honored greeting of: *"Hail, full of grace, the Lord is with thee: blessed art thou among women."* This is also *why* while *Jesus* is dying on the cross on Calvary (*Golgotha* in Hebrew) *Jesus calls His loving mother Mary* **"woman,"** in John 19:26-27 and then *"saith to the disciple: Behold thy mother."* So, if *you* are *a disciple of Jesus,* ***"Behold thy mother."***

Remember, *Mary* is the *woman* prophesized in Genesis 3:15 *who (with her seed) shall crush the head of the serpent.* Mary with baby Jesus inside the farm house was literally *clothed in the sun* with the 30-90% more *sun light* detected outside the farm house, while *"lightnings"- the lightning energy* - were recorded inside the room. This portrait of *Our Loving Mother* together with our *new* medical and scientific *data* collected emerges as *three combined pictures* namely of the *ark of his testament, "lightnings"* (Rev 11:19) and *"a woman clothed in the sun"* (Rev 12:1). All three pictures remarkably combined together into one picture, as *"the temple of God was opened in heaven"* (Rev11:19) to John, **is** indeed the *new data* recorded of *Our Loving Mother's apparitions.* Historically, we now know that in the Middle Ages Monks partitioned the Book of Revelation into chapters. Initially in John's writings there were no chapters. The two verses in sequence Rev 11:19 and Rev 12:1 were indeed read one verse right after the other with no chapter separations. So, if you read these two verses in sequence exactly the way John wrote it, it makes (good and logical) sense that *the portrait of Our Loving Mother* combined *with* our *new medical and scientific data* actually *fits the same description* of what *John was allowed to see in a vision* as *"the temple of God was opened in heaven"* (Rev 11:19). John *mystically saw the Jerusalem Temple* all safe and sound in *heaven,* before the earthly Jerusalem Temple was to be destroyed in 70 A.D. by the Romans under Titus. I believe John was really comforted and assured knowing that the true *temple of God* and *the ark of the new covenant* were safe and sound in the safest place ever, namely *heaven. "A woman clothed in the sun"* (Rev12:1) **is** *Mary with baby Jesus, Our Loving Mother.* And *Jesus* **is** the *new covenant "a man child, who was to rule all nations with an iron rod: and her (Mary's) son was taken up to God, and to his throne"* (Rev 12:5; but, also see Psalms 2:9 and 109/110:1).

Now the word *covenant* leaped out from these pages, as I began to read about *the Ark of the Covenant.* So, *what* does the word ***covenant*** really mean, especially between God and man? When I researched the word *covenant,* I learned that centuries around the time and even before Abram lived and way before the gentile

Abram became *Abraham* (who is the father of the Jewish people through Isaac and subsequently the father of the Christians and also the father of the Muslims through Ishmael), there was an *accepted practice among the peoples* of that time period called *the cutting of a covenant.* This was apparently recognized as the highest form of making an agreement or compact that is seriously binding between two people, two tribes or two nations or *with God.* This usually involved a formal ceremony. A *covenant* was used by the tribal heads or chiefs, who wanted to enter into a mutual peace treaty or just wanted to formally demonstrate a deep trust or love between two people involved in *making a total commitment with each other.* (Many thanks to the Messianic Jewish couple, who introduced me to StanTelchin's own personal and dramatic Jewish family's conversion story and a historical account of *covenant relationships* in his engaging new book called: *Betrayed!)*

Invariably, the two new partners or parties would exchange gifts even weapons and names pledging to one another their total assistance, strength and sometimes even their identity. Thus, while *making a covenant - the (formal) cutting of a covenant* - was indeed *a very serious matter.* The two persons, parties or tribes making the covenant would first recite the rules of the covenant with certain *blessings* given for keeping the covenant and with certain *curses* for breaking any of the covenant rules. Interestingly, the word *cutting* means that *actual blood must be shed.* This was done in several ways. One of the more popular ways of *cutting* used in those days was to cut their arms and let the blood drip into a bowl, where the blood was then mixed from both parties to indicate that they were both now *of one blood.* Both new partners of the covenant would drink the newly mixed blood from the same bowl. Then, they would *seal* the cutting of the covenant by rubbing ashes into their wounds, in order to leave a scar as a reminder of the covenant. A *memorial* was then set up after the *sealing of the covenant* in order to remind the new partners of *the covenant.* And finally the new covenant partners would sit down to eat together like a new family to enjoy *the covenant meal.*

As I read about the ancient traditions on the *making of a covenant* in the days of Abram (later named *Abraham* by God) and the early history of the Jews, I could not escape the obvious and very perplexing question. In history *when and where was the cutting* or the *shedding of blood on God's part of the covenant?* We see in Genesis 17:1-27 details of the entire cutting of the covenant for Abram and man's part of the covenant as God gave Abram a new name - ***"...Abraham: because I have made thee a father of many nations"*** (Genesis 17:5). *God* also said to Abraham in Genesis 17:10-11: ***"This is my covenant which you shall observe, between me and you, and thy seed after thee: All the male kind of you shall be circumcised: And you shall circumcise the flesh of your foreskin, that it may be for a sign of the covenant between me and you."***

We know that for several thousands of years *God* has asked *His chosen people* (the Jews) for man's part of the *formal cutting of the covenant* with the *cutting of the foreskin* called *circumcision. God asks Jews for the shedding of blood* to honor the covenant *He* made with Abram/Abraham thousands of years ago. So, now I ask again - when and where in history **is** *God's part* in the *shedding of blood? Where* is *God's part* in the *formal cutting of the covenant?* Now think hard and ponder. Just like in Stan Telchin's: *Betrayed!,* I for one cannot escape *the passion imagery of Jesus crucified on Calvary.* Just ponder *the image of Jesus,* Who I believe **is** the true Jewish Messiah, the Lamb of God Who takes away the sins of the world and suffers *the passion* for us, as was prophesized in Isaiah 53: ***"and by his stripes we are healed,"*** in Psalm 22:17: ***"they have pierced my hands and feet,"*** and in Zachariah 12:10:***"and they shall look upon me, whom they have pierced."*** Now see *the crucifixion of Jesus - as the (formal) cutting of God's part of the covenant and as man's part simultaneously* for all sins, transgressions and iniquities. See *the shedding of blood on the cross by Jesus* - as truly fulfilling Bible prophecy and completing *the covenant* - God made with Abram/Abraham.

So, is *Jesus* truly *the Jewish Messiah?* Is Jesus *the living Son of God?* Is Jesus *the God-man* in, Isaiah 9:6? The prophet Zachariah may have said it best. See the following verses in Zachariah 12:8-10:"**In that day shall the Lord protect the inhabitants of Jerusalem ...and *the house of David, as that of God, as an angel of the Lord in their sight* ...And I will pour out upon the house of David, and upon the inhabitants of Jerusalem, *the spirit of grace, and of prayers:* and *they shall look upon me, whom they have pierced*: and *they shall mourn for him as* one mourneth for *an only son,* and they shall grieve over him, *as the manner is to grieve for the death of the firstborn.*** " In Zachariah 13:6:*"And they shall say to him:* ***What are these wounds in the midst of thy hands?*** And **he shall say: With these I was wounded in the house of them that loved me."** Here it is very difficult to escape *the imagery of Jesus crucified* in the *passion of the Christ, Who was nailed to a tree by His hands* and feet/*crucified /pierced* by a lance.

If you look very carefully at all *the evidence* I have presented to you thus far accepting and believing that *the passion and crucifixion of Jesus* **is** *God's part* of *the cutting* and *the shedding of blood of the old and new covenant,* then the ancient Holy Scriptures are indeed truly fulfilled by ***the Jewish Messiah, the Christ*** *Jesus,* Whose name in Hebrew means *salvation* or *God saves.* Now in John's Gospel see Mother *Mary and John the disciple* at the foot of *the cross,* two Jewish eyewitness of *the cutting* and *the shedding of blood* on *God's part of the covenant* that God made with Abram/Abraham, as it is written by Moses in the Book of Genesis. So, in *the cutting of the covenant* - see *the passion of the Christ* Jesus.

Looking at the sequence above in the *making of a covenant* in terms of the *Holy Mass* and the *Holy Eucharist* celebration, *"the sacrifice of praise" – Jesus* (Psalm 106:22), *Who* offers to God as *the high priest* and *is offered up to God as the victim* (the Eternal Lamb of God) in the daily Mass, I pondered. Then it hit me. Each Holy Mass is a *memorial service* to Father God. *The ashes* used in *sealing the covenant* is now *the incense (or ashes) burned* over the altars for *sealing* our *covenant with God* at the Mass. The *cutting of the covenant* is finally completed with *Jesus on Calvary* approximately 2,000 years ago. Many scholars say *Jesus is the same yesterday, today and tomorrow* as *God the Son. Jesus* says in John 10:15: *"...I lay down my life for my sheep."* But since *God is outside of time,* I can now see how *His* most awesome *sacrifice of love* as the *Good Shepherd* with *His* unfathomable *mercy* for us is *perpetual* and *ongoing daily* for all our sins, iniquities and all our transgressions. I truly believe *Jesus fulfills this prophecy* of Ezekiel 34:11: **"For thus *saith the Lord God: Behold I myself will seek my sheep,* and *will visit them."***

Now recall that in order to complete a *covenant,* there is the *drinking of the blood* of the covenant and the *eating of the covenant meal* as celebrated by both *new* partners of the covenant. So, *why* does the priest *lift up* the consecrated cup of *wine* (the true blood of Jesus, *"the blood of the grape",* Genesis 49:10-11)? The priest first *offers the cup - to God the Father* - and *then, the blood* of the covenant is *offered - to us,* who partake of this covenant by the *drinking of the blood (the blood of the grape).* Prior to this, the priest first *lifts up the* consecrated *bread - offering it to God the Father, then he offers the* consecrated *bread -"the holy flesh"* or *"meat indeed"* (John 6:56) - *"the living bread which came down from heaven"* (John 6:41, 51), *Jesus - to* all of *us.* As prophesized, in Jeremiah 11:15: *"...* **shall *the holy flesh* take away from thee thy crimes, in which thou hast boasted?"** Then, in Jeremiah 11:19: "And **I was as a *meek lamb*, that is carried to be a *victim:* and I knew not that they had devised counsels against me, saying: Let us put *wood*** *(the cross)* **on *his bread*** *(His holy flesh)*, **and cut him off from the land of the living, and let his name be remembered no more."** In the Holy Mass, *the priest first offers* the consecrated bread of heaven, the *covenant meal, to God the Father* and *then the priest* offers the *covenant meal - the Eucharist - to us.*

It is *the eating* of the *new covenant meal (the Eucharist)* then, that actually *completes the celebration* of the *new covenant* God made with us. If you believe *Jesus* is indeed the true God-man (Isaiah 9:6), then *in* or *with the cutting of Jesus, both the old and new cutting of the covenants are completed and fulfilled,* respectively. *Jesus* simultaneously sheds *His Precious Blood* as *the Son of the living God (as God Himself)* and also *sheds the blood of the Son of man,* which is already thoroughly mixed within and inside Jesus *(the God-man).* Thus, the two species of blood *(God and man)* are shed at once - in the cup - *as one blood.* Ponder this. *The blood of God* and *the blood of the Son of man* poured into one bowl or cup.

Thus, *with the formal cutting of Jesus, the God part of the cutting concerning the old covenant God made with Abram/Abraham is now completed. So, simultaneously with the cutting of Jesus, a new God part* and *a new man part of the new covenant,* as *God foretold* - in Jeremiah 31:33 - **is** also now *fulfilled.*

Note: If you believe *Jesus is the Son of the living God* and also One with God: *Jesus* the Lord God, the second person of the Holy Trinity, part of the One God, then the above information will hopefully help you better understand the real true importance of the *Holy Eucharist,* the daily communion and *covenant meal* in the daily Holy Mass. *Jesus* ***is*** *the new covenant* prophesized in Isaiah 42:6 and 49:8. *Jesus* ***is*** *the new covenant* and the *new covenant meal* described and alluded to in Jeremiah 31:33.

The drinking of the blood - *Jesus* shed for us on Calvary - is seen in John 6:55:*"He that eateth my flesh, and drinketh my blood, hath everlasting life: and I will raise him up in the last day."* And the *eating of the new covenant meal* - *Jesus* gives to us - is seen in John 6:52: *"...and* ***the bread*** *that I will* ***give,*** *is my flesh, for the life of the world."* This completes the celebration of *the new covenant meal.* But now, we who partake of the *new covenant meal* must also abide by *the rules of the new covenant.* So, we need to know *what the rules are.* Besides *loving God with all your might, heart, soul and mind* and *obeying the Ten Commandments, Jesus* summed it up in John 15:12**: "This is my commandment, that you love one another, as I have loved you."**

It now makes perfect sense to me that *"the ark of his (new) testament (covenant)"* (Rev 11:19) is *the Blessed Virgin Mary,* since *Jesus* ***is*** *the incarnation of wisdom, the law of God, the word of God and the bread of God (the Eucharist)* all combined together to make up the very much awaited, heralded and prophesized *new covenant* (Jeremiah 31:33). Recall, inside the blessed womb of Mary is *Jesus* (Luke 1:42) *the word of God, the fountain of wisdom, everlasting commandments,* which **is** *the law of God* (John1:1; Rev 19:13; Ecclesiasticus 1:5) and **is** *"the bread of God"* (John 6:33) *made flesh* (John 1:14; John 6:35, 38, 47-59). *Jesus* twice said, *"I am the living bread which came down from heaven"* (John 6:41, 51), so this must be important. Thus, *Mary's blessed womb* **is** like the inside the *Ark of the Covenant* God instructed Moses to build, but much better since *she was created perfect* and *fashioned* solely *by the hands of God.* Inside the Ark in the *holy of holies* in the Temple, we see the placement of the actual *testimony* or *testaments of God (the word of God),* see Exodus 25:16, 20-21. Later, a jar or small urn was filled with *a gomer of manna,* **the bread of heaven** *God* had instructed to be kept inside the *tabernacle* for all future generations to see (see Exodus 16:33-34) and *traditions* say the jar with manna was later placed inside of the *Ark of the Covenant* by the high priests along with *the staff* of Aaron and Moses that *blossomed.*

If the above is true, then *Mary* **is** *the living ark of the new testament/covenant* or *the ark of Jesus* simply because of *Who* **is** *living inside her most blessed womb* (Luke 1:42). First - *"the word of God,"* (Rev 19:13) *"made flesh"* (John1:14) and second - the *"living bread which came down from heaven"* (John 6:41, 51) or *"the bread of God"* (John 6:33) both *the Word* & *the Bread* dwell and live inside *Mary's* *most blessed womb* just like what is inside - the Ark of the Covenant in the Holy of Holies. If J*esus is the* prophesized *new covenant* (Jeremiah 31:33), then *Mary is the first living "ark of his testament"* (Rev 11:19), *the ark of the* ***new*** *covenant,* the first *living tabernacle* and *living temple of the new covenant* (Luke 1:31). This is probably *why* so many of *the early Christians* like Elizabeth (Luke 1:41-43), who understood *Mary's role in God's Divine salvation plan for all of mankind,* saw her as *the first living human tabernacle of God (Jesus),* and so *honored Mary* accordingly; by naming many of the first early churches after her name all throughout the world. They acknowledge *Mary* as the *Mother of God, Theotokos.*

Yes, even though her baby Son *(Jesus)* created *Mary, the virgin gave birth to the Son of God, the second person of the Holy Trinity-Jesus/Emmanuel/God with us,* Isaiah 7:14. *Mary* in fact **is** *the first living tabernacle of God* (Psalm 18:6). Think and just ponder this *truth. Mary* is the first living *creature created by God to have* the true living *God living inside her blessed womb.* See *"the woman"* in Genesis 3:15 **is** indeed the *Blessed Virgin Mary,* as was prophesized by Moses. *Mary* is carrying *the seed of a woman.* In Luke 1:35 the Archangel Gabriel said to Mary: ***"The Holy Ghost shall come upon thee, and the power of the most High shall overshadow thee. And therefore also the Holy which shall be born of thee shall be called the Son of God."*** So, the *seed of God* comes ***in*** *"the living water"* (John 4:10), via *the Holy Spirit of God* - as ***"water shall flow out of his bucket, and his seed*** *(the seed of God)* ***shall be in many waters"*** (Numbers 24:7; 3 Kings 18:34-38); and then *"he that believeth in me (Jesus/the seed/ the Word of God/the Son of God and Son of* ***wo****man, Mary)* as the scripture saith, *"Out of his belly shall flow rivers of living water"* (John 7:38). I now believe this is *why* the *greeting in Hebrew* that *David gives to the ark of the Lord* (2 Kings 6:9), when the *ark* is recovered from the Philistines, **is** *identical in meaning to the greeting Elizabeth gave* to *the pregnant virgin Mary* carrying *"the Holy"* - the *Son of God - Jesus* (Luke 1:35), when Mary visited her (Luke 1:43). To assist in God's great master plan, I believe *Our Loving Mother* is continuingly trying to bring *the true light of the world* (John 1:9) - *her baby Jesus - the Son of God* - back to the United States of America and to the whole world in order to give us a greater *faith* - through *His Divine Will,* immeasurable *Love, Divine Mercy* and *Awesome Power (the Holy Spirit).* So now, this is your chance to believe in the *one true God, the Holy Trinity,* as our amazing *new medical and scientific data* supports - *the truth (Jesus) - to the absolute max!*

So, now come and believe in *the One He sent – Jesus.* If you are still not a believer---do realize that I have just meticulously presented to you a multitude of true medical and scientific facts, so that the *loving graces* and *Divine Mercy of the Almighty God* can help you (just like it did me) *take a huge grasshopper-like leap towards faith* and *"be not disbelieving (faithless) any longer but believing"* (John 2:7). Remember, how the *doubting* apostle Thomas (John 20:28) was the first to confess *Jesus: "My Lord, and my God."* So, just like in the days of Noah, make up your mind to get into *the ark* or suffer the flood. *Mary,* as *the ark,* can now be portrayed and looked upon as a true living and floating hospital for all the sick souls (sinners) of this world - through the blood of the cross - of her Son, *Jesus.* Recall, all the different types of animals that entered *the ark of Noah.* Mary's role as the *ark* is really no different, but is really similar to Noah's ark. Because, I believe, *the ark of Noah* was a *foreshadowing* of just how accommodating, receptive, merciful and loving *Mary,* the *ark of the new covenant,* **is** to all sinners - like the beasts, *tame or wild* that entered *the ark of Noah.* Even the most hardened, vicious and ruthless sinners, any of them by *just asking God for forgiveness* like prodigal sons and daughters *may attain Mary's maternal office as Mother of the Redeemer,* then *Mary lovingly goes to work - to help you* - by *interceding, pleading and praying to God - for you.* Thus, *Mary* is the true *blue print* of the *Church of her Son Jesus,* especially with her pure, selfless virtues and most generous self-sacrificing love and mercy. *Jesus and Mary living in the Divine Will of God* are indeed our perfect role models for living a *good life* here on earth, according to *God's laws/commandments of love.* I firmly believe this is what *God* originally intended for us from *the beginning* even after sin entered the world, in order to help us live *good holy lives.*

In the first miracle *Jesus* performed in Cana of Galilee, recall that it was simply *after the prayers of Mary* asking *her Son Jesus* to help the wedding party, when there was no more wine, that six water-pots of stone filled with water to the brim were miraculously changed *by Jesus* into *"good wine"* (John 2:1-10). Now *Mary is bringing Jesus "the true light"* (John 1:9) *to us* - in our sinful generation, while a rapidly growing veil of darkness covers, invades, deceives and corrupts our country and the judicial system in America like a fast growing malignant cancer that shakes us to the very core and tries to destroy our nation's moral fiber and that of the free world. Just look at all the anger, the hatred, the conflicts, the battles, the wars and terrorism amongst God's children. Look at the seemingly never ending and ever increasing *rebellion and rejection of God* in this increasingly *secular world,* especially here in America. Can you imagine *the Laws of God – The Ten Commandments* being thrown out of our Judicial Courts in the USA? Sadly enough it has already happened and is now part of history. So, let us all wake up. Wake up *America!* Wake up *"free" world!* Or you will soon lose your dearly treasured freedoms. Today the *Judeo-Christian faith* is currently under the most vicious and cruel demonic attack from the very depths of *hell* itself (Psalm 2:1-2; Isaiah 14:9) deceiving the best intellectual minds from all sides especially the very liberal left, the communists, the atheists, the secularists, relativists, *new age* proponents, radical Islamists, abortionists, activist judges, all *pro-choice* legislators and all who promote a *culture of death* in America and throughout the world. Especially, all who are working so hard *to throw God out of* our nation, our government, our judicial court system, our laws, our communities, our schools, our churches, our homes and even our hearts. *Wake up America! Wake up free world!* You are not really *free* any longer. *Wake up Jews & Christians everywhere!* Some of the most radical Islamists have declared *Jihad* a holy war against you and our nation for many years, and we have seemingly slept through most of it, not giving it the real importance or the gravity announced by *the war of words.* So, we sadly awakened one beautiful morning in the USA to our nation's horrific 911. Now *imagine* an even *more vicious foe* that is *invisible,* much more notorious, powerful and sinister, who has declared a *holy war (Jihad) against your very own souls* (and this includes *the souls* of all Muslims too) *from the very first moment of your life* - your *conception in the womb* (Jeremiah 1:5). The attacks begin here, since *conception* is now medically and scientifically proven to be *the true beginning of human life,* as it has always been taught by the Church. Recall, this evil foe, *"the serpent,"* Lucifer knew *God* - *the Triune God* - *in heaven* before being cast down to earth. So, be very careful and please do not ignore the most important *holy war* ever declared---against your very own *soul*---or else you too will have your very own horrific, private, personal and forever tragic 911. Please be very careful, indeed. Remember, this *subtle* notorious and vicious foe **is** the *father of lies,* the *master of all deception,* and *a murderer* who *masterfully mixes truth and lies* to a point where even the most intelligent minds cannot tell them apart. Now, maybe and hopefully, you will see the true merits of *Mary* or at least get a better understanding *why Mary is crying* and trying so desperately to bring God back into our lives---for all her beloved Jews and Gentiles alike. *Mary* **is** God's *"handmaid of the Lord"* and God's *holy vessel* (Gen 3:15; and God's *bucket,* Numbers 24:7). So, *ask Mary* ***to pray*** *to her Son Jesus for you* just as she did for the family in the *wedding of Cana* heralding *the first miracle of Jesus* then dip, soak and totally immerse yourself, your family, all your relatives and friends into the unfathomable bottomless ocean of *Divine Mercy* thru the *Precious Blood of Jesus* - and remove all stain of sin, and *then learn to live in His Divine Will.*

* * *

III. "The light" (energy) - as a Hebrew phrase has a mathematical value = 613.

A. On June 13th, 1993 in Conyers, Georgia, USA, at high noon during the *heavenly visits* or *apparitions* of the *Blessed Virgin Mary bringing baby Jesus* with the living heavenly court of holy angels and saints, including the two times *Jesus appeared* in the apparition room, *the light energy* recorded in the room's atmosphere increased astronomically in various parameters as was already shown in Chapters 3, 4 and 5. Also in the adjacent room to the apparition room later on that same day of 6/13, we recorded astronomical *increases in the light energy* only during the *heavenly visit* or *apparition of Jesus alive on the cross* on the wall with the pulsating coherent bursts or *near-infrared (maser-like) laser signals of radio light emanating* from the *resin model corpus of Jesus on the wood cross,* that simulated true bioelectrical type pulsations of a human heart beat, when placing the probe on the chest or heart area of *Jesus.* Later, when *the probe* was placed over the *resin model head of Jesus crowned with thorns on a wood cross,* we recorded the amazing bioelectrical type pulsations of the *light energy* with a frequency typical of normal adult brain waves emanating from *the resin/wood crucifix.* Wow! These *pulsations* were made up of frequent sequential rhythmic harmonic fluctuations in the *near-infrared light radiation energy fields* as was clearly demonstrated by Dr. Callahan. Remember, the *other probe* that was placed in the atmosphere of both rooms recorded *the light radiation energy fields* in the range of the North American Aviation Radio Band Spectrum of 800-1000 Hz as a *baseline* measurement that *increased 3-4 fold* up to 2,000-4,000+ Hz *only during heavenly visits* or *apparitions (in His Living Presence).* This *peaceful light energy* recorded generated a definite relaxing, calming and very peaceful atmosphere in the surrounding or round about environment that was used by dentists in the 1800's for dental procedures called *electrical anesthesia.*

Of great interest is the fact that *the light energy radiation field spectrum* we recorded actually includes the detection of 97% of the *invisible light range* (from the *gamma* high radiation energy fields to the *low radiation* energy fields of infrared, *radio,* and *the extremely low radiation* energy) and the detection of 3% of the *visible light range* (which includes the 30-90% *more sun light energy* recorded on the professional photographs and the amazing concentrated *increased coherent bursts of white laser light* captured on Dr. Velasquez's video) all which were detected only *in His Living Presence.* Recall, the *gamma* radiation energy fields though detected did not increase in a statistical significant manner. And thus, *no one was harmed* by *the heavenly visits* or *visions* or *apparitions.* Also of great interest is the phrase in Hebrew *the light* which has a numerical value of 613. Each one of the following phrases in Hebrew: "*Moses our teacher*" = 613 and *"the Lord God of Israel"* = 613. Now I ask, *"What did Moses teach?" Moses* was the *teacher of the law.* In fact the Jewish *prayer shawl* interestingly has a *total of 613 knots, each knot for each law, commandments, precepts,* and *statutes in the Bible –Torah.* Thus, 613 - the numerical Hebrew value = *"the light"= "the law" = "the Lord God of Israel."* Now remember, we completed these medical and scientific studies uncovering (discovering) *the light* on June 13th (6/13), while *in His Living Presence.* Is this just a coincidence or another *God-incidence?*

Dr. Callahan recorded *Schumann waves* of 14 Hz and *Soliton waves* of 1 mV at Nancy's aura/atmospheric-skin boundary radiation energy fields *before* the *heavenly visits* or *apparitions. During the heavenly visits* of the *Blessed Virgin Mary bringing baby Jesus,* the *Schumann waves* dropped abruptly to 4 Hz, while the *Soliton waves* sky-rocketed up to 25-40 mV. *During the apparitions of Jesus* in the adjacent room to the apparition room, the *Schumann waves dropped abruptly to 3-4 Hz range* (averaging 3.0-3.3 Hz), while the *Soliton waves* astronomically increased upwards to 80-90 mV. Thus, the entire surface area of Nancy's atmospheric-skin boundary radiation *light* energy fields or the intensity/power of *the light* energy at the surface of Nancy's skin (aura) was astronomically increased to levels beyond comprehension. Nancy's *aura was* literally *set ablaze* with *the fire/reflection/the light* of *Jesus - in His Living Presence.* The *fire/the light/lightning energy* was *invisible* to most of our eyes *during the testing* in the room *except for the chosen souls.* But *the light energy* was *not invisible to the scientific probes* and *recording equipment* that had repeatedly detected and documented these very extraordinary and astonishing *supernatural events.* Can you imagine *the fire/the light/lightning* light energy *of Jesus* being recorded at the surface of Nancy's skin? Yes, this is indeed *what* was recorded. *Nancy was* literally *set on fire or set ablaze in His Living Presence - in the living presence of the Son of God, but yet not burned* just like Sidrach, Misach and Abdenago in Daniel 3:91-93. Recall, *what Jesus says* in Luke 12:49: ***"I am come to cast fire on earth: and what I will, but that it be kindled?"***

Thus, the science of Nancy's (aura) atmospheric-skin boundary radiation *light* energy fields recorded *on an earthling* fulfills this prophetic verse. Can you imagine or even fathom *why* God has so lovingly and mercifully done this for us? *What* does *fire* bring to the dark, darkness *on earth?* The obvious answer is *the light.*

Question: So, what does Jesus and "the light" have in common?

B. The Old Testament is replete with numerous prophetic verses of the *Jewish Messiah* coming as *the light of the world.* In fact there are so many verses on *the light* as *our Lord and salvation* that to mention all of them would probable make up an entire book by itself. But, I have selected a few verses below to show you how *fire* and *the light* is indeed connected *as one with God.* Starting with Genesis, we revisit Gen 1:3: ***"And God said: Be light made. And light was made."*** If you stand back just a little and look at this verse again you can see that the very *first words* ever recorded as *spoken by God Himself* in the Bible were *"Be light made." Or "Light be made."* So, at the *first* moment of time from *the beginning, the Word of God* was, is, and always will be – ***the light!*** In the next verse, Genesis 1:4:"And God saw *the light* that it was *good;* and he divided *(separated) the light* from the darkness." So, God calls ***the light* - *good*** *which =* ***life*** *in* Deuteronomy 30:15: "...I have set before thee this day *life* and *good..."* A careful review of the top two sections on ***the sun light*** and ***the lightning light*** energy will indeed show you many Bible verses concerning ***the light*** of God, which has been already presented in the previous chapters.

See below, how I selected some very special Bible verses that give knowledge on the mystery and *glory of God's fire* and *light.* Recall, Genesis 1:3:*"Be **light** made.* And light was made." Genesis 15:12-17: *"...* ***a deep sleep fell upon Abram****...*And when ***the sun*** was ***set,*** there arouse a dark mist, and *there* ***appeared a smoking furnace*** and ***a lamp of fire...*"** This *apparition* and *heavenly vision* *given to Abram, while in a* **deep sleep** *(sound familiar),* is just like what I recorded with Nancy and the two other *chosen souls* tested. I believe this *apparition of a smoking furnace* seen by Abram is *a prophecy of the law of God* to be *given to Moses* that is fulfilled in Exodus 19:18. The *apparition of a lamp of fire* seen by Abram is *a prophecy of the word of God* to be *given to Elijah (and the prophets)* and is fulfilled in 3 Kings 18:37-39. See Exodus 19:18:"And all mount Sinai was on a smoke: because *the Lord was come* down upon it *in fire,* and the smoke arose from it as out of a *furnace..."* Exodus 20:18:"And all the people *saw the voices* and *the flames,* and the sound of the trumpet, and *the mount was smoking..."* Exodus 24:17:"And the *sight of the glory of the Lord* was like *a burning fire* upon the top of the mount, in the eyes of the children of Israel." Also recall, a famous verse in Exodus 3:2:*"And* ***the Lord appeared*** *to him (Moses)* ***in a flame of fire*** *out of the midst of a bush:* and he saw that **the bush was on fire and was not burnt**." Numbers 24:17:*"I shall see him, but not now: I shall behold him, but not near.* A STAR SHALL RISE *out of Jacob* and *a sceptre shall spring up from Israel..."* Deuteronomy 4:12:"And *the Lord spoke to you* from *the midst of the* **fire."** Deut 4:24: *"...****the Lord*** *thy God* **is a consuming fire,** *a jealous God."* Deut 4:36: And *upon earth he (the Lord God)* **shewed thee** ***his exceeding great fire, and thou didst hear his words out of the midst of the fire..."*** Deut 5:4: *"He (God)* **spoke to us** *face to face* in the mount ***out of the midst of fire."*** Deut 9:10: "And the Lord gave me two tablets of stone *written with the finger of God,* and *containing all the words that he spoke to you* in the mount *from the midst of the fire..."* Thus, in summarizing the above verses *I believe "the finger (or hand) of God," all the words written on the two tablets* and *"the voices and the flames" of God spoken* and *seen by "all the people"* (Exodus 20:18) **is** indeed the *"exceeding great fire"* (Deut 5:25) and ***the light*** *of the Lord thy God (Jesus). The fire* and *the light of God* is seen while *Moses blesses the children of Israel,* Deut 33:2:*"The Lord came from Sinai,* and from Seir he rose up to us: *he hath appeared from mount Pharan, and with him thousands of saints.* ***In his right hand a fiery law."***

When *God* spoke to Job, *the Lord* asks this probing question in Job 38:19: *"Where* is **the way** *where light dwelleth,* and where is the place of darkness..." And with all our *new data* and amazing scientific evidence, I now believe ***the way*** *where light dwelleth* **is** *Jesus.* Then *the Lord* showing Job the things that *He* has made, since man cannot even comprehend *His power and wisdom,* asks in Job 38:32: *"Canst* thou bring forth the *day star* in its time, and make the *evening star* to rise upon the children of the earth?" The Davidic Psalms are definitely replete with multiple references to ***the light*** of God. See Psalm 11:7: *"The words of the Lord* are *pure words:* as silver tried by the *fire,* purged from the earth, *refined seven times."* In Psalm 18:9: ***"The justices of the Lord are right,*** rejoicing hearts: *the commandment of the Lord* **is** *lightsome, enlightening* the eyes." The famous Davidic Psalm 26 (27):1 also asks a most important question: ***"The Lord is my light and***

my salvation, whom shall I fear?" David understands the *goodness of God* in Psalm 35:10: *"For* with thee is the *fountain of life;* and *in thy light we shall see light."* Psalm 88:16*: "They shall walk,* O Lord, in *the light of thy countenance."* Psalm 89:8: *"Thou* hast set our iniquities before *thy eyes:* our *life* in *the light of thy countenance."* Psalm 96 (97):1-11: *"The Lord hath reigned, let the earth rejoice...justice* and *judgment are the establishment of his throne. A* ***fire*** *shall go before him,* and *shall burn his enemies round about. His* ***lightnings*** *have shone forth to the world: the earth saw and trembled.* The *mountains melted like wax, at the presence of the Lord: at the presence of the Lord* of all the earth. *The heavens declared his justice:* and *all the* people saw *his glory...* ***Light is risen*** to the just, and joy to the right of heart.*"* Psalm 103 is intriguing and very prophetic in regards to *the testing* of Nancy, as seen in verses 1-4: *"Bless the Lord, O my soul:* ***O Lord my God,*** *thou art exceedingly great.* Thou hast put on praise and beauty: and *art clothed with light as with a garment...* ***Who makest*** *thy angels spirits: and* ***thy ministers a burning fire."*** Recall how *the probe* placed on Nancy's atmospheric-skin boundary (aura) actually measured astronomical increases in the radiation light energy fields *only in His Living Presence* that set Nancy literally *ablaze, on fire with His lightning. So, Nancy is like His* ***dart -*** *that goes forth as lightning!* Ponder this. God has made *His ministers (like Nancy) a burning fire* - set ablaze – but *only in His Living Presence.* Wow! Now for other references on *the light,* see Psalm 111:4:"To the righteous *a light* is risen up in darkness*..."* Psalm 116 (117):27: *"The Lord* is God, and he hath *shone upon us."* Psalm118 (119):105**: *"Thy word is a lamp to my feet,* and *a light to my paths."*** In the fulfilling of God's promises made to David, see Psalm 131:17: "There will I *(the Lord, God) bring forth a horn to David:* I have prepared *a lamp* for *my anointed."* A *lamp* in those days is a ***fire and light.*** *God's anointed* **is** *the Messiah* or *the Cristos* in Greek, *the Christ – Jesus.* David praises *God* for *His* wonderful works and special providence over *His servants* in Psalm 135 (136):7-9: *"Who* made ***the great lights:*** for *his mercy* endureth for ever. *The sun* to rule *the day:* for *his mercy* endureth for ever. *The moon and the stars* to rule *the night:* for *his mercy* endureth for ever." In Psalm 138 (139):12: *"But* darkness shall not be dark to thee *(Lord),* and *night shall be light* as *the day:* the darkness thereof, and ***the light*** thereof are alike to thee.*"* Finally, David exhorts us *not to trust in men, but in God alone.* Psalm 145 (146):5-8: *"Blessed is he who* hath the *God of Jacob* for his helper, whose hope is in *the Lord* his *God: who made heaven and earth, the sea, and all things that are in them. Who keepeth truth for ever: who executeth judgment* for them that suffer wrong: *who giveth food* to the hungry. *The Lord looseth* them that are fettered: *the Lord enlighteneth the blind."*

In the Book of Proverbs or the parables of Solomon, son of David and king of Israel, a series of verses exhorting *the wisdom of God* also shed some ***light*** on the nature of *the light* of God. Proverbs 4:18-19: *"But the path of the just,* as ***a shining light,*** goeth forwards and increaseth even to perfect day. The way of the wicked is darksome: they know not where they fall." Proverbs 6:23: *"Because* ***the commandment*** *(of God)* is ***a lamp,*** and ***the law a light,*** and *reproofs of instruction are* ***the way of life."*** Proverbs 7:2: *"Keep my commandments*, and thou shalt *live:* and *my law* as the apple of thy eye." Proverbs 13:9: *"The light* of the just giveth joy: but the lamp of the wicked shall be put out." Proverbs 15:3, 9, 30: *"The eyes of the Lord* in every place *behold the good and the evil...*The way of the wicked is an abomination to the Lord: *he that followeth justice (Jesus) is beloved by him (God the Father)...****The light*** of the eyes rejoiceth the soul." Proverbs 16:2, 5-7: "All the ways of a man are open to *his eyes: the Lord is the weigher of spirits...The beginning* of a *good way* is to do *justice (Jesus);* and this is more acceptable with *God,* than to offer sacrifices. By *mercy and truth (Jesus) iniquity is redeemed:* and *by the fear of the Lord men depart from evil.* When the ways of man shall please the Lord, he will convert even his enemies to *peace (Jesus)."* Proverbs 17:3: "As silver is tried by ***fire,*** and gold in the ***furnace:*** so *the Lord* trieth the hearts." Proverbs 20:20, 27: *"He* that curseth his father, and mother, his *lamp* shall be put out in the midst of darkness...***The spirit of a man is the lamp of the Lord, which searcheth all the hidden things of the bowels."*** Lastly Proverbs 30:4-5: ***"Who hath ascended up into heaven, and descended? Who hath held the wind in his hands? Who hath bound up the waters together as in a garment? Who hath raised up all the borders of the earth? What is his name, and what is the name of his son, if thou knowest? Every word of God is fire tried: he is a buckler to them that hope in him."***

So, *what* is *the name of His Son?* I do believe *His name* **is** *Jesus.* Other Books of the prophets also share in *revealing* ***the light*** *of God.* Ecclesiastes 2:13: "And I saw that *wisdom* excelled folly, as much as *light* differeth from darkness." The Book of Wisdom is believed to be written by Solomon and contains *prophecies of the coming of Christ, His Passion, His Resurrection* and other Christian mysteries. Here are some sentiments of Solomon on the subject of *light.* Wisdom 3:7: "The just shall *shine*, and shall run to and fro like *sparks* among the reeds." Wisdom 3:9: "They that trust in him *(the Lord),* shall understand *the truth:* and they that are *faithful in love* shall rest in him *(the Lord): for grace and peace is to his elect."* Wisdom 6:23: *"Love* ***the light*** *of* ***wisdom,*** all ye that bear rule over peoples." Wisdom 7:26, 29: *"For she* ***(wisdom)*** **is** the ***brightness of eternal light,*** and *the unspotted mirror of God's majesty,* and *the image of his goodness...*For she *(wisdom)* is more beautiful than ***the sun,*** and above all the order of ***the stars:*** being compared with ***the light,*** she *(wisdom) is found before it."*

Ecclesiasticus, which contains admirable lessons on all virtues, has a lot of very insightful knowledge and *prophecy* concerning ***wisdom.*** Ecclesiasticus 1-10 is especially so revealing that I now understand where St. John the Gospel writer might have received some of his *insights like a soaring eagle in the heavens* concerning *the word of God.* Please just read the following below then read the first

5 verses of John. Ecclesiasticus 1:1, 4-5, 8-10: ***"All wisdom is from the Lord God, and hath been always with him, and is before all time... Wisdom hath been created before all things,*** and the understanding of prudence from everlasting. ***The word of God on high is the fountain of wisdom, and her ways are everlasting commandments...*** There is *one most high Creator Almighty,* and a *powerful king,* and greatly to be feared, *who sitteth upon his throne,* and is *the God of dominion. He (God)* created her *(wisdom) in the Holy Ghost (Holy Spirit),* and saw her, and numbered her, and measured her. And *he (God) poured her (wisdom) out upon all his works,* and *upon all flesh according to his gift,* and hath given her *(wisdom)* to them that love him *(God)."* Thus, *the word of God* **is** *the fountain of wisdom,* and ***the way*** *of wisdom* **is** *the everlasting commandments of God.* Now remember what we really need in order to know *the way?* The *answer* is: we need ***the light.*** Read Ecclesiasticus Chapter 24 slowly. Ponder and praise the majesty, the dignity and *divinity* of ***wisdom*** *(the word of God).*

For some choice excerpts from this very prophetic Chapter 24 in Ecclesiasticus please read the following selected verses 5-8, 12-16, 22-37, 40-47 while reflecting on *the life of Jesus* and some of the famous quotes of *Jesus* in the New Testament Gospel of John:

"I (wisdom) came out of the mouth of *the most High, the firstborn before all creatures: I* (*wisdom) made that in the heavens there should rise* ***light*** *that never faileth...I (wisdom)* dwelt in the highest places, and *my throne* is in *a pillar of a cloud. I (wisdom)* alone have compassed the circuit of heaven, and have penetrated into the bottom of the deep, and have *walked in the waves of the sea...*and *he that made me, rested in my tabernacle...* And *he (God)* said to *me (wisdom):* Let *thy dwelling be in Jacob,* and *thy inheritance in Israel,* and *take root in my elect.* From ***the beginning***, and *before the world, was I (wisdom)* created, and unto the world to come *I (wisdom)* shall not cease to be, and in the holy dwelling place *I (wisdom) have ministered before him (the most High).* And so was *I (wisdom)* established in Sion...And *I (wisdom) took root in an honourable people,* and *in the portion of my God his inheritance,* and *my abode is in the full assembly of saints...I (wisdom) stretched out my branches...*As ***the vine*** *I (wisdom)* have brought forth a pleasant odor...In *me (wisdom)* is all ***grace*** of ***the way*** and of ***the truth,*** in *me (wisdom)* is all hope of ***(the) life*** and of virtue...They that ***eat me*** *(wisdom),* ***shall*** yet ***(not) hunger:*** and they that ***drink me*** *(wisdom),* ***shall*** yet ***(not) thirst...***They that *explain me (wisdom) shall have* ***life everlasting.*** All these things are ***the book of life***, and ***the covenant of the most High,*** and the ***knowledge of truth.*** *He (God) appointed to David his servant to raise up of him a most mighty king (the seed of David),* and *sitting on the throne of glory for ever. Who sendeth knowledge as* ***the light... I, wisdom,*** *have poured out rivers. I (wisdom)...came out of paradise...I (wisdom)* ***will water abundantly*** the fruits of my meadow...*For I (wisdom)* ***make doctrine to shine forth*** to all ***as the morning light...****I (wisdom) will penetrate to all the lower*

parts of the earth, and will behold all that sleep, and ***will enlighten*** *all that hope in the Lord.* ***I (wisdom) will*** yet pour out *doctrine as* ***prophecy,*** *and will leave it to them that seek wisdom, and will not cease to instruct their offspring* even to the holy age. See ye that *I (wisdom) have not laboured for myself only, but for all that seek* ***the truth."*** Notice *wisdom* ***is*** *a person* in these writings. So, *Who is wisdom/the Word of God/the light?"* I hope you answered - *Jesus, the name of His (God's) Son.*

Now, I will turn to one of the greatest prophets of the Lord for more pearls and prophecy on the splendor, majesty and glory of ***the light of the Lord.*** In Isaiah there are numerous verses that prophesize to *the light of the Lord*:

Isaiah 2:2-5: "And *in the last days the mountain of the house of the Lord shall be prepared on the top of mountains, and it shall be exalted above the hills, and all nations shall flow unto it.* And many people shall go, and say: Come and let us go up to *the mountain of the Lord,* and *to the house of the God of Jacob,* and *he will teach* us *his ways*, and we will walk in *his paths: for* ***the word of the Lord*** from Jerusalem...O house of Jacob, *come ye,* and ***let us walk in the light of the Lord."***

Isaiah 9:1-2, 8:"At the first time the land of Zabulon, and the land of Nephtali was ***lightly touched***...The *people that walked in darkness, have seen* ***a great light:*** *to them that dwelt in the region of the shadow of death,* ***light is risen ...*** *The Lord sent* ***word*** *into Jacob, and it hath* ***lighted*** *upon Israel."* Isaiah 10:17:"And ***the light of Israel*** *shall be* as ***a fire,*** and ***the Holy One*** *thereof* as ***a flame..."***

Isaiah 26:19:"...my slain shall rise again: awake, and give praise, ye that dwell in the dust: for thy dew is *the dew of the light..." Christ* Jesus who according to his humanity is *the servant of God,* in Isaiah 42:1, 6, 13, 16, 21:***"Behold my servant, I will uphold him: my elect,*** *my soul delighteth in him:* ***I have given my spirit upon him,*** *he shall bring forth judgment to the Gentiles*...I the Lord have *called thee in* ***justice,*** and *taken thee by the hand,* and *preserved thee.* And *I have* ***given thee for a covenant of the people, for a light of the Gentiles...The Lord shall go forth as a mighty man,*** as a man of war *shall he stir up zeal: he shall shout* and *cry: he shall prevail against his enemies*...And I will *lead the blind* into ***the way*** which they know not: and *in* ***the paths*** which *they were ignorant of I will make them walk: I will make darkness* ***light*** *before them,* and *crooked things straight*...And *the Lord was willing to sanctify him*, and *to magnify* ***the law,*** and *exalt it."*

Isaiah 49:5-6:"And now saith the Lord, that ***formed me from the womb*** to be his servant...And he said...*Behold, I have given thee to be* ***the light of the Gentiles,*** that thou mayest be ***my salvation*** even to the farthest part of the earth." Interestingly, the name *Jesus* in Hebrew means *salvation* or *God saves.*

Isaiah 51:4-5:"...for ***a law shall go forth from me,*** and *my judgment shall rest to be* ***a light of the nations. My just one*** is near at hand, ***my saviour is gone forth****..."* Isaiah 60:1-3: "Arise, be ***enlightened,*** O Jerusalem: for ***thy light is come,*** and ***the glory of the Lord is risen upon thee.*** For behold darkness shall cover the earth, and a mist the people: but ***the Lord shall arise upon thee,*** and ***his glory***

shall be seen *upon thee.* And ***the Gentiles shall walk in thy light,*** and ***kings in the brightness of thy rising."*** Isaiah 60:19:*"Thou shalt no more have* ***the sun*** for thy *light by day, neither shall the brightness of the moon enlighten thee:* but ***the Lord shall be unto thee*** *for* ***an everlasting light,*** and *thy God for thy glory."* Isaiah 62:1-3:*"For Sion's sake* I will not hold my peace, and for the sake of Jerusalem, I will not rest till *her* ***just one come forth as brightness,*** and *her* ***saviour*** be ***lighted as a lamp.*** And ***the Gentiles shall see thy just one,*** and *all kings* ***thy glorious one:*** and *thou shalt be called by a* ***new name,*** *which the mouth of the Lord shall name.* And *thou shalt be a crown of glory in the hand of the Lord,* and *a royal diadem* in the hand of God." So, have *the Gentiles seen - thy just one?*

And finally, in Isaiah 66:15:*"For behold* ***the Lord will come with fire...*** *and his rebuke with* ***flames of fire."*** In the above verses I only added the words within parenthesis for clarity. I hope this made it clearer for you. Many other prophets also give *glory to* ***the light*** of the Lord God.

In Baruch 4:1-2:"This is the book of the commandments of God, and ***the law,*** that is for ever: *all they that keep it, shall come to life:* but they that have forsaken it, to death. Return O Jacob, and take hold of it, *walk in* ***the way*** *by its* ***brightness, in the presence of the light*** *thereof."* Baruch 5:9:*"For God* will bring Israel with joy in ***the light*** of *his majesty, with mercy, and justice,* that cometh from him." In the glorious vision of Ezekiel we can see a glimpse of *the light* and glory of God. Ezekiel 1:25-27:*"For* when ***a voice*** came from *above the firmament,* that was over their heads...And above the firmament ...was the *likeness of a throne,* as the appearance of the sapphire stone, and ***upon the likeness of the throne,*** was a likeness as of the ***appearance of a man*** above upon it. And I saw as it were the resemblance of amber as the ***appearance of fire*** within it ***round about:*** from his loins and upward, and from his loins downward, I saw as it were ***the resemblance of fire shining round about."*** Recall, *the description of Jesus* by the seminarian.

The story of three righteous men (Sidrach, Misach and Abdenago) that were thrown into *the burning furnace* by King Nabuchodonosor as is written in the Book of Daniel is indeed very revealing as to the true divinity and glory of the Son of God. Daniel 3:91-92: "Then Nabuchodonosor the king was astonished, and rose up in haste, and said to his nobles: Did we not *cast three men bound* into ***the fire****?* They answered the king, and said: True, O king. He answered, and said: Behold *I see four men loose, and walking in the midst of the fire,* and *there is no hurt in them,* and ***the form of the fourth is like the Son of God."*** Later, Daniel ***beholds a man,*** Daniel 10:5-6:"...and ***his face*** as the ***appearance of lightning,*** and ***his eyes*** as ***a burning lamp..."*** *Who* is this *man?* Hosea 6:3:"...***on the third day he will raise*** *us up,* and we shall live in his sight. We shall know, and we shall follow on, that we may know *the Lord.* ***His going forth is prepared as the morning light,*** and ***he will come to us as the early and the latter rain to the earth."*** Sophonias 3:8:*"Wherefore* ***expect me, saith the Lord, in the day of my resurrection*** that is to come...for ***with the fire of my jealousy shall all the earth be devoured."*** Finally, in Micah 7:8: *"...**I shall arise,** when I sit in darkness,* ***the Lord is my light."***

C. In the New Testament the Gospel of John Chapter 1, we clearly see a man sent by God to be a *witness to give testimony* of **the light,** *the true light of the world.* This man's name was John *(called John the Baptist).* John 1:1-10: *"In the beginning* was *the Word,* and *the Word was with God,* and *the Word was God.* The same was in the beginning with God. All things were made by him: and without him was made nothing that was made. *In him (the Word) was life*, and **the life** *was* ***the light of men.*** And **the light** *shineth in darkness, and the darkness did not comprehend it.* There was a man sent from God, whose name was John. This man came for a *witness, to give testimony of the light, that all men might believe through him. He was not the light, but was to give testimony of* **the light.** *That was* ***the true light,*** *which enlighteneth every man that cometh into this world. He was in the world, and* ***the world was made by him,*** *and the world knew him not."* John identifies *Jesus* as **the light** and *the Word of God (Wisdom).* Now in the next few verses, we will see *Who* – the *Word of God* and *the light* truly is.

According to John 1:11-18: *"He (the light)* came unto his own *(the Jews),* and *his own received him not. But as many as received him, he gave them power to be made the sons of God, to them that believe in his name. Who are born,* not of blood, nor of the will of the flesh, nor of the will of man, but *of God.* And ***the Word was made flesh, and dwelt among us,*** *(and we saw his glory,* the glory as it were of ***the only begotten of the Father,) full of grace and truth.*** *John beareth witness of him,* and crieth out, saying: This was he of whom I spoke: *He that shall come after me, is preferred before me: because he was before me.* And of his fullness we all have received, and grace for grace. For *the law was given by Moses;* ***grace*** *and* ***truth*** *came by Jesus Christ. No man hath seen God* at any time: *the only begotten Son who is in the bosom of the Father, he hath declared him."* For more insight into John the Baptist's *witness of Who Jesus* really and truly *is,* read John 1:28-34: "...in Bethania, beyond the Jordan, where John was baptizing...John saw *Jesus coming* to him, and he saith: ***Behold the Lamb of God , behold him who taketh away the sin of the world.*** This is he, of whom I said: After me there cometh a man, who is preferred before me: because he was before me. And I knew him not, but that he may be made manifest in *Israel,* therefore am I come baptizing with water. And *John gave testimony, saying: I saw* **the Spirit coming down, as a dove from heaven,** *and he (the Holy Spirit)* ***remained upon him*** *(Jesus).* And I knew him not; but *he (God) who sent me to baptize with water,* said to me: He upon whom thou shalt see *the Spirit* descending, and remaining upon him, *he it is that baptizeth with the Holy Ghost (Holy Spirit).* And *I saw, and I gave testimony*, that **this is the Son of God."** Wow! John the Baptist was a true eye witness to *"the Spirit coming down, as a dove from heaven"* descending and remaining upon *Jesus, the Son of God.*

In the Book of John Chapter 3, *Jesus* has an encounter with a man of the Pharisees named *Nicodemus,* a ruler of the Jews. Here *Jesus* teaches on the subject matter concerning *the Son of God* and **the light.** John 3:16-21:*"For God* so loved the world, as to give his only begotten Son; that *whosoever believeth in him, may not perish, but may have life everlasting.* For *God sent not his Son into the world, to judge the world, but that the world may be saved by him.* He that believeth in him is not judged. But he that doth not believe, is already judged: because he believeth not in the name of the only begotten Son of God. And this is the judgment: because ***the light is come into the world,*** and men loved darkness rather than *the light:* for their works were evil. For every one that doth evil hateth *the light,* and cometh not to *the light,* that his works may not be reproved. But ***he that doth truth, cometh to the light, that*** his works may be made manifest, because they are done *in God." Jesus* says it best in a famous verse of John 8:12:*"...**I am the light of the world:** he that followeth me, walketh not in darkness, but shall have **the light of life."*** John 12:35-36:*"Jesus* therefore said to them*:* Yet a little while, ***the light*** is among you. Walk whilst you have *the light,* that the darkness overtake you not. And he that walketh in darkness, knoweth not wither he goeth. Whilst you have *the light,* ***believe in the light,*** that you may be *the children of light..." The Messiah, the Christ Jesus* is described vividly by John in Rev 1:13-16:"And in the midst of *the seven golden* ***candlesticks,*** one like *the Son of man...* and his eyes were as ***a flame of fire,*** And *his feet* unto fine brass, as in ***a burning furnace.*** And *his voice as the sound of many waters.* And *he had in his right hand seven* ***stars.*** And *from his mouth came out* ***a sharp two edged sword:*** and ***his face* was *as the sun*** *shineth in his power."* And finally, in Rev 22:16*:"I Jesus...* ***I am*** the root and stock of David, ***the bright and morning star."*** Wow! ***Jesus is*** *indeed* ***– "the light."***

Reflections on "the light" and Wisdom

I am not a physicist, but I did complete 1 year of pre-med physics. Now ponder this. Scientists in the realm of physics today are scrambling to come up with a *grand unified wave theory* to explain how the universe really works. Of great interest to all of us is that *light or light particles* called **photons** may in fact be *the cornerstone for every creation in the entire universe.* Can you imagine the implications? Examples of this are in the subatomic particles, atomic structures, galactic formations, genes, DNA and even *thought* as a process of electromagnetic wavelengths that travel within the brain's complex circuitry of neuro-connections and neuronal pathways. Where does the *evolution theory* go on the subject matter of *light?* Nowhere. Interestingly, in the *creation theory* God, the Almighty Creator, actually says *His first* ***word*** ever recorded - in Genesis 1:3:*"Be* ***light*** made. And *light* was made." How about that for a *Big Bang!* So, is *God's Word light?* See in Gen 1:4:"And *God* saw *the light* that it was *good..."* So, ***the light*** was ***good.*** In the *eyes of God - good is* ***life.*** Recall as it is written in Deut. 30:15:*"…I have set* before thee *life* and *good,* and on the other hand *death* and *evil."*

Now carefully re-reading the last section **III "the light"– energy**, we can see how ***the light*** *of God* **is** synonymous with: *"the burning furnace," "the lamp of fire," "a flame of fire," "a fire," "a flame," "the sun," "the bright and morning star," "the morning light," "the day star," "the true light," "a great light," "brightness of eternal light," "lightning," "an everlasting light," etc.* We can also see how ***the light*** *of God* ***is*** *synonymous with* **the word of God/wisdom** - starting with the *first word spoken by God* in Gen1:3:*"Be* ***light*** made." So, ***God's Word is light, a living light!*** In Proverbs 30:5:*"Every word of God* is ***fire*** *tried…"* Wisdom 6:23:*"Love* ***the light*** *of wisdom…"* Wisdom 7:24-26***:"For wisdom is more active than all active things:*** and ***reacheth everywhere*** *by reason of her purity.* For *she (wisdom) is a vapour of the power of God,* and *a certain pure emanation of the glory of the almighty God:* and therefore no defiled thing cometh into her. For *she* ***(wisdom) is the brightness of eternal light,*** and *the unspotted mirror of God's majesty,* and *the image of his* ***goodness."*** Ecclesiasticus 1:5, 9-10*:"**The word of God on high is the fountain of wisdom,** and **her ways** are **everlasting commandments** …He (Father God)* created *her (wisdom) in the Holy Ghost (the Holy Spirit),* and saw her, and numbered her, and measured her. And *he (God) poured her (wisdom) out upon all his works, and upon all flesh according to his gift,* and *hath given her (wisdom) to them that love him (God)."*

So, we can see above that ***the word of God*** *is* in fact ***wisdom*** = ***"the brightness of eternal light,"*** *which is* indeed ***the light of God.*** In Proverbs 8:22-35: *"The Lord* possessed *me (wisdom)* in *the beginning of his ways, before he made any thing from the beginning. I (wisdom)* was *set up from eternity,* and *of old before the earth* was made. *The depths* were not as yet, and *I (wisdom/the word of God /the light)* was already conceived, neither had *the fountains of waters* as yet sprung out…*He (God)* had not yet made *the earth…*When *he (God)* prepared *the heavens, I (wisdom) was present:* when with a certain law and compass *he (God)* enclosed *the depths…* When *he (God) established the sky above,* and *poised the fountains of waters:* When *he (God) compassed the sea with its bounds,* and *set a law to the waters* that they should not pass there limits: when *he (God) balanced the foundations of the earth; I (wisdom) was with him (God) forming all things*: and was delighted every day, *playing before him (God)* at all times; Playing in the world: and *my (wisdom's) delights were to be with the children of men…Blessed are they that keep my ways (**the way** of wisdom)… Blessed is the man that heareth me (wisdom),* and *that watcheth daily at my gates,* and *waiteth at the posts of my doors (**the door** of wisdom). He that shall find me (wisdom), shall find* ***life,*** *and shall have* ***salvation*** *from the Lord…"*

Notice above how once again ***wisdom*** *is a person* in these extraordinary verses from Solomon's Proverbs. So, *just* ***Who is this person*** called ***wisdom*** *(the*

Word of God/the light) that existed before heaven and *earth was formed in the beginning "from eternity"* and *"of old?"* Could this *person called wisdom* indeed possibly be *the Son of the living God?* Recall that in Genesis 1:1 the written name of God in Hebrew is *Elohim (the Hebrew plural noun for God: Gods): "In the beginning God (Elohim/Gods) created heaven, and earth."* Now again, re-read Proverbs 30:4:*"Who* hath *ascended up into heaven,* and *descended? Who* hath bound up the waters together as in a garment? *Who* hath raised up all the borders of the earth? ***What is his name,*** and ***what is the name of his son,*** if thou knowest?" In Proverbs 30:5:*"Every* ***word of God*** *(wisdom/the light)* is ***fire tried*** *(that is,* ***most pure****, like gold purified by fire)..."* Could it be that **"*the name of his son"* is = to *wisdom/the Word of God/the light?*** So, ***just Who* is *this person, the Son of God?*** If you believe in *One God* as I do, then *wisdom/the Word of God/the light* was and is *not only with God from the beginning,* but must also *be God from eternity* and *of old.* ***God's Word*** is not only part of *God* - but ***was, is and will always be God/ One with God.*** *In Holy Scriptures* ***wisdom/the Word of God/the light is:*** *"the brightness of eternal light," "the image of His goodness," "a vapour of the power of God," "the unspotted mirror of God's majesty," and the "pure emanation of the glory of the Almighty God"* (Wisdom 7:24-26). In Ecclesiasticus 1:9:*"He (God)* created *her (wisdom) in the Holy Ghost (Holy Spirit)."* So, *wisdom/the Word/the light* - was, is and always will be - ***God.*** *Father God opens His mouth* and *speaks His first Word* ever recorded in Genesis 1:3: ***"light"*** and in Genesis 1:4: *"...God* saw *the light* that it was ***good (life)..."*** Now can you imagine *what* happens when *God's Word/wisdom/the light* - the most pure *active creative living energetic matter* along with *God's* all powerful *living breath (breath of life: the Holy Spirit)* becomes simultaneously animated unto a *life giving holy flesh and blood* as *the personification of wisdom, the Son of God?* And those who find *wisdom, the Son of God, "shall find* ***life,*** *and shall have* ***salvation*** *from the Lord (Proverbs 8:35)." So Who* is *the Son of the living God-the Word-wisdom-****the light****? Who is* ***"the life"*** *and* ***salvation*** as it is written in Holy Scriptures? *What* is his name? **Hint:** According to our new medical and scientific studies, meticulously performed, *His living words in the light* spoken by *Jesus in light* and *His Living Presence* both produced/evoked the same amazing, unprecedented and astonishing *new data.* Both manifestations generated the same powerful source of energy with ***the light*** detected. Thus, *His Living Words in light* and *His Living Presence in light* are *One.* See Jeremiah 23:9. Recall, *in Hebrew* **the name *Jesus* means *salvation*** or ***God saves****; saves our* ***life.***

In the New Testament John the Gospel writer is an eyewitness to the ministry life, passion, crucifixion, death and resurrection of *the Christ Jesus.* John was one of the three eyewitnesses to actually *see the kingdom of God while still on earth* at Mt. Tabor during *the transfiguration of Jesus* with a *deep sleep* (sounds familiar). Later after the resurrection of Jesus, John was briefly on taken up to heaven and over a time given the prophetic words to write in the Book of Revelation. Recall in

John 1:1:*"In the beginning* was *the Word,* and *the Word was with God,* and *the Word was God."* Clearly just like in Solomon's writings on *wisdom* this verse personifies *the* W*ord of God* as being *One with God* and *being God* Himself. Now carefully read John 1:3-4:"All things were made by him *(the Word):* and without him *(the Word)* was made nothing that was made. **In him *(the Word)* was life,** and ***the life*** *was* **the light of men."** *Jesus* Himself says in John 4:24*:* ***"God is a spirit..."***

So, if *"God is a spirit"* and *the Word of God* **is** *God;* and *"the word of God"* **is** *wisdom;* and *wisdom* **is** *"the brightness of eternal light," "a vapour of* the *power of God," "a certain pure emanation of the glory of the almighty God," "the unspotted mirror of God's majesty, and the image of his goodness* (Wisdom 7:25-26)*,"* then we can say that ***the Word*** *of God,* ***the life*** *and wisdom* **is** *God,* ***the light*** *of men.* Thus, *the Word of God – the life - the light - wisdom* **is** *One with the spirit of God* and **is** *"more active than all active things: and reacheth everywhere by reason of her purity* (Wisdom 7:24)*." Ecclesiasticus 1:9-10: "He (God) created her (wisdom) in the Holy Ghost"* and **is** *"poured...out upon all his (God's) works, and upon all flesh according to his (God's) gift."* Thus, ***the light*** *of God,* which is, was and will always be *God, is in everything - that is.* Now, just ponder this and think about ***photons.***

In physics *a photon* is composed of two main loops (fields), one transverse and one perpendicular *(forming* ***a cross of light****),* which together create *a single wave* particle *(with three colors or wavelengths per loop)* and is composed of the smallest known formation of organized ***active*** *energetic (electro-magnetic) matter. In astronomy* observers see that galaxies decay just like other *objects decay into a photon formation.* Scientists believe *this means that* ***the photon*** *is composed of basic, pure, and essential active energetic matter. The photon* may in fact actually be ***the primary raw formation of all active energetic matter.*** Since *the photon* is also known to be in perpetual movement, scientists believe that the natural behavior of energetic matter (*the photon* or *the light* particle) is one of continuous activity and also *continuous creative living activity.* Thus, many physicists today believe *energetic matter* like **the photon** or **the light** *particle* is the ***most active*** and ***creative living matter.*** Again just think of all the *active* and *creative living matter* implications presented here. So, with the above scientific understanding of *the photon* or *the light particle,* it really makes more sense to me *now* when I read the following verses like in Proverbs 20:27: ***"The spirit of a man* is *the lamp* (the light) *of the Lord,*** which *searcheth all the hidden things of the bowels."* In Wisdom 7:24*:"For wisdom* (the word of God/the light) *is more active than all active things..."* Wow! **The life** in ***the Word*** *of God/* ***wisdom/ the light*** *of the Lord* **is** *One with God's Spirit* and is in everything that is and *"is more active than all active things."* That is *why* it says in Wisdom 12:1:*"O how good* and sweet is *thy spirit, O Lord, in all things."* In other translations: *"For your imperishable spirit is in all things."*

So, we see that *the Word of God* **is** *the light* or *light particles (photons) in all things.* Since *the spirit of a man* **is** *the light* or *the lamp of the Lord (God) that* **is** *in* *all things,* then this may help explain *what* is written in the following verses. Isaiah 9:8:*"The Lord* sent a ***word*** into Jacob, and it *hath* ***lighted*** *upon Israel."* In John 1:14: *"...****the Word was made flesh, and dwelt among us...full of grace and truth."*** If *Jesus* **is** *the Word of God "made flesh"* (John 1:14) and ***the Word*** *of God/the Bible/* the *Holy Scriptures* ***is light,*** then one of the unpublished and undated messages *Jesus* gave to Nancy rings so true: *"I Am light. Without My light the world is in complete and total darkness. There is no other light. I Am light."* So, *Jesus* **is** truly *"the light of the world"* (John 8:12).

Each the following phrases in Hebrew: ***"the light,"*** *"the law," "Moses our teacher," and "the Lord God of Israel,"* has a value of **613.** Amazingly, the number 613 is equal to the same number of commandments, laws, decrees, precepts and statutes--- all totaling 613--- as written in the Holy Bible, *the Torah* (five Books of Moses). **613** is also the *number of knots* in the Hebrew prayer shawl, *the Tallit.* Please remember and ponder that we recorded ***the light*** on June 13th, 1993--- (**6/13**/1993). Is this *yet* another co-incidence or another *God-incidence?*

Many physicists believe that perhaps all *active* energetic (electro-magnetic) matter (waves) ---as independent single-waves (quantum) of energy--- actually composes everything. Astronomers and physicists also believe that galaxies create stars, stars create atoms and atoms create molecules that create all the structures we know. It can then be postulated that all *active* energetic matter (*the photons* or ***the light*** *particles*) probably help to create everything that is. So, *Who is the Creator of light?* Of interest, *light (photons)* has no place in the *theory of evolution.*

Now, a very important observation and clear distinction must be and needs to be made about ***the light of God.*** According to Genesis 1:1-3, *"In the beginning,* God**..."** *Elohim first* created *the matrix* or rather *the raw building blocks for all life to begin* as we know it in these first three verses. *First verse: "In the beginning, God (Elohim) created heaven, and earth." Second verse: "And the earth was void and empty, and darkness was upon the face of the deep; and the spirit of God moved over the waters." Third verse: "And God said: Be light made. And light was made."* Now take careful notice of the first verse of Genesis. See how the *Hebrew* plural noun version of God, *Elohim = Gods (the Holy Trinity/the One Triune God*; as drawn by David in the *Star of David)* is used. *Elohim first* created *time* and then created the raw material and building blocks for *life* using *"heaven, and earth."* Then *second, "the spirit of God (the Holy Spirit)* moved over *the waters."* So, God created *"the waters" and the wind--- as He moved over the waters.* In medicine and science *water* is the most basic and necessary liquid matrix for all *life* forms to be sustained *in, through and with. Water* is *the purest solvent in all living things.* Then *third,* "And God said: Be *light* made. And *light* was made.*" God (Elohim)* must have existed before *the beginning,* since **God first created time** *in Genesis 1:1 verse:* ***"In the beginning."*** *Elohim/Gods as written* in the Bible is ***"the*** *purest holiest* ***light"*** *that always existed from eternity.* So, *what* is *the light* that *"was made?"* Obviously a definite and clear distinction must be made between *the light* of *Elohim* (Gods: plural noun) - *the* ***uncreated*** *eternal light that always existed before time was made* (Wisdom 7: 29) and *God's* ***created*** *light (photons and the light particles).*

Now see if you can guess which of the two is ***the light*** we recorded and documented *repeatedly* in our scientific studies - *in His Living Presence*? In search of the answer to this important question, I found some Bible verses that may hopefully help shed some *light* on this matter. In the Book of Wisdom Chapter 7, King Solomon son of David makes the distinction between *the light* of *wisdom (the word of God)* and God's *created light.* In Wisdom 7:10, Solomon says: *"I loved her (wisdom)* above health and beauty, and chose to have *her (wisdom) instead of light*: for *her* ***(wisdom's) light cannot be put out."*** In Wisdom 7:29, he says*: "For her (wisdom)* is ***more beautiful*** **than** ***the sun,*** and ***above*** **all the order of** ***the stars:*** **being** ***compared with the light,*** *she* ***(wisdom) is found before it."***

So, we can clearly see how ***the light of God*** *(Elohim)* and *God's Eternal Word/Wisdom* is indeed *different from* ***God's created light*** which is emitted from *the sun/the stars/photons. The light of God* is an *everlasting light, "the brightness of eternal light"* (Wisdom 7:26) that *"cannot be put out"* (Wisdom 7:10). This is in stark contrast obviously to *created light that can be put out* like a dying star or a fire or flame. In the Book of Revelation 21:9-11, John was shown *"the bride, the wife of the Lamb"* and was taken *"up in spirit* to a great and high mountain: and he shewed me *(John)* the *holy city Jerusalem coming down out of heaven from God,* Having the glory of God, and *the light* thereof..." In Rev 21:22-25 John then says: *"And I saw* no temple therein. For *the Lord God Almighty is the temple thereof, and the Lamb.* And *the city hath no need of* **the sun,** *nor of the moon,* to shine in it. For ***the glory of God*** **hath** ***enlightened*** **it, and** ***the Lamb*** **is** ***the lamp*** **thereof.** And the nations shall walk in *the light* of it...for there shall be *no more night there."* This is exciting. God's *created light* is but a *mire glimpse of God's true reflection.* Mankind, man the creature and all of creation is a *reflection of God*---as in the *Star of David.*

God's *created light* is ***the light*** that is *seen* (3% visible light) *and unseen* (97% invisible light) of the *entire light radiation energy field spectrum* and also *the light* that is *in all active creative energetic matter,* recall *photons* and *the light particles* information given above. God's *created light* is *the light* of *the sun with* reflections of the *moon* and *the stars, the lightning* that we see in electrical thunderstorms and even all the *lamps of fire.* So, *what* did we measure? I believe **God's** ***created light*** **is** ***the light*** we ***measured*** in our scientific studies. **God's** ***uncreated*** *eternal* ***light,*** *"the brightness of eternal light"* (Wisdom 7:26), the essence and *"pure emanation of the glory of the Almighty God"* (Wisdom 7:25), *wisdom/the word of God/the Eternal Word* **is** ***immeasurable!*** *God's uncreated light is way beyond our ability to measure (Wisdom 7:29)* ***just like God's love and mercy is immeasurable.***

I believe it is *the uncreated eternal light* that always existed - that is *the spirit of man* and is *"that by which he (man) is most especially in God's image"* (CCC: 363).

As it is written in Proverbs 20:27: *"The spirit of a man* is *the lamp (the light) of the Lord (God), which searcheth all the hidden things of the bowels (the spirit/within)."* Thus, *man's life* is very *blessed and sacred to God* and indeed different from all other living creatures, since we have the *immeasurable uncreated everlasting eternal living light of God within us.* This is confirmed in Genesis 1:26 where *God (Elohim)* says*: "Let us* make man to *our image and likeness..."* And God, so wonderful in all *His works* especially *in man,* is singularly exalted by the *Incarnation of Christ Jesus, the Son of God.* We can see in David's psalm a confirmation of man's nature in creation. Psalm 8:4-8: *"For I will behold thy heavens,* and *the works* of *thy fingers: the moon* and *the stars* which thou hast founded. *What* is *man* that *thou art mindful of him?* Or *the son of man that thou visitest him?* Thou hast *made him a little less than the angels,* thou hast *crowned him with glory and honour:* and hast *set him (man) over the works of thy hands.* Thou hast *subjected all things under his feet..."* So, it is ***the works*** *of God, His Almighty created light* and the various awesome *manifestations of the living presence of God to man,* as recorded throughout history, that *we were so blessed to measure* - for *His name's sake, His Divine Will, His wisdom/the living Word, His love & mercy* and *His glory.* For **God's *uncreated eternal light,*** *His Eternal Word, His tender love, His* unfathomable *Divine Mercy, His Divine Will* and awesome *everlasting glory* **is *immeasurable.***

Now a short message *Jesus* gave Nancy way before we even started the *baseline medical and scientific tests* in 1993 makes sense to me. Jesus said, ***"Watch what I will do."***

The *operant word* in this incredibly *prophetic message of future works is* **do.** *Please recall the results of our tests,* the amazing unprecedented and astonishing medical and scientific *new data* collected following *His message.* Again and again for the benefit of mankind so that *man can be saved, Jesus will* ***do*** *the works of God.* In the Gospel of John *Jesus speaks* to his disciples, the multitude and the Jews on different occasions concerning *the works of God.* In John 4:34: *"Jesus* saith to them: ***My meat is to do the will of him*** *(Father God)* ***that sent me, that I may perfect his*** *(Father God's)* ***work."*** In John 5:36: *"But I (Jesus)* have a greater testimony than that of John *(the Baptist):* for *the works* which *the Father hath given me to perfect; the works themselves, which I do, give testimony of me,* that *the Father hath sent me."* In John 6:28-29 the multitude said to Jesus: *"...*What shall we *do,* that we may *work* the *works of God?* Jesus answered, and said to them: *This is the work of God,* that you *believe in him whom he (Father God) hath sent."* In John 9:4-5: ***"I (Jesus) must work the works of him (Father God) that sent me,*** whilst it is day: the night cometh, when no man can *work.* As long as I am in the world, ***I am the light of the world."*** Finally in John 10:37-38: *"If I (Jesus)* do *not* the works of *my Father (God), believe me not.* But if I *do,* though you will not believe me, *believe the works:* that you may *know* and *believe that the Father is in me (Jesus), and I in the Father (God)."* Throughout the history of mankind, our merciful *God* continues to love man beyond measure and way beyond our understanding or comprehension. *God the Almighty* has given us many memorable manifestations of *His awesome power and glory,* and *His miraculous works* among man *in His Living Presence,* as it is written in the Holy Bible. I believe *it is these same* awesome *manifestations of God's living presence,* made known to *man* through ***the holy word of God*** *given to Moses* and *the prophets, whom God is now* so generously *permitting us to measure* - using our medical and scientific equipment. Can you imagine, *God* actually allowed us to record ***His tangible living presence.*** *Why?*

Recall the *Blessed Virgin Mary's* first message to America, Sept. 2nd, 1990:

"There is too little faith here. I am very sad." Maybe this is *why.*

I believe God's *created light* is responsible for *the light show* extravaganza witnessed and recorded during the medical and scientific tests done on Nancy and the *chosen souls.* In our modern day society where *faith* is so hard to find, especially within the medical and scientific community, *the light* show extravaganza is *just what the Divine Healer - the Great Physician* ordered. I believe *God* wants to increase our *faith, hope* and *trust in Him.* So, now I ask: Was there another form of *light* present during the scientific tests - *in His Living Presence* that Nancy and the other *chosen souls* witnessed, which we simply could *not measure?* The answer to this last question is most emphatically – **yes!** For God's *uncreated eternal light* **is** *immeasurable* (Wisdom 7:29) and also written in Wisdom 7:10: *"cannot be put out."*

I believe *God in His* relentless *insatiable love for man* has allowed the results of our medical and scientific studies to match so closely with the recorded manifestations of *God's living presence in the Bible* just to help us *build a great case with good solid evidence that demands a verdict* on the *One Who He sent, Jesus the Messiah, the Christ.* Just ponder this. *The Almighty God Creator of heaven and earth,* even took on willingly the full price of *our redemption for all our sins,* to the point of accepting death on *a tree /a cross,* so that *man* (you and I) can have a chance at acquiring *salvation* and *eternal life.* Recall, *the light of God* **is** *the living fire of God* and *the living Word of God* (Gen 1:3). Remember, the *voice* is made up of three elements: *wind, water* and *fire.* So, *the Breath of God - the Rua -* as *Father God opens His mouth* and *breathes* is presented as *the wind* which moved over *the (living) waters (the rain/the dew)* and both represent *the Holy Spirit of God* and *the power of the Most High Almighty God.* Now comes the most creative *living word of God – light,* the *living fire of God* in Gen 1:3. With those three elements: *wind, water* and *fire*: *"their* voices *(voices of God)...Their sound* hath gone forth into all the earth (Psalm 18: 4-5)." David must have known *the Holy Trinity – the One Triune God.* Imagine *as God speaks, the Lord* ***creates photons, the light*** **particles**: *the primary raw formation of all active energetic creative living matter!*

So, *what* is *"the light?"* The best answer is written in John 1:1-5 (thank you St. Jerome), please read it slowly. In John 1:3-4:"All things were made by *him (the*

Word/the light): and without *him (the Word/the light)* was made nothing that was made. In *him (the Word/ the light)* was *life*, and ***the life*** was ***the light* of men.*"** Now this requires ***wisdom***, imagine *what* a ***Big Bang*** *God created with His* ***Word,*** Gen 1:3:*"Be* **light** *made."* Sorry evolution. Sorry atheists. Now *through the eyes of science* herself, I can see *wisdom* in the words written in John 1:1:*"In the beginning* was *the Word (the light),* and *the Word (the light)* was *with God,* and *the Word (the light)* was *God."* Maybe, this is *why Jesus* said to Nancy, *"I am light."* Please note, I added the words in parenthesis for clarity in the verses above. So, ***Jesus in light is:*** *God saves, the Messiah, the Christ,* **the Eternal Word,** *the way, the truth and* ***the life,*** *the light of God, the light of the world, wisdom and* ***the light of men.***

IV. "The *living* word of God"

A. All our medical and scientific studies have repeatedly and clearly demonstrated that whenever *Jesus speaks* whether *audibly* or *interiorly* to Nancy or the seminarian, *His living words in the light* actually produces or evokes the amazing unprecedented *new data* already mentioned meticulously throughout this book in association with all the *supernatural events - in His Living Presence.* Recall *the light show* extravaganza recorded and documented by Dr. Callahan and Dr. Velasquez during the *heavenly visits, visions* or *apparitions* and all the medical and neurophysiological studies of the *chosen souls* recorded by me and later by Dr. Agosto and Dr. Dalmau when *Jesus speaks.* Let us not forget the very thorough psychiatric evaluations performed by Dr. Hogben or the neuropsychophysiological studies done by Prof. Castanon clearly demonstrating no evidence of any mental illness or psychiatric pathology *before, during or after the heavenly visits.* Recall the astonishing *deep sleep stages with awake and alert EEG topographic patterns* associated with the now famous mathematical and numerical sequence of **333!** This EEG pattern of 333 was indeed repeatedly evoked with every specific stimulus of *Jesus speaking His living words in the light* - to Nancy and the seminarian.

Question: So, what does *Jesus* and "*the* (living) *word of God*" have in common?

B. Starting with Genesis, remember that *God's* first *word* and *voice* spoken in *the beginning* --- was *light.* Gen 1:3*: "Be light made..."* In Gen 1:4: *"And God saw* ***the light*** *that it was* ***good...*"** Then, we see in Exodus 20:18*: "And all the people (the children of Israel) saw the voices* and *the flames..."* While *God spoke to Moses from heaven* and wrote down the *Ten Commandments* with *the finger of God/ flames of burning fire of God's voices/ God's words of light,* the children of Israel were *"terrified and struck with fear, and stood far off..."* Repeatedly throughout *the Torah* it is written: *"And the Lord* said to *Moses (face to face) ..."* This is in contrast to how *God* communicates with the *other prophets of the Lord.* Frequently prophets like Isaiah write, *"And I heard* ***the voice*** of the Lord, saying: ..." And Jeremiah writes: *"And* ***the word*** *of the Lord* came to me, saying: ..." Though not face to face, *God's voice* and *word* came to all the prophets as it is written in the Holy Books. Both *the voice of the Lord (the voice of God as God speaks) and the word of the Lord (the word of God)* ***is*** indeed ***light.*** A secretary learned in *the law,* a man of noble extraction and a disciple of the prophet Jeremiah was named Baruch. He wrote one of the best verses that describe *the word of God.* See Baruch 4:1-2: "This is *the book of the commandments of God (the word of God),* and *the law,* that is for ever: *all they that keep it, shall come to* ***life:*** but they that have forsaken it, to death. Return, O Jacob, and take hold of it, ***walk in the way*** *by its brightness,* ***in the presence of the light*** thereof." This last verse clearly illustrates the magnitude, majesty and glory of ***the word of God.*** *The word of God* is *the law and the light of God.* In Ecclesiasticus 1:5: *"The word of God* on high is *the fountain of* ***wisdom,*** and her *ways* are ***everlasting commandments."*** Proverbs 30:5:*"Every* ***word*** *of God is* ***fire tried***..." Wisdom 6:23: *"Love the light* of wisdom *(the word of God)..."* Wisdom 7:26: *"For she (wisdom/the word of God)* is the *brightness of* ***eternal light***...*the image of his (God's)* ***goodness."*** Again recall that ***God equates life with good*** as it is written in Deuteronomy 30:15: *"Consider that I (God)* have set before thee this day ***life*** *and* ***good,*** and on the other hand *death and evil."* Again reviewing the Holy Scriptures ***good*** *or* ***goodness*** in the eyes of God is ***life or living.*** Now go back and check out Genesis 1:4: *"And God* saw ***the light (the*** *first* ***word of God*** *ever spoken)* that it *was* ***good..."*** So, ***in the light/the Word was life.***

We know from Holy Scriptures that *the word of God* is ***the truth*** *and* ***just,*** since in Hebrew *"to do* ***truth****"* is *"to do what is* ***just****"* or ***righteous*** or *"to do* ***justice."*** So, then ***the word of God*** is ***the light, the way, the truth*** and ***the life*** or ***living*** for all of us simply because it is ***good*** in God's eyes. Now recall a famous verse that truly magnifies *what it means* to say ***the living word of God,*** as it is written in Deuteronomy 8:3: *"He* afflicted thee with want, and *gave thee* ***manna*** *for thy food,* which neither thou nor thy fathers knew: to shew that ***not in bread alone doth man live, but in every word that proceedeth from the mouth of God."*** So, man *lives - in every word spoken by God,* because *there is* ***life*** *in every word of God.* Since ***there is life in the Word of God,*** *we can say - this is* ***the living Word of God.*** Psalms and Proverbs are *full of wisdom* that adds to the purity, glory and magnificence of *the living word of God.* Psalm 11:7: ***"The words of the Lord*** are ***pure words***: as silver ***tried by the fire,*** purged from the earth, ***refined seven times."*** Psalm 18:2-5:*"The heavens shew forth the glory of God,* and the firmament declareth the work of his hands. Day to day *uttereth* speech, and night to night sheweth knowledge. *There are no speeches nor languages, where* ***their voices*** *(the voices of God/Elohim/Father, Son and Holy Spirit) are not heard.* ***Their sound hath gone forth into all the earth:*** and ***their words unto the ends of the world".***

In *the beginning* (Gen1:3:*"Be* ***light*** *made"),* we know that ***the voices of God*** *"uttereth"* ***the first sound, the Word of God – light!*** Please ponder *the creation theory and photons or light particles in the grand unified wave theory.* Sorry evolution. Sorry atheists. Now, how about that for a **Big Bang!**

Here I unwittingly uncovered or discovered *the truth* about what is meant by *the life giving and living* **Word of God** after combining all the *hardcore science* available with amazing *Holy Bible connections* as it is written. *Wow!* What a *revelation* this was and is for me. And hopefully this will also be a *source of revelation and truth* for you too as you *journey science to faith.* Now as we continue to journey see Psalm 32:4, 6, 9:*"For the word of the Lord* is *right (truth/just)...*By *the word of the Lord (the Word of God/Jesus) the heavens* were established; and *all the power* of *them ("their voices"/Elohim* created *"the heavens")* by *the spirit (the Holy Spirit) of his (Father God's) mouth...*For he *(Father God) spoke (the Word of God/Jesus)* and *they were made:* he *(Father God) commanded* and *they were created."* Can you see *the Holy Trinity of God* - the One Triune God - concealed here in this second verse 32:6? Again I added the words in parenthesis for clarity only. Psalm 67:12:*"The Lord* shall give ***the word*** to them that preach *good (life) tidings with great power."* I suspect this is what *evangelization* throughout the world, and preaching *the gospel* ***good news*** of a *just* redeeming *Saviour (Jesus)* and *eternal salvation through him* - is all about. In the New Testament *Jesus often speaks in parables.* See a prophetic verse foretelling that *God* will speak *in parables* to his people, in Psalm 77:1-2:"Attend, O my people, to *my law:* incline your ears to *the words of my mouth.* I will open my mouth *in parables:* I will *utter propositions* from ***the beginning."*** Also, see *the works of the word* in Psalm 88:35:*"Neither will I profane my covenant*: and *the words that proceed from my mouth I will not make void."* Isaiah 55:10-11 also makes this point clearly as we shall see below. Psalm 106:20: *"He (Father God) sent his* ***word*** *(Jesus),* and ***healed them:*** and *delivered them* from their destructions*."* A famous Psalm verse concerning *the word of God* is now one of my favorites too, Psalm 118 (119):105: **"*Thy word*** *(Jesus)* ***is a lamp to my feet, and a light to my paths."*** Proverbs 6:23:*"Because the commandment* is *a lamp,* and *the law a light,* and the reproofs of instruction are ***the way of life."*** Again we see such strong connections with *the word of God* as *a lamp* or *a light that shows us the way of life. Also* ***the Word of God*** *is life giving /living, thus a true living word.* Proverbs 8:6-8: "...and my lips shall be opened to preach *right* things. My mouth shall meditate *truth,* and my lips shall hate wickedness. ***All my words are just (truth),*** there is nothing wicked nor perverse in them*."* Finally, we revisit *the purity of the word of God* in Proverbs 30:5: ***"Every word of God is fire tried..."*** Thus, ***the Word of God*** **is** *pure life giving,* a *good light,* an *eternal everlasting light* and ***a living light.***

Much of the three + years of the *public ministry of Jesus* over 2,000 years ago were spent on *prayer, teaching the good news, healing* and *miracles.* There are numerous accounts of *Jesus* healing the sick, opening the eyes of the blind, cleansing the lepers, making withered limbs strong, casting out demons, delivering those from destruction of the pit, showing authority over the elements like calming the storms and even raising *the dead asleep.* Indeed, in the New Testament it is correct to say that *Jesus* **is** *the greatest miracle healer* and *wonder worker ever.* Thus, it should not surprise you that in Ecclesiasticus 1:5:"***the word of God*** *on high (Jesus),* is the fountain of ***wisdom,"*** and ***the Word*** *works wonders* and **heals.** See Wisdom 9:11:*"For she (wisdom)* knoweth and understandeth all things, and shall lead me soberly in my *works,* and shall preserve me by her *power."* Wisdom 9:19:"**For by *wisdom* they were *healed,*** whosoever have pleased thee, *O Lord,* from *the beginning."* Wisdom 10:4: *"...**wisdom healed it*** **again,** directing the course of *the just* **by *contemptible wood."*** This last verse foreshadows the *healing* of *the just* by ***the cross*** *(Jesus/wisdom* ***heals,*** *directing the way of the just by contemptible wood - the cross).* If *Jesus* **is** *the Word of God* made flesh (John 1:14) and *the word of God* **is** *wisdom incarnate,* and we see how *the word of God* and *wisdom* ***heals*** in *the Bible,* then it should be *no surprise* to anyone that *Jesus (the Word of God/Wisdom Incarnate)* spent so much of *His* ministry *healing the sick, delivering souls* from destruction and the pit, *preaching good tidings,* while working wondrous *miracles* with *God's* awesome *power* and *love of man - in His Divine Will.*

Now I will conclude this section with some verses from the great prophet Isaiah that may help you to make *holy* connections with *the word of the Lord (God), the light, a (new) covenant, a law, my judgment, a light, my just one, my saviour, my arms, my arm, my salvation, my justice, arm of the Lord, his bread, my mercy, the covenant of my (God's) peace, an everlasting covenant* and *my* ***(God's) word.*** Isaiah 9:8:*"The Lord* sent a ***word*** into Jacob, and it hath ***lighted*** upon Israel.*"* Isaiah 45:23-26:*"...**the word of justice*** shall go out of my mouth, and shall not return: *For every knee shall be bowed to me, and every tongue shall swear.* Therefore shall *he (the word of justice)* say: *In the Lord are my justices* and *empire: they shall come to him,* and *all that resist him shall be confounded. In the Lord shall all the seed of Israel be justified and praised."* So, *Who* is *he (the word of justice)?* Isaiah 49:6, 8:*"...Behold, I have given thee* to be ***the light*** of *the Gentiles, that thou mayest be* my ***salvation*** even to the farthest part of the earth...and *given thee to be* ***a covenant*** *of the people,* that thou mightest *raise up the earth,* and *possess the inheritances that were destroyed."* Isaiah 51:4-6, 9, 14: *"...* for ***a law*** *shall go forth from me,* and ***my judgment*** *shall rest* to be ***a light*** *of the nations.* ***My just one*** is near at hand, ***my saviour*** *is gone forth,* and ***my arms*** shall judge *the people: the islands shall look for me, and shall patiently wait for **my arm**... **my salvation** shall be for ever,* and ***my justice*** shall not fail...Arise, arise, put on strength, O thou ***arm of the Lord,*** *arise as in the days of old,* in the ancient generations. Hast not *thou (Jesus) struck the proud one (Satan), and wounded the dragon?* ...neither shall ***his*** *(Jesus)* ***bread*** *fail."* Isaiah 54:10*: "...**my mercy*** shall not depart from thee, and ***the***

covenant of my peace *shall not be moved:* said the Lord that hath mercy on thee." Isaiah 55:3-5, 10-11: *"Incline your ear* and come to me: *hear* (*the word of God) and your soul shall* **live,** and *I (God) will make* **an everlasting covenant** *with you,* the faithful mercies of David. Behold *I (God)* have given *him (the word of God)* for *a witness* to the people, for *a leader* and *a master to the Gentiles. Behold thou shalt call a nation, which thou knewest not:* and *the nations that knew not thee shall run to thee,* because of *the Lord thy God,* **and** for *the Holy One of Israel,* for *he (the word of God/the Holy One of Israel) hath glorified thee...*And *as* **the rain** (see Numbers 24:7:*"his seed shall be in many waters")* ***and the snow*** *come down from heaven,* and return no more thither, but *soak the earth, and water it,* and *make it to spring, and* ***give seed*** *(Jesus) to the sower,* **and** ***bread*** *(Jesus/the word of God) to the eater:* ***So shall my word be,*** *which shall go forth from my mouth (God's): it (the Word) shall not return to me (God) void, but it (the Word) shall do whatsoever I (God*) please *(His Divine Will),* and *shall prosper in the things for which I (God) sent it (the Word)."* So, *Who* is *the Word,* the *living* word of God, *"the Holy One of Israel," "my just one," "my saviour,"* and *"the covenant of my peace?"* This next section should answer this important, pivotal and crucial *life saving* question.

C. All the four Gospels, Acts, the letters of Paul, James, Peter, John and Jude as well as *The Apocalypse - Book of Revelation* written by John the Apostle make the clearest case in the Bible New Testament that acknowledges ***Jesus is the living Word of God (personified) - "made flesh, and dwelt among us" (John 1:14),*** *"the Son of God," "the Messiah," "the Christ," "the Orient from on high," "the Sun of Justice," "the true light of the world," "the Holy One of Israel," and "the way of peace."* Starting in Luke Chapter 1, we see the famous prophecy of the *Jewish priest Zachary filled with the Holy Spirit* concerning his son named *John (later known as John the Baptist).* The name John was given to Zachary by the angel *(archangel)* of God Gabriel who *appeared to him* during his priestly duties of offering incense in the Temple of the Lord, *"standing on the right side of the altar of incense,"* (Luke 1:9-25). Zachary's wife was *of the daughters of Aaron* named *Elizabeth.* Both were *just* before *God,* barren with no son and advanced in years. Elizabeth was a cousin of Mary, who was the *mother of Jesus.* The *angel Gabriel* said to Zachary, Luke 1:13-17: *"Fear not, Zachary,* for *thy prayer is heard;* and thy wife Elizabeth shall bear thee a son, and thou shalt call his name *John:* And thou shalt have joy and gladness, and many shall rejoice in his nativity. For he shall be *great before the Lord;* and shall drink no wine nor strong drink: and *he shall be filled with the Holy Ghost (Holy Spirit), even from his mother's womb.* And *he shall convert many of the children of Israel to the Lord their God.* And *he shall go before him (the Lord) in the spirit and power of Elijah;* (see Malachi 4:5-6) *that he may turn* the hearts of the fathers unto the children, and *the incredulous to the wisdom of the just* (*"the Sun of justice,"* Malachi 4:2), *to prepare unto the Lord a perfect people."*

But because Zachary was an *old man* advanced in years and *did not believe* these words from *the angel Gabriel who stands before God, Gabriel* said in Luke 1:20: *"And behold,* thou shalt be dumb, and shalt not be able to speak until the day wherein these things shall come to pass*..."* And when the time came Elizabeth brought forth a son. Then on the eighth day came the time to circumcise and to name the child. Zachary wrote on the table, *"saying: John is his name* (Luke 1:63)*."* Luke 1:64:*"*And immediately his *(Zachary's) mouth was opened,* and *his tongue loosed,* and *he spoke, blessing God."*

This miracle occurred while *"Mary (pregnant with Jesus) abode with her about three months"* (Luke 1:56). Filled with *the Holy Spirit* the Jewish priest Zachary prophesied in Luke 1:68-79:***"Blessed be the Lord God of Israel;*** because ***he hath visited*** and ***wrought the redemption of his people*** *(Psalm 73:12):* And *hath raised up an* ***horn of salvation*** to us, *in the* ***house of David*** his servant *(Psalm 131:17; Jeremiah 23:5-6, 30:10):* As *he spoke by the mouth* of *his holy prophets,* who are from *the beginning: Salvation* from our enemies and from the hand of all that hate us: *To perform mercy* to our fathers, and *to remember his holy testament,* The oath, which he swore to *Abraham our father,* that he would grant to us *(Genesis 22:16; Jeremiah 31:33),* That being delivered from the hand of our enemies, we may serve him without fear, In holiness and justice before him, all our days. And thou, child, shalt be called *the prophet of the Highest: for thou shalt go before the face of the Lord to prepare his ways:* To give *knowledge of salvation* to his people, *unto the remission of their sins* (Malachi 4:5):*Through the bowels of the mercy of our God,* in which ***the Orient from on high hath visited us*** (Zach 3:9, 6:12; Malachi 4:2): ***To enlighten*** *them that sit in darkness,* and in the shadow of death: ***to direct our feet into the way of peace."*** I added the parenthesis above to show you the incredible depth of this *Spirit filled prophecy* concerning Zachary's new born son *John (the Baptist)* and the *prophecy of the Highest, Lord, the Orient from on high, Who hath visited us* (**Mary who was pregnant with Jesus** *came to visit Elizabeth in her sixth month).* Zachary joyously goes on to announce how *the Orient from on high* will *enlighten his people* and *direct their feet into the way of peace.* Over 2,000 years ago *Zachary, the Jewish priest,* at that moment in history *fully understood the promises of God to Abraham, to David,* and *to his people* were being fulfilled. And his son *John "shalt go before the face of the Lord to prepare his ways"* (Luke 1:76), *"in the spirit and power of Elijah"* (Luke 1:17), and *"shalt be called the prophet of the Highest"* as it is written in Malachi 4:5-6. Zachary, the *Jewish high priest,* truly understood ***the Messiah is Lord, the living Son of God.***

In the Gospel of John, the beloved *disciple of Christ Jesus, John the Apostle,* the son of Zebedee and Salome, who stood by *Jesus* at *His crucifixion* clearly writes about *John the Baptist* in John 1:6-10: *"...a man sent from God...This man came for a witness, to give testimony of* ***the light,*** *that all men might believe through him. He was not the light, but was to give testimony of* ***the light. That was***

the true light, *which enlighteneth every man that cometh into this world. He (the true light) was in the world, and the world was made by him, and the world knew him not."* In fact *"when the Jews sent from Jerusalem priests and Levites"* to ask him who he is, *John* the Baptist *"confessed: I am not the Christ* (John 1:19-20)." However, when they pressed him on further, *"Who art thou?"* In John 1:23: *"He said: I am the voice of one crying in the wilderness, make straight the way of the Lord, as said the prophet Isaiah (Isaiah 40:3)." John* the Baptist *proclaims Jesus* to us in the Gospel of John 1:29-36: *"Behold the Lamb of God, behold him who taketh away the sins of the world.* This is *he, of whom* I said: *After me there cometh a man, who is preferred before me: because he was before me.* And *I knew him not, but that* ***he (the true light)*** *may be made manifest in Israel,* therefore *am I come baptizing in water...I saw the Spirit coming down, as a dove from heaven,* and ***he (the Spirit) remained upon him.*** And...***he (God the Father)*** *who* ***sent me to baptize with water,*** *said to me: He* ***(Jesus)*** *upon whom thou shalt see the Spirit descending, and remaining upon him,* ***he it is that baptizeth with the Holy Ghost (Holy Spirit).*** *And I saw, and I gave testimony, that* ***this is the Son of God."***

John the Baptist (see above) I believe also knew something about *the Holy Trinity,* as John proclaims the three ***he -*** *in- One:* ***God the Father, the Spirit and the true light/ Lamb of God/Son of God Who baptizes with the Holy Spirit as the One Almighty God, the Triune God.*** John the Baptist further describes ***the Christ*** in John 3:28-36: *"I said, I am not the Christ,* but that *I am sent before him (the Christ Jesus).He that hath the bride, is the bridegroom ...*He must increase, but I must decrease. ***He that cometh from above, is above all...He that cometh from heaven, is above all****...He that hath received his testimony, hath set to his seal that* ***God is true.*** *For* ***he whom God hath sent, speaketh the words of God:*** for God doth not give the Spirit by measure. ***The Father loveth the Son:*** *and he (the Father) hath given all things into his (the Son's) hand.* ***He that believeth in the Son (Christ Jesus), hath life everlasting; but he that believeth not the Son, shall not see life (eternal life); but the wrath of God abideth on him (that believeth not the Son)."***

Notice how *he (Christ Jesus) whom God (the Father) sent* not only *speaks the words of God,* but has been *given all things from God (the Father) into his hand,* which is all of the universe and mankind, and all that is seen and unseen. Note also this very generous promise made to us all - that *anyone who believeth in the Son of God (Jesus) will have life everlasting, eternal life.* John the Baptist and John the Apostle are among two of the greatest eye witnesses to the *divinity, glory* and *the humanity of the Son of God, Jesus* the true *God-man.* Jesus, *the Son of God* (Psalm 2:7, 44:2-8, 88:2- 8,110:1; Proverbs 30:4; Wisdom 2:13,18; Daniel 3:92) and *the Son of man* (Psalm 8:5; Daniel 7:13), both Johns know *the Word of God was made flesh* (John 1:14). John the apostle and the other 11 apostles know *Jesus is the living bread of God made flesh* (John 6:41, 51) in the *virgin womb of Mary*

(Isaiah 7:14). John the Apostle and the other 11 apostles were with *Jesus* during the 3+ years of His public ministry spreading *the good news* to *His people,* first to the Jews, then the Gentiles. John and all the apostles all saw the awesome miracles, the signs from heaven, the incredible healings and deliverance from demons. He even saw *Jesus walking on water,* showing *His* authority over nature and the weather. John twice saw *Jesus multiply* scanty *loaves of bread* and *fishes* into more than enough food to feed thousands of hungry people. He *witnessed Jesus raising the dead.*

Recall, *John the Apostle* was present with Peter and James for *the transfiguration of Jesus* (Matthew 17:1-9; Luke 9:27-36). John *the Apostle* stood beside Jesus during his crucifixion and saw *blood and water coming out of Jesus* immediately after *"one of the soldiers with a spear opened his side"* (John 19:34), while Jesus *"was already dead"* (John 19:33) on the cross. And John was also present with the other apostles, when *Jesus revealed His Glory* - after *His resurrection* three days after *His death* (John 20:19, 26-27), just as *Jesus* had foretold on several occasions. John and all the apostles (minus Judas) were present at the *ascension of Jesus into heaven* (Luke 24:51). John was the only apostle given the duty by *Jesus Himself to take care of Mary, the mother of Jesus* (John 19:27). Later, John received the *Revelation of Jesus Christ* (Rev 1:1). Also, John *"hath given testimony to* ***the word of God,*** and *the testimony of* ***Jesus Christ,*** what things soever he hath seen*"* (Rev 1:2). No wonder John *the beloved disciple of Christ* is depicted as *an eagle that soars above the heavens* giving all of us, Jews and Gentiles alike, *the testimony of* **the truth** - with *God's love and mercy.* John the Apostle knowing that *the word of God (Jesus)* was *made flesh* in the *virgin's womb Mary* of the *House of David* in the *city of David (the city of Bread, Bethlehem, Israel)* writes in John 1:14*: "And the Word was made flesh, and dwelt among us..."* John knows *the word of God* **is** *the light, "the true light,* which enlighteneth every man that cometh into this world*"* (John 1:9); and ***the Word - the light*** is *good and gives* ***life.*** John acknowledges ***the life in the Word of God, wisdom and the light*** - was, is and will always be - ***the light of men,*** and he also understands that ***in the Word of God is life*** *(eternal life).*

Thus, it is indeed fair to say that John *hath given* his *testimony* that ***Jesus is the Word!*** More insights into John's deep understanding of ***the truth*** are given in the next verses picked below. See John 4:25-26: *"The woman* saith to him *(Jesus):* I know that *the Messias (Messiah) cometh* (who is called *Christ)*; therefore, when he is to come, he will tell us all things. ***Jesus saith*** to her: ***I am*** he, ***who am*** *speaking with thee."* John 8:51: *"Amen,* amen I say to you: *If any man keep my word, he shall not see death for ever."* John 5:19-33: *"Then Jesus* answered *(the Jews),* and said to them: Amen, amen, I say unto you, *the Son* cannot do any thing of himself, but what he seeth *the Father* doing: for what things soever he doth, these *the Son* also doth in like manner. For *the Father* loveth *the Son,* and *sheweth* *him all things* which himself doth: and greater works than these will he shew him, which you may wonder. For as *the Father raiseth up the dead, and giveth life:* so *the Son* also *giveth life to whom he will.* For neither doth *the Father* judge any man, but hath *given all judgment to the Son.* That all men may honour *the Son,* as they honour *the Father. He who honoureth not the Son, honoureth not the Father, who hath sent him.* Amen, amen I say unto you, that ***he who heareth my word, and believeth him that sent me, hath life everlasting;*** *and cometh not to judgment, but is passed from death to life.* Amen, amen I say unto you, that *the hour cometh, and now is, when the dead shall hear the voice of the Son of God,* and *they that hear shall live.* For as *the Father* hath life in himself, so he hath given to *the Son* also to have life in himself: And *he hath given him power to do judgment, because he is the Son of man.* Wonder not at this; for the hour cometh, wherein all that are in the graves shall hear *the voice of the Son of God.* And *they that have done good things, shall come forth unto the resurrection of life;* but they that have done evil, unto the resurrection of judgment. *I cannot of myself do any thing. As I hear, so I judge: and my judgment is just; because I seek not my own will, but the will of him (Father God) that sent me (Jesus).* If I bear witness of myself, my witness is not true. There is another that beareth witness of me; and I know that *the witness* which he witnesseth of me is true. You sent *(people)* to John *(John the Baptist, a Jew),* and he *gave testimony to* **the truth."**

Finally, in John 12:44-50: *"...Jesus* cried, and *said: He that believeth in me,* doth not *believe* in me, but *in him (Father God) that sent me.* And ***he that seeth me, seeth him*** *(Father God)* ***that sent me. I am* come *a light* into the world;** *that whosoever believeth in me, may not remain in darkness.* And if any man ***hear my words,*** and keep them not, I do not judge him: ***for I came not to judge the world, but to save the world.*** He that despiseth me, and receiveth not *my words,* hath one that judgeth him; ***the word*** that I have spoken, the same *(the Word)* shall judge him ***in the last day.*** *For I have not spoken of myself;* **but the Father who sent me, he gave me *commandment* what I should say, and what I should speak. And I know that *his*** *(God's)* ***commandment*** *(the word of God)* ***is life everlasting. The things therefore that I speak, even as the Father said unto me, so do I speak."***

Recall that our medical and scientific studies recorded the same amazing *new data* whenever *Jesus speaks His living words in the light* to Nancy or the seminarian. This *data* is identical to all the *new data,* we recorded *in His Living Presence* repeatedly. Thus, ***the living words of God*** *in the light* and ***His Living Presence are One.*** Now connect *the word of God /wisdom - to the sweetness of honey* and *the Eucharist.* Psalm 119:103: *"How sweet are* **thy words** *to my palate: more than* ***honey to my mouth."*** Psalm 80:11 -17*: "For I am the Lord thy God...open thy mouth wide, and I will fill it...And he (God)* ***fed*** *them with* ***the fat of the wheat*** (the Bread of life / the Eucharist), and ***filled*** *them* ***with honey*** (wisdom) *out of the rock* (the Church)*."* So, eating *the Bread of life* nourishes us *with wisdom.*

I believe it is *the sin of man* (Genesis 3:1-6) at the level of the mind and heart of man *(a personal and conscious decision to rebel or sin against the Divine Will, the laws/commandments of God)* that inadvertently causes misunderstandings and corruption of ***"the*** (incorruptible) ***Word of God"*** (Rev 19:13), *"And the Word was made flesh, and dwelt among us"* (John 1:14). I believe *sin* lead God from the very beginning (Genesis 3:15) to *divinely* plan to plant His Seed *through, in and with His Spirit* (Numbers 24:7; 3 Kings 18:34-39; Isaiah 55:10-11)) in *the woman, the new Eve, a virgin* (Isaiah 7:14). God *gave us* His *new covenant.* Jeremiah 31:33:*"I will* ***give my law*** *in their bowels,* and I will *write it in their heart."* Now, see how *His new covenant* is indeed *personified* as *Emmanuel* (Isaiah 7:14), which is interpreted *"God with us"* (Matthew1:23). ***Honey fed Emmanuel*** (Isaiah 7:15), I believe **is** *Jesus - in the Holy Eucharist - the pure incorruptible word of God, the law* of God in the most approachable form ever imaginable – ***bread and wine.*** *Jesus* says, ***"I am the living bread which came down from heaven,"*** *twice* in John 6:41 and 6: 51.

Jesus, ***the new covenant*** *as the living bread and wine* gloriously fulfills the great prophecy of Jeremiah 31:33. Now *God (the Father)* with *His new covenant* ***Jesus,*** *the only begotten Son of the living God with the power of* the Holy Spirit of God *(the Holy Spirit)* can truly nourish their *(your)* souls with *His living Word* and *His law* directly *within you/inside you. "The living bread and wine"* literally writes *in their bowels/in their spirit/in their heart* **the Word** bypassing (or passing over) *the brain, the mind of man,* the centrifuge of the human intellect, memory, will, understanding and reasoning - through which *the stain of sin corrupts* and misinterprets *the Word of God.* I believe God truly wants to *directly communicate* and *commune* with each one of us in a very special way without the interference of our mind and *sin.* Sin corrupts. So now by drinking the *"blood of the grape,"* God *"will write it (the law/the Word of God) in their heart"* and in your heart too, if you only *let God in.* Ok, so how do you let God *in?* It is indeed very simple. Pray for forgiveness. Pray for God's mercy to wash away all your sins and iniquities. Repent. Invite God inside *thy spirit/thy bowels* and *heart.* Then, taste and see the *goodness of the Lord.*

David said: *"Create a new heart in me,* O God: and *renew a right spirit within my bowels* (Psalm 50:12).*"* Thus, *"thy spirit"* is in *"thy bowels"* or *"within you."* So, let us all now *commune, communicate* and *have communion* with *our Lord thy God.* Remember what *Jesus* said in John 6:55: *"He that eateth my flesh (the living bread), and drinketh my blood (the blood of the grape), hath everlasting life:* and I *(Jesus, the Son of the living God) will raise him up in the last day." The last day* some Biblical scholars have identified as *the last millennium or the seventh day,* since both David (Psalm 89:4) and later Peter acknowledged, 2 Peter 3:8: *"that one day with the Lord is as a thousand years, and a thousand years as one day."* Hebrew scholars recently identified a mistake in the calculation of the Jewish calendar years that actually places the true date very near to 6,000 years since *the beginning.* So, we are now very near to *the last day.* Bible prophecy foretells that *the Jewish Messiah will come (back) in the last day,* the *day of rest* or the seventh millennium period of *peace*. So, *what* are *you* waiting for? Please do not continue to be so foolish. At judgment day the *eternal life of your soul will desperately want and need to know* **the truth** *"and the truth shall make you free"* (John 8:32), free from the bondage of *sin,* and free from *death and evil* (Deut 30:15). So come, taste and see the true *goodness of the Lord, thy God. Let God come into your heart.* Let God *nourish and communicate* ***His pure incorruptible*** *fire tried* ***living Word, the Eucharist,*** in *your bowels/ your spirit/within you.* So, if you are *hungry* and *thirsty for God,* please *come eat and drink --- the* ***new everlasting covenant of peace.*** *Come eat and drink the* ***living Word*** *of God* **in** *the* ***living bread*** and **in** *the* ***blood of the grape*** *of God.* And as promised (John 6:55) *Jesus* will raise you up *"in the last day," the coming* years of **peace** *(of rest).* John 6:59:"This is *the bread* that came down *from heaven*...***He that eateth this bread, shall live for ever."*** What a promise! Please, now read John 3:16.

V. "The living bread" of God

A. Recall Chapter 8 for a more in depth account on the series of medical and scientific studies completed by Dr. Norma Agosto and Dr. Teresa Dalmau in the city of Cuenca, Ecuador in November 17-19th, 1994 that I examined and interpreted; and the clinical neuropsychology tests and battery of neuropsychophysiology studies completed by Prof. Castanon in June 10th, August 12th, and November 17-19th, 1994, on the *chosen soul* Patricia Talbot. I interviewed and neurologically examined Patricia in her home. The young and beautiful Patricia (Pachi) was tested extensively by a medical research team approach; and all the neurological examinations, the clinical neuropsychology battery of tests and the in depth neuropsychophysiological testing were **normal.** The ambulatory EEG intensive monitoring demonstrated awake patterns and sleep stages for her stated age of 22 yrs. that were also **normal.** While she was awake with eyes closed, *normal* alpha rhythms of 10 Hz were recorded in the posterior head regions bilaterally. During prayer and meditation, while awake and alert and leading a group in prayer, we recorded *normal* beta rhythms in the 18-20 Hz range with eyes open bilaterally. Yet, during her private Holy Communion service the moment *the Eucharist ("the bread of life", John 6:35)* touched Patricia's tongue, while still very much *awake,* the ambulatory EEG recorded the unprecedented *3 Hz delta rhythms* with a *deep sleep pattern* topography and the same identical mathematical and numerical EEG pattern of **333!** Accentuated *beta rhythms,* typical for an awake and alert with eyes open and focused attention EEG patterns were seen and recorded overriding the *deep sleep delta* (*mostly 3 Hz rhythms* with a range of 3-4 Hz). Thus, the *oxymoron* of EEG patterns previously seen in our *new data* is once again recorded. An *awake* *and alert with focused attention* EEG pattern is again seen overriding a very *deep sleep* EEG pattern. What *a contradiction* of EEG physiological states. *Awake and alert while* simultaneously being *in a deep sleep.* This now famous 333 EEG pattern was again recorded, when Patricia receives *Holy Communion - the Eucharist ("the bread of God,"* John 6:33*),* just like it was repeatedly recorded and documented in all our studies of the *chosen souls,* when they are *in His Living Presence.* Recall, Patricia's *deep sleep pattern while awake lasted ~20 minutes.*

Question: What does Jesus and the "living bread of God" have in common?

B. I believe *the Holy Spirit* has led me to a very interesting series of *connections* between certain special *words in Holy Scriptures* that may help us see prophetically a real true glimpse of *the wisdom of God.* I will ***highlight*** the *words* for you in this section of *Bible verses* from the Old Testament that helps answer the above question. Starting with the Book of Genesis as it is written in Chapter 3, it appears that immediately after *God* realized Adam and Eve had eaten the *forbidden fruit, God* made *His divine plan for salvation* of the human race at that very moment. *God's plan included something never seen* elsewhere *in Holy Scriptures.* Can you imagine *the seed of the woman?* Throughout *the Bible* it is always *the seed of a man* that is heralded to be *the children of God's inheritance,* except here. So, *what* does *the seed of the woman* really mean? And *who* is *"her seed,"* that along with *the woman "shall crush thy head"* (Gen 3:15), the head of the *"more subtle"* (Gen 3:1) the *old serpent, Satan?* And *why* does *God's plan to send the seed of the woman to us* begin right after man commits *the first sin?* Please ponder this, as you read this section. It indeed appears *the seed of the woman* is a virtual *time bomb* for all the *children of God, children of the light.* Recall, the *children of God's inheritance* and especially *the coming of the Jewish Messiah* in the Bible is *prophesized to come through the seed of Abraham, the seed of Isaac, the seed of Jacob* and *the seed of David.* So, *who* is *the seed of the woman? And who is the woman?* I will try to answer these questions later; but first re-read the last reflection. Starting with the first Book of Genesis 1:26-27: *"Let* ***us*** *(God/Elohim)* make man to *our* image and likeness...And *God created man to his own image: to the image of God he created him: male and female he created them."* After the first *sin was* committed in paradise we can see how *God's* unfathomable *love and mercy given (as a gift) to man* is truly at work. Genesis 3:15: *"I will* put enmities between thee and *the woman,* and thy seed and *her seed:* she *(he)* shall crush thy head, and thou *(serpent)* shalt lie in wait for her *(his)* heel.*"* Genesis 12:1-3: "And *the Lord said to Abram:* Go forth out of thy country...and come into the land which I shall shew thee. And *I (God) will make thee a great nation, and I will bless thee...*I will bless them that bless thee, and curse them that curse thee, and **IN THEE *shall all the kindred***

of the earth be blessed." *"IN THEE,"* here means *in thy seed* (Genesis 22:18), the seed of Abram/Abraham respectively.

Genesis 14:18-20:*"But Melchisedech the king of Salem,* bringing forth ***bread and wine,*** for he was *the priest of the most high God,* Blessed him *(Abram),* and said: *Blessed be Abram by the most high God, who created heaven and earth.* And blessed be the most high God, by whose protection the enemies are in thy hands. And he *(Abram)* gave him the tithes of all." So, *who* is this character *king Melchisedech, who* is the *priest of the most high God* and *brings forth* ***bread and wine*** for the *anointing* and *blessing* of Abram? Read Psalm 109 (110):1-4 for further insight into *"the order of Melchisedech."* Notice this *priestly order* existed by *faith* centuries before Moses brother *Aaron's priestly line* was ever established by *the law of God* during the Exodus from Egypt. Now see Genesis 49:10-11: *"The septre* shall not be taken away from Juda, nor a ruler from his thigh, till *he (Messiah/Christ) come that is to be sent,* and *he (Messiah/Christ Jesus)* shall be *the expectations of nations.* Tying his *foal* to the vineyard, and his *ass,* ***O my son,*** to ***the vine.*** He ***shall wash his robe in wine,*** and ***his garment in the blood of the grape."*** Oh passion.

Now for more on *the bread of God,* see Exodus 16:15: "And when the children of Israel saw it, they said to one another: Manhu! Which signifieth: *What is this!* for they knew not what it was. And Moses said to them: This is ***the bread,*** *which the Lord hath given you to eat."* Exodus 16:31-35: "And the house of Israel called the name thereof ***Manna:*** and it was like *coriander seed* ***white,*** and ***the taste*** *thereof* ***like to flour with honey*** *(sweet and mild).* And Moses said: This is ***the word,*** *which the Lord hath commanded:* Fill a gomor of it, and let it be kept unto generations to come hereafter, that they may know ***the bread,*** *wherewith I fed you in the wilderness,* when you were brought out of the land of Egypt. And Moses said to Aaron: Take ***a vessel,*** *and put* ***manna*** *into it,* as much as a gomor can hold: and lay it up before the Lord to keep unto your generations, as the Lord commanded Moses. And Aaron put it in ***the tabernacle*** to be kept. And the children of Israel ate ***manna*** forty years, till they came to a habitable land: ***with this meat*** *were they fed,* until they reached the borders of the land of Chanaan." Hebrew traditions teach that this gomor of *manna* was later placed into the *Ark of the Covenant* when the Temple was built. Now notice how in the above verses *manna* is referred to as *meat.* In Numbers 11:7: *"Now* the ***manna*** was like coriander seed, of *the colour of bdellium (white and bright)."* Now to connect *bread/manna/milk/honey/meat/food* with *the word of God,* see the famous verse in Deut 8:3: *"He* afflicted thee with want, and ***gave*** thee ***manna*** for thy ***food,*** which neither thou nor thy fathers knew: to shew that *not in* ***bread*** *alone doth man live, but in every* ***word*** *that proceedeth* ***from the mouth of God."*** *God* also *promised His children "a land that floweth with* ***milk and honey"*** (Exodus 3:17). In Hebrew, *milk=the word of God /honey=wisdom.*

In the David's Psalm 77(78) we can see further insights into *the bread of heaven,* 20-25: "... Can *he (God)* also give ***bread,*** or provide a table for his people?

...And ***he*** *(God)* had *commanded the clouds from above,* and had ***opened the doors of heaven.*** And *had* ***rained down manna*** *upon them to eat,* and had ***given them the bread of heaven.*** Man ate ***the bread of angels: he*** *(God)* ***sent them provisions in abundance."*** Psalm 85:5: *"For thou, O Lord, art* ***sweet*** *and* ***mild:*** and *plenteous in mercy* to all that call upon thee." Now see this very interesting verse in a Psalm where *David praises God's mighty works,* Psalm 103:13-15, 30: "...the earth shall be filled with *the fruit of thy works* ...That *thou mayest bring* ***bread*** *(the Anointed One) out of the earth*: and *that* ***wine*** may *cheer the heart of man.* That he may *make the face cheerful with* ***oil:*** and *that* ***bread*** may *strengthen man's heart...Thou shalt* ***send forth thy spirit,*** and *they shall be created:* and *thou shalt renew the face of the earth."* Psalm 106 (107):1, 9, 20-22: *"Give glory to the Lord, for he is* ***good*** *(life): for his mercy endureth for ever...*For *he hath* ***satisfied the empty soul,*** and *hath* ***filled the hungry soul*** *with good things...He sent his* ***word*** *(Jesus),* and ***healed*** them: and ***delivered*** them *from their destructions. Let the mercies of the Lord give glory to him:* and *his wonderful works* to the children of men. And *let them sacrifice* ***the sacrifice of praise*** *(Jesus):* and *declare his works with* ***joy."*** See manna/*bread of heaven/provisions* in abundance/*the Word*---**Jesus.**

Now to revisit earlier Psalms that may *shed light* on these connections. Starting with Psalm 2:1-8: *"Why* have the Gentiles raged, and the people devised vain things? The kings of the earth stood up, and the princes met together, against ***the Lord,*** and against ***his Christ (****against* ***his Anointed One, Messiah). Let us*** break their bonds asunder: and ***let us*** cast away their yoke from ***us.*** *He that dwelleth in heaven* shall laugh at them: and the Lord shall deride them. *Then shall he speak* to them in *his anger,* and trouble them in *his rage.* But ***I*** *(Messiah)* **am** *appointed* **king** *by him (God) over Sion his holy mountain, preaching his commandment. The Lord* hath *said to me (Messiah/ Christ):* ***Thou art my son, this day have I begotten thee.*** *Ask of me (God), and I will give thee the Gentiles for thy inheritance,* and the utmost parts of the earth for thy possession." Psalm 41 (42):2-3: "As the hart panteth after the fountains of water; so *my soul panteth after thee, O God. My* ***soul*** *hath* ***thirsted after*** *the strong living* ***God..."*** Psalm 44 (45):2-8: *"My heart* hath uttered a ***good word:*** *I speak my works* ***to the king ...Thou art*** *beautiful* ***above the sons of men...O thou most mighty...*** ***Thy throne, O God,*** *is forever* and ever: the sceptre of ***thy kingdom*** is a *sceptre of* ***uprightness.*** *Thou hast loved* ***justice,*** and hated iniquity: **therefore *God*** *(the Son, Jesus),* ***thy God*** *(Father God),* ***hath anointed thee*** *(Christ/Messiah)* ***with the oil of gladness*** *(the Holy Spirit)* ***above thy fellows*** *(sons of men)."* Psalm 49 (50):14-16: *"Offer to (Father) God* ***the sacrifice of praise*** *(Jesus):* and *pay thy vows to the most High (Holy Spirit).* And *call upon me in the day of trouble: I will deliver thee,* and thou shalt glorify me. But to the sinner *God* hath said: *Why dost thou* declare *my justices,* and ***take my covenant*** *(Jesus)* ***in thy mouth?"*** Now please pay close attention to this next verse. Psalm 51 (52):12-13: ***"Create a clean heart in me, O God:*** and ***renew a right spirit within my***

bowels. Cast me not away from *thy face (thy presence);* and *take not* ***thy holy spirit*** *from me."* Ponder these last two verses. Now read the following verses with all the above perspectives given in this section, Psalm 109 (110):1-4:***"The Lord*** *(Father God)* ***said to my Lord*** *(my Son):* ***Sit thou at my right hand:*** Until I make thy enemies thy footstool. *The Lord* will send forth *the sceptre of thy power* out of Sion: *rule thou in the midst of thy enemies. With thee is the principality (Holy Spirit) in the day of thy strength: in the brightness of the saints:* ***from the womb before the day star I*** *(God)* ***begot thee.*** *The Lord* hath sworn, and *he will not repent:* ***Thou art a priest for ever according to the order of Melchisedech."*** Psalm 110 (111):3-9:***"His work is praise*** *and magnificence:* and ***his justice*** *continueth for ever and ever...he hath* ***given food*** *to them that fear him. He will* be *mindful for ever of* ***his covenant:*** *he will* shew forth to his people *the power of his works... He hath sent redemption* to his people: *he hath commanded his* ***covenant for ever.*** *Holy* and *terrible is his name:* ***the fear of the Lord is the beginning of wisdom."*** Psalm 118:103: *"How sweet* are ***thy words*** to my palate! more than ***honey to my mouth."*** Finally, in Psalm 131 (132):15-18: *"...I will satisfy her (Sion's) poor with* ***bread.*** *I will* clothe *her (Sion's) priests with* ***salvation:*** and *her saints shall rejoice* with exceeding great joy. *There will I bring forth* ***a horn to David:*** *I have prepared* ***a lamp for my anointed*** *(Messiah/Christ)* His enemies I will clothe with confusion: but *upon him (Messiah/Christ Jesus/my Son) shall my* ***sanctification*** *flourish."*

In Proverbs 9:4-5: *"Whosoever is a little one, let him come to me.* And to the unwise *she (wisdom)* said: *Come,* ***eat my bread,*** *and* ***drink the wine*** *which I have mingled for you."* Proverbs 16:24: ***"Well ordered words*** are ***as a honeycomb: sweet to the soul,*** and *health to the bones."* Proverbs 24:13-14:***"Eat honey***, ***my son***, because ***it is good*** *(life)*, and *the honeycomb most* ***sweet to thy throat: So*** *also* ***is the doctrine of wisdom to thy soul:*** which *when* thou hast *found, thou shalt have hope in the end,* and *thy hope shall not perish."*

The prophet Isaiah gives an important clue to the nature of *Emmanuel, "God is with us"* (Isaiah 8:10) in the *prophecy of the virgin birth.* See Isaiah 7:13-15:"And he said: Hear ye therefore, *O house of David...*Therefore *the Lord himself shall give* you *a sign.* ***Behold a virgin shall conceive, and bear a son, and his name shall be called Emmanuel. He shall eat*** butter ***(milk)*** *and* ***honey, that he may know to refuse the evil,*** and ***to choose the good."*** *So, how does eating butter (which comes from* ***milk****) and* ***honey*** let you know *how - to refuse the evil, and to choose the good? Ponder.* Now if *a virgin conceives a son,* we can see the prophecy of Moses Gen 3:15 and Isaiah 7:14 fulfilled. Recall, ***the seed of the woman! A virgin*** *(Mary) that* ***conceives -*** *fits that prophecy.* In David's Psalm 77(78) seen above, Isaiah 45:8 also describes *a special* ***rain*** *from heaven: "Drop down* ***dew,*** ye ***heavens,*** *from above,* and ***let the clouds rain the just: let the earth be opened,*** *and* ***bud forth a saviour*** *(my Son/the Word)****..."*** In Isaiah 49:1-18 ***the word*** *of the Lord God* speaks of ***his servant:*** *"formed...* ***from the womb****...to be* ***the light*** *(my*

Son) of the Gentiles... ***my salvation*** *even to the farthest part of the earth...* ***the Lord the redeemer*** *of Israel (my Son), his Holy One...* ***the Holy One of Israel...given thee to be a covenant*** *of the people,* ***that thou*** *mightest* ***raise up the earth,*** *and possess the inheritances that were destroyed...* ***They shall not hunger, nor thirst...for he*** *that* ***is merciful...shall be their shepherd,*** *and at the fountains of waters he shall* ***give them drink****...Give praise, O ye heavens, and rejoice, O earth...the Lord hath comforted his people, and* ***will have mercy on his poor ones****...Behold,* ***I have graven thee in my hands...Lift up thy eyes*** *round about, and* ***see...I live, saith the Lord..."*** These verses (like many from Isaiah) are just brimming over and over flowing with *prophecies of Jesus.* In Isaiah 51:14:***"He*** *(my Son/Christ)* ***shall*** *quickly* ***come*** *that is going to open unto you...* ***neither shall his bread fail."*** Finally in Isaiah 63:2-3, we see another *prophecy* similar *to* what Moses had written in Genesis 49:10-11. Both verses are seen as being fulfilled by *the passion, crucifixion and death of Jesus* as portrayed in Rev 19:13. See Isaiah 63:2-3: *"Why* then is *thy apparel* ***red,*** and ***thy garments*** *like theirs that* ***tread*** *in* the winepress? *I have trodden the* ***winepress*** *alone..."* Recall, *the blood of the grape!*

Jeremiah and Ezekiel have some fascinating *prophetic verses* that make major connections in trying to understand the *hidden mysteries,* and abundant mercies and graces of *the living bread of God.* In Jeremiah 11:15, 19: *"...****shall the holy flesh take away from thee thy crimes,*** in which thou hast boasted? ...**I was** as **a** ***meek lamb,*** that is carried to be **a** ***victim:*** and I knew not that **they had devised counsels against me,** saying: **Let us put** ***wood*** **(the cross)** ***on his bread*** **(holy flesh/ meat),** and *cut him off from the land of the living..."* In Ezekiel chap. 2 and 3, I believe we finally start to see *what* the *Almighty God* wants to show us *in His Divine Mercy and Divine Will.* Ezekiel 2:2, 8-9: *"...And* ***the spirit entered into me*** *after that* ***he spoke to me****...do not provoke me, as that house provoketh me:* ***open thy mouth,*** *and* ***eat what I give thee.*** *And I looked, and behold,* ***a hand was sent*** *to me, wherein was* ***a book*** *rolled up: and he spread it before me, and it was* ***written within and without:*** *and there were written in it lamentations, and canticles, and woe."* Ezekiel 3:1-4, 10: *"And he said to me: Son of man,* ***eat*** *all that thou shalt find:* ***eat this book, and go speak to the children of Israel****. And I opened my mouth, and he caused me to eat that book: And he said to me: Son of man,* ***thy belly shall eat, and thy bowels shall be filled with this book,*** *which* ***I give thee.*** *And* ***I did eat it:*** *and* ***it was sweet as honey in my mouth.*** *And he said to me: Son of man, go to the house of Israel, and thou shalt* ***speak my words to them****...And he said to me: Son of man,* ***receive in thy heart,*** *and* ***hear*** *with thy ears,* ***all the words*** *that* ***I speak*** *to thee..."* Now we can see and understand more vividly *what God truly wills* for *His new covenant* in Jeremiah 31:33, 25: *"But this shall be the (new)* ***covenant*** *that I will make with the house of Israel...saith the Lord:* ***I will give my law*** *(the Word of God)* ***in their bowels,*** *and* ***I will write it in their heart:*** *and* ***I will be their God,*** *and they shall be my people... For* ***I have***

***inebriated the weary soul:** and **I have filled every hungry soul.**" So, how does* our merciful loving *God give His law (the Word of God/Jesus) "in their bowels"* and *"write it in their heart?"* Think about *the Word* and *the Bread of God* from heaven.

Ponder this. ***Honey*** is *imperishable food* just like *the Eucharist.* It is ***sweet*** and ***mild.*** The works of worker bees perfect honey. But it is *the works of God* that perfect *the Eucharist.* Now see ***milk and honey fed Emmanuel*** *as the book/new covenant/my law /milk=the word/honey=wisdom/manna/meat/food/holy flesh/victim/ meek lamb/bread/wine/salvation* and *the life* **is *the Eucharist.*** *The corn of the elect and wine* that gives/preserves purity so wonderfully *budding forth virgins* (just look at all the *nuns* and *religious orders* that *offer God* their life *of purity* and *chastity*), as in Zach 9:17:*"For what is the good thing of **him,** and what is his beautiful thing,* but *the corn of the elect (the Eucharist), and wine (His Blood) springing forth virgins?"*

C. *Jesus* answers this question in the Gospel of Luke during *the last supper* and on the *road to Emmaus.* Also in the Gospel of John, *Jesus* gives us one of the best pictures of *prophecy fulfilled* from the series of verses shown in **section b).** Starting with Luke 22:15-20: "And he *(Jesus)* said to them: *With* desire *I have desired to eat this pasch* with you, *before I suffer (Jesus foretells His Father's Will and His own Will to suffer the passion and death willingly for all the sins of man. Thus, Jesus is the true Lamb of God, Who takes away the sins of the world. Since these foretold events so neatly coincides with the original Pasch, I believe this is no mere coincidence, but a divinely planned God-incidence. Check out the original Pasch calendar dates with the passion, death and resurrection dates of Jesus)."*

"For I (Jesus) say to you, that from this time I will not eat it, till it be fulfilled in the kingdom of God. And having *taken **the chalice,*** he *gave thanks,* and said: Take, and divide it among you: For I say to you, that *I will not **drink** of the **fruit** of **the vine** (Jesus is 'the vine', John 15:5), till the kingdom of God come.* And taking ***bread,*** he *gave thanks,* and brake; and gave to them, saying: ***This is my body,*** which is ***given for you****. Do this for a commemoration of me.* In like manner the chalice also, after he had supped, saying: ***This is** the chalice, the new testament in **my blood,** which shall be **shed for you** (Jesus - foretells His passion and death)."*

Reflections on the Pasch and Special Jewish Calendar Dates

For those of you who are interested in the Jewish calendar just check out these special dates. It is indeed intriguing to me how *God* uses certain Jewish calendar dates possibly I believe to make a point. Historically, for instance in the holy month of Nissan 10th day the high priest goes from Jerusalem to the *city of David, Bethlehem,* to pick out an *unblemished lamb* and brings it back to the Temple with a chorus of people singing with jubilation placing palm tree leaves in front of *the high priest and the unblemished lamb* for preparations for the upcoming *Pasch.* This is exactly the time and date in history that *Jesus* rode into Jerusalem on an ass with the chorus singing *"Hosanna in the highest"* and *"Blessed is He who comes in the name of the Lord"* while placing palm tree leaves before *Jesus*. This fulfilled the famous prophecy of Zachariah 9:9: "BEHOLD THY KING will come to thee, *the just* and *saviour:* he is poor, and *riding upon an ass,* and upon a colt the *foal* of an *ass."*

Now think *Palm Sunday,* which first occurred on the 10th day of Nissan. Once *the lamb* is in the Temple, the lamb is carefully studied by the Jewish priests for 4 days to make sure it is indeed spotless and without blemish. Then on the 14th day of Nissan *between the eves,* which is exactly at 3 o'clock mid-afternoon, *the lamb is sacrificed.* Recall how in the Bible accounts Jesus *(the Lamb of God)* is also studied for 4 days by the Jews in the Temple, the Jewish priests, the Roman rulers and finally, *Jesus* was studied very closely indeed by the Roman soldiers during *His passion and crucifixion,* Zachariah 9:11:*"Thou also by the blood of thy testament hast sent forth thy prisoners out of the pit, wherein is no water."*

Thus, *Jesus shed His Precious Blood for you and me,* willingly accepting death on ***a cross*** of wood *(a tree).* Yes, *His holy flesh/the bread of life* (Jeremiah11:19) was *put on wood, gave up His spirit* and *died at exactly 3 o'clock (the same time the Pasch lamb is sacrificed)* on the 14th day of Nissan. This occurred during *the eclipse of the sun* which lasted from ~12 noon to 3 o'clock (Isaiah 13:10: *"...the sun shall be darkened in his rising").* Then, *3 days later the glorious resurrection of Jesus* was fulfilled on the 17th day of Nissan, according to the Jewish calendar exactly as foretold by many of the prophets: David in Psalm 3:6, Psalm15(16):10, Isaiah 33:10, Hosea 6:3, Sophonias 3:8, Ezekiel 37:3-14 and then by *Jesus Himself* in the Gospels of the New Testament. Of even further interest the 17th day of Nissan is considered by Jewish rabbis to be *a holy day of salvation for the Jews* throughout their history. For example *Noah's ark* landed on a mountain top safely on the 17th day of Nissan*; Moses* along with *all the children of Israel* crossed the miraculously parted *Red Sea* and were all safe and sound on the other side of the Red Sea *(saved by God)* on the 17th day of Nissan; the evil Aman was hanged on the same gibbet, he had prepared for Mordochai after *Queen Esther* petitioned king Assuerus for *salvation* of all her people the Jews on the 17th day of Nissan. So, are these very specific Jewish calendar dates yet another coincidence or a true *God-incidence?*

C. (Continued) In the Gospel of John Chapter 6 in the New Testament, we see how *Jesus twice* proclaims to the multitude and *His disciples:* ***"I am the bread of life"*** (John 6:35, 48); and says: ***"I am the living bread which came down from heaven"*** (6:41, 51). I can only imagine that when *Jesus* says something *twice,* it must be important. Now see how in *His* famous discourse as is written *Jesus* actually connects specific prophecy/*foreshadows of things to come* from Moses and the prophets of the Old Testament with *Himself* in the New Testament with the following words: *manna* (Exodus 16:15), *bread from heaven* (Psalm 77(78):24), *bright* and *white* (Numbers 11:7), *"the* taste thereof *like to flour with* ***honey"*** (Exodus 16:31), *meat* (Exodus 16:35), *holy flesh* (Jeremiah 11:15), *"the blood of the grape"* (Genesis 49:11), *"thou, O Lord,* art *sweet* and *mild"* (Psalm 85:5), *"Eat honey, my son,* because it is *good"* (Proverbs 24:13), Emmanuel - *"God is with us"*- *"he* shall eat butter *(milk) and honey"* (Isaiah 7:14-15), *new covenant, "I will give my law in their bowels,* and I will *write it in their heart"* (Jeremiah 31:33), *"a book* rolled up...written within and without" (Ezekiel 2:9), *"thy bowels* shall be filled with *this book,* which I *give thee.* And I did eat it: and it was *sweet as honey in my mouth"* (Ezekiel 3:3). *Jesus* says it best in John 6:32-33: *"...**my Father giveth** you* ***the true bread from heaven.*** For ***the bread of God*** is that which *cometh down from heaven,* and ***giveth life to the world."*** And in John 6:35: ***"I am the bread of life: he that cometh to me shall not hunger: and he that believeth in me shall never thirst."*** In John 6:48-52: ***"I am the bread of life.*** Your fathers did eat ***manna*** in the desert, and are dead. *This is the* ***bread*** *which cometh down from heaven; that if any man eat of it, he may not die.* ***I am the living bread which came down from heaven. If any man eat of this bread, he shall live for ever;*** and ***the bread*** *that* ***I will give, is my flesh, for the life of the world."*** And finally in John 6:54-59: **"...Except you *eat the flesh* of the Son of man, and *drink his blood,* you shall not have life in you. *He that eateth my flesh, and drinketh my blood, hath everlasting life: and I will raise him up in the last day.*** For ***my flesh is meat*** indeed: and ***my blood is drink*** indeed. ***He that eateth my flesh,*** and ***drinketh my blood, abideth in me, and I in him.*** As *the living Father (God) hath sent me,* and *I live by the Father;* so *he that eateth me, the same also shall live by me.* This is ***the bread*** *that came down* ***from heaven.*** Not as your fathers did eat *manna,* and are dead. ***He that eateth this bread*** *(Jesus),* ***shall live for ever."***

Now ponder *Jesus on the way to Emmaus* (Luke 24). *After the resurrection of Jesus,* two disciples *"knew him in the breaking of bread"* (Luke 24:34-35). In Luke 24:30-31: "And it came to pass, whilst *he (Jesus)* was at the table with them, *he (Jesus)* took ***bread,*** and ***blessed,*** and ***brake,*** *and* ***gave*** *to them. And their eyes were opened,* and they knew *him (Jesus): and he (Jesus) vanished out of their sight."* But, did *he (Jesus)* really vanish from them? No, because in John 6:32-33 *he* ***is*** *the true bread from heaven* and *the bread of God.* So, *Jesus* on *the way to Emmaus* completes the ***circle of life*** through *the bread of life (the Eucharist)* namely *Himself* as *He had proclaimed* and *foretold* to *His disciples* in John 6:35: ***"I am the bread of life."*** In the Acts of the Apostles, it is written concerning the infant church of Christ Jesus - that *all the new converts* in Acts 2:42-47: "...were persevering in the doctrine of the apostles *(of Jesus),* and *in the* ***communi****cation of the breaking of* ***bread,*** *and in prayers.* ...And continuing ***daily with one accord in the temple,*** and ***breaking bread*** from house to house, *they took* ***their meat*** *with gladness* and simplicity of heart; Praising God..." And John 4:34: ***"Jesus saith*** *to them:* ***My meat is to do the will of him that sent me,*** *that I may perfect his work."*

Thanks to EWTN, Mother Angelica, for showing authors Dr. Scott Hahn's *The Lamb's Supper -The Mass and the Apocalypse* and Mike Aguilina's *The Mass of the Early Christians,* so we can see how *the early church* formed most of the actual *liturgy of the Mass* from *The Apocalypse* (Rev). They understand (like Nancy through her visions) that *the Mass* ***is*** *where heaven truly meets earth.* Dr. Hahn demonstrates in great detail how verses from *The Apocalypse* (Rev) are intertwined within the *liturgy of the Mass.* The early Christians obviously utilized John's holy writings *The Apocalypse* to create the *liturgy of the Mass* with and for *the Eucharistic celebration.* See in the following verses below, how the early Christians developed *the Mass.*

Start with Rev 4:4-5: *"And round about the throne* were four and twenty seats; and upon the seats, *four and twenty ancients* ***(presbyters)*** *sitting,* ***clothed in white garments,*** *and* ***on their heads were crowns of gold.*** And from the throne preceded *lightnings, and voices, and thunders;* and *there were* ***seven lamps burning*** *before the throne..."* Rev 1:12-13: *"...*I saw ***seven golden candlesticks****...*And in the midst of the seven golden candlesticks, one like the Son of man *(Jesus)..."* Rev 8:3-5: *"And another angel came, and stood before the altar, having* ***a golden censer;*** *and there was given to him much* ***incense,*** *that he should offer of the prayers of all saints upon the golden* ***altar,*** *which is before the throne of God. And* ***the smoke of the incense of the prayers of the saints ascended up before God*** *from the hand of the angel. And the angel took the* ***censer,*** *and* ***filled*** *it* ***with the fire of the altar, and cast it on the earth..."*** Rev 15:5: *"...and behold, the temple of* ***the tabernacle of the testimony*** *in heaven* ***was opened****..."* Rev 15:7: *"And one...gave...* ***seven golden*** *vials* ***(chalices)****..."* And finally Rev 19:9: ***"Blessed are they that are called to the marriage supper of the Lamb..."*** So, ***Jesus is - the Eucharist*** *- the Lamb of God, Who takes away the sins of the world.*

VI. 666: "That old serpent"- Satan the father of lies and deception.

A. Recall the EEG results of the August 20th 1993 testing of two *chosen souls* in my state-of-the-art neurodiagnostic laboratory suite at the Doctor's Specialty Center, St. Joseph's Hospital of Atlanta. I recorded two separate EEG epochs of 6 Hz theta rhythms forming the 666 EEG brain wave activity pattern evoked only in the living presence of Satan - *that old serpent.* Also recall how one of the videos documented the *white (snake) serpent* seen only by Nancy during *the testing* was attested to by the testimony of two Jewish doctors, who wish their names to remain anonymous. As both doctors, during the video viewing time of the 666 EEG pattern, vividly identified a *white (snake) serpent on top of the cross* seen only by Nancy.

Question: What does Satan and the mathematical and numerical sequence of 666 have in common with "the serpent" of Genesis 3:4-5 and 3:14-15?

B. Our first introduction to *"the Father of lies"/ "the serpent"* is in Genesis 3:1-15, as the serpent's *subtle* craft and seduction assisted ***the fall*** of our *first parents.* Then, see a prophetic foreshadow of things to come *within the spiritual kingdom* in Numbers 21:4-9: "And *speaking against God* and *Moses (God's chosen soul)...*Wherefore *the Lord sent* among the people *fiery serpents, which bit them* and *killed many of them...**Moses prayed** for the people. And the Lord said to him: Make **a brazen serpent,** and set it up **for a sign** (read John 3:14-16): **whosoever being struck** (by fiery serpents/seduced by Satan) **shall look on it** (look on Jesus the sinless Lamb of God on the cross, who took on all our sins, see Isaiah 53:1-12 and believe), **shall live."*** See Satan in Job: 6-12; Psalms 12:3-5; 21(22):17; 24(25):19; 39(40):13; Isaiah14:9-15; 26:14; 27:1; 42:13; 51:9. Read Isaiah 14.

Isaiah 14:9:***"Hell** below* was ***in an uproar*** to meet thee ***at thy coming,*** it stirred up*..."*

C. Read Matthew 4:1-11; Rev 13:18: *"Here is wisdom.* He that hath understanding, let him *count the number of the beast (that great dragon, that old serpent, the devil, Lucifer, Satan).* For it is *the number of a man:* and *the number of him* **is** *six hundred sixty six (666)."* Rev 12:9: "And that *great dragon* was cast out, that *old serpent,* who is called *the devil* and *Satan, who seduceth the whole world;* and he was cast out unto earth, and his angels were thrown down with him.*"* Rev 19:19-20 and Rev 20:1-2: "And I saw *an angel coming down from heaven,* having the key of the bottomless pit, and a great chain in his hand. And he laid hold on *the dragon the old serpent,* which is *the devil* and Satan, and bound him...And he cast him into the bottomless pit, and shut him up*..."* Rev 20:9-10: "And there came down *fire from God out of heaven,* and *devoured them; and the devil, who seduced them,* was *cast into the pool of fire and brimstone ...the beast And the false prophet shall be tormented day and night for ever and ever."* So, Satan is indeed a liar, a murderer, a thief, a seducer, *the most proud one, the deceiver* and *a false light.*

VII. 444: "The Ark of the New Covenant," the holy "Incarnation," and "A woman clothed with the sun."

A. During the medical and scientific studies whenever the special *chosen souls* Nancy and the seminarian claim to be seeing *the Blessed Virgin Mary* lovingly caressing and *bringing her baby Jesus to us,* I recorded an unprecedented 4 Hz brain wave activity in a topographic *deep sleep like pattern,* while they were still fully awake and alert with focused attention and with the now famous *stimulus specific evoked EEG pattern of 444.* And when *Mary appeared alone,* a *reflective state alpha* pattern with eyes open in the 8-9 Hz range (mostly 8 Hz) was recorded.

Question: What does the Blessed Virgin Mary bringing her baby Jesus to us and the mathematical and numerical sequence of 444 have in common

with the "ark of the covenant," the holy "Incarnation" and "A woman clothed with the sun?"

B. In the Jewish Sabaoth celebration *the woman* of the house brings *the light back to us* by lighting two candles representing: *Moses and the law* and *Elijah (the prophets) and the word of God.* The first woman *Eve lost the light* of paradise, so *"the woman"* of Gen 3:15 *Mary brings the light/the law /the word of God/Jesus back to us* through *two great lights: Moses and Elijah,* as it is written in Holy Scriptures (See Gen 15:17-18; Exodus 25:10-27; 37:1-15; and 3 Kings18: 1-39, respectively). See 4-4-4 gold parts of the *Ark of the Covenant;* and the 4-4-4 *buckets filled with water* that foretells of *the Holy Incarnation.* See *reflections* on *Mary* in Chapter IX.

C. Rev 11:19 and 12:1 clearly shows that *the ark of God's testament* was seen by John in *God's temple in heaven* with *"lightnings, and voices (God and His court)...and great hail (Hail Mary)."* Then, John describes *the ark* as: *"A woman clothed with the sun, and the moon under feet, and on her head a crown of twelve stars."* Bible scholars have identified a total of 456 prophecies (see Stan Telchin's *Betrayed!*) they say *are truly fulfilled by* - the birth, life, passion, crucifixion, death, resurrection and ascension of *Jesus.* In our studies, *the Blessed Virgin Mary being with child* and bringing Jesus to us **is** *"clothed with the sun" (with 30-90%* more *sun light* detected) and *"lightnings"* (detected inside the apparition room). Yes, with *"the moon under her feet,"* reflecting *the sun light - Jesus* - in the darkness of the night; recall the *chosen soul's* 444 EEG pattern recorded. *"And on her head a crown of twelve stars," see the 12 bright stars,* the 12 Apostles, also reflecting *the sun light - Jesus - the word of God* – who preach *the gospel.* So now, add it up and see: (Mary bringing Jesus- *the moon*) 444+12 (Apostles-*a crown of twelve stars*) = 456!

VIII. 333 "The Way of Peace"

A. Remarkable as it may seem the repeatedly unprecedented EEG *deep sleep* topographic pattern, while yet fully awake and alert with focused attention and the stimulus specific evoked EEG brain wave pattern of 333 recorded only *in His Living Presence – the living presence of Jesus in light,* still baffles me and many medical scientists today. Remember, all the different holy and tangible manifestations of *His living Presence* that we were so graciously allowed to test and measure from *the baseline studies* in my medical office in Atlanta, Georgia, USA to Pachi's reception of *the Eucharist* in Cuenca, Ecuador, South America. All the *holy* and *tangible manifestations* of *the living Son of God, Jesus - the second person of the Holy Trinity* produced the same identical physiological, neurophysiological and EEG changes that until now were always considered to be a *physiological impossibility* and *a contradiction* of known neurophysiological principles. But, since there is really *nothing impossible for God* or *"nothing to hard for God,"* the impossible becomes possible. Just imagine again the obvious oxymoron of being awake, while in a *deep sleep EEG pattern* only *in His Living Presence.* The *delta deep sleep* brain wave pattern is still considered to be the most relaxed, tranquil, calm, and profoundly *peace*ful brain wave activity state. Thus, *the living presence of Jesus* in light evokes the most profound *peace* ever imagined *in the chosen soul* and *the atmosphere.* One must marvel - seeing a glimpse of *God's peace, love* and *glory.* So, *Jesus* the prophesized *"Prince of Peace"* (Isaiah 9:6) *evokes peace,* ***the way of peace*** **- 333!**

Question: What does Jesus and the mathematical and numerical sequence of 333 have in common with *the way of peace*?

B. Starting with a prophetic verse concerning Juda that clearly infers *peace/Jesus* **is *"the expectation of nations"*** in Gen 49:10: "The sceptre shall not be taken away from Juda, nor a ruler from his thigh, till ***he come that is to be sent,*** and ***he shall be the expectation of nations."*** *Peace* is indeed *what* all the nations are waiting for and so much *desire.* See the prophet Aggeus 2:8: *"...AND THE DESIRED OF ALL NATIONS SHALL COME..."* Please read Chapter 3 in Leviticus concerning God's *peace offerings* instructions to Moses and the children of Israel. Recall animals of a herd like *the lamb* used for a sacrifice *of* ***peace*** *offerings* had to be *without blemish before the Lord.* In connecting *(deep) sleep* with *peace* David writes in Psalm 4:9:*"In* ***peace*** in the selfsame I will ***sleep,*** *and* I will ***rest."***

The *holy connections of the word of God/Jesus with the new medical and scientific data are* indeed *truly awesome.* David later writes about the general corruption of man before our *redemption by Christ Jesus* in Psalm 13:3:"They are all gone aside... there is none that doth good, no not one...with their tongues they acted deceitfully...Their mouth is full of cursing and bitterness; their feet are swift to shed blood... and ***the way of peace*** *(Jesus)* they have *not known..."* A *prophecy* of *the coming Christ* is seen in Psalm 71(72):3-8: *"Let the mountains* receive ***peace for the people:*** and *the hills* ***justice...he shall save*** the children of the poor... ***he shall continue with the sun,*** and before the moon, throughout all generations. ***He shall come down like rain*** upon the fleece...***In his days*** *shall* ***justice*** *spring up,* and ***abundance of peace,*** till the moon be taken away. And *he (Jesus) shall rule from sea to sea... unto the ends of the earth."* Another *prophecy* of *the coming of Christ Jesus* bringing *peace and salvation* to man in Psalm 84(85):7-12:"Thou wilt turn, O God, and ***bring us to life****...Shew us,* O Lord, *thy mercy;* and grant us ***thy salvation***...for *he (Jesus)* will speak ***peace*** *unto his people:* And *unto his saints:* and *unto them that are converted* to the heart...***Mercy and truth*** have met each other: ***justice and peace*** have kissed. ***Truth*** *(Jesus)* is sprung out of the earth..." In Psalm 118(119):165: *"Much* ***peace*** *have they that love* ***thy law,*** *and to them there is no stumbling block."*

Of all the prophets Isaiah has written the most about *peace,* starting with

Isaiah 9:6-7: "For a CHILD IS BORN to us, and ***a son*** *(of the living God) is given to us...*and *his name* shall be called, Wonderful, Counsellor, ***God the Mighty,*** *the Father of the world to come, the* ***Prince of* Peace.** *His empire* shall be *multiplied,* and *there shall be no end of* ***peace."*** In Isaiah 32:17-18: "And *the work of justice (Jesus) shall be* ***peace...***And *my people* shall sit in ***the beauty of peace...***and in ***wealthy rest*** *(like deep sleep)."* Isaiah 39:8: *"Only let* ***peace and truth*** *be in my days."* Isaiah 41:2-3: *"Who* hath raised up ***the just one*** from the east...*he shall rule over kings...he shall pass in* ***peace."*** Isaiah 45:7: *"I form* ***the light,*** *and create darkness, I make* ***peace...I the Lord*** that do all these things." Isaiah 52:7: *"How* beautiful upon the mountains are *the feet of him* that *bringeth* ***good tidings,*** and that ***preacheth peace...****that preacheth* ***salvation."*** Ponder *His passion,* Isaiah 53:5: *"But he was wounded for our iniquities, he was bruised for our sins: the chastisement of our* ***peace*** *was upon him,* and ***by his bruises (stripes)* we are *healed."*** Isaiah 54:10-13: *"For the mountains* shall be *moved,* and the *hills shall tremble;* but ***my mercy*** *shall not depart from thee,* and ***the covenant of my peace*** *(Jesus)* ***shall not be moved...***All thy children *shall be taught of* ***the Lord*** *(Jesus):* and ***great*** *shall be the* ***peace*** *of thy children."* Isaiah 55:10-11:*"So shall* ***my word*** *(Jesus) be, which shall go forth from my mouth: it shall not return to me void, but it shall do whatsoever I please, and shall prosper in the things for which* ***I sent it****. For you shall go out* ***with joy,*** *and* ***be led forth with peace...***and ***the Lord*** *shall be named for* ***an everlasting sign,*** *that shall not be taken away."* Isaiah 57:2: ***"Let peace come..."*** In Isaiah 59:8:"They have not known ***the way of peace..."*** In Ezekiel 34:25: "And I will make ***a covenant of peace*** with them." Micah 5:5: *"this man* shall be ***our peace."***

C. John recognizes *Jesus* as *the one God sent* of whom *Moses* and the *prophets did write* about. See John 1:45*: "Philip* findeth Nathanael, and saith to him: We have found *him* of whom *Moses in the law, and the prophets did write, Jesus* the son of Joseph of Nazareth." So, if the Old Testament *did write* about the *Son of man,* Who *God sent* and *anointed to be* their *peace,* then ***Jesus* is *peace.*** That is *why Jesus* said in John 14:27: ***"Peace*** I leave with you, ***my peace I give unto you:*** *not as the world giveth, do I give unto you.* Let not your heart be troubled, nor let it be afraid." The *peace Jesus gives* us **is** indeed *a peace* the world cannot give.

Imagine, the *peace Jesus brings unto us* was actually recorded repeatedly and *only in His Living Presence* in a topographic delta brain wave activity EEG pattern of *deep sleep* with the stimulus specific evoked EEG pattern of 333. Recall, the *peaceful* light, the relaxing *electrical anesthesia* atmosphere *Jesus* brings *around us.* The 333 pattern was and is revealed in our (my) medical and scientific research as well as by *Jesus* Himself, see the following *333 pattern* in John's *Revelation.*

Rev 22:13: *"**I am** Alpha and Omega, the first and the last, the beginning and the end."* **1 2 3 *///*** **1 2 3 *///*** **1 2 3 *///* = 333!**

IX. 333 "The Holy Trinity"

A. The greatest *mystery of all mysteries* is *the Holy Trinity,* the Almighty God - *Elohim: The Father, the Son and the Holy Spirit:* I AM WHO AM (Exodus 3:14). In the *Reflections* below see how all the fundamental building blocks, all *intelligent designs of creation* and all *basic patterns of life, for life* and *in life* of *heaven and earth* are indeed intertwined and *deeply rooted in an amazing pattern* of ***Three in One.*** Throughout our entire meticulous medical and scientific research, and despite the many numerous repeated *tests* performed on the *three chosen souls* by different experts from different countries, using different testing equipments in different locations, *one truth remains* that is undeniably unprecedented: the astonishing *new stimulus specific EEG evoked brain wave activity pattern of 333 is always and only produced while being in His Living Presence.* This *EEG pattern of 333* was *only* recognized repeatedly while Nancy, the seminarian and Patricia Talbot were experiencing a *supernatural event of the most pure, mild and sweet (like honey) Lord God, while feeling the most profound peace, love and joy of God.*

Question: What does Jesus and the mathematical and numerical sequence of 333 have in common with *the Holy Trinity*?

B. Starting with *the beginning* of Genesis 1:1-3 in *the first three verses* alone you can see the mystery of *the Holy Trinity.* As mentioned in *this book,* see *God/Elohim first created time "In the beginning"* then *"created heaven and earth"* in the first verse. In the second verse *"the spirit of God (the Holy Spirit)* moved *(like the wind, the breath of God) over the waters".* And finally in the third verse *"light (a fire, the light or the living flames)* was made.*"* So, *just Who* **is** *"the light," "the light of the world," "the living flames of love," and "a fiery law?"* Re-read Part I - III of this outline again. See, after I carefully connected all *the new medical and scientific data* recorded and documented in our research *with Holy Scriptures, how* I then fully recognized without a shadow of a doubt thru *hard-core science,* that *the only plausible answer to this loaded question is ---* ***Jesus.*** Thus, *the Holy Trinity* is proclaimed in the first 3 verses of Genesis. Now, see how several verses in Genesis *the Lord God/Elohim* proclaims *Himself* as *"us," "our"* and *"as one of us"* in the first 3 chapters of Genesis starting with Gen 1:26:*"Let us* make man to *our* image and likeness,*"* Gen 2:18: *"let us* make him a help like unto himself,*" and* Gen 3:22:*"Behold* Adam is become *as one of us,* knowing good and evil.*"* Also in Gen 11:7:*"let us go down,* and there confound their tongue.*" Why* does *the Lord God Almighty* refer to *Himself* as *"us," "our"* and *"as one of us." Why?* Can it be that *the Lord God* **is** indeed *One God in Three - the Holy Trinity?* See *the image of the Trinity* in Abraham's encounter with *the three angels, three men* - ***the Lord*** in Genesis 18:1-19:"And *the Lord appeared to him* in the vale of Mambre...*three men* standing near him...And ***they said:*** *Do as thou hast spoken...*but he stood by *them* *under the tree.* And when *they (the Lord) had eaten,* **they said** to him: *Where is Sara thy wife? ...And* **he** *(the Lord)* **said** *to him: I will return and come to thee at this time, life accompanying, and Sara thy wife shall have a son...Why did Sara laugh, saying : Shall I who am an old woman bear a child indeed? Is there any thing hard to God? ...*And when *the men rose up...*and *Abraham walked with them...And the Lord said...*he shall become a great and mighty nation, and ***in him*** *(the seed of Abraham)* ***all the nations of the earth shall be blessed...*"** See these verses show *three men/the Lord speaking* to Abraham twice *in unison* and once alone.

In Exodus 3:14: *"God/Elohim* said to Moses: **I AM WHO AM.**" I believe this is another *holy name* for *the Holy Trinity.* It has three parts to one basic name **I AM I WHO I AM,** the basic name **I** *is one of three parts*: AM WHO AM! In Exodus 20:2, 18: ***"I am*** *the Lord thy God....*And *all the people* ***saw the voices*** *and the flames."* Even the phrase *I am-the Lord-thy God* has 3 parts; and *the voices (Three in One).* In Numbers 24:7: *"Water (the Holy Spirit) shall flow out of his (Father God's) bucket (Mary) and his (Father God's) seed (Jesus) shall be in many waters."* In this vivid *Messianic prophetic verse* from Moses I added the words in parenthesis only, to show you *what the Holy Spirit has shown me* these words *(of God)* mean. Also see *the Trinity plus Mary* in this last verse. Now see *the Trinity* in ***the Shema*** as it is written in Deut. 6:4:*"Hear, O Israel, the Lord (1) our God (2)* ***is one*** *Lord (3)." Three in One unite,* since the word *"Hear"* in Hebrew also means *unite* or *come together.* Thus, the *Shema* with *10 words (10 = the number of salvation in Hebrew)* truly proclaims a *Tri-fold Unity* or *Three-fold Unity, the Holy Trinity of God,* that *truly saves us, who believe in the one true God.* In *the last words of David,* see *the Holy Trinity* in 2 Kings 23:1-4:*"The man* to whom it was *appointed* concerning *the Christ (the Messiah) of the God of Jacob...The spirit of the Lord (the Holy Spirit)* hath spoken by me and *his (God's) word (Jesus)* by my tongue. *The God of Israel (Father God)* said to me...As *the light (Jesus) of the morning,* when *the sun riseth, shineth in the morning* without clouds..."

Now **see *the Trinity*** in the following Psalm verses. Psalm 18:2-4:*"The heavens* shew forth *the glory of God...* There are no speeches nor languages, where *their voices* are not heard." Psalm 44 (45):8:*"Thou* hast loved *justice,* and hated iniquity: **therefore *God*** *(the Christ/the Messiah/the Son of the living God/Jesus),* ***thy God*** *(Father God),* **hath anointed thee with *the oil of gladness*** *(the Holy Spirit)* above thy fellows." Psalm 49:14:*"Offer to God (Father God)* the *sacrifice of praise (the Christ/Jesus):* and *pay thy vows* to *the most High (the Holy Spirit)."* Psalm 67:12: *"The Lord (Father God)* shall give *the word (the Christ/Jesus)* to them that *preach good tidings* with *great power (the Holy Spirit)."* Psalm 109 (110):1-3: *"The Lord (Father God)* said to *my Lord (the Christ/Jesus):* Sit thou at *my right hand...*With thee is *the principality (the Holy Spirit)* in the day of *thy strength: in the brightness of the saints: from the womb* **before the day star I begot thee."**

See *the Trinity,* in Wisdom 9:17:*"And who* shall know *thy (Father God's) thought,* except *thou give wisdom (the word of God/Jesus),* and *send thy Holy Spirit* from above.*"* See *the Trinity* in Ecclesiasticus 1:9:*"He (Father God)* created *(begot) her (wisdom/the word of God /Jesus)* in the *Holy Ghost (the Holy Spirit),"* and in Ecclesiasticus 15:19:*"For the wisdom (the word of God /Jesus)* of *God (Father God) is great,* and *he (Jesus)* is *strong in power (the Holy Spirit), seeing all men without ceasing."* See *the Trinity* as presented in Isaiah 48:16:*"Come ye near unto me,* and *hear this: I have not spoken in secret from the beginning:* from the time *before it was done, I was there,* and now *the Lord God (Father God) hath sent me (the Christ/the Messiah/Jesus), and his spirit (the Holy Spirit)."* And in Isaiah 6:3, 8: *"Holy, holy, holy, the Lord God of hosts (Holy is hailed x* ***3!*** *Why?);" "and who shall go* ***for us****?"* **Ponder *the majesty and the glory* of *the Holy Trinity.***

C. After *Jesus resurrected* and just before *Jesus ascended He appeared* to *His* eleven disciples on a mountain in Galilee. And *Jesus* said to them in Matthew 28:18-19:*"...All power is given to me in heaven and in earth. Going therefore, teach ye all nations; baptizing them in the name of* ***the Father,*** *and of* ***the Son,*** *and of the Holy Ghost* ***(the Holy Spirit)."*** I believe *Jesus reveals* to us *the Holy Trinity,* **His signature - 333** in Rev 22:13. So, does *333 reflect* ***the Divine Will*** *relationship of the "Holy, Holy, Holy," the Tri-fold Unity, the Triune God – Three-in-One?*

Reflections of "Three in One"

If God **is** *"Three in One,"* and in Genesis 1:26 God says: *"Let us* make man to our image and likeness...,*"* then God's architecture for *His creation* should reflect *the three in one image and likeness* in its total concept. We need to look not far to find out *the truth.* Just look at us. We are three dimensional, but one body; we have a mind, body and soul or a body, soul and spirit in one whole person. To locate us in space with a satellite we need three coordinates: altitude, longitude and latitude; we are indeed mainly made up of water-H2O three parts in one water molecule; we come from one embryo that has three parts namely ectoderm, mesoderm and endoderm tissues; we are time travelers indeed ruled by the past , present and the future. Time is always presented in three parts of one whole: like seconds, minutes and hours or days, weeks and months or years, decades and centuries etc. We eat plants that come from a seed made up of three parts in one seed; we eat birds like chicken, duck, goose that come from one egg made up of three parts; and Ireland's St. Patrick was credited to have helped convert many pagan Druids and Celtics to the One Triune God by displaying the *clover leaf* as a symbol of One God - the Holy Trinity: three parts to one leaf. Just look at David's Star *(the Jewish Star),* it has one triangle pointing upwards (which a Jewish rabbi said represents God) and has another triangle pointing downward (which the same Jewish rabbi said represents God's creation or God's reflection, namely man). Interestingly, both triangles are seemingly locked in a *life-death grip battle* as God's reflection man continues on a downward spiral, a destructive path towards death, while simultaneously God's immeasurable love and mercy continues to rescue us and lock us in at (you guessed it) three points (the Holy Trinity). Just look at the Jewish star carefully and see how the two triangles that make up David's star are going in two opposite directions but merge at three corners of the one triangle pointing upwards. Thus, the triangle pointing upwards (God) continually tries to prevent us from going down towards the pit of death and brings us (man – the triangle pointing downward) upwards towards *life (with God).* Pope John Paul II has said: *"Only the Holy Trinity can save us."*

The Star of David graphically explains his statement (if you believe in the One Triune God). The sign of a triangle in Greek is the sign of *Delta,* which interestingly in neurophysiology terms, is the predominant EEG brain wave activity of the *deep sleep* pattern we recorded *only in His Living Presence. Delta* we also know represents: *Three* sides that form *one* triangle. Now doing simple mathematics will also reveal to us that when 3 is divided into 1 the result equals = *.333...to infinity!* Well if all of God's creation including man is in the *"three in one"* format of God's reflection, then God's ministry to man (us) should show the same *image* and *likeness.* This is probably *why* we can see that in God's *ministry* there are *3 pillars of truth* or *3 ways God ministers* to us:

1) *Traditions* – the *oral laws of God* given to Moses and the prophets of God.

2) *Holy Bible* – the *written laws of God* given to Moses in the commandments, precepts and statutes, and *the word of God* given to the prophets as lessons, guidelines, pathways or ways of God.

3) *"The Church of the living God"* – which St. Paul said in 1Timothy 3:15: *"is the pillar and foundation of all truth."* Thus, *the Church with the Holy Sacraments* **is** the main *pillar of truth* and has *the fullness of* ***the truth*** *(Jesus).* See Matthew 16:15-20.

We can also see that the *nine angelic celestial choirs in heaven* have been set up in God's *image* with a similar pattern of *a triad of three tiers,* three – three – three (3-3-3):

1) Seraphim, Cherubim and Thrones.

2) Dominions, Powers and Virtues.

3) Principalities, Archangels and Angels. Even *the Temple* in Jerusalem, in its simplest architecture, had a three in one design with an outer court, a middle court and an inner court, where within *the Holy of Holies* was kept the *ark of the covenant (the testimony).* One of Jeremiah's most famous *prophetic* verses invites us all to *call* upon *the Lord our God* at anytime by simply dialing 3-3-3. So, for those who are interested in calling *God's* private, hot line and direct *number* --- just dial **Jeremiah 33:3:"Cry to me and I will hear thee: and will shew thee great things, and sure things which thou knowest not."** God really has a *good* sense of humor. Even our *human pregnancy* with 9 months *to be born* has *3 month trimesters:* 3 – 3 – 3!

X. 333 "The circle of God" – "The circle of life"

A. Recall the multiple times we recorded the unprecedented and astonishing EEG *delta deep sleep* topography *pattern of 333* in the *three chosen souls* while awake and alert repeatedly, and always or only *in His Living Presence. The living presence of Jesus in light* was *"round about"* them and was *around* us, the medical and scientific research team, as was repeatedly documented by *the* blazing *light* show and dramatic changes in the atmosphere radiation energy fields all *around* us during the two separate series of testing on June 13th, 1993. Recall *how* in November 19th, 1994, *the same EEG pattern of 333* was recorded *at the reception of the Eucharist* - lasting *a total of 20 minutes.*

Question: What does Jesus and the mathematical and numerical sequence of 333 have in common with "the circle of God?"

B. Follow **the circle *round about:*** In Exodus 16:13 we see a *new revelation* concerning *manna: "...*and in the morning a ***dew*** lay ***round about*** the camp.*"* So, *what* is this *dew?* See Isaiah 45:8:*"Drop down dew,* ye *heavens, from above,* and let the clouds *rain down* ***the just:*** let the *earth be opened,* and *bud forth* ***a saviour..."*** The *dew* foreshadows *a coming down of the Word of God/Bread of God by the Holy Spirit -* ***"round about"*** the camp - to *bud forth* the just- *a saviour.* David in Psalm 96(97):2-3 truly rejoices at the glorious *coming and reign of Christ: "Clouds* and darkness are ***round about*** him: ***justice*** and ***judgment*** are the establishment of his throne. A ***fire*** shall go before him, and shall burn his enemies ***round about."*** In Isaiah 60:1-4: *"*Arise, *be enlightened,* O Jerusalem: for *thy light is come,* and the *glory of the Lord is risen* upon thee...*the Lord shall arise* upon thee...And *the Gentiles* shall *walk in thy light,* and kings in the *brightness of thy rising.* Lift up thy eyes ***round about,*** and see...*"* In *the vision of the likeness of the glory of the Lord,* Ezekiel describes in great detail, 1:26-28:*"*a likeness as of the appearance of *a man...* upon the likeness of *a throne...*the resemblance of amber as the appearance of ***fire*** *within it* ***round about:*** from *his* loins and upward, and from *his* loins downward, I saw as it were the resemblance of ***fire shining round about.*** As the appearance of the *rainbow* when it is in a cloud on a rainy day: this was the appearance of ***the brightness round about."*** In Zachariah 2:1-5 he describes the spiritual Jerusalem, the future church of Christ, and the *new Jerusalem* in heaven: *"...*Jerusalem shall be inhabited without walls (see Rev 21:22-28)...And ***I will be to it, saith the Lord, a wall of fire round about:*** and *I will be* ***in glory*** *in the midst thereof."*

C. Now see the 333 pattern in what *Jesus* said to John, in Rev 22:13: *"I am Alpha and Omega, the first and the last, the beginning and the end." I am* means now, present tense, so I am (1) Alpha (2) and Omega (3); I am (1) the first (2) and the last (3); I am (1) the beginning (2) and the end (3) = 333. But how can *Jesus* be in all three time zones all at once? Jesus once said to Nancy, *"I am a circle. I am infinity..."* Just look at a *circle.* It is truly a *sign of infinity!* As a *circle* Jesus can truly be "Alpha and Omega, the first and the last, the beginning and the end." *Jesus* is proclaiming ***His signature – 333.*** Based on the ELS Hebrew Bible codes *circumference line* is found in the first 5 verses of Genesis 1:1-5. The *line of a circumference = diameter,* so the word *line (diameter)* in Hebrew *kav= 106.* Recall in geometry *the diameter* of a circle X *pi* (constant of all circles) = *the circumference* of a circle. Thus, ***kav 106 x pi 3.1415926 = 333.*** (Thanks Yacov Rambsel, a Messianic Jew and Hebrew Bible scholar, for *The Genesis Factor)*

Of interest in Zachariah 2:1-5 we see a series of 3 circles in 3 planes and 3 different dimensions that altogether make up one sphere: "And I lifted up my eyes, and saw, and *behold a man,* with a *measuring line in his hand.* And I said: Whither goest thou? And he said to me: *To measure Jerusalem,* and to see how great is ***the breadth*** thereof, and how great ***the length*** thereof... Jerusalem shall be inhabited without walls...And *I will be to it, saith the Lord,* ***a wall of fire round about*** *(a circle)****:*** and ***I will be in glory in the midst thereof."*** The *breadth is both the height* and *width,* and with *the length* we have 3 distinct dimensions to be measured with a *measuring line.* In Hebrew a *measuring line (kavah) = circumference.* And it has the numerical value of 111. So, can you imagine 3 circles or 3 circumferences (3 measuring lines) in 3 different planes and 3 different dimensions in the basic three positions just like the three coordinates used in space for finding any location? This truly makes *an outline* of *3 circles,* each with a 111 value for each circle = 333 *in one sphere.* Just think about all the stars and planets, even the sun and the moon. Indeed, they are all in a shape or outline of a sphere. *God creates* us in *His image* in ***the circle of life!*** God is *love,* infinity, *a circle,* a sphere, *the light, delta* sign, *peace* and *so much more.*

AND NOW FOR MY FINAL COMMENTS

HAIL MARY- FULL OF GRACE – PRAY FOR US AND BRING US "THE LIGHT"- YOUR BABY JESUS

Hail (Mary), full of grace, the Lord is with thee *(Luke 1:28).* ***Blessed art thou amongst women and blessed is the fruit of thy womb, Jesus*** *(Luke 1:42).****Holy Mary*** *(Luke 1:30),* ***Mother of God*** *(Luke 1:35),* ***pray for us sinners now, and at the hour of our death. Amen.***

Basically, *4 verses* from God's words in Luke *and an earthly petition* – is added by the Catholic Church - to our heavenly Mother – *asking Mary to pray for us* - **is** indeed, the *"Hail Mary"* prayer.

The name *Jesus* is implied in Luke 1:42. But the actual name *Jesus* was given to *Mary* in a city of Galilee called Nazareth by the *archangel Gabriel sent from God* as it is written in Luke 1:31:

"Behold thou shalt conceive in thy womb, and shalt bring forth a son; and thou shalt call his name Jesus."

The purist may add that the *"Hail Mary"* is actually *five verses* taken from Luke 1:28-42-31-30-35. The next 4 verses in Luke explain further the origin of Jesus *(our true Christmas gift)* as it is written in Luke 1:32-35:

"He shall be great, and shall be called the Son of the most High (His Heavenly Father God); ***and the Lord God shall give unto him the throne of David his father*** (His earthly father); ***and he shall reign in the house of Jacob for ever*** (the Jewish Messiah). ***And of his kingdom there shall be no end*** (God's Kingdom has no end, it is everlasting).

"And Mary said to the angel (Gabriel): ***'How shall this be done, because I know not man?'*** (Meaning *she has had no relations with a man* according to the Biblical scholars)

And the angel (Gabriel) ***answering, said to her: The Holy Ghost*** (Holy Spirit) ***shall come upon thee, and the power of the most High shall overshadow thee. And therefore also the Holy*** (Jesus) ***which shall be born of thee shall be called the Son of God."***

So, according to Luke - and now Nancy - *Jesus is the living Son of God.* And just like the apostle Thomas approximately 2,000 years ago had to place his fingers literally into the sacred wounds of the *resurrected Jesus,* in order for Thomas to believe *Jesus* really resurrected and *is alive, after His passion and crucifixion,* I too placed my fingers (I must admit) and plunged my doubts, my hands, arms and legs deep into the *holy wounds of Jesus,* in order to believe and know *the truth.* My hardened disbelieving skeptic fingers pierced deeply into the precious and sacred wounds of our *Lord Jesus;* just like Thomas did.

Just recall the meticulous medical and scientific research, and the slow, difficult but fruitful steps I climbed during the mountainous Biblical research the past (>10) years of my life. Finally, just like in the epiphany of Thomas, this previously super-doubting Thomas to-the-max (namely me) now kneels frequently, freely and fervently with great love, peace and joy, bowing down low before *Jesus* with all my heart, mind, body, and soul, and with all my strength, privilege and honor to shout out *my joyous epiphany:*

"My Lord, and my God!"

See John 20:24-29: ***"Now Thomas, one of the twelve, who is called Didymus, was not with them when Jesus came*** (to visit the apostles after His death and resurrection). **The *other disciples therefore said to him: We have seen the Lord. But he said to them: Except I shall see in his hands the print of***

the nails, and put my finger into the place of the nails, and put my hand into his side, I will not believe *(check out this deep sentiment expressed by Thomas, it really sounded like me and unfortunately it sounds like most of us in our modern world today).* ***And after eight days*** (eight is the number that in Hebrew symbolizes a new beginning) ***again his disciples were within, and Thomas with them. Jesus cometh, the doors being shut, and stood in the midst, and said: Peace be to you.***

"Then he (Jesus) ***saith to Thomas: Put in thy finger hither, and see my hands; and bring hither thy hand, and put it into my side; and be not faithless, but believing.***

"Thomas answered, and said to him: 'My Lord, and my God.'

"Jesus saith to him: **Because thou hast seen me, Thomas, thou hast believed: blessed are they that have not seen, and have believed."**

For the pure of heart and the faithful *"blessed are they,"* but for the rest of us doubters and the many hardened faithless skeptics (like me) this very special blessing of *proof for believing* with lots of medical and scientific *evidence that demands a verdict* is now extended to you by all the hard-core *new data* uncovered (discovered) in this body of work.

So, now when I come to **Jesus** *in the Holy Eucharist (a true supernatural event),* I also come to *the Father and the Holy Spirit together* as One Holy Undivided Substance, the Holy Three-fold Unity, the One Triune God (symbolized by the delta triangle in the Star of David), *the Holy Trinity.* Praise the Lord our Almighty God *in His Living Presence in the Eucharist.* Thus, God's *living presence* in *the Eucharist, the bread of life* and the true living *Peace of God - received via the Holy Mass -* **is** truly *heaven on earth for our souls.* I can only imagine what majestic glory and blessings actually descend from heaven upon each soul *made new* - after receiving *the Eucharist.* See Rev 21:5:"And *he that sat on the throne,* said: **Behold, I make all things new**..." In this passage ***"he that sat on the throne"*** **is** ***Jesus: "the King of kings, and Lord of lords"*** (Rev 19:16). This verse fulfills the prophecies in Isaiah 9:6:

"**For a child is born to us, and a son is given us** *(the Son of man),* ***and the government is upon his shoulder: and his name shall be called, Wonderful, Counsellor, God the Mighty*** *(the Son of God),* ***the Father of the world to come, and the Prince of Peace."*** And in Rev 21:6-7***:"And he*** *(Jesus)* ***said to me*** *(John)*: **It is** ***done. I am Alpha and Omega; the beginning and the end. To him that thirsteth, I will give of the fountain of the water of life*** *(the Holy Spirit),* ***freely. He that shall overcome shall possess these things, and I will be his God; and he shall be my son."***

Now I ask you, how can *Jesus* make all things *new?* And *what* does *Jesus* mean when *He says:* ***"It is done."*** *The answer* to these two questions *is in - the passion, crucifixion and death of Jesus* (*He* freely submitted to - for all of our sins) *and in His resurrection.* Remember *the empty tomb* and the 500 eye witnesses of Jesus (1 Corinthians 15:3-8) after the passion, crucifixion, death, burial and resurrection.

Yes, it is the awesome *resurrection-power* of Jesus *plus our believing in Him, as well as following* and *imitating* the One *(Jesus)* He *(Father God)* sent – that will perpetually break wide open our heavy shackles of bondage in *sin* and set us free. Thus, the *resurrection-power* of *Jesus* is *what* truly *transforms* death into a *new* life, the life of sin into a *new* life growing and maturing in the image and likeness of God, and a war torn world filled with terrorism into a *new* reign of *peace.* So, do not be enslaved by sin any longer. Stop being *bitter* in the slavery of sin, but be *better* by overcoming all sin with the *resurrection-power* of *Jesus.* And do not be a *victim of sin* any longer, but be a *victor over sin* in the name - that is above all names, *Jesus.*

I now understand that it's not about *who you are* that is so very important, but it's really about *whose you are* that is so crucially pivotal and vital in reaching *everlasting peace, life in paradise* and gaining our *eternal salvation.* And *whose you are* is in the name of the One He sent, *Jesus.* Remember, *you were purchased with His Precious Blood.* So, when we invite *Jesus* into our hearts, *Father God adopts us as His very own* (Rev 21:7). So, let us now shout it together - come Lord *Jesus!* O come, O come Emmanuel (Isaiah 7:14)! Come *"God the Mighty, the Father of the world to come, Prince of Peace"* (Isaiah 9:6)! And come *Holy Spirit, "spirit of truth," (John 14:17)!*

* * *

Is Jesus God? Is Jesus - *the Messiah* - God? The answer to this question is in this *(His)* book. Just look at all the *new medical and scientific data, the Bible* and the *Hebrew ELS Bible codes.* Interestingly, the very name of *Jesus* in Hebrew means*: salvation* and *God saves.* But just in case you still do not get it, nor understand or still do not know the *true* answer to this most crucial *life of the soul* saving question, **my** very enthusiastic **answer** *via the Holy Spirit* **is** now a genuinely *truthful,* honest and powerfully resounding **–** ***yes!***

Jesus is Lord! (1 Corinthians 12:3) Please acknowledge this *truth* is in sync with *the God-man, Jesus as the 2nd person of the Holy Trinity* of the *One Triune God.* So, now… *drum roll* please… and just like Thomas, I will *shout it out* from the top of my lungs…

Jesus is "my Lord," (Psalm110:1) **"and"** *the Eternal Word Incarnate* is **"my God!"**

P.S. Hopefully the title of this *(His)* book will maybe make more sense to you now and be more meaningful and fruitful in your own personal *life journey to faith.* May God bless you (your home, family, and country) and graciously give you the *great gift* of *faith.* And I pray that you may always *hear the word of God.* My parting thoughts on this *life* journey comes from *Jesus* in John 3:16**: "For God so loved the world, as to give his only begotten Son; that whosoever believeth in him, may not perish, but may have life everlasting."** Also in John 10:10: **"I am come that they may have life, and may have it more abundantly."** So go on...do not be afraid to use all the *science* God gave us (me) to have *faith*...but believe *in the One He* (Father God) *sent* and *live.* Invite *Jesus the living flame of love* into your *bowels and into your heart.* Recall, *Jesus* said in Luke 12:49: **"I am come to cast fire on the earth."** And *Father God* and *the Holy Spirit* said through Isaiah 10:17: **"And *the light of Israel* (Jesus) shall be as *a fire,* and *the Holy One* thereof as *a flame.*"** So, believe *in the One He sent. Invite Jesus into your life, Who* **is** One with *Father God* and **is** One with *the Holy Spirit* of God *in His Will.* And ***let Jesus,*** *a fiery law, the flame of love, the Holy One, the light of Israel,* and *the true light of the world* ***live within you forever.*** Fear not. Be not afraid to let *the Peace of God,* a science confirmed, tangible and most profound *peace, Jesus-the Prince of Peace,*

along *with Father God* and *the Holy Spirit* – ***His Signature 333*** *–The Holy Trinity* - remain *within you* always and *live.* **Say yes to *God!* And *live forever*** in eternal bliss ***in His*** unfathomable ***Divine Mercy and Divine Will: the way*** *of peace, love & joy,* ***the truth and the life*** *(eternal life)* ***and be always In His Living Presence!*** **Amen. Amen. Amen.**

Please re-read John 3:16-18: ***"For God so loved the world, as to give his only begotten Son; that whosoever believeth in him*** **(Jesus),** ***may not perish, but may have life everlasting. For God sent not his Son into the world, to judge the world, but that the world may be saved by him. He that believeth in him is not judged. But he that doth not believe, is already judged: because he believeth not in the name of the only begotten Son of God*** **(Jesus).*"* Amen.**

May everything be for *the glory of God* and for the fulfillment of *His Divine Will.*

The End

is truly the Beginning

ISBN 142515955-9

9 781425 159559